ACCOUNTING: an introduction

Accounting:
an introduction

Arthur HINDMARCH
Miles ATCHISON
Richard MARKE

First published 1977 by
THE MACMILLAN PRESS LTD
London and Basingstoke
Associated companies in New York Dublin
Melbourne Johannesburg and Madras

ISBN 0 333 15023 6 (hard cover)
0 333 19167 6 (paper cover)

Text set in 10/11 pt Photon Baskerville, printed by photolithography and bound in Great Britain at The Pitman Press, Bath

Editor's Introduction

This series is a direct outcome of the opportunities and challenges created by the rapid expansion of higher and further education in the past decade.

The expansion involved changes in the structure of advanced education, through the CNAA, the Polytechnics, the Regional Management Centres and the professional bodies which encouraged staff to develop new and experimental teaching. Substantial changes have taken place in the definition, scope and methodologies of the social, administrative and management sciences leading to modifications in the presentation of these subjects. Many new full-time students and staff have questioned traditional approaches and methods and have established more open discussion and debate on their courses. Demands for qualified manpower led to an expansion in part-time education and increased questioning by students in full-time jobs of the relevance of their studies.

Each of these developments has had a profound impact on the structure and content of courses and given fresh impetus to the discussion and modification of curricula and teaching methods in polytechnics, universities and colleges of further education. The editor and authors of the books in this series have made a deliberate attempt to respond to these changes.

The books set out to provide a comprehensive and up-to-date introduction to the ideas and methods of their subjects for specialist and non-specialist students in fields such as business and management studies, social science and administration. Their aim is to help students who have little or no previous knowledge of them to achieve a mastery of the scope and basic techniques of their subjects and to use them critically and with imagination for further study or for practical professional applications. They also seek to make some contribution to discussions of teaching and learning problems in their field.

Many introductory books present their subjects as a coherent body of knowledge of which the logic is self-evident and the concepts and methods clear to the careful reader. Students do not always find this so. Confronted as they are by a well-established discipline which has developed a particular method that may not bear any obvious relationship to the way in which they have been accustomed to think or to realities as they see them, students often have difficulty in comprehending the significance and detail of the forms of analysis it employs.

The editor and authors of the series felt that they should not take for granted the 'self-evident logic' of their subjects, but try to demonstrate to readers the ways in which their disciplines provide an effective framework for the analysis of problems in their field. When abstractions or concepts are introduced their functions and limitations are explained. Where methods or techniques are described the authors show why they take the form they do and the ways in which they may be used for particular tasks of analysis.

Students often criticise courses because their subjects or parts of them do not have any obvious, or immediate, practical applications. They may present what appear to be unnecessarily complicated ways of dealing with quite straightforward problems or, paradoxically, they may be regarded as over-simplifying or ignoring difficulties which are experienced in real situations. Criticisms of this sort are due to misunderstandings about the nature of subjects. Systems of knowledge provide generalisations which are derived from a variety of abstractions and models. Some of these yield tools of description and analysis that have direct applications. Others suggest ways of looking at problems that, however fruitful, may have only limited or indirect applications.

The authors have tried to make clear the relevance of their subjects. Where concepts and methods have direct applications they show how, and under what circumstances, they can usefully be applied. Where they are of indirect use they show how a process of simplification may isolate and draw attention to the important characteristics of a complex problem, or how the study of complicated or abstract aspects of a problem may throw fresh light on it.

The authors have rejected a view, reflected in many basic textbooks, that students at an introductory level should concentrate on 'learning up' the information and techniques of their subjects and not be troubled with discussions of concepts and analytical method. This 'descriptive' approach, which divorces the study of techniques from that of conceptual and analytical structures, makes it more rather than less difficult for students to appreciate how a technique has developed, why it takes a particular form and how it functions. As a result students can spend a considerable time trying to understand, with limited success, a method of describing and presenting information or a method of analysis and fail to achieve any real facility in using it. The discussion of concepts and analytical method also acquaints a student with some of the difficulties and controversies surrounding the ideas and techniques he is studying. Without such knowledge he is unlikely to appreciate their limitations or establish any real ability to discriminate between alternative approaches and methods.

One of the more important aims of education is to develop a student's capacity to formulate and solve theoretical and practical problems. It is clear that few business and administrative problems are in practice separable into the neat categories represented by disciplines such as economics, accounting, law, sociology, psychology and computing. But most courses are based on combinations of studies in these and similar discrete disciplines which are rarely effectively integrated. It is recognised that the development of bodies of knowledge which provide rigorous rather than superficial integrative approaches will be a long and difficult task. The editor and authors of the books in this series are aware of this problem and within their limitations have attempted to indicate points at which contributions from other disciplines are necessary to the analysis of the problems with which they are dealing. It is thus hoped that in the long run the series will make some contribution to the development of interdisciplinary approaches.

The problems outlined above are common in the teaching and learning of many subjects which, although emerging historically as systems for analysing and solving practical problems, have developed advanced methodologies and a logical order of presentation that may not bear an obvious relation to the practical problems with which they are supposed to be concerned.

The study of accounting appears to many to approximate closely to the actual practices and problems of the accounting profession. And yet many students have great difficulty in grasping its methods of analysing and presenting data. Perhaps this is due to a general problem of numeracy and an inability to understand relationships between variables presented in a quantitative form. Or perhaps it is that the student has in his early stages to study many complex methods of presenting data which can only at a later stage be used for more interesting and complete analyses of the economic performance of organisations. The power of the concepts and tools of accounting to analyse and explain the structure and operations of an organisation should, however, be of interest to anyone who follows economic and business affairs. It is hoped that the present exposition, by helping students to achieve a more effective command of modern basic accounting, will encourage them to investigate further its methodology and potential.

The editor and authors of the books in this series are conscious of their limitations in attempting to implement their ideas in writing and teaching and do not suppose that their presentation will solve students' learning problems. They do not ignore the critical importance of motivation and sustained and disciplined study as factors in effective learning. But they felt that if subjects were presented in a way that made their form and justification explicit rather than implicit this would aid teaching and learning.

In seeking to achieve their aims the books in the series have been subjected to a great deal of critical scrutiny. Each is written by more than one author. This has enabled authors to combine a comparison of views with a considerable, and sometimes uncomfortable, degree of mutal criticism. The editor and authors have all, in recent years, had considerable experience of designing and teaching new CNAA honours degree, diploma or professional courses. Their manuscripts have been discussed with colleagues in education and the professions and have been tested in classes with students.

My thanks as editor are owed to the authors who responded to my request to write the books in the form that I have outlined. This has involved them in an extremely demanding process. The fact that we shared some basic assumptions about education and learning was of great help. The editors and staff of Macmillan with whom we have worked have showed great patience and could not have done more in difficult circumstances to encourage the series. My thanks are also due to George Brosan, Maurice Peston and Bruce May, who through many discussions have significantly influenced my educational ideas, and to my wife Diane, who has kept a discerning eye on my activities and the progress of the series.

February 1976 ALAN HALE

Contents

Introduction

The book will provide a foundation in accounting for those courses where the emphasis is on analysis rather than description. We believe that the book could provide the basis for a one-year course for a specialist accounting student or a two-year course for the student on a less specialised course such as business studies.

This should make it suitable for:

- undergraduate degree courses in business studies, accounting or economics
- H.N.C. and H.N.D. courses in business studies
- foundation courses required by the professional accounting bodies
- other courses providing an introduction to accounting, e.g. for managers or for postgraduate students on conversion courses in accounting or business studies.

We have written this book in an attempt to bridge a gap in the literature available to students of accounting. Until recent years introductory courses in accounting concentrated on the methods and techniques of the subject. Students who progressed to more advanced work were then introduced to the on-going discussion of the conceptual basis of accounting. The literature also exhibits this dichotomy. There are many books which deal in varying detail with technical aspects of accounting and also many at an advanced level with conceptual and theoretical topics. We believe that the teaching of accounting should conform to a logical pattern of introducing the conceptual foundations of the subject before building the superstructure of accounting methods. Thus we have written an introductory text which does not avoid the difficult conceptual problems but which attempts to present them in language and style which will be easily understood by those unfamiliar with accounting. We realise that in a single text it is not possible to cover the comparatively wide topic areas we have attempted and to reach a high level of sophistication simultaneously. Thus we have concentrated on giving a sound introduction to the topic areas and have supplemented each chapter with references to further reading of a more advanced nature.

We have taken as our starting-point the common definition of accounting as the measurement, recording and communication of economic data. Accounting has evolved from the needs of business and its concern is chiefly with the solution of business problems. The definition of business in this context is widely drawn to include any organisations which use accounting information, e.g. firms, government or trades unions. Business problems are usually multi-dimensional and their solution requires an understanding of a range of disciplines, in addition to accounting, such as economics, quantitative methods, law and behavioural science. Thus the study of accounting should ideally be related to the study of these other disciplines. We have in the text, wherever possible, highlighted the relationship of accounting to these other disciplines.

The accountant's area of major contribution is in the measurement of costs and benefits of business problems and the planning and control of business strategy and operations. To meet this challenge the subject-matter is continually evolving in an attempt to improve this measurement and to satisfy the changing demands of business. Our view is that the study of accounting can be an interesting and stimulating experience. We hope that the student will appreciate both the potential of accounting as a means of recording, analysis and communication of information, but also recognise the boundaries of the subject and the limitations of accounting measurement.

The book is divided into three parts: Measurement, Planning and Control. This division recognises that we have identified three clusters of problems in accounting, and that for clarity of exposition and analysis these clusters should be considered together. The parts on planning and control build on concepts developed in the measurement part, as both these processes clearly rely on measurement:

MEASUREMENT – the measurement of profit and value is regarded as a central theme of accounting; the conceptual basis is established in the first two chapters of Part I and the detailed implications are explored in the rest of Part I. Throughout Part I we emphasise that the need to provide published accounting information has been a strong influence on the measurement concepts adopted by accountants, but that many of these concepts are inappropriate for planning and control decisions.

PLANNING – the definition of planning adopted includes both short-term and long-term decision-making; this obviates the need for a distinction which is often made between decision-making and planning.

CONTROL – it is recognised that control and planning are closely linked but we have attempted to isolate the particular problems of control. These are seen as a process of monitoring and evaluation. Hence we include in this section the interpretation of financial statements and a discussion of the role and content of published financial information. This emphasises that the analysis of historical, or at best current, information is the major means of control in many organisations and is perhaps the only means of control available to external interested parties.

The content includes topics found in courses on financial and management accounting. Where only a financial accounting course is required it may be appropriate to consider Chapters 16 and 17 in addition to Part I. The book incorporates several features which we hope will facilitate its use as a textbook for a course. Each Part is introduced with a chapter on the concepts to be explored in that Part and it is recommended that each subsequent chapter is read in conjunction with the concepts chapter. We have attempted to build a coherent structure by consciously linking each chapter, either through the summary of the preceding chapter or in the introduction to the chapter. This should help to demonstrate the coherence of a lecture programme based on the chapters of the book. At the end of each chapter there are notes and references relating to points in the chapters, suggestions for further reading and a set of questions and problems. The further reading has been selected to assist the student who wishes to go into more depth in a particular area and would be appropriate reading for a seminar paper based on a particular aspect of the chapter. As well as going into more depth a student may be interested in learning more about the wide variety of existing book-keeping techniques and specialist accounting systems, such as those for partnership, which are used for handling accounting data. We have analysed the principles of the structure and processing of accounting data in Chapters 3 and 4 but have not considered in any detail the numerous possible book-keeping applications. We hope that with the general principles developed in these chapters, students will be able to understand any specialist applications they may encounter in practice. As teachers we recognise that one of the major obstacles to understanding accounting is its use of a terminology which is in many areas imprecise and ambiguous. We have attempted to be consistent in our use of terminology and we must admit the exercise has increased our sympathy towards students who are commonly faced with various usages of terms such as capital, profit, cost, returns or stock. As a learning and a teaching aid we have included as the first of the questions at the end of each chapter a review of important terminology used in the chapter. This and the other questions and problems have been designed to provide a basis for personal assessments, seminar papers or seminar and tutorial discussion.

Finally we would like to recommend the idea of triple authorship for anyone who wishes to embark on a critical self-analysis of what he thinks he understands about accounting, but not for anyone who wishes to write a book in a reasonable time. We would like to acknowledge our debt to our long-suffering wives and children, and to all those who helped with the typing of the manuscript.

1976
ARTHUR HINDMARCH
MILES ATCHISON
RICHARD MARKE

Part I
MEASUREMENT

1
Concepts of Value
and Profit

1.1 Introduction

Accounting was defined in the Introduction as the measurement, recording and communication of economic data. All three aspects of accounting are examined in Part I with particular emphasis on problems of measurement.

Economic data is information about an individual, firm or organisation, which can be expressed in monetary terms. Thus for an individual this might include earnings from his job, ownership of a house or a car, or expenditure on food and clothing. A firm's economic data could include payment of wages, expenditure on materials used in its products, receipts from the sale of these products, its ownership of land, buildings and motor vehicles, or a protected market for its products.

The emphasis on the expression of data in monetary terms is the basis of accounting information and is an important factor in defining the boundaries of the subject of accounting. Some important areas of a firm's activities will be difficult to express in monetary terms, e.g. its reputation with customers, or the state of its industrial relations. It is important that students of accounting should be critically aware of the limitations of accounting measurement, as well as its potential for reflecting the performance of the firm in monetary terms.

This chapter is concerned with the general problem of measurement. The remainder of Part I analyses the application of the basic concepts developed in Chapter 1 to the measurement of past performance. In Parts II and III the concepts are applied to the analysis of future performance.

1.2 Objectives of measurement

The question of what information accounting attempts to measure is perhaps best illustrated by reference to the needs of users of the information.[1] A knowledge of a country's legal, financial, taxation and social structure would be needed to appreciate fully the wide variety of potential users. (Some evidence can be found in App. A on Legal Aspects of Accounting for Companies and App. B on Taxation.) However, some general comments can be made which do not rely on specialised knowledge.

An individual may wish to discover his financial situation, for instance, when reviewing the family budget or deciding whether to buy a new car. If he runs his own business then he is even more likely to require such information. There may also be others who are interested in his position, for example, the taxation authorities or the local authority which fixes his children's education grants.

If instead of the individual or the one-man business we consider a large firm involved in complex manufacturing and trading operations, with a large number of employees and relying on large quantities of borrowed finance, then the number of potential users grows. They include managers, owners (if different from managers), lenders of finance, taxation authorities, other government bodies, trade unions and employees. In addition there may be others who are interested because they are considering joining one of these categories. There are thus a number of categories of users of accounting information who have a legitimate interest in the affairs of a firm. As a result the firm may be said to be accountable to these users. The concept of accountability[2] has been an important factor in the development of accounting information.

It is likely that the different users will be interested in different aspects of the accounting information. The manager may be concerned to prove to the owner what a good job he has done, or he may wish to evaluate alternative courses of action; the owner wants to know if he is getting a fair return on his investment, the lender whether his loan is safe and the trade union whether the firm can justify not giving an increase in wages. In addition accounting information forms the basis by which government monitors its control over wages, prices and monopolies.

If accounting is to provide an adequate service then accounting measurement of a firm's economic information should be concerned with the needs of these users. With needs as diverse as these is it possible to set up a satisfactory model for accounting measurement? We shall see that it is possible in terms of general propositions, but that alternative interpretations of the model[3] may be required to satisfy particular needs.

The interested parties mentioned above are concerned about the 'health' of the firm, or at least with different aspects of its 'health'. The main question they are interested in is: What is the firm's current (financial) position and what effect will the choice of a particular course of action have on the present position? There are two other questions closely linked with this one: How has the firm done recently? How is it likely to do in the future? In one sense these last two questions are subsumed in the first. Obviously the recent performance of the firm will have had some effect on the current position. Less obviously, but perhaps even more important, is the fact that the present position is dependent in many ways on the future performance of the firm. For example, consider two firms which are identical except that Firm A has signed a favourable long-term sales contract whereas Firm B has not. Because of this it might be said that Firm A is in the better position, even though the increase in sales will not start until next year.

Therefore an analysis of the current position should include an estimate of future prospects. We have here one of the dilemmas of accounting measurement in that while information on recent performance that contributes towards the present position is largely factual, information on prospects is inevitably based on estimates.

Just as the individual will visit a doctor periodically to obtain information about his health, so the users of accounting information require regular reports on the health of the firm. The desirable frequency of these reports will vary from user to user. For example, the manager may wish to know each week how the firm is performing, whereas the taxation authorities may be satisfied with annual reports. In Sect. 14.2 we discuss the criteria for the determination of what constitutes a desirable frequency.

Thus an objective of accounting measurement is to provide various users with information on the state of the firm. The state of the firm can be expressed as in Fig. 1.1 in a simple diagram which will prove useful and be referred to again later in the chapter.

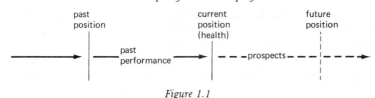

Figure 1.1

In Fig. 1.1 the arrows represent the passing of time and the vertical lines the points in time at which the firm's position is assessed. Where the lines are solid this indicates that measurements can be based on factual information while the dashed lines represent estimates.

1.3 Introduction to Value and Profit

In Sect. 1.2 the terminology used in describing what is measured was kept intentionally simple, using terms such as 'current health' or 'how the firm has done recently'. Here we introduce more specific concepts which will form the basis for much of what follows.

The economic position or health of an individual or firm can be restated in terms of what they are worth. The use of the term 'worth' in turn implies a notion of value. In Fig. 1.2 value is used to replace the term 'position' used in Fig. 1.1.

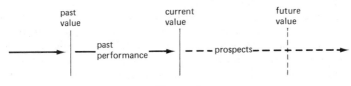

Figure 1.2

If value is taken as the measure of the health or well-being of a firm (or individual) then it follows that a measure of whether the past performance in Fig. 1.2 is good, i.e. beneficial to the well-being of the firm, is its effect on the value of the firm. The measurement of this performance in financial terms will be the increase or decrease in the value of the firm. The term used for this financial measure of performance is 'profit'. Strictly speaking the term 'profit' is only valid where the value has increased, but this can be overcome, either by referring to negative profit or to loss, where value has decreased. Fig. 1.2 can now be amended:

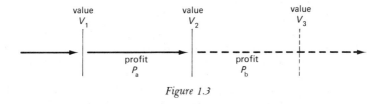

Figure 1.3

Using the symbols in Fig. 1.2 and assuming that V_2 represents value at the current date, and V_1 say a year earlier, with V_3 the estimate for a year hence, then the profit (P_a) for the past year is $V_2 - V_1$ and the estimated profit (P_b) for the next year is $V_3 - V_2$. This simply restates that profit is a change in value over time and defines profit in a simplified way which is sufficiently accurate for our present purposes. It can be expressed as a simple model: $P_t = V_t - V_{t-1}$ where P_t represents the profit for the year t (or period t) and V_t is the value at the end of the year t and V_{t-1} the value at the end of the previous year. There are two possible approaches to the measurement of value and profit used in this model. Assuming the value at V_{t-1} is known then the value at V_t can be measured thus providing a figure of profit (P_t) by solving the equation. The alternative approach is to estimate P_t, thus providing the closing value V_t as the result of the equation. Both approaches, we shall see later, are used in accounting to measure profit and value.

It is important to understand the conceptual difference between value and profit as illustrated by this model. The nature of the concept of value is that it is static, a monetary figure placed on an item or group of items at a particular point in time. Values may of course change over time but these represent measurements taken at different times. Profit on the other hand is a measure of performance over a period of time: in our model, the time linking two sets of valuations. This idea of a stock (value) and a flow (profit) concept form the basis for the major accounting statements and for most accounting systems of recording events. Its application can be seen in Sect. 1.6 on accounting statements later in this chapter.

1.4   The Concept of Value

The concept of value is examined by considering its application first to an individual, using familiar examples, and then to a firm where more specific valuation problems are introduced. An individual asked what he is worth, would probably attempt to value his possessions, his house, furniture, car, etc. If he has borrowed money from the bank to buy his car then the amount he still owes should be deducted to arrive at his net worth or value. Included in this example are three concepts basic to accounting measurement: assets, liabilities and net worth.

The dictionary defines an asset as any possession and also any useful quality. The idea of possessions is clearly relevant to the measurement of value, for example, a firm may possess assets such as cars, buildings, or machinery. Care must be taken in measuring one's value to identify those assets whose possession also implies ownership. For example, a borrowed car would not normally be included; however if it was, then a corresponding liability to the owner of the car should also be included. A liability in accounting terminology is the financial representation of an obligation owed to another individual or firm.

The question of whether a useful quality should also be included in measurement of an individual's value is more problematical. Good health and a sense of humour are useful qualities but there are obvious difficulties in estimating their monetary value. It may even be questioned whether they have any monetary value. In the sense that they could not be sold directly for money, then they have not, although indirectly they may be sold; for example, a man may get a better job if he has good health and this obviously has monetary implications. These are examples of extremely difficult measurement problems. In the context of a firm there are similarly difficult problems, for example, in valuing management, the labour force, customer relations or the reputation of its products.

Thus there are problems both of measurement and of deciding which items to include in a list of assets or liabilities, and we shall see in Chapter 2 that the accounting answer to many of these problems is simply one of practicality and easy verification. There are further fundamental questions of valuation to be considered which identify possible solutions to these problems.

If a number of people were asked to value a common object, say a car, it is likely that there would be many different values proposed. This may be because they have different levels of knowledge about cars, but it is also probable that they used different approaches to the valuation. Consider some of the possibilities:

(1)	Its cost – when new two years ago	£1300
(2)	Its cost when new – less an allowance for two years' use	£920
(3)	What it would now cost to buy a similar two-year-old car	£900
(4)	What it could be sold for – privately	£850
(5)	– to a garage, straight sale	£830
(6)	– to a garage, traded for a new car	£860
(7)	The owner's estimate of its usefulness	£950

There are seven different values shown and it is possible to detect four different basic approaches or different concepts of value:

(*a*)   Original cost – that is, an item's value is represented by its original cost. Values (1) and (2) are variations of this approach.

(*b*)   Replacement cost – instead of considering the original cost of the specific item, this approach looks at the current purchase price of similar items, i.e. value (3).

(*c*)   Selling price – an estimate of what could be received for the item if it were sold now, i.e. values (4), (5) and (6).

(*d*)   Future utility – a monetary estimate of the item's potential usefulness, which could, for example, be based on the estimated fares saved by having a car, i.e. value (7).

The implications of the use of these alternative approaches to valuation in specific areas is explored in later chapters, but we can here consider some general points:

Original Cost

The attraction of original cost is that it is the only one of the four where a transaction has taken place. At least two people have agreed on a value at some time and have been prepared to act on it, e.g. in the purchase of a car, a house or a factory. In most commercial transactions there will be evidence of what took place – a contract, bill or a receipt – and it is therefore usually possible to verify an original cost value by reference to such evidence. This means that the valuation does not have to be based on estimates but relies on impartial and objective evidence. Unfortunately reliance on a transaction approach which is the strength of the original cost concept leads also to its two major weaknesses.

The clue to the first weakness was given in the previous paragraph by the phrase, 'At least two people have agreed on a value at some time . . .'. A list of assets of an individual or a firm will include items acquired at different times in the past. It is therefore obvious that use of the original cost concept implies using values which to a lesser or greater extent are historical. The only exception to this would be where all the items being valued were acquired at the precise time of valuation, but it is clear this would be an unlikely exception. This aspect of the original cost approach will be referred to in more sophisticated terms in later chapters but perhaps the simplest explanation of the problems is that such values become out of date because prices change as supply and demand conditions change and the assets deteriorate through wear and tear. There are ways around this problem such as revaluing the original transaction figures by considering any changes in price levels or making adjustments to the data to allow for wear and tear but this destroys, or at least limits, the objectivity of the valuation.

The second major weakness is that using the original cost in a transaction as the basis for valuation eliminates anything which did not arise from a transaction. If an individual builds a car out of spare parts collected from other discarded vehicles, then it would seem that it has no value, using an original cost approach. It is possible to estimate what the parts would have cost him and to put a value on the leisure time he has spent but these estimates would not qualify as transactions or be objective evidence of value. The example may seem unrealistic but there are many such instances in firms of items of value which have not arisen from specific transactions and thus have no 'original cost'. For example, a firm has an idea for a new product which could take over the whole market in its field, or has built up a reputation and customer relationship which is the envy of all its competitors, or has developed a group of managers who are far more efficient than those of its competitors. None of these items, which could be the difference between a firm succeeding or going out of business, would be included in a valuation of the firm using original cost principles.

Replacement Cost
Using the cost which would have to be incurred to replace an asset has the attraction of giving an up-to-date valuation. To some extent it also uses objective criteria in that, if possible, the replacement costs are based on current market prices. However, there are many areas where the replacement cost concept is difficult to apply. Taking the example of the car, this particular type may have been discontinued and there may be few second-hand cars being sold; or it may have particular characteristics, such as excessive usage, accident damage, etc., which make an accurate replacement price difficult to gauge. An important issue is whether the replacement cost should be based on an identical item or merely one which is similar to the original in terms of the services it provides. In practice it will usually be based on a similar item. For example, an insurance company's estimate of replacement cost would be based on the make and year of the car and might virtually ignore all its other characteristics. In a firm there may be assets whose market replacement cost is difficult to ascertain, among them the examples given in the paragraphs on original cost; the idea for a new product, reputation, customer relations and efficient management are all apposite here. Replacement cost is easiest to apply where there is a recognised market in which the asset is bought and sold, e.g. standard commodities, motor cars, houses, etc., but it works less well where the asset has qualities which make it peculiar to the firm, e.g. a purpose-built factory with specialised machinery.

Selling Price
The advantages of this concept of value are similar to those for replacement cost in that it provides an up-to-date value and in some circumstances an objective one. The qualification on objectivity is necessary because a selling price calculated using existing market prices is only reliable where the asset is one identical to those being sold in the market.

As with replacement cost, where the asset has individual characteristics there may be a wide divergence between the owner's idea of value and what the asset would realise if sold. If an individual has recently bought a suit, its selling price is unlikely to be an acceptable measure of value. Similarly, if a firm builds a stretch of road to give better access to its factory, the selling price of the road may not be a reasonable measure of its value. In general the market selling price is likely to be least adequate where the prime purpose for owning an asset is not resale; for example, a firm's machinery, offices and factories.

Future Utility

The term 'utility', as used here, has a meaning similar to its use in economics, i.e. usefulness to the owner of the asset or the satisfaction derived from the benefits arising out of the asset. For this reason the concept is sometimes termed 'value in use'.

Original cost, replacement cost and selling price are similar to each other in at least one important respect: they are all variations of a market price, albeit at different points in time. Of course they differ in that original cost is the actual market price for the purchase at some time in the past, replacement cost is a simulated current market purchase price, and selling price is a simulated current market selling price. In each case the valuation is based on what the valuer ascertains to be the market's evaluation of the asset, given the different stated circumstances.

The concept of future utility is different from the other three in that it attempts to value the asset by assessing its qualities in monetary terms independently of market considerations. What this entails is estimating the present value of future benefits arising from the asset. The implication of this approach is that nothing has any value unless it is of some future benefit; for example, one buys a suit, car or a house for the benefit they will provide subsequent to the purchase, and a firm buys land, buildings, machinery, etc., for similar reasons.

The definition of benefits can be widely drawn to include tangible things which are easily expressed in monetary terms; for example, income from sales or cost savings from increased efficiency; and non-tangible items such as convenience, pleasure, etc. Thus if the asset is a ton of coal owned by a coal merchant its value could be the money benefits to be received from selling it. In this example the value is the same as in the selling price approach. If, however, the asset is a piece of machinery, its value may be the money earned from the sale of products produced on it. This may be very different from the selling price of the machinery itself.

An illustration of this approach is given in Fig. 1.4.

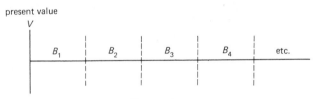

Figure 1.4

V is what we are trying to measure, i.e. the value of the asset using future-utility and B_1, B_2, B_3, B_4, etc., are the benefits arising in future periods 1, 2, 3, 4, etc. A simple mathematical expression to calculate the value is $V = B_1 + B_2 + B_3 + B_4$, etc. In practice the values of B would not simply be added without adjustment, because a sum received in period B_1 will not be the same as an equivalent money sum received in period B_4, i.e. benefits received in later years would have a lower weighting than those received in early years. For example the value of £950 estimated for the car on page 7 is equivalent to cash benefits of £300 p.a. for 4 years where the weighting is assumed to be measured by a rate of interest of 10%. A more sophisticated explanation of this point is given in Chapter 12 in connection with discounted cash flow techniques, and an explanation of the mathematical basis of the technique is included in App. C. The term 'present value' is usually used when value is calculated using the future-utility approach.

The estimation of B will be easiest where the benefits are cash returns, e.g. the cash proceeds from selling the coal or the products produced on the machinery. There will of course be estimation problems because the benefits may be spread over many future years. Far greater problems arise in estimating B where the benefits are not obviously cash benefits. Consider for example the valuation of a painting where the benefits are at least partially aesthetic, or the situation of a firm which builds a sports pavilion for its employees. It may do so in the hope that its firm's commercial performance will improve because of reduced staff turnover, more loyal or healthy employees. It will be extremely difficult to put a monetary value on these benefits.

It was stated earlier that this approach of considering future benefits was different from the other approaches which use some variant of market prices. However, this difference should not be over-emphasised because market prices are themselves the result of supply and demand for an asset and demand is generated by the future benefits used in the future-utility approach. For example, the individuals who constitute the market for motor cars are prepared to pay the market price because of the benefits they estimate they will receive from these items, and an elementary knowledge of economics will show that these individuals may influence the price if they value the benefits sufficiently highly to compete and push up the price.

The approach of using future utility enables the asset to be valued using the benefits as defined by the owner of the asset whether the owner is an individual or a firm. This makes such a valuation a subjective one. For example, an individual may derive more pleasure from a painting than anyone else and his valuation of it will be higher than anyone else's. Similarly, if a firm has a group of assets including land, a factory, machinery and a labour force, it may put a high value on them because it considers it can use them in combination to obtain large future monetary benefits. On the other hand because others estimate less potential in the assets, or have different opportunities for their use, they may put a much lower value on them. Once market values are discarded and replaced by individual estimates of potential inherent in an asset, it will be more difficult to achieve a valuation which is generally acceptable.

RELEVANT VALUE CONCEPT

In this chapter four concepts of value have been considered. We have seen that it is unlikely that the application of each concept would result in the same value for an asset. We shall see in the remainder of the book that it will not be possible to advocate one concept which will be the most relevant in each situation. Relevance must be related to the needs of the users of accounting information. We can, however, suggest a method of assessing which concept might give the most relevant valuation in a particular situation. The method, which is based on the work of Bonbright[4] and Solomons,[5] is to consider what the loss would be to the owner of the item being valued if he was deprived of it. This is sometimes referred to as 'deprival value' or 'opportunity value', being the value of the lost opportunity and thus similar to the economist's definition of opportunity cost.[6] This gives an indication of the value to the owner.

Applying this criterion to the example of the car, we can examine which of the four approaches might be the most appropriate. Assume initially that the car is identical with many others freely available on the second-hand market. If the owner intends to sell, then it is the selling price he would lose if he were deprived of the car. If he intends to keep the car, then its replacement cost would be relevant because that is what he would have to pay out if he were deprived of this car and had to replace it. This assumes that the future utility value as calculated by the owner is at least as high as the replacement cost. If it is not, then the future utility value may be the relevant value because were he deprived of the car he would not replace it at a cost higher than its future utility to him. Similarly in the unlikely situation of the selling price being above the replacement cost, the maximum sacrifice of losing the car must be the replacement cost because he could always buy another car at this price and resell it at the higher price. The conclusion from this analysis is that where we are dealing with an homogeneous item which can be easily replaced by an identical item then replacement cost is the maximum value that could be attributed to the item, but that selling price or future utility value if lower could be more appropriate, depending on whether the intention was to sell or retain the item. Original cost has not been mentioned in this analysis because it cannot, except by coincidence, be the most appropriate measure of what the owner would lose if deprived of the car. He has already paid out the original cost and what he loses must be based on a current estimate of value. However, as mentioned earlier in this chapter and elsewhere in this book, original cost may be the most appropriate measure because it is easily verified and because of the defects of the other measures in practical situations.

The same criterion of deprival value can be applied in situations where the item is not homogeneous with other products and cannot be readily bought or sold in a recognised market. In this situation, however, it is more difficult to state that the replacement cost is the maximum value because it may not be possible to replace with an identical item. For example, if a car is a unique custom-built model, or if its owner had placed high sentimental value on it, then the future utility may be the most appropriate because the selling price may not reflect the owner's high utility value and it could not be replaced with an identical model.

In conclusion, the relevant value concept will depend on the circumstances of the valuation but the concept of deprival value will be a useful guideline to the choice of valuation method.[7]

1.5 The concept of profit

By referring again to Fig. 1.3 we can see that profit and value are closely related concepts. It was stated earlier that the well-being of an organisation is measured by its worth or value and that changes in this value over time is what is defined as profit (or loss). The measurement of profit will thus be closely linked with the concept of value employed.

It may seem that this explanation of profit is unnecessarily complicated because most people have an idea what profit is. For example, a dictionary definition of 'profit' is simple – 'a pecuniary gain or the excess of returns over outlay'. This definition, though it is acceptable, still leaves the problem of defining gain, returns and outlay. The simplest view of making a profit is that of selling an article for more than its cost. The terms gain, returns and outlay are represented here by profit, sales and cost and the notion of valuation seems unnecessary. There is a valuation process involved but it is easily overlooked,

$$V_0 \longrightarrow V_1$$

V_0 represents the starting-point of the transaction, when the valuation is that of the cost of the article, or at least of the value of whatever was given in return for the purchase, most likely cash. The distance between V_0 and V_1 is the time the article was held before resale and V_1 is the value of the proceeds of the sale. Profit is V_1 less

V_0. If all transactions and commercial operations could be considered in this simple form then it might indeed be unnecessary to consider profit in terms of changes in value. However, there are complicating factors in practice which we will now consider:

(a)   Usually it is not simply a single transaction that is being accounted for but the total affairs of an individual or organisation.

(b)   Although in the final analysis most commerce can be thought of as buying and selling, the actual processes tend to obscure this. In operating a business, say a shop, the owner buys and sells his products but he must also buy things he does not intend to sell, e.g. a cash register, shop fittings, or the services of an assistant. Extending this example to a manufacturing organisation, then the products sold are entirely different from those purchased by the firm. For example, a motor manufacturer buys steel, rubber, glass, etc., and sells motor cars. In addition he must buy many things he does not sell, e.g. labour, factory buildings, office furniture, etc. Thus the single arrow is insufficient to illustrate the normal activity for which profit calculations are required. This can be seen in Fig. 1.5 which shows several activities, some of which are concerned with running the business but only indirectly with actual selling. Before we discuss Fig. 1.5 in detail there are further complicating factors.

(c)   A third complication which arises to some extent out of the second is that of the time span of the various activities mentioned in (b) above. Let us take the example of the activities involved in running a sports shop, e.g. purchase of the lease on the shop, provision of shop fittings, of counters, shelves, etc., payment of wages to an assistant and two product lines – table tennis bats and billiard tables, and consider the time element in each. The business may have a definite time span but it is more likely to be open-ended; the owner may wish to hand it on to his son when he retires. The lease will have a definite time span, say ten years, but the owner may have the option of renewing the lease. The time span of the shop fittings will depend on how long the owner decides they are serving their purpose, but let us assume this is three years. The assistant may be paid weekly and be on a week's notice so that the purchase of his labour and the payment for it takes place at weekly intervals. The table-tennis bats are usually in stock for about a month but the billiard tables may be held for two years before they are resold.

One of the objectives of measurement referred to earlier was to provide regular reports on the health of the firm. If this was not necessary and we could wait, for example, until the business ceased operating before we worked out how it had done, i.e. what profit it had made, then the problems introduced above could be minimised.[8] However this is clearly impracticable and regular measurement of profit is necessary and it is obviously much more difficult now to compare returns and outlays as suggested in the original definition of profit.

The complications explained in (c) above can perhaps be best expressed in a diagram. Fig. 1.5 shows the activities of the business by means of arrows, the length of the arrows representing the time period involved in each activity. Activities which are regularly repeated are shown by a series of arrows; for example, the payment of weekly wages and the turnover of table-tennis bats and billiard tables. As mentioned above, measuring profit would be much easier if we could wait until the business closed, or in terms of the diagram until each arrow had ended, i.e. the lease had run out, the shop fittings disposed of, the assistant paid off and remaining products sold. However, information is required at intermediate times. Profit has to be measured for interim periods in the life of the business and there are various unexpired activities at the end of these periods. In Fig. 1.5 the periods are assumed to be years represented by the vertical lines.

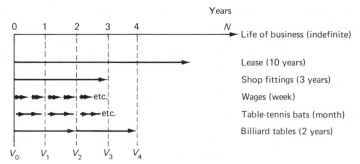

Figure 1.5

It should be clear that measuring profit for a particular period in the life of an organisation is a difficult task. Taking Year 1 in Fig. 1.5 as an example, it is possible that the only 'returns' are from the sale of some of the table-tennis bats. The 'outlay' to set against these returns could be expressed in terms of the cost of the lease, shop fittings and wages; but what part of this cost? The chief difficulties arise because the various activities are not coterminous with the period for which profit is being measured. It is rather like looking at a 10,000-metres race over thirty laps of the track and, instead of waiting until the end to decide the winner, taking a particular lap and evaluating the performance of the runners. The speed over the lap and position at the end of the lap are only partial indications of the runners' performance, and likelihood of success in the competition. It would not be surprising if two commentators arrived at different estimates of the performance of an athlete for the lap in question, for there can be no definite answer until the race is over. Similarly the question of what is the profit of a firm for a particular period is unlikely to have a single definite answer until the life of the organisation is over and all its activities ceased, and we have the benefit of hindsight. This does not of course preclude meaningful estimates of profit, just as some commentators may accurately predict the end of the race. It is because the measurement of profit is so difficult that it is useful to consider it as a problem of valuation at points in time and to see profit as the reason for changes in these values. If this is so, then the approach to valuation, discussed earlier, will have a direct effect on the profit measured. The dictionary definition was, 'pecuniary gain or the excess of returns over outlay'. Pecuniary gain in the terms of our analysis is an increase in value and similarly returns and outlay are increases and decreases in value respectively.

1.6   Accounting statements

Measurement of profit and value was introduced at the beginning of the chapter as a means of providing information on the state of an organisation. In some respects the types of user of this information and their requirements depends on the form of organisation involved. A common classification of organisations, by reference to their legal status, is sole trader, partnership and company. Details of these types of organisations and their relevance to the presentation of accounting information can be found in Chapter 17 and App. A. Although the requirements of the users of accounting information will vary depending on the type of organisation, the usual means of communicating the information is by means of accounting statements, e.g. the balance sheet (also known as the position statement, especially in the U.S.A.) and the profit statement. The more usual U.K. terminology for the latter is profit and loss account but profit statement is preferred in the text because we consider it less confusing for students new to accounting. (See Sect. 4.4 for further explanation of this terminology and Sects D.1 and D.2 for examples of the profit and loss account and balance sheet of Marks & Spencer Ltd.)

The terms 'assets' and 'liabilities' were introduced earlier in the chapter as the items which should be included in a calculation of value. The total monetary value of a firm's assets less its liabilities is usually known as its 'net worth'. Net worth is also known as 'owners' equity', which represented the firm's liability to the owner. It has been explained that there are problems of what to include in a list of assets or liabilities and of how to put a monetary value on them, but for the moment we will ignore the problems. The term used in accounting for the statement which records these assets and liabilities is the 'balance sheet'. Thus the simplest form of balance sheet would be:

Balance Sheet of ABC company at 1 January 19X1

	£
Assets	3000
Liabilities	500
Net Worth (or Owners' Equity)	£2500

Referring to Fig. 1.3 this balance sheet could represent the company's position at V_1. If we assume that V_2 is one year later, the next balance sheet could be:

Balance Sheet of ABC company at 1 January 19X2

	£
Assets	3700
Liabilities	600
Net Worth (or Owners' Equity)	£3100

If the definition of profit is the change in value over the time then it is clear that the company has a profit of £600 (£3100 − £2500) for the year 19X1, the period between the two balance-sheet dates. (There are situations where the £600 may not be the profit, i.e. where the owner has introduced or withdrawn assets from the firm. This is explained further in Sect. 3.4.) The purpose of the profit statement is to show in detail how the £600 has been earned; for example, it may be the net result of buying and selling products, and the associated outlay and returns:

Profit Statement of ABC Company for the year ended 1 January 19X2

	£
Revenue – Sale of Products	4000
Less	
Expense – Cost of Products Sold	2400
	1600
Less	
Expense – Cost of Wages	1000
Profit	£ 600

In accounting terminology outlay and returns are usually referred to as expenses and revenues. The balance sheets and profit statement shown above were presented in the simplest possible form and reveal little of the nature of the company and what its net worth represented. In practice the balance sheets would show much more detail (see App. D.2) and below they are expanded to give more information and also to introduce terminology which will be useful in subsequent chapters:

Balance Sheet of ABC company at 1 January

Assets	19x1	19x2
	£	£
Land	1000	1000
Buildings	800	1300
Inventory	400	600
Debtors	300	500
Cash	500	300
Total Assets	3000	3700
Liabilities		
Creditors	500	600
Net Worth (or Owners' Equity)	£2500	£3100

The balance sheet now shows details of the assets and liabilities owned and owed by the company. The value of the company at the two dates is the total assets less the single liability. Terms which may require an explanation are 'inventory', 'debtors' and 'creditors'. Inventories are products held with the intention of selling them, e.g. groceries in a supermarket or coal held by a coal merchant. Debtors represent the amount owed to the firm by customers who bought on credit, and creditors the amount owed by the firm where it, in turn, has bought on credit from its suppliers.

A feature which may initially cause problems is the fact that although the company has made a profit of £600 for the year the cash owned by the company has fallen from £500 to £300. This need not cause any problems if it is remembered that profit was defined as an increase in total value or the total of the assets less liabilities, and there may be various changes in individual assets, of which cash is one, and the fall in cash is compensated by increases elsewhere, e.g. in buildings.

It should be emphasised that in introducing these accounting statements, nothing has been said about the basis on which the figures contained in them are derived. They do show a value for the company and a profit, but discussion of what value and profit concepts are used in accounting statements will be considered in detail in Chapter 2.

1.7   Summary

The chapter began by examining the question of the objective of accounting measurement. This objective was to be the measurement of the health or well-being of the organisation. It was accepted that a judgment of what constitutes well-being will depend to some extent on who is making the judgment, because different groups of people, e.g. owners, investors, trade unions, may have different objectives. However, it was decided that the measure likely to be most satisfactory was the concept of value linked to the concept of profit. Four alternative concepts of value – original cost, replacement cost, selling price and future utility – were considered and the underlying concept of deprival value was suggested as a criterion for choosing the relevant approach in a particular situation. These concepts were examined without specific reference to their accounting interpretations, which is the subject of Chapter 2. The likely forms of organisation being accounted for were introduced, partly as an aid to understanding the terminology in subsequent chapters on practical measurement problems. For similar reasons the basic accounting statements were also introduced.

Notes and References

1. G. Macdonald, *Profit Measurement: Alternatives to Historical Cost* (London, Haymarket, 1974) chap. 4, and Accounting Standards Steering Committee, *The Corporate Report* (London, Accounting Standards Steering Committee, 1975) sect. 2.
2. P. Bird, *Accountability: Standards in Financial Reporting* (London, Haymarket, 1973).
3. For a general introduction to the nature of models see P. M. Rigby, *Models in Business Analysis* (New York, Macmillan Co., 1969).
4. J. C. Bonbright, *The Valuation of Property* (New York, McGraw-Hill, 1937; reprinted by The Michie Co., Charlottesville, Va, 1965) vol. I, chap. 4.
5. D. Solomons, 'Economic and Accounting Concepts of Cost and Value', in M. Backer (ed.), *Modern Accounting Theory* (Englewood Cliffs, N.J., Prentice-Hall, 1966).
6. See most introductory economics texts, for example R. G. Lipsey, *An Introduction to Positive Economics*, 2nd ed. (London, Weidenfeld & Nicolson, 1971).
7. Sandilands, *Inflation Accounting: Report of the Inflation Accounting Committee*, Cmnd 6225 (H.M.S.O., 1975). Provides a comprehensive analysis of the four concepts of value and of deprival value, which it refers to as 'value to the business'.
8. Professor David Solomons has written: 'all the problems of income [i.e. profit] measurement are the result of our desire to attribute income to arbitrarily determined short periods of time. Everything comes right in the end; but by then, it is too late to matter.' ('Economic and Accounting Concepts of Income', *Accounting Review*, vol. XXXVI (1961) 374–83; reprinted in *Readings in the Concept and Measurement of Income*, ed. R. H. Parker and G. C. Harcourt (Cambridge University Press, 1969).)

Further Reading

Arthur Andersen & Co., *Objectives of Financial Statements for Business Enterprises* (Chicago, Arthur Andersen & Co., 1972).

A. M. Bourne, 'Valuation and Profit', in A. M. Bourn (ed.), *Studies in Accounting for Management Decision* (London, McGraw-Hill, 1969).

H. C. Edey, 'Accounting Principles and Business Reality', *Accountancy* (July 1963); reprinted in *Modern Financial Management*, ed. B. V. Carsberg and H. C. Edey (Harmondsworth, Penguin Books, 1969).

H. C. Edey, 'The Nature of Profit', *Accounting and Business Research*, no. 1 (Winter, 1970).

R. H. Parker and G. C. Harcourt, *Readings in the Concept and Measurement of Income* (Cambridge University Press, 1969).

R. Sidebotham, *Introduction to the Theory and Context of Accounting* (Oxford, Pergamon, 1970).

E. Stamp and C. Marley, *Accounting Principles and the City Code: The Case for Reform* (London, Butterworth, 1970).

Accounting Standards Steering Committee, *The Corporate Report* (London, Accounting Standards Steering Committee, 1975).

Sandilands, *Inflation Accounting: Report of the Inflation Accounting Committee*, Cmnd 6225 (H.M.S.O., 1975).

T. A. Lee, *Income and Value Measurement: Theory and Practice* (London, Nelson, 1974).

Questions and Problems

1.1 What do you understand by the following terminology?

Value	Selling price	Balance sheet
Accountability	Future utility	Profit statement
Present value	Deprival value	Net worth
Profit	Opportunity cost	Owners' equity
Assets	Objective evidence	Expense
Liabilities	Sole trader	Revenue
Original cost	Partnership	Inventory
Replacement cost	Company	Debtor
		Creditor

1.2 List the different individuals or groups who might be interested in accounting information. What different aspects might they be interested in?

1.3 What, in your view, constitutes a healthy company?

1.4 Draw a diagram which illustrates that value is a stock, and profit a flow, concept.

1.5 A firm borrows £10,000 on 1 January. During January it buys goods for £6000 and then sells half of them for £5000. All transactions are in cash and the firm has no other assets and liabilities. What is the value of the firm at the beginning of January and at the end of January and what is the profit for the month? Make what assumptions you think are necessary. Show that it is possible to arrive at the same profit calculation in two ways.

1.6 Four alternative approaches to valuation are suggested in Chapter 1. Discuss how these might be applied to: a private car, a company car, a field, an automated production line, a computer, a footballer, or a company's reputation for good workmanship and efficient service.

1.7 Why are accounting statements produced annually or at more regular intervals? What problems arise because of the necessity for such regular reporting?

1.8 Prepare a balance sheet from the following information, which is for the Anderson Company as at 30 June 19X3.

	£
Creditors	5000
Debtors	6000
Inventory	4000
Bank overdraft	2000
Machinery	5000
Buildings	4000

1.9 The Anderson Company in 1.8 has been in business for two years only. It started on 1 July 19X1 with £4000 cash borrowed from the bank. At 30 June 19X2 it had inventory £2000, debtors £3000, machinery £3000, and a bank overdraft of £3000. What is its profit for each of the two years to 30 June 19X3?

2
Accounting Concepts

2.1 Introduction

In Chapter 1 it was stated that the central objective of accounting measurement was to provide information about the well-being of the firm. This could be best expressed in terms of value and profit and the accounting statements which present this information are the balance sheet and profit statement. The discussion of the measurement of value and profit emphasised the following problems:

(a) The most suitable concept of value. Four alternatives were considered: original cost, replacement cost, selling price and future utility.

(b) The items which should be included in the list of assets to be valued.

(c) The most suitable approach to the problem of the need for periodic profit measurement of the firm's activities, many of which are only partially completed.

(d) How measurement can be related to the needs of the users of the information.

The aim of this chapter is to consider the concepts which have been adopted or developed in accounting, to measure and record information about firms and to attempt to evaluate these concepts, especially in the context of the problem areas listed above.

2.2 Need for a conceptual framework

Accounting information is prepared for an organisation for internal and external use. Internally it forms the basis for an evaluation of past performance and is a guide for decision makers. External users include investors, lenders, taxation authorities, trade unions and government departments. It was made clear in Chapter 1 that the task of regular measurement of the position and profit of a firm is a difficult one and that there are conceptual as well as practical problems. It might be possible for each accountant to work out his own solution to these problems but this would clearly be an unacceptable method of operating. There is a need for a set of assumptions and rules which provide a conceptual framework to be used as a guide to preparing accounting information.

It seems sensible that there should be some degree of consistency about the way in which accounting information is prepared. This makes it easier for those preparing and interpreting the information. It also limits the area of discretion open to the accountant or to the firm to present information in a biased manner. The strength of this last comment depends of course on the sanctions provided against not working within the framework. Perhaps the most important reason for having a conceptual framework is that it is more likely to establish confidence in accounting information. This is very necessary when it is remembered that the various users of the information both internal and external are expected to use it as the basis, for example, for investment decisions, calculating taxation, or evaluating management performance or as a guide to government policy.

There are conflicting views as to what the nature and content of such an agreed framework should be. One possibility is to accept that the content does not matter provided it is generally acceptable. For example, temperature is measured on a thermometer using a standard gauge. In the U.K. this gauge has in the past been Fahrenheit while in other European countries it is Centigrade. The use of two standards operates satisfactorily provided everyone using the information understands the basis of measurement. There are in fact differences between countries on approaches to the accounting measurement of value and profit and as with Fahrenheit and Centigrade it is important to understand the basis of the measurement before using data from different countries. The alternative view is that the conceptual framework must measure the underlying reality and it is thus not sufficient that it is merely generally acceptable. This view assumes that there is an underlying reality and thus a correct value for the accounting information being measured.

2.3 Development of a conceptual framework

The analysis in Sect. 2.2 of the need for a conceptual framework for accounting information could apply equally to information for internal or external use. However, it will be shown that the conceptual framework developed for preparing information for external use, or for measuring past performance, is not necessarily the most appropriate for internal use, e.g. by management in making decisions for planning and control. The rest of this chapter is concerned with conceptual framework which has developed primarily for external reporting and in the rest of Part I we analyse the application of the framework to particular types of accounting information. In Parts II and III where we develop the theme of accounting measurement into the areas of planning and control we shall examine further the relationship of accounting information for internal and external purposes.

While we may agree that a framework is necessary, deciding what it should consist of is likely to be more difficult. There are various ways in which a framework could evolve. It could be set out in a formal legal document such as an act of parliament which shows it either as a broad statement of principle or as a detailed set of working rules. Alternatively it could be a voluntary code of practice evolved by agreement, implicit or explicit between the various interested parties, for example, professional accounting bodies, shareholders' associations, company representatives or the Inland Revenue. In practice, of course, these two possibilities are closely related because a law which is not based on the agreement of the parties to which it relates may not be very useful.

The role of the accounting profession in connection with auditing[1,2] is particularly important in the development of a conceptual framework. In the U.K. companies are required each year to publish copies of their financial statements, i.e. the balance sheet and profit statement. The content of these statements is an important source of information for a variety of users (see App. D). It is thus important that there should be some means of reassuring the user that the information can be relied on. Part of this reassurance is that the statements have been prepared using an agreed conceptual framework. The role of the auditor in preparation of the auditor's report (see App. D.4) as determined by company law is to report to the shareholders on the statements and in particular to state whether, in accordance with Section 149(1) of the Companies Act, 1948: the balance sheet 'gives a true and fair view of the state of affairs of the company as at the end of its financial year, and the profit and loss account of the company gives a true and fair view of the profit or loss of the company for the financial year'.

The interpretation of what constitutes a true and fair view[3] is left to the accounting profession and in particular to the auditor. A review of the history of reported accounting information will show that the interpretation has changed over time.[4] It is based on a conceptual framework which has in the past been recognised as consisting of a set of generally accepted accounting principles. It is of course difficult in practice to say what a rather vague term like 'generally accepted' means but a major influence in the U.K. has been the Institute of Chartered Accountants. This body has issued over the past thirty years a series of 'Recommendations on accounting principles'. These are not rules which members must follow but are, in the words of the Institute, 'persuasive in intent'. The accounting profession has been the subject of criticism for having a conceptual framework which was not generally understood and which gave too much latitude in producing accounting information. As a result the profession has since 1970 issued a series of 'Statements of Standard Accounting Practice' (S.S.A.P.) which it expects its members to observe. It is likely that these statements will be an important influence on accounting information and they are considered in more detail later in this chapter and in Chapter 17.

The Government influences the standards and content of accounting information directly through acts of parliament such as the Companies Acts (see App. A), or it may, by the implied threat of legislation in areas where it is thought necessary, persuade the profession to amend their standards.[5] Its indirect influence is shown, for example, in setting regulations for taxing of business profits which may influence how those profits are measured for other purposes. The Council of the Stock Exchange, as the body responsible for regulating the public issue of shares and their subsequent trading, is also influential and in fact has its own rules on the reporting of accounting information which go beyond the legal requirements. Finally public opinion as expressed in the press, on radio and television may be the motivating force in obtaining changes in the basis of accounting information.

In many respects the U.S.A. has led the way in developing accounting concepts. The influences on accounting information in the U.S.A. are similar to those in this country but there are features which merit special attention. In 1934 in the wake of the depression the Securities and Exchange Commission (S.E.C.) was set up as a government 'watchdog' over the operation of companies. It has been particularly concerned with the content of financial statements and has the authority to prescribe the accounting principles used in these statements. It has not explicitly used this authority to any great extent but the knowledge that it is there seems to have prompted the American Institute of Certified Public Accountants (A.I.C.P.A.) into taking a more positive role in defining accounting principles. This they did by setting up the Committee on Accounting Procedure in 1938 which was replaced in 1959 by the Accounting Principles Board, in turn replaced in 1973 by the Financial Accounting Standards Board. The opinions on accounting principles issued by the board constitute authoritative statements in the U.S.A. and are known as 'generally accepted accounting principles'. There may, however, be additional principles which are acceptable provided they have sufficient support from accountants and businessmen.

The Netherlands and West Germany have concepts and practices similar to the U.K. and U.S.A. In countries where the accounting professions are less well developed and do not have as much influence as in the U.K., as for example in Spain and Portugal, the idea of generally accepted accounting concepts does not have the same force. Two recent developments may help to reduce the differences between countries. One was the establishment of the European Economic Community and its programme to harmonise company law in the Community. This should lead to more standardisation of accounting practices of countries and companies within the E.E.C. (The impact of the E.E.C. on the U.K. is discussed further in Chapter 17.) The other development was the setting up in 1973 of an International Accounting Standards Committee to consider the establishment of standards where companies are operating across international boundaries.

2.4 Content of a conceptual framework

The terminology used to describe this area of accounting is often a source of confusion. It is perhaps ironic that in the area of 'generally accepted accounting principles' there appears to be no generally accepted terminology. So far we have used the terms 'concept', 'conceptual framework' and 'principles'. Other terms which are used include 'conventions', 'rules', 'doctrines', 'postulates' and 'standards'. Attempts have been made by various writers[6] to sort out this confusion by distinguishing between, on the one hand, fundamental theoretical principles and, on the other, applications or 'rules of thumb' which are the expedients of practice. The S.S.A.P. no. 2, 'Disclosure of Accounting Policies', issued in 1971 attempted to reduce the extent of this confusion of terminology. The foreword to the statement says:

It is fundamental to the understanding and interpretation of financial accounts that those who use them should be aware of the main assumptions on which they are based. The purpose of this Statement . . . is to assist such understanding by promoting improvement in the quality of information disclosed. It seeks to achieve this by establishing as standard accounting practice the disclosure in financial accounts of clear explanations of the accounting policies followed in so far as these are significant for the purpose of giving a true and fair view.

In the Statement a distinction is made between:

(1) Fundamental accounting concepts
    These are defined as 'broad basic assumptions which underline the periodic financial accounts of business enterprises'. Their fundamental nature is, however, qualified by the further comment that 'they are practical rules rather than theoretical ideals and are capable of variation and evolution as accounting thought and practice develop'.
(2) Accounting bases
    Defined as 'the methods which have been developed for expressing or applying fundamental accounting concepts to financial transactions and items'. We shall see in later chapters that because of the wide diversity of business situations there may be several bases for dealing with particular items and this is the reason for the third category:
(3) Accounting policies
    These are 'the specific accounting bases judged by business enterprises to be most appropriate to their circumstances and adopted by them for the purpose of preparing their financial accounts'.

This terminology will be adopted for the remainder of the book to describe the accounting conceptual framework of principles and practices (see App. D.3). The relationships between these aspects of the accounting framework is shown by Fig. 2.1.

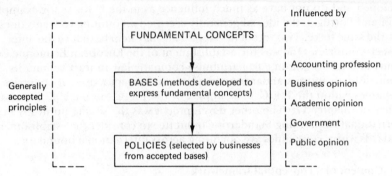

Figure 2.1   Accounting framework

Fig. 2.1 shows that what constitutes generally acceptable concepts and bases is subject to a variety of influences, i.e. the professional accounting bodies, government, business, academic and public opinion. The effect of these influences is difficult to assess. In this chapter we are chiefly concerned with accounting concepts. Accounting bases and policies are considered further in Chapters 5–9, and 16 and 17.

S.S.A.P. no. 2 singled out four concepts for special mention: going concern, accruals, consistency and prudence. It is pointed out in a footnote to the Statement that it was considered expedient to recognise only these four concepts as having general acceptance at that time (i.e. November 1971) but that a more theoretical approach would include other concepts. Further evidence that these four concepts may not form an exhaustive list is to be found in the U.S.A. The American Institute of Certified Public Accountants in *Accounting Research Study 7 (1965)* listed ten basic concepts and other lists have also been compiled in the U.S.A. by other professional accounting bodies and by individual writers. These lists have slight variations in terminology and the number of concepts but the following seem to have general support:

Going concern
Matching (or accruals)
Consistency
Conservatism ⎱
Realisation   ⎰ (or prudence)
Entity
Objectivity
Materiality
Money measurement (including an assumption of a stable monetary unit)

The first five concepts are similar to the four singled out in S.S.A.P. no. 2. Going concern and consistency survive with the same title; the accrual concept becomes the matching concept and the concept of prudence approximates to a combination of conservatism and realisation. There is reason to assume that the other concepts listed apply to the U.K. as well as to the U.S.A. and may thus be included in subsequent Statements. For this reason an explanation is given below of each of the concepts listed above. As stated, the framework consists of generally accepted concepts, bases and policies. The framework is thus an attempt to specify the underlying ideas which are believed to guide accountants in their measurement of accounting data.

2.5 The concepts defined and illustrated

We will now examine and define the accounting concepts listed above.

Going Concern. It is assumed that, unless there is evidence to the contrary, the business will have a continuing existence. This is important in the valuation of assets, especially those which have little use outside the business. Such assets may have little selling price value but with the going-concern assumption their value in use is more significant.

Matching (or Accruals). Profit has been defined as change in value, expressed in the profit statement as revenue less expenses. Profit is usually measured and profit statements prepared at regular intervals. The process of matching is an attempt to ensure that the revenues recorded in a period are matched with the expenses incurred in earning them.

Consistency. Accounting information should be prepared on a consistent basis from period to period and within periods there should be consistent treatment of similar items. This at first sight seems too obvious to be regarded as a concept but it will be seen to be important when it is realised that there may be several alternative bases for dealing with similar situations.

Conservatism. This is difficult to define because it is an expression of a general attitude that it is thought should be applied to accounting measurement and reporting. It is equivalent to taking a cautious or prudent approach to valuation. It will be a matter of judgment and experience as to what constitutes a conservative approach in a particular situation but it is a concept which seems firmly entrenched and underlies most of the other concepts. If it is possible to measure with accuracy then conservatism has little impact, but there are many situations where accuracy cannot be achieved and in such situations this concept should prevent optimism.

Realisation. Increases in the value of assets should not be recognised in accounting statements unless they have been realised by an exchange of assets. This means that revenues and profits will not be recognised until realised. What constitutes realisation is not always clearly definable. For example, the sale of an asset for cash is clearly a realised revenue and a sale on credit will also usually be recognised as realised. However, where assets appear to have increased in value when judged by a market price, this will usually not be recognised as a realisation unless the asset is actually sold. On the other hand a different view may be taken of assets which have fallen in value. These expenses may be recognised immediately though the asset is not yet sold. This is an example of the realisation and conservatism concept working together.

Entity. If accounting information for a unit of organisation is to be meaningful it is important to identify the entity of the unit and distinguish it from other units. For example, a sole trader's business unit should be distinguished from his domestic activities. Furthermore only those economic events which affect the business unit are recognised whilst costs and benefits which do not are excluded in its financial statements, e.g. expenses imposed on the locality by the business's smoky chimney. These effects are normally termed externalities.

Objectivity. Accounting information should be based as far as possible on objective evidence. This means that it should be free from bias, based on factual evidence, and capable of independent verification. It should be clear that it is again a matter of judgment whether these qualities are present. The importance of this concept is based mainly on the need for a system of auditing as explained earlier in this chapter.

Materiality. The accounting treatment of an item may be determined by its materiality, i.e. its relative value or importance. In Fig. 1.5, it was shown that assets with a life longer than the accounting period would have to be valued at the end of each period to ascertain the total net assets and thus derive the profit for the period. However, if the item is of small value in relation to the size of the organisation it may be treated differently, e.g. a spanner may last several years but it might be regarded as an expense of the period in which it was purchased and its end-of-period value ignored, the resulting inaccuracy being regarded as immaterial.

Money Measurement. Accounting information is expressed in terms of money. Money is the common denominator which enables diverse types of activity to be compared and combined. It follows that only those items or activities which can be expressed in money terms are included in accounting statements. This may exclude things like quality of the product, customer satisfaction or employee dissatisfaction which may be relevant information for running a business. Another disadvantage is that although money may be an adequate common denominator between diverse activities, it is a less than satisfactory common denominator between different periods of time because of changing price levels and purchasing power.

Stable Monetary Unit. At the present time accounting statements are prepared as if the monetary unit was stable. Development of this problem is discussed in Chapter 8.

An illustration of an application of some of the concepts is shown in Fig. 2.2.

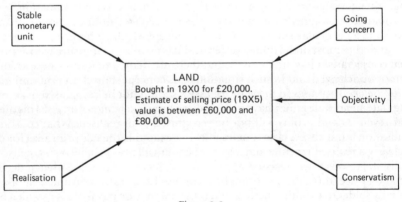

Figure 2.2

Assuming we were preparing a balance sheet at the end of 19X5, there are at least five concepts influencing the valuation of land to be included in the balance sheet. The value of the land may have risen because there has been general inflation and because it is sited in an area where building land is in great demand.

If the *stable monetary unit* concept is followed then rises in value due to rises in general prices should not be recognised and, in any event, the *realisation* concept may not allow unrealised profits to be included while the land is still held by the company. If this seems unrealistic and misleading, then it could be pointed out that the *going concern* concept assumes that the company will continue its existence and may need the land for its own use and thus any possible market value for the land is irrelevant to the balance sheet. A counter argument to this might be that if the market value of the land was shown in the balance sheet, the owners might decide to discontinue the business, sell up and retire to the south of France! The concept of *objectivity* is now introduced into the argument. In this situation it will usually be taken that the original cost of the land of £20,000 paid in 19X0 is objective evidence because it is based on a transaction which actually took place and for which there is documentary verifiable evidence. Whether the varying estimates of current market value constitute objective evidence is a question on judgment. If an identical piece of land has recently been sold and there is proof of the price, then this may be taken as acceptable evidence. It is becoming increasingly common to accept the opinion of an accredited valuer as objective evidence of changes in land values. (App. D.3, Note 8 shows properties value on a basis other than original cost.) If there are complications, such as the fact that the land has factory buildings on it, then it may be impossible to estimate a market value of the land without the buildings. Underlying this discussion is the concept of *conservatism* which may lead to the rejection of the estimates of market value if they cannot be ascertained with reasonable certainty.

2.6 The concepts evaluated

It should be clear from the example in the previous section that while the accounting concepts provide guidance in measuring value and profit the interpretation of the concepts in specific situations is still a matter for the judgment and skill of the accountant. In some situations it is possible that the concepts may be in conflict. For example, if the market value of an asset falls well below its cost shortly after it is purchased then it might seem that, using conservatism, the most cautious view would be to decrease the value from cost to market value. However, if the company intends to use the asset rather than sell it then the going-concern concept might deem the market value to be irrelevant.

A further explanation of the applications of the concepts will be given in relation to specific situations in the remaining chapters of Part I. We now consider the concepts adopted in accounting and evaluate them in the context of the problem areas specified at the beginning of the chapter:

(a) *Which concept of value is most suitable: Original cost, replacement cost, selling price or future utility?*

The concept of value accepted and used in the great majority of situations in practice is original cost. Some of the reasons for this can be found in the requirements of the accounting concepts. Objective evidence has perhaps the strongest influence.[7] This is emphasised by a quotation from recommendation N15 of the Institute of Chartered Accountants in England and Wales ('Accounting in relation to changes in the purchasing power of money') issued in 1952: 'An important feature of the historical [i.e. original] cost basis of preparing annual accounts is that it reduces to a minimum the extent to which the accounts can be affected by the personal opinions of those reponsible for them.'

With this approach it is unlikely that the idea of future utility will be acceptable as this must be based on estimates of future performance. To a lesser extent replacement cost and selling prices may not be based on objective evidence where the asset in question has not been replaced or sold. This latter view can be challenged where there is a recognised market with known prices for the asset in question. The use of original cost is also supported by the realisation concept which if rigidly applied prevents recognition of any increases in value over original cost unless these are realised by sale. The concept of conservatism and of a stable monetary unit also add support to this recognition of original cost as measure of value. This is especially true of the conservatism where cost tends to give a lower value than the other concepts and in periods of rising prices the original cost is likely to be lower than current costs for the same asset.

It has been asserted that original cost is the most suitable value concept for the expression of accounting concepts. This does not necessarily mean that it is the most suitable in a wider sense. For this we must decide whether the accounting concepts themselves are suitable. This question is discussed further in (*d*) below and in Chapter 9.

(*b*)   *What items should be included in the list of assets to be valued?*

It might seem that valuation of a company would be incomplete without the inclusion of all assets. Intangible assets such as good customer relations, a product of superior quality to its competitors, an efficient management team, may be what makes a particular company superior to its rivals. Such assets could be included in a valuation only where objective evidence of value can be shown. In most cases this is not possible because in the examples quoted, although these qualities may improve future performance, it is unlikely that they could be bought and sold as with physical assets, and thus there will be no specific original cost. Consequently such assets or qualities are unlikely to be found in a balance sheet. There are exceptions, for example, where the rights to market a product have been purchased from the inventor, then the cost of the rights may be included.

(*c*)   *What is the most suitable approach to the problem of the need for periodic profit measurement of the firm's activities many of which are only partially completed?*

It was explained in Chapter 1 that one of the major problems in profit measurement is that we are measuring the progress of a series of activities which are partially completed. These activities involve the use of assets and incurring of liabilities, and thus profit measurement consists of valuing these at the end of each period. The matching concept is one which is relevant because it attempts to make this process most meaningful by relating, for each period, revenues (which cause increases in assets) with relevant expenses (which cause decreases in assets or increases in liabilities). The concept of consistency also helps by ensuring that the methods used in profit measurement in each period do not change without good reason.

(*d*)   *How can measurement be related to the needs of the users of the information?*

The users of accounting information on value and profit as reported in the balance sheet and profit statement include internal management and external users such as tax authorities, shareholders, creditors and lenders, trade unions and customers. What are these groups looking for? The tax authorities use the annual reported profit to assess the tax payable by the firm. They have on the whole accepted the accounting profit as a basis for this assessment but with adjustments to satisfy their own requirements (see App. B). Shareholders are concerned with the safety and profitability of their investment in the future. Creditors and lenders want to know if their loans to the firm will be repaid at the appropriate time in the future and if the interest on the loan can be met. Trade unions may have a variety of reasons for being interested in a firm's financial statement. On the one hand they may be concerned to see that the firm has done well in the past and that this is expected to continue so that an improvement in wages and conditions is justified. On the other hand they may be interested in collecting evidence on the effect of price increases or redundancies on firms as supporting facts for a particular union policy. The internal management will be interested in the effect of their past decisions on the value and profit of the company but they will be more concerned with obtaining the sort of information which will provide the proper basis for decisions on the future activities of the company.

One of the requirements of users which underlies much of what was said in the last paragraph is that they need information which will give them an indication of what is *going to happen* to the firm. It can be seen from the earlier discussion of the concepts underlying the information on value and profit that their application is likely to result in measures which are based mainly on past events. This is especially true of the application of conservatism, realisation and objectivity. In many cases past events may be a useful guide to the future but clearly they are not necessarily so. Two important reports which have emphasised the need to relate the content of accounting statements to the needs of the users of these statements are the 'Sandilands Report'[8] and 'The Corporate Report'.[9] Both reports emphasised the need to replace or at least supplement historic information with current values and forecasts of future events.

2.7 Summary

This chapter has considered the conceptual framework which has been developed by the accounting professions in the U.K. and in other countries. The framework discussed is that developed to provide information by means of published financial statements for external users. We shall see in subsequent chapters in Part I that this framework determines to a large extent the type of information provided by accounting systems. In Parts II and III it will be shown that this information, which is largely based on historical measurement of original cost, is not adequate for management's planning and control decisions which are essentially concerned with the future. Indeed the analysis showed that in several respects the conceptual framework also has shortcomings in the provision of adequate information for external users.

Notes and References

1. P. Bird, *Accountability: Standards in Financial Reporting* (London, Haymarket, 1973) chaps 7–9.
2. P. Bird, 'The Scope of the Company Audit', *Accounting and Business Research*, no. 1 (Winter 1970).
3. H. Edey, 'The True and Fair View', *Accountancy* (August 1971).
4. P. Bird, *Accountability: Standards in Financial Reporting*, chap. 2.
5. An example of a significant government initiative was the setting up in 1974 of the committee of enquiry which produced the 'Sandilands Report' (see below for reference to the Report).
6. R. Sidebotham, *Introduction to the Theory and Context of Accounting* (Oxford, Pergamon, 1970) chap. 4.
7. M. Mumford, 'Objectivity and the Accounting Profession', *Accounting and Business Research*, no. 4 (Autumn 1971).
8. Sandilands, *Inflation Accounting: Report of the Inflation Accounting Committee,* Cmmd 6225 (H.M.S.O., 1975).
9. Accounting Standards Steering Committee, *The Corporate Report* (London, Accounting Standards Steering Committee, 1975).

Further Reading

T. Keller and S. Zeff, *Financial Accounting Theory II – Issues and Controversies* (New York, McGraw-Hill, 1969).
P. Garner and K. B. Berg, *Readings in Accounting Theory* (Boston, Mass., Houghton Mifflin, 1966).
E. S. Hendrikson, *Accounting Theory* (Homewood, Ill., Irwin, 1968).
P. Bird, 'Standard Accounting Practice', in H. C. Edey and B. S. Yamey (eds) *Debits, Credits, Finance and Profits* (London, Sweet & Maxwell, 1974).

Questions and Problems

2.1   What do you understand by the following terminology?

Conceptual framework	Matching (or accruals)
Auditing	Consistency
Generally accepted accounting principles	Conservatism
True and fair view	Realisation
Accounting bases	Entity
Fundamental accounting concepts	Objectivity
Accounting policies	Materiality
Statements of standard accounting practice	Money measurement
Going concern	Stable monetary unit

2.2   Which of the justifications for the existence of an agreed conceptual framework do you find most convincing?

2.3   What is the role of the professional accounting organisation?

2.4   Is it possible to give a true or a fair view of a company's position using accounting information?

2.5   Give examples of situations where the accounting concepts referred to in Chapter 2 might be in conflict with each other.

2.6   Discuss the four approaches to valuation suggested in Chapter 1 in the context of the accounting concepts in Chapter 2.

2.7   Value the following for balance sheet purposes by applying the accounting concepts:

(a)   Land bought for £10,000. The company has had an offer of £20,000 but it doesn't wish to sell as the land is needed to build a new factory and it is estimated that a similar piece would cost £25,000.

(b)   A building left to the owner of the company by an aunt. He spent £5000 converting it and now lives in half and uses the other half for the business.

(c)   An inventory which consists of 1000 units of a product which cost £6 per unit. The company has a contract to sell 600 at £12 each but expects that the remainder will have to be sold off at £5 each and even then there may not be any buyers.

(d)   The company is being sued by an employee for wrongful dismissal without redundancy payments. These could amount to £500 if the employee wins his case and other damages may be awarded. The company believes it will win the case.

2.8   Explain what you think are the chief weaknesses in the accounting concepts as described in Chapter 2.

3
The Structure of Accounting Data

3.1 Introduction

The applications of the concepts of value in Chapters 1 and 2 relied on the ability of the firm to collect data to provide evidence for increases or decreases in value or net worth. The preparation of such financial statements as the balance sheet and profit statement in order to show this data in a coherent manner is an integral part of accounting. The accounting concepts on which these statements are prepared were examined in Chapter 2, and this chapter examines some of the procedures for their preparation.

It has been emphasised that due to the accounting concepts used in the accounting framework not all economic events would be reflected in the balance sheet and profit statement. This in turn implies that the preparation of these statements will be based mainly on an analysis of historical data which reflects original costs and the benefits from past transactions. Thus this chapter examines some of the interrelationships between assets, liabilities and owners' equity first introduced in Chapter 1, and Chapter 4 provides an examination of the problems of processing accounting information for preparation of the profit statement and balance sheet.

3.2 Fundamental accounting equation

The analysis of procedures for preparation of financial statements will begin by considering some transactions and their effect on the firm. If we assume for simplicity that the first resource that a firm receives is cash, we can see that the effect on the financial position of the firm is twofold. Not only does the firm now own an asset, namely the cash, but it has also established a relationship with the person from whom the cash came. The provider of the cash can be thought of as having a claim against the firm. This twofold effect on accounting data is termed 'duality'. If the cash was provided by one of the firm's owners, the owner would have a financial interest in the firm equal to the amount of cash. It is conventional to refer to this as the owners' claim or owners' equity. Although the owner now has a claim against the firm it is not normally termed a liability because of the restricted legal claims which owners have against a firm's assets. If the cash was obtained by borrowing, the firm would owe the lender that sum; the lender's interest in the firm is its liability. The underlying contrasts of these different forms of providing a business's assets are discussed in Sect. 7.3. At this stage it is sufficient to note that the firm will find it useful to distinguish between these qualitatively different relationships.

By applying the idea of duality and recognising the two distinct types of claims against the firm, the following equation can be derived:

$$\text{Assets} = \text{Liabilities} + \text{Owners' Equity}$$

It is termed the 'fundamental accounting equation' because these relationships are so central to the analysis and presentation of accounting information. We will now use this basic framework to begin the analysis of accounting information.

3.3 Examples of analysis using the fundamental accounting equation

In Sects 3.3, 3.4 and 3.5 we will examine the relationship between assets, liabilities and owners' equity and we will see how their respective values change as a result of a firm's transactions. Exs 3.1, 3.2 and 3.3 provide an initial illustration of some transactions and their implications for assets, liabilities and owners' equity. We will see how accounting information which is collected about changes in value is reflected in accounting statements.

Example 3.1   Changes in Assets and Owners' Equity
Cotton Company commences business on 1 January 19X1, and the owner immediately provides £500 in cash. The balance sheet for the firm at the end of 1 January would be:

Balance Sheet Cotton Company at end of 1 January 19X1

Assets	£
Cash	500
Total Assets	£500

Owners' Equity	
Capital	500
Total Owners' Equity	£500

We can see from this example the duality effect and that the analysis maintains the equality of the fundamental accounting equation. The owners' equity on commencing business is described as capital (see Sect. 3.4). It is convenient to continue our analysis by using the data and balance sheet of Ex. 3.1.

Example 3.2   Changes in Assets and Liabilities
On 2 January Cotton Company borrows £900 in cash from the bank as an interest-free loan, which is provided on the same day. This information could be reflected in a revised balance sheet:

Balance Sheet Cotton Company

	At end of 1 January 19X1	At end of 2 January 19X1
Assets	£	£
Cash	500	1400
Total Assets	£500	£1400
Liabilities		
Owed to bank	—	900
Owners' Equity		
Capital	500	500
Total Liabilities and Owners' Equity	£500	£1400

In Ex. 3.2 we can again see the duality effect operating and that the equality of the fundamental accounting equation still holds.

The results of Exs 3.1 and 3.2 can be summarised as follows:

Ex.	Assets	=	Liabilities	+	Owners' Equity
	£		£		£
3.1	+500 =				+500
3.2	+900 =		+900		
Total	£+1400 =		£+900		£+500

There will clearly be a series of other combinations of changes which affect assets, liabilities and owners' equity, but the principles can be illustrated by considering a limited set of combinations.

Example 3.3   Changes in Assets Only

The following is a summary of the transactions of Cotton Company during the rest of January 19X1:

1. Pays £300 in cash for inventory.
2. Lends £200 in cash to Mr Morris as an interest-free loan.

The balance sheet for the end of the month can be calculated as:

Balance Sheet Cotton Company

	At end of 2 January 19X1	Transactions		At end of 31 January 19X1
	£	£	£	£
Assets				
Cash	1400	−300	−200	900
Inventory		+300		300
Debtors			+200	200
	£1400			£1400
Liabilities				
Owed to bank	900	no change		900
Owners' Equity				
Initial	500	no change		500
	£1400			£1400

The transactions in Ex. 3.3 alter the amounts of assets that are classified into particular categories; again we can see that the equality in the fundamental accounting equation is not changed.

3.4   Owners' Equity

As explained in previous sections the owners' equity represents the owners' interest in the firm, i.e. the net worth, or assets less liabilities. For simplicity in Chapter 1 we explained the change in net worth as being profit, but we will now clarify some important assumptions underlying our preliminary analysis.

The changes in owners' equity over time can be classified into capital and profit changes such that:

$$\text{Owners' Equity} = \text{Capital} + \text{Retained Profit}$$

A firm will receive assets from its owners at its inception and may periodically receive further assets from its owners during its life. These direct flows between the owners and the firm normally termed 'capital inputs'. It is possible that assets which were formerly associated with capital inputs may be returned to the owners, perhaps when a firm no longer requires the assets or ceases its activities. Although the term 'capital' has many uses in accounting we will restrict its use to this context.

The change in the value of the firm which is associated with changes in capital can be distinguished from the circumstances in which it changes as a result of earning a profit, or a loss. When the value of the assets and liabilities changes, to reflect profits or losses (see Sect. 1.6), the owners' equity will absorb the change. This analysis reflects contemporary legal, social and economic considerations as a result of which the owners' claim extends to profit. The legitimacy of the claim to all profit is challenged when parties other than owners consider that all or part of the profits is available for their claim, e.g. employees in a profit-sharing scheme.

Clearly then the net worth of the firm will increase when profits are earned over time. The firm may decide to distribute part or all of the profits earned in a period to its owners. These distributions, termed 'dividends' in the case of companies, are flows of assets from the firm to the owners, and thus the owners' equity will be correspondingly reduced. The retained profit of a period is the excess of a period's profit over distributions. Where a firm earns profits over several periods and not all are distributed the amount of retained profit for past and current periods will accumulate into the total retained profit. Thus the net worth of a firm will consist of capital and retained profits for all periods in the past. In Sect. 7.4 we examine factors which affect a firm's decisions about distributions of profit.

It is important to distinguish between capital and profit when a firm transfers assets to its owners, who must be able to decide whether they are receiving a payment of capital or a distribution of profit. This may be useful in their evaluation of the performance of the firm, in the same way that it is useful to distinguish between a bank deposit and its associated interest.

Furthermore, as a means of reassuring creditors that the owners have a continuing and non-withdrawable financial interest in a company, it is illegal for a company to repay capital to shareholders, except in liquidation (see App. A.5). Thus the separation of capital and retained profit is a legal disclosure requirement under the Companies' Acts, 1948 and 1967 (see App. D.3, note 14). Alternative legal frameworks for providing some assurance to creditors other than by making capital non-repayable are suggested by European Communities Law.

Thus some of the changes in net worth of a firm during an accounting period may be the result of capital, or profit and distributions. The profit model first introduced in Sect. 1.3 must be modified to:

$$C + (P_t - D) = V_t - V_{t-1} \qquad \text{re-arranged to}$$

$$P_t = V_t - V_{t-1} + D - C$$

where D_t and C_t are, respectively, the distributions and new capital for a period. Where profit is explained in terms of change in value over a period, it is assumed that D and C are both zero.

Revenues and Expenses

The profit of a period is the net result of increases and decreases in the firm's assets − liabilities, i.e. net worth. It is useful to separate the profit into those elements which cause increases (+), termed 'revenues', and those which are decreases (−), termed 'expenses'.

Example 3.4   Revenues and Expenses
The following is a chronological summary of the transactions of Cotton Company during February 19X1:

1. Paid £600 in cash for inventory.
2. Received £1200 in cash for selling all inventory, i.e. opening inventory and month's purchases.
3. Paid £80 in cash to an assistant for working during February.

The balance sheet for the end of February could be calculated:

Balance Sheet of Cotton Company

	At end of 31 January 19X1	Transaction 1	2	3	At end of 28 February 19X1
Assets	£	£	£	£	£
Cash	900	−600	+1200	−80	1420
Inventory	300	+600	− 900		—
Debtors	200				200
	£1400				£1620
Liabilities					
Owed to Bank	900				900
Owners' Equity					£
Capital	500			£	500
Profit – revenues (note 1)			+1200	= 1200	
– expenses (note 1)			−900 −80	= −980	
– retained (note 2)					220
					720
	£1400				£1620

Notes: (1) Revenues are shown as positive (+) as they are increases in profits, and expenses are shown as negative (−) because they reduce profits.
(2) No profit is distributed during February and therefore all is retained.

It will be useful to examine these transactions to see their effect on the firm's net worth.

Transaction 1. An exchange of assets: cash for inventory.

Transaction 2. There are two aspects of this exchange: the generation of revenue of £1200 which increases the assets and increases the profit (owners' equity) and the use of an inventory, an expense which reduces the assets and the profit (owners' equity). Fig. 3.1 illutrates the two-directional flow:

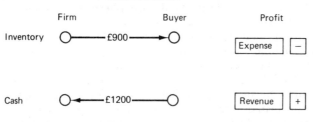

Figure 3.1

Transaction 3. The cash payment of £80 as wages was in exchange for the resource of labour provided by the assistant; if it is assumed that this payment related to services for February only, there would be no future services owing to the firm at the end of February and hence no assets at that time. The value of the firm's assets would thus fall by £80 during February.

We can see within the balance sheet of 28 February that the excess of revenues over expenses is £220 (all retained within the firm, as no distribution of profit was made). In this example we have summarised the increases and decreases of profit within the balance sheets. Information about the causes of changes in profit would normally be sufficiently important and contain enough items to warrant a separate profit statement, which would show details of the calculation of the £220 retained profit.

To indicate this approach to calculation of profit is identical in principle to that described in Chapter 1, we can calculate valuations at two points in time. Using the data from Ex. 3.4 we can see that:

$$P = V \, (28 \text{ February } 19XI) - V \, (31 \text{ January } 19XI), \text{ with } D \text{ and } C \text{ as nil}$$
$$P = (\pounds1620 - \pounds900) - (\pounds1400 - \pounds900)$$
$$P = \pounds720 - \pounds500$$
$$P = \pounds220$$

If the profit of £220 was calculated in this manner in practice it would not provide sufficient information about the causes of the changes in value of the firm during February 19X1.

Although the previous process of profit computation may appear a routine arithmetical manipulation, the conceptual framework of accounting has been used implicitly in limiting our analysis to information which is considered relevant for purposes of profit computation and valuation of net worth. Thus the data in Ex. 3.4 reflects those historical events which are considered as falling within the accounting framework, and ignores other information which may have been relevant for valuation purposes had some of the other concepts of value been applied, e.g. alternative uses for the inventory which were forgone, or the effect of the transactions on the good name of the firm.

3.5   Assets and Expenses

This section analyses the inherent relationship between the assets and expenses of a firm. In Chapter 1 we saw that a major problem of valuation of assets was in estimating the extent to which a firm was to derive future benefits from owning an asset. The discussion of Fig. 1.5 showed that measurement was easy if a sufficiently long period was taken over which to calculate profit. This is because all asset lives would have ended within the period and there would be no need to estimate future benefits. In Sect. 3.4 the process of profit calculation involved *inter alia* the valuation of assets. Where assets fall in value over time, this fall is a reduction in profit. As was explained the reduction in the profit of a firm is termed an expense.

For certain assets, whose useful life for the firm is longer than the period over which profit is measured, it will be necessary to calculate an interim valuation for the asset at points in time between acquisition and disposal. For example, if a firm acquires a van which it expects to use for three years, and it wishes to calculate its profit annually, it will be required to value the van after one year to enable it to calculate its profit for the first year. The fall in value of the van during this first year is an expense of the firm during the first year of the van's ownership.

Other types of assets which the firm acquires, such as the assistant's commitment to work in Ex. 3.4, may be without value at the end of the period over which profits are calculated. Where assets are acquired and used up within the period, no asset exists at the end of the period for which profit is measured. Because of this, the payment is considered as an expense at the time of payment. This latter treatment is essentially a shortened form of analysis. At the time the payment is made (let us assume for simplicity it is payment in advance for wages) an asset exists in the form of a requirement by the assistant to provide future services. Thus a balance sheet prepared at that point would consider the wages paid as an asset. The period of time over which profit was calculated in Ex. 3.4 was of such a length that the asset was completely used up by the end of the period. Thus the analysis recognised the payment of £80 wages as an expense rather than as an asset which later became an expense. This can be shown as:

	assistant's wages
underlying flow	payment ⟶ asset ⟶ expense
assumed flow	payment ⟶ expense

There are many transactions which are often recognised as expenses at the time of payment, e.g. rent, wages and salaries and rates.

The accounting concepts of Chapter 2 provide some additional guidance to the accounting analysis of a firm's acquisition of assets. A firm may incur costs (as payments or accruals) in exchange for expected future benefits which may not be classified as assets in the valuation of net worth because of the accounting concepts. These costs may thus be considered as expenses when incurred, rather than as assets. Some examples discussed in later chapters are costs of research and development (Chapter 5) and costs of production (Chapter 6).

Costs classified as long-lived assets are sometimes termed 'capital expenditure' by accountants, and those which are classified as expenses are 'revenue expenditure'.

It has now been established that the relationship between assets and expenses is that the costs of most assets will eventually become expenses. The initial classification of costs will depend on the length of time over which profit is being calculated and the application of the accounting concepts.

3.6 Analysis of accounting data for financial statements

The processes adopted so far in this chapter for measuring the effect of the firm's transactions during an accounting period have required the calculation of a new balance sheet, through the addition and subtraction of amounts from the previous balance sheet. This method as presented in Ex. 3.4 will become increasingly difficult as the number of transactions to be processed increases. In Ex. 3.5 a more complex problem is considered, where the number of transactions precludes the methods of Ex. 3.4. As a more useful and generally applicable alternative to representing the effects of transactions horizontally, a vertical system is adopted. This change in the system helps to solve the problem of processing data and does not require any changes in the principles previously established.

Example 3.5
Crisp Company commenced business on 1 July 19X1, and the following transactions occurred during July:

Transaction	Date	Description
1	1st	Received £1000 in cash from owners
2	2nd	Purchased van for £600 in cash
3	8th	Purchased inventory for £200 in cash
4	10th	Sold all inventory for £300 in cash
5	12th	Paid £50 in cash for clerical labour
6	20th	Purchased inventory for £500 in cash
7	23rd	Sold all inventory for £800 in cash
8	27th	Purchase inventory of £500 : £200 in cash and £300 to be paid in August
9	31st	£100 paid in cash to the owners of the firm as part of the estimated profit for July

Notes: (1) The van's useful life is estimated as five years, and it will have no sale value at that time, and will be disposed of. (2) The firm owes £50 for the rent of the shop which it used during July.

As in the previous example, we can calculate the profit for July by an analysis of the transactions of the firm and by using the other information which the firm may have available to enable it to conform to accounting concepts in its valuation procedures. This information can be systematically processed as shown in Fig. 3.2.

The two-part analysis indicates that the process of profit calculation involves an initial analysis of the transactions data, followed by inspection of and recalculation through analysis of any adjustments to the valuations of assets and liabilities so calculated, to establish whether they conform with all the accounting concepts. In terms of Ex. 3.5, the total valuations given to assets after the transactions' analysis proposes a valuation of £600 for the van and £1200 for the inventory. Liabilities are also understated by £50 at this stage. The adjustments' stage reflects the application of accounting concepts in the form of adjustments to the primary data.

Explanation of the Analysis in Ex. 3.5

Each transaction or adjustment was analysed to show the effect on the various classifications within the fundamental accounting equation. If the processing of the data has been arithmetically correct the equality of the fundamental accounting equation will hold. This accuracy is illustrated by the check total.

The separation of the effects on individual categories of assets, liabilities, or owners' equity as shown in the columns (or accounts) in Fig. 3.2 is the basis of what is termed the accounts of a firm. The nature of the accounts and the accounting systems for processing data are examined in Chapter 4. In Ex. 3.5 we assumed that the Crisp Company had just commenced business and there were no assets, liabilities or owners' equity at the beginning of the period. In the subsequent period the starting-point of the analysis will be the amounts of assets, liabilities and owners' equity at the end of the previous period.

Transactions Analysis

Analysis of transactions 1 to 9 can be understood with the knowledge of the fundamental accounting equation previously established. Further explanation may be useful for transactions 4 and 7: the receipt of cash in both transactions is an increase in the assets of the firm and the revenue (owners' equity). The inventory expense of generating this revenue is calculated as adjustment 1. In practice this procedure may be necessary because the expense is not known at the time of sales (see Sect. (ii) 6.4). The £100 distribution of profit of transaction 9 is not considered as

Assets   =   Liabilities + Owners' Equity

Transaction	Cash	Van	Inventory	Creditor	Capital	Revenue	Expense	Distribution
1	+1000				+1000			
2	−600	+600						
3	−200		+200					
4	+300					+300		
5	−50						−50	
6	−500		+500					
7	+800					+800		
8	−200		+500	+300				
9	−100							−100
Sub-total	+450	+600	+1200	+300	+1000	+1100	−50	−100
Adjustments								
1			−700				−700	
2		−10					−10	
3				+50			−50	
Total	+450	+590	+500	+350	+1000	+1100	−810	−100

Check total

$$+1540 = +350 + 1190$$
$$+1540 = +1540$$

+290 (bracket joining Revenue +1100 and Expense −810)

Figure 3.2. Analysis of accounting data from Ex. 3.5.

Note (1) The negative sign attached to expenses and distributions under this system of processing indicates that they are reductions in owners' equity.

an expense of the firm, but rather as a payment to owners which reduces their claims against the firm.

Adjustments Analysis

This recognises that some assets no longer exist (in an accounting sense) or that some assets should be revalued. The various accounting concepts dictate revaluation of some assets.

Adjustment 1. The inventory obtained in transaction 8 is still available, and, as an asset, will be included in the balance sheet. Inventory acquired in transactions 3 and 6 (£200 + £500 = £700) has been used up and is hence an expense. Further discussion of the flow of costs in inventory follows in Sect. 6.2. This adjustment reclassifies the asset as an expense, i.e. cost of goods sold.

Adjustment 2. The van purchased under transaction 2 was estimated to have a life of five years. If it is assumed that one month later the van has an estimated life of five years less one month; 1/60 of its life will have expired, and hence 1/60 of its original cost of £600 is an expense of July 19X1, i.e. £10. This type of expense is termed 'depreciation'. Further discussion follows in Chapter 5.

Adjustment 3. The firm owes £50 for rent; the accruals concept requires the inclusion of this data, as benefits have flowed from renting the shop, even though they have not been paid for; there is an expense flow though there is no associated cash payment. The opposite treatment is necessary for prepayments.

3.7   Presentation of the Balance Sheet

The numbers used in the balance sheet below correspond with the totals of the columns presented in Fig. 3.2.

The presentation of balance sheets that are clear and informative is of importance. There is, however, no standard format for the balance sheet that has been adopted for management use or in published accounts in practice; App. D.2 provides an illustration of a balance sheet designed to satisfy statutory reporting requirements. Two alternative presentations of the data from Ex. 3.5 are outlined below.

HORIZONTAL PRESENTATION

Though historically the most popular form of presentation, this form of presentation is frequently being replaced by a vertical form.

Balance Sheet of Crisp Company at 31 July 19X1

	£	£		£	£
Owners' Equity			*Fixed Assets*		
Capital	1000		Van at cost (note 1)	600	
Retained Profit			*Less* Accumulated		
(reserves)	190		Depreciation	10	
		1190			590
Long-term Liabilities		—			
Current Liabilities			*Current Assets*		
(note 3)			(note 2)		
Creditors		350	Inventory	500	
			Cash	450	
					950
		£1540			£1540

VERTICAL PRESENTATION

Presentation of the balance sheet vertically is now widely adopted, as comprehension of data so presented is considered easier.

Balance Sheet of Crisp Company at 31 July 19X1

	£	£
Fixed Assets		
Van at cost (note 1)	600	
Less Accumulated Depreciation	10	
		590
Current Assets (note 2)		

	£		
Inventory	500		
Cash	450		
		950	
Current Liabilities (note 3)			
Creditors		350	
Net Current Assets			600
			£1190
Financed by			
Owners' Equity			
Capital		1000	
Retained Profit (reserves)		190	
			1190
Long-term Liabilities			
—			—
			£1190

Terms Used in Balance Sheets

A brief summary of some of the terms used in balance sheets will be useful at this stage.

Term	Definition	Example	Considered further in Chapter
Fixed asset	Asset acquired by firm for use rather than sale	Buildings, Machinery	5
Current asset	Asset acquired by firm, but retained for short periods conventionally up to one year	Inventory, Cash	6 7
Current liability	A liability which will normally be repaid within a short period, conventionally one year	Wages payable	7
Net current assets	Assets and liabilities which are frequently changing, i.e. current assets–current liabilities; sometimes known as working capital		7

| Reserves | A synonym for retained profit | | 7 |
| Long-term liability | A liability which will normally be repayable after more than one year | Five-year loan | 7 |

Notes on Presentation

(1) The original cost and the accumulated depreciation associated with fixed assets are shown separately. The accumulated depreciation is the amount of the asset treated as an expense up to the date of the balance sheet. The balance sheet will then show which assets have been depreciated. By examination of the balance sheet it may then be possible to obtain an estimate of the age structure of the fixed assets, and perhaps gauge the extent of future usefulness of assets.

(2) The sequence of current assets is in order of increasing liquidity (closeness of conversion into cash); current assets are separated from fixed assets.

(3) Current liabilities are separated from long-term liabilities.

The type of presentation chosen should be based on an understanding of the needs of users of the financial statement. The format of statements will vary greatly according to whether they are for use within the firm by its management or are for external users such as shareholders. Where statements are published they have to satisfy legal reporting requirements laid down by the Companies' Acts, 1948 and 1967, but little guidance is given as to methods of presentation. The annual survey of published accounts gives an indication of the wide range of possible formats that have been adopted by British public companies.[1] Various Statements of Standard Accounting Practice (S.S.A.P.) are now being issued by the Accounting Standards Steering Committee (A.S.S.C.) in an attempt to standardise aspects of presentation.

3.8 Presentation of the Profit Statement

The analysis of profit in Fig. 3.2 does not reveal sufficiently clearly the causes and details of revenues and expenses. The profit statement is an additional statement which is usually provided to give an analysis and presentation of this information. An example of a published profit statement appears in App. D.1.

The revenue, expense and distribution data from Fig. 3.2 can be formed into a profit statement by a slight rearrangement:

Profit Statement of Crisp Company for one month ended 31 July 19X1

		£	Notes
Sales Revenue		1100	
Less Cost of Goods Sold (inventory expense)		700	
Gross Profit		400	(1)
Less Other Expenses:	£		
Clerical	50		
Depreciation	10		
Rent	50		
		110	
Net Profit before Extra-ordinary Items		290	
Extra-ordinary			(2)

Net Profit after Extra-ordinary Items	290
Distributions	100
Retained Profit	190 (3)
Retained Profit from Previous Periods	—
	£190

The classifications used in the profit statement will depend on the proposed use of the report. In Chapter 4 we discuss the problems of classification of accounting data. This format of the profit statement is normally termed the 'vertical form'.

Notes on Presentation

(1) The terms 'gross' and 'net' profit are used to distinguish between different categories and classifications of profit, the former after deduction of the cost of goods sold, and the latter after other expenses have been deducted.

(2) If comparisons are to be made between the profit statements of periods it will be useful to be able to distinguish the extent to which exceptional or extraordinary factors in a period may affect profits. Extraordinary, i.e. non-recurring revenues or expenses, will disguise any underlying trends in data if the effects are material and unidentified. While the idea of an extraordinary item implies that we have some concept of normality, our notion of extraordinary revenues and expenses is narrowly drawn. It will cover only those items which are material in their influence on profit, and which will not recur. For full details see S.S.A.P.6.[2] (There are no extraordinary items in Ex. 3.5).

(3) The profit retained from previous periods is often most conveniently incorporated into a period's profit statement so we can show the effect on the cumulative retained profits of a period's profits and dividend. The total of retained profit for the period and the previous periods will be part of the owners' equity in the balance sheet. As the firm commenced business in the period under consideration there was no retained profit from the previous periods.

Comparison with the financial statements of Marks & Spencer Ltd
It will be useful at this stage to examine the statements shown in Apps. D.1, D.2, and D.3.

3.9 Profit and Cash Flow

It may be useful in the understanding of the nature of profit to compare the amount of a firm's profit with the flow of cash into and out of a firm. The cash flow of a firm can be measured by the comparison of the cash position at the beginning and the end of a period of time. The cash flow into the firm will normally comprise the receipt of cash from owners, lenders, and those who purchase the goods and services of the firm. The cash flow out of the firm will be the payments of cash for assets and expenses provided to the firm, payments to the creditors, and also any distributions of profit or capital to the owners.

The net cash flow of Crisp Company during July 19X1 can be calculated as:

	£
Cash at commencement of business	Nil
Cash on 31 July	450
Net cash flow IN (into firm)	£450

An analysis of the cash transactions indicates:

Cash flow IN	£	Cash flow OUT	£
From owners*	1000	Purchase of van	600
From sales	300	Purchase of inventory	200
From sales	800	To obtain clerical services	50
		Purchase of inventory	500
		Purchase of inventory	200
		*To owners: Distribution	
		of profit	100
	£2100		£1650

The net cash flow is £450 inwards to the firm.
  Further examination reveals that:

Cash flow relating to capital and distributions of profit	+900 marked*
Cash flow relating to operations	−450 all others
Net Cash-flow In	£450

The accounting profit was £290; the difference of £740 between profit and operations cash-flow could be explained thus:

	Transactions Adjustments	Cash £	Profit £	Difference £
			Expenses	
Purchase of van	TR2 AD2	−600	− 10	−590 (1)
Purchase of inventory	TR3 AD1	−200	−200	−
Clerical services	TR5	− 50	− 50	−
Purchase of inventory	TR6 AD1	−500	−500	−
Purchase of inventory	TR8 AD1	−200		−200 (2)
Rent	AD3		− 50	+ 50 (3)
			Revenues	
Sales of inventory	TR4	+300	+300	−
Sales of inventory	TR7	+800	+800	−
		£−450	£+290	£−740

Notes on differences: (1) −£590: this reflects the unused future life of the van which the accounting concepts adopted recognise as an asset. (2) −£200: as this inventory has future use, and thus value because it can be sold to earn revenue, it will be an asset. (3) +£50: the matching concept leads to the inclusion of rent as an expense, even though there has been no cash flow.

  The importance of the relationship between these measurements of the changes in the firm's value is that the concepts applied give a clearer guide to the total change in the value of the firm and include all the firm's assets, while the cash-flow position is closely related to a firm's liquidity, e.g. its ability to pay its creditors (see Sect. 7.9 for a fuller analysis). The performance of the firm must satisfy several criteria, and these two analyses have useful, though complementary, roles to play. An objective of the firm may be to earn profits, but it may also wish to maintain its liquidity. To provide a full measure of a firm's health, both liquidity and profitability are important.

3.10 Summary

This chapter provided an introduction to some of the problems of analysis of financial information and the application of the accounting concepts of previous chapters in preparing accounting statements. The selection of events which are of concern to the accountant is limited by the accounting concepts, at least in his evaluation of performance, although not in a decision-making context. Their effect can be analysed within the framework provided by the fundamental accounting equation. The format of accounting statements should be determined by the needs of users, rather than by convention or legal considerations. The problems of developing a system to process accounting data are examined in Chapter 4.

Notes and References

1. *Survey of Published Accounts 1974–1975* (General Educational Trust of the Institute of Chartered Accountants in England and Wales, 1974).
2. See S.S.A.P.6, 'Extraordinary Items and Prior Year Adjustments' (Accounting Standards Steering Committee, Institute of Chartered Accountants, 1975), for a fuller explanation.

Further Reading

H. Bierman and A. R. Drebin, *Financial Accounting: An Introduction* (London, Collier–Macmillan, 1970).
R. Sidebotham, *Introduction to the Theory and Context of Accounting* (Oxford, Pergamon, 1970).

Questions and Problems

3.1 What do you understand by the following terminology?

Owners' equity	Revenue	Accumulated depreciation
Duality	Expense	Cash flow
Accounting information	Transaction	Liquidity
Capital	Adjustments	Gross profit
Retained profit	Accounts	Net profit
Distribution	Fixed asset	Fundamental accounting
Dividend	Current liability	equation
Depreciation	Net current assets	
Long-term liability	Cost of goods sold	
Working capital	Extraordinary item	

3.2 The following are transactions relating to Crow, a wholesaler, during January 19X1:

   (a) Commences business with £400 of his own cash, and £600 borrowed at an interest rate of 3% per quarter.
   (b) Purchases a van for the firm for £800 on credit.
   (c) Purchases inventory for resale for £400 on credit.
   (d) Sells three-quarters of inventory for £1000, £500 on credit and £500 for cash.
   (e) Purchases inventory for £200 in cash.
   (f) Pays rent for first six months of £500.

(g) Incurs wages of £180 in cash, but in addition is still owing £50 at the end of January.

(h) Purchase a vintage car for the firm for £300 in cash but decides that it is not necessary and sells it for £700.

(i) The depreciation expense for the van for the first month is £50.

(j) Withdraws £60 as a share of the anticipated profit for January.

Analyse this information using the fundamental accounting equation and prepare a profit statement and balance sheet. Explain the relationship between the cash flow of the firm and its profit for January 19X1.

3.3 Crab Ltd is already in business and has prepared its balance sheet and profit statement for 19X1. The following data has not been reflected in these statements. Explain what effect there would be on the profit statement and balance sheet if the data was included:

(a) Debtors are valued at £1000 in the balance sheet but 10% are expected to be unable to pay.

(b) A vehicle is valued in the balance sheet at £60 but its resale value is nil.

(c) The firm owes £200 for purchases of goods which it did not use during 19X1.

(d) £586 was entered in the 'cash' and 'revenue' accounts for a transaction in error. The correct data is a credit sale of £865.

3.4 Should a company be required to have a minimum amount of capital?

3.5 An accountant values a firm at two points in time:

$$V_0 \quad £1000 \qquad V_1 \quad £1500$$

What assumptions are necessary to calculate the profit for the period? If you were informed that £300 new capital was introduced and distributions were £200, would this affect your calculations?

3.6 What criteria determine the format of the balance sheet and profit statement?

3.7 'The entity concept delineates the area of the firm's responsibility too narrowly. The accounts of a firm should reflect the firm's social responsibilities by having both an owners' equity and social equity classification, from which it could produce a social profit statement'. What benefits would such a proposal bring? What problems would there be in the implementation?

3.8 'The owners' equity concept is redundant in the analysis of the accounts of nationalised industries and local authorities'. Do you agree?

4
The Processing of Accounting Data

4.1 Introduction

This chapter continues the analysis of the preparation of accounting statements begun in the previous chapter. The discussions of the previous chapter involve an underlying assumption that the data required in the process is available in the necessary form and with sufficient frequency. We will see that the required data will emerge from an information system which is designed to enable us to prepare the accounting statements. An information system has three identifiable components: data collection, data processing and data communication, and it is in this form that we will examine methods of translating accounting data into statements. We begin by considering the most widely used method of analysis of accounting data.

4.2 Double-entry Book-keeping

The double-entry book-keeping system was long considered as the central and most important procedure for processing accounting data. The term 'double entry' is an alternative term for the idea of duality described in Chapter 3: the twofold effect on the firm of transactions (and adjustments). The reference to the term book-keeping' is perhaps an anachronism. The processing of accounting data with the use of books and clerks which was the forerunner of the modern accounting system has largely been replaced by mechanical and electronic techniques.[1]

PROCEDURES

The procedures of double-entry book-keeping require the same analysis of transactions and adjustments as was required by the procedure outlined in Chapter 3. These could be formally stated as:

(a) The identification of which components of the fundamental accounting equation are affected: assets, liabilities or owners' equity?

(b) The identification of which classification within a component is affected: e.g. within assets – cash?; within owners' equity – sales revenue? The individual classification is an account.

(c) The identification of the direction of change in an account, i.e. an increase or a decrease?

The account referred to in (b) is a detailed analysis of the results of transactions and adjustments relating to that classification. The accounts of a firm are central to any accounting system.

In a double-entry book-keeping system an account is not represented by a column as in the solution to Ex. 3.5, but by a column divided down its centre; this is termed a 'T' account, because of its physical similarity to the letter T. As shown in Fig. 4.1 the description of the classification that the T account represents is written along the top of the T. The account will show a detailed analysis of all increases and decreases of the relevant classification.

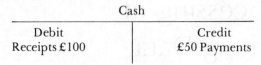

Cash	
Debit	Credit
Receipts £100	£50 Payments

Figure 4.1   Example of a T account

Increases or decreases in an account are denoted by entering the details and amount of the transaction on either the left or right side according to a set of rules. These are not normally presented or thought of as a set of rules, but as we are considering a systematic approach to the analysis of transactions it is useful to consider them as rules, which are the result of our formulation of the fundamental accounting equation.

Rules for Recording Transactions and Adjustments in Accounts

Rule 1. Increases in the value of assets, liabilities and owners' equity accounts are entered on the side of the T account corresponding to their side in the fundamental accounting equation of the previous chapter, i.e. increases in assets on left, increases in liabilities and owners' equity on right.

Rule 2. Decreases in the value of assets, liabilities and owners' equity accounts are entered on the side of the T account opposite to their side in the fundamental accounting equation of the previous chapter, i.e. decreases in assets on the right, decreases in liabilities and owners' equity on left.

Summary of entries in accounts from Rules 1 and 2

Assets	= Liabilities + Owners' Equity
Left (debit)	*Right (credit)*
Increases in assets	Increases in liabilities
	Increases in owners' equity, e.g. revenues, capital
Decreases in liabilities	Decreases in assets
Decreases in owners' equity, e.g. expenses, distributions	

Notes: (1) Entries on the left side of any account are termed 'debits' (commonly abbreviated to Dr); entries on the right side of any account are termed 'credits' (commonly abbreviated to Cr). (2) In each transaction or adjustment the value of debit entries will equal the value of credit entries in the accounts, and this maintains the equality of the fundamental accounting equation.

The above analysis is based on the assumption that a system of T accounts is being used. The use of the terms 'debit' and 'credit' may also arise even when columnar accounts are being used, e.g. in a computer system although there is neither left nor right side. The interpretation in the summary of entries in accounts still has the same meaning.

Rule 3. The balance of an account is the numerical difference between the sum of the debit entries and the sum of the credit entries. If the sum of debit entries exceeds the sum of credit entries it will be a left (debit) balance, and vice versa.

Summary of balances from Rule 3

Σ debit entries $>$ Σ credit entries = left balance (debit)
Σ credit entries $>$ Σ debit entries = right balance (credit)
Σ debit entries $=$ Σ credit entries = nil balance

It should be clear from the above analysis that the following examples of balances can be derived:

Examples of balances derived from above rules

Left (Dr)	Right (Cr)
Assets	Liabilities
Expenses	Capital
Distributions	Revenue
Accumulated losses	Retained profits

THE USE OF DOUBLE-ENTRY PROCEDURE AND T ACCOUNTS

The use of T accounts and the rules of double entry offer us many advantages over the methods of processing data discussed in Chapter 3. In industrial or commercial accounting it will be necessary to provide classifications of assets, liabilities and owners' equity into many accounts to produce useful accounting statements, e.g. if we have to provide a classification of revenues and expenses in a profit statement. Furthermore it is necessary to control the processing of information to ensure accuracy in the data and to eliminate as far as possible the need for correction of errors. Large volumes of data will often be processed by many methods within an organisation, and control becomes more difficult as the operation of the accounting system becomes de-centralised.

The procedures we have explained in this chapter will enable those responsible for preparing accounting statements to use as many accounts as they find necessary by creating (termed 'opening') a T account for each classification necessary. Where there is a large volume of data the tasks of entering (termed 'posting') data into particular accounts may be split up among several individuals, e.g. Mr A responsible for cash, Mr B for inventory data. In modern processing some of the accounts may be prepared by computer and some by manual methods. All these requirements will make the procedures of the previous chapter inappropriate as the system described was not sufficiently flexible to satisfy the likely demands that would be made on it, nor would control of accuracy be maintained. Increases in the volume of data and decentralisation of account preparation increase the likelihood of errors.

A major source of error may be where data is given an incorrect sign before it is entered in the accounts, such as could occur using the system of Chapter 3. In Chapter 3 we decided on the sign of a number in an account according to whether it was an increase or decrease in assets, liabilities or owners' equity. Thus, for example, if we increased an asset (+) we could either decrease another asset (−) or increase a liability (+). Therefore:

+ followed by − is correct
+ followed by + is correct

It would not be possible for someone unskilled in understanding the fundamental accounting equation to tell whether a + entry should be followed by a + sign or a − sign unless he knew whether the first and second accounts were assets, liabilities or owners' equity. This raises the great possibility of error, e.g. a message such as: 'Cash + £50, Debtors + £50', which the unskilled would not recognise as incorrect unless he knew that both cash and debtors were assets.

The use of the terms 'debit' and 'credit' in accordance with the rules of double entry eliminates this problem. For any transaction (or adjustment) we will know that the sum of the debit entries into accounts will equal the sum of credit entries:

'Dr Cash £50, Cr £50 Debtors'
'Dr Cash £50, Cr £50 Creditors'

are correct messages. The incorrect message:

'Dr Cash £50, Dr Debtors £50'

would be immediately recognisable as incorrect by anyone irrespective of their knowledge of the component of the fundamental accounting equation being altered. The elimination of this type of error is of considerable importance in an accounting system as the costs of correcting errors are high, and errors are difficult to identify in both large or decentralised systems. It is equally important that the numerical accuracy of entries can be checked by calculating that the total debit and total credit entries for a transaction are equal.

4.3 Double-entry Procedures

Double-entry procedures are routines using a set of rules which lend themselves to flow-chart presentation. If a book-keeping routine were to be written for a computer it could be based on a flow chart, or a flow chart could be used if it was necessary to define a clerical routine very precisely.

The procedures to be adopted in using this system are reflected in Fig. 4.2. This flow chart is a diagrammatic representation of the actions and decisions that are necessary to process transactions and adjustments data using T accounts. It is termed a 'logical' flow chart as it indicates the underlying decisions and actions relating to solving a processing problem. It can be contrasted with a 'system' flow chart which would give more information about the medium used to carry out the sequences, e.g. man, machine, etc.

Five symbols are used in this simple representation:

Symbol	Description	Notes on symbols
⬭	Begin or end	Relates to the whole system
▭	Action	Contains action number and description
◇	Decision	Contains question number and description
○	Junction	Meeting of various flows channelled into one flow
→	Direction of flow or movement	Proceed through flow chart in this direction

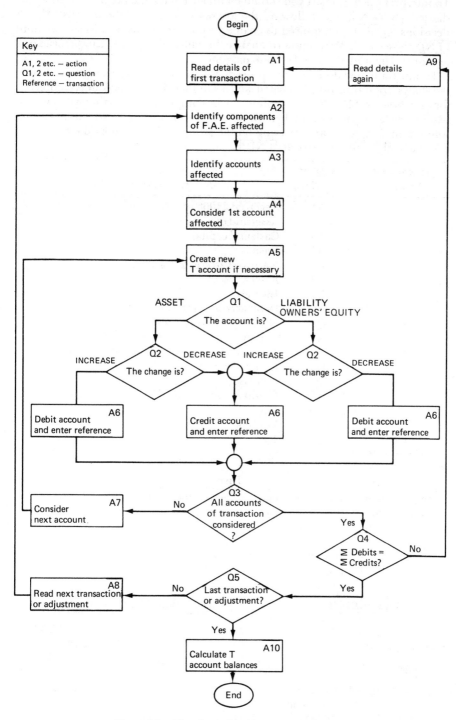

Figure 4.2   Flow chart of double-entry procedures

To interpret the flow chart you should commence the sequence at the symbol indicated [BEGIN], and following the arrows you can see the actions 'A' and decisions 'Q' that are required to enable you to process data satisfactorily until [END] is reached. We will now re-analyse the data from Ex. 3.5, using a series of T accounts. The student should refer to page 36.

To illustrate how double-entry procedures can be used we have shown below the analysis of transaction 1 in detail, and a summary of the T accounts completed for the whole problem. The T accounts can be completed by imagining that we are reading each transaction and then the adjustments in the same order as in Ex. 3.5 solution in Chapter 3, and carrying on the sequence indicated by the flow chart automatically until we arrive at [END]:

Transaction Number	Stage of Flow Chart	Interpretation of Flow Chart
1	A1	Received £1000 in cash from owners
	A2	Asset and owners' equity
	A3	Cash and capital
	A4	Cash
	A5	Necessary to create T account 'cash'
	Q1	Asset
	Q2	Increase
	A6	Debit account; ref. 'TR1, 1000'
	Q3	No; owners' equity not yet entered
	A7	Capital
	A5	Necessary to create new T account 'capital'
	Q1	Owners' equity
	Q2	Increase
	A6	Credit account '1000 TR1'
	Q3	Yes
	Q4	Yes $1000 = 1000$
	Q5	No

T Accounts for Ex. 3.5

Assets

Cash

TR1	1000	600	TR2
TR4	300	200	TR3
TR7	800	50	TR5
		500	TR6
		200	TR8
		100	TR9
	£2100	£1650	

Balance £450

Inventory

TR3	200	700	AD1
TR6	500		
TR8	500		
	£1200	£700	
Balance £500			

Van

TR2	600
Balance	£600

Accumulated depreciation (note 1)

	10	AD2
	£10	Balance

Liabilities

Creditor

	300	TR8
	50	AD3
	£350	Balance

Owners' Equity

Capital			Cost of Goods Sold			Clerical Expense		
	1000	TR1	AD1	700		TR5	50	
	£1000	Balance	Balance	£700		Balance	£50	

		Depreciation Expense			Rent Expense		
		AD2	10		AD3	50	
		Balance	£10		Balance	£50	

Sales Revenue				Distribution		
	300	TR4				
	800	TR7		TR9	100	
	£1100	Balance		Balance	£100	

Note: (1) Accumulated depreciation related to van (see Sect. 3.7) is an asset valuation account, and the numbers in this account cannot be meaningfully considered separately from the van account itself.

Every transaction and adjustment has been processed and cross-referenced through its transaction or adjustment number, e.g. TR1, AD1. The transaction reference may in other cases indicate the name of the account in which the double entry is to be found, or alternatively, as above, a reference number to the original transaction or adjustment. This latter procedure is very useful in the search for errors, and in tracing the source of the numbers in an account.

The procedure for calculating balances (A10) can be seen by considering an example. We show two 'balancing procedures' below, the 'short form' on the left, which is simple and clear to understand, and 'balancing and ruling' on the right, which accords with good book-keeping practice. Throughout the text we use the 'short form'.

Short Form				*or*	*Balancing and Ruling*			
Inventory					Inventory			
TR3	200	700	AD1		TR3	200	700	AD1
TR6	500				TR6	500		
TR8	500				TR8	500	500	Balance carried forward (cf)
	£1200	£700				£1200	£1200	
Balance 31 July 19X1	£500				Balance 31 July 19X1 (bf)	£500		

The debit balance on this account is the valuation at the end of the period, termed 'closing balance'. To accommodate the situation where a firm already has assets, etc., at the beginning of an accounting period, these 'opening balances' will appear in the accounts having been 'brought forward' from the previous period.

4.4 Preparation of financial statements

In this section we will examine how the data which results from the double-entry procedures previously considered can be used in the preparation of financial

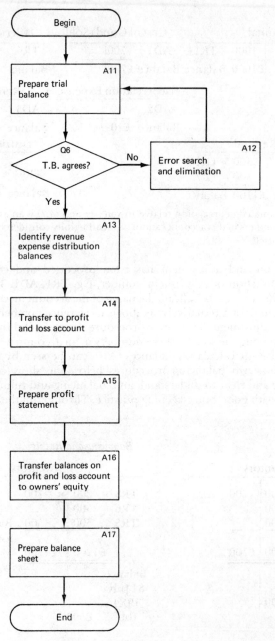

Figure 4.3   Flow chart of preparation of financial statements

statements. In Chapter 3 we examined the format of these statements and in this section we examine the question of providing a routine system for their preparation. In Fig. 4.3 we show the various stages through which we must pass in the form of a flow chart. As with Fig. 4.2 we will follow the routine from ⎡BEGIN⎤ to ⎣END⎦. Data from Ex. 3.5 illustrates. The three major stages are the preparation of a trial balance, profit and loss account, profit statement and balance sheet.

Preparation of Trial Balance (A11, Q6, A12)
A trial balance is a list and summation of accounts and their respective balances which have been used in a double-entry procedure. Using the data from pages 50 and 51 the trial balance would be:

Trial balance at 31 July 19X1

See A13 & A14

	Debit	Credit	Profit and Loss, Retained Profit	Balance Sheet
	£	£		
Cash	450			✓
Inventory	500			✓
Van	600			✓
Accumulated depreciation		10		✓
Creditor		350		✓
Capital		1000		✓
Rent expense	50		✓	
Depreciation expense	10		✓	
Clerical expense	50		✓	
Cost of goods sold (expense)	700		✓	
Sales revenue		1100	✓	
Distribution	100		✓	
Retained profit	—	—		✓
	£2460	£2460		

The equality of the trial balance arises because the sum of debit and credit entries for every transaction or adjustment processed will be equal, and all accounts used are listed. The trial balance provides a mechanism for ensuring the arithmetical accuracy of the entries in accounts (e.g. Q4 in Fig. 4.2 has been correctly answered), and ensures that all accounts used in processing are listed for use in the preparation of financial statements (e.g. in a large de-centralised processing system some accounts may be accidentally ignored). In the event of a trial balance not balancing it will be necessary to carry out logical checking procedures, for example:

(1) Is the trial balance correctly added?
(2) Have all the accounts used been listed?
(3) Have all the accounts been correctly balanced?
(4) Has procedure Q4 in Fig. 4.2 been adhered to?

The trial balance will not, however, indicate whether the analysis of A2, A3, Q1, Q2 in Fig. 4.2 has been correct.

Preparation of the Profit (and Loss) Account (in Flow Chart A13, A14)
We will need to identify those accounts in the trial balance which are to be transferred to the profit (and loss) account (P & L a/c). This account (which is summarised in a profit statement) brings together revenue and expense accounts to calculate the profit (or loss) for the period under consideration. Revenue and expense accounts are temporary in so far as once the balances are transferred to the profit (and loss) account they will have nil balances. The balance on the profit (and loss) account is then transferred to the retained profit account to become part

of the retained profit. The balance on the distribution account is also transferred to the retained profit account as distributions come not from the profits of the current year but from the cumulative retained profit. The balance on the retained profit account is part of the owners' equity at the end of the period. The profit (and loss) account and the distribution accounts are thus also temporary. All the accounts with balances at the end of a period relate to the balance sheet. Fig. 4.4 shows the process of transferring revenue, expense and distribution balances within the accounts to arrive at the retained profit at the end of the period.

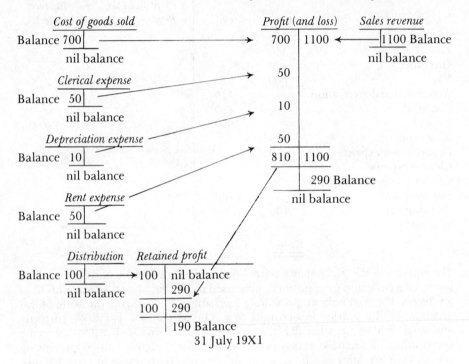

Figure 4.4   Transfer of revenue, expense and distribution balances

The profit statement based on this information was shown in Sect. 3.8.

A new trial balance could be prepared at this or any stage if additional checks were considered necessary; the revised trial balance after calculation of the change in retained profit is shown here for illustrative purposes only.

Trial Balance at 31 July 19X1

	Dr	Cr
	£	£
Cash	450	
Van	600	
Accumulated Depreciation		10
Capital		1000
Creditors		350
Inventory	500	
Retained Profit		190
	£1550	£1550

The accounts shown in this trial balance will all relate to the balance sheet. All the other accounts previously prepared were temporary, and the balance sheet shows a summary of the balances on accounts at the end of the period. At the beginning of the next period these balances will appear as opening balances in the accounts. The balance sheet can now be prepared in accordance with Sect. 3.7, but we will not repeat the exercise in this chapter.[2]

4.5   Total accounts

In many practical applications of the analysis of transactions the volume of processing is such that it is necessary to incorporate controls or checks into the system to ensure accuracy. For example, a mail-order company may have upwards of 50,000 credit customers for whom it must keep separate individual records. It will also be important for the firm to know both the total of individual debts to the firm and the aggregate total of debtors. The firm could thus keep a total account, termed a 'control account', into which it would enter data about aggregate cash receipts, credit sales, etc., and it would also keep individual accounts. This could be shown in terms of T accounts:

Total Debtors (Debtors' Control)

Bal £6000	£100 Receipts

Debtor A		Debtor B		Debtor C	
Bal. £1000	£50 Receipt	Bal. £2000	£30 Receipt	Bal. £3000	£20 Receipt

The individual accounts are not part of the major double-entry system, and hence no misunderstanding about duplication of entries should arise. The major advantages which accrue to the user of the total accounts are that they provide a check on the correctness of entries in total to the individual accounts and also a total or aggregate valuation of the asset or liability under consideration. The use of total accounts can be applied to any part of an accounting system where summaries and additional accuracy checks are required, e.g. inventory, creditors, and fixed assets.

4.6   Classification of accounting data

In Chapter 1 we saw that the major purpose of accounting was to provide financial information about the firm to those who required it. In the preparation of the balance sheet and profit statement it was necessary to provide a classification of our information into various categories. In the balance sheet in Sect. 1.6 we classified assets into land, buildings, etc. In the profit statement we were also involved in the classification of revenues and expenses. The classification system we choose, as in all problems of taxonomy, should be designed to illustrate information in a form most useful to a user's range of needs. For example, we could classify our fixed assets by geographical location, or age, if such information would be useful. The accounts used in the recording system will be designed around a certain predetermined classification system chosen in the light of anticipated requirements. Accounting data is thus concerned not only with recording financial values but also with their classification.

One useful way of classifying data for the management of a firm is by identifying parts of organisations or functions which have been responsible for incurring costs or expenses. This is useful for purposes of business control. The profit statement in Sect. 3.8 used a 'natural expense classification' such as 'clerical' and 'depreciation'.

In Fig. 4.5 we have reclassified the expense data formerly classified under natural accounts into a 'functional classification'. To enable us to reclassify we would need evidence, to determine certain criteria, which would help us established an equitable allocation of expenses and costs to functions. In Sect. 6.2 (3) we have paid special attention to the process of reclassification of data in determining the costs of production.

Natural		Functional		
		Production (Cost of goods sold) £	Administration £	Marketing £
	£			
Clerical labour	50		20	30
Depreciation	10			10
Rent	50		10	40
Cost of goods sold	700	700		
	£810	£700	£30	£80

Figure 4.5   Alternative classification of expenses

A profit statement using a functional classification could be:

Profit Statement of Crisp Company for One Month ended 31 July 19X1

		£
Sales Revenue		1100
Less Cost of Goods Sold (production)		700
Gross Profit		400
Less Other Expenses:		
Administration	30	
Marketing	80	
		110
Net Profit		£290

4.7   Information and accounting systems

It is useful to consider the information used in preparation of accounting statements as part of an overall information system. An information system has three central components: it will collect, process and communicate information. Fig. 4.6 outlines the relationship between the components of an information system. Illustrations from accounting systems are discussed at a later stage.

Data Collection
The term 'data collection' (sometimes termed 'data capture') involves the identification of the information that is required, the search for this information and designing a means for its collection. As we can see in Fig. 4.6 the objective of data collection is ultimately to satisfy our data users. The users or potential users of data

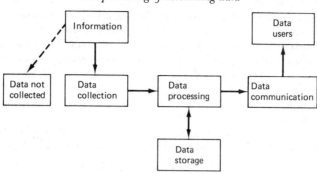

Figure 4.6   Information system

will thus be the determinants of the data that the firm collects. Furthermore Fig. 4.6 shows that information exists in a firm's environment which it does not collect. It may be that it is thought not to be relevant to its needs or it may be too difficult to collect. In Chapter 2 it was emphasised that not all economic events were of relevance for accounting purposes and thus not all economic data is collected, and thus conventional accounting statements cannot reflect the over-all position.

Data Processing and Storage

Data once collected will need to be processed into a form suitable for the user. The concept of processing can be applied to any manipulation of data which has been collected, for example it may involve arithmetical manipulation, sorting or merely permanent recording. The procedures explained in Figs 4.2 and 4.3 all fall within the concept of processing.

Storage of data is an important part of an information system. A firm will store data because it is not required immediately. The use of stored data at a later stage may be in conjunction with newly collected data. For example, the firm may collect information about its production of inventory and continuously update its records about the levels of its inventory. Information about levels of inventory may only be used occasionally and the results of the continuous processing must be recorded or otherwise the information may be lost. The process of storage requires the creation of files to which a system of access (or data retrieval) will be necessary to enable future users to identify where the data they require is stored.

The decision about file creation is complex as it involves predicting which data will be required in the future. The firm will incur storage costs if it creates files, but it will also incur cost if it does not have data available when required, either from further searches for data or from the loss of opportunities.

Data Communication

The information that is required by users of a system is the determinant of the data that is collected and processed. Communication of the results of processing is the final stage in the system. Data that is communicated can be drawn either from files or from data which is collected and processed and immediately.

ACCOUNTING SYSTEMS

The firm may have separate systems for collecting data for various parts of its organisation, e.g. for production and marketing data. Accounting data may be collected and processed as a separate system. In some firms the various systems have grown up independently and therefore there may be a degree of duplication.

It may be possible to develop a system which gives all the functions of the firm access to the same data due to the development of computer technology.

The demands made upon accounting systems have been shown so far to relate to the preparation of financial statements. Later in this book we will examine how accounting systems will be required to provide data for planning and control purposes. The accounting systems which we will now examine will be designed primarily around the requirement to provide an analysis of historical data for purposes of profit measurement and valuation.

These procedures are summarised in Fig. 4.7 where it can be seen that the various stages in our information system correspond to an accounting system:

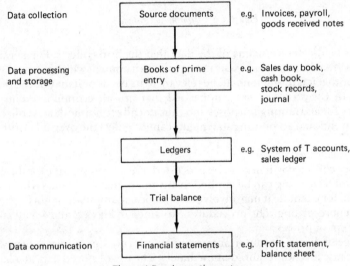

Figure 4.7   Accounting system

As can be seen, data is initially collected from source documents, some of which, e.g. invoices received, will be created externally, and some which will be created internally, e.g. payroll, goods received notes. The books of prime entry summarise the data in a convenient form for processing through the T accounts in the ledgers.[2] This leads to the trial balance and financial statements.

The system described can rely on manual-, mechanical- or computer-based methods of data collection, processing and communication. Manual-based systems rely on clerks and handwritten books and are common in small firms. As firms grow in size and sophistication mechanical and computer technology can improve the speed and accuracy of accounting systems and provide economies in operation. Though ledgers are often thought of as referring to handwritten books, they can take the form of computer files on magnetic tape or discs. The sophistication of the mechanisms found in a firm will depend on the demands made on the system and the applicability of information technology to the particular problems of the firm. Individual systems will be tailor-made and may reflect the idiosyncrasies of particular organisations.[3]

4.8 Summary

This chapter has examined how the use of a system of double-entry accounting using T accounts has developed and improved the flexibility and reliability of our system of processing accounting data. The procedures leading to the preparation of the balance sheet rely on the collection and processing of data, all of which are ultimately determined by the needs of users of information. An understanding of the processing of data can only be developed in the context of an overall accounting system which in some firms may be related to other information systems. The mechanisms of particular accounting systems are likely to be substantially different between firms, though the underlying characteristics of the system will be the same.

As we have now examined the problems of preparation and presentation of financial statements in the context of data analysis, we shall turn to the examination of some of the more important underlying conceptual problems in the following four chapters.

Notes and References

1. For background to the origins and history of accounting see B. S. Yamey, 'Some topics in the history of financial accounting in England, 1500–1900', *Studies in Accounting Theory*, 2nd ed. (ed. W. T. Baxter and S. Davidson) (London, Sweet & Maxwell, 1962); B. S. Yamey, 'Pious inscriptions; confused accounts; classification of accounts: three historical notes', *Debits, Credits, Finance and Profits*, ed. H. C. Edey and B. S. Yamey (London, Sweet & Maxwell, 1974).
2. For a more extensive coverage of problems of double-entry book-keeping there are many detailed texts to choose from; see, for example, *Spicer and Pegler's Book-keeping and Accounts*, 17th ed. (ed. W. W. Bigg and R. E. G. Perrins) (London, H.F.L., 1971).
3. T. A. Macrae, *The Impact of Computers on Accounting* (New York, Wiley–Interscience, 1964).

Further Reading

P. A. Losty, *The Effective Use of Computers in Business* (London, Cassell, 1969).

Questions and Problems

4.1　What do you understand by the following terminology?

Double-entry book-keeping	Ledger
T account	Temporary account
Debit	Profit (and loss) account
Credit	Total account
Balance	Control account
Trial balance	Functional classification
Information system	Natural classification
Books of prime entry	Data collection
Journal	Data processing
Accounting system	Data communication

4.2　Examine the advantages and disadvantages of the use of T accounts for the processing of accounting data.

4.3　Many firms use computers to process and record accounting data. Is the analysis of transactions into 'debit' and 'credit' still meaningful and useful?

4.4　Using the data from Question 3.2 prepare the T accounts, trial balance, profit (and loss) account and profit statement and balance sheet.

4.5 You are responsible for an accounting system which processes the following volume of data on a daily basis:

    1000 cheques received
    £5000 received in cash in 30 tills
    300 cheques paid to suppliers
    5000 items of inventory received from suppliers

How would you ensure the accuracy of the system?

4.6 Explain any problems which may arise in a small transport firm in classifying the following expenses into functional areas:

(a) petrol for lorries and cars from the firms pumps
(b) insurance
(c) electricity
(d) rent for the garages, haulage yard and offices
(e) the accountant's salary
(f) the managing director's salary
(g) interest

4.7 Explain how and why you would collect the following data about a firm to assist in the preparation of its financial statements:

(a) wages paid
(b) rent paid and owing
(c) the useful life of a van
(d) level of inventory in a warehouse
(e) amount of oil in an oilwell
(f) inventory being delivered to a firm
(g) the effect of a research and development programme
(h) changes in the demand for a firm's products

5
Fixed Assets

5.1 Introduction

Chapters 5–8 analyse selected areas of measurement and recording starting in this chapter with an analysis of fixed assets. We can consider that fixed assets are a category of assets that are owned by the firm normally for more than a year. They provide the means by which the firm carries on its operations rather than being held for processing and selling. In most firms they form a significant part of the total assets. Examples of fixed assets are:

Factory buildings
Ships
Shares owned by a pension fund
Lorries owned by a manufacturing firm (when owned, for example, by a lorry
   dealer they may be current assets)

The methods of measuring fixed assets can have a significant effect on the assessment of a firm's value and therefore its profit.

Most fixed assets will have a finite life. There are exceptions to this, one example of which is land. Even with land the specific quality for which it is held – e.g. its use as farming land – may wear out. The finite life of an asset may be determined by the lapse of time – e.g. leases and patents – or because of their use – e.g. cars and machinery. Other assets may no longer be required because they do not produce sufficient benefits, e.g. where the market for the products manufactured no longer exists. Some assets have a physical existence; some are a document of title, e.g. a patent; others have no evidence for their existence other than people's opinion, e.g. a retail shop's good name.

An example of the classifications of fixed assets made by a firm in its published accounts is given in App. D.3, notes 8 and 9. Firms summarise their fixed assets into a broad classification when presenting information to interested parties, e.g. land and buildings, plant and machinery.[1] In the financial statements of Marks & Spencer Ltd a distinction is made between properties and fixtures and equipment. A distinction is also made between freehold properties, long-lease and short-lease properties. Some of these distinctions are required by law,[2] others are made as a compromise between giving detailed information on all assets and giving one summary figure for total assets.

5.2 Value considerations

In Chapter 1 four possible concepts of value were considered – original cost, replacement cost, selling price and future utility. The choice of the concept used in financial statements depends on the application of the accounting concepts which were discussed in Chapter 2. For the various reasons mentioned in earlier chapters the valuation concept applied in practice to value assets in financial statements is normally original cost, though it is becoming more common for those fixed assets that appreciate in value to be valued at selling price (see Chapter 8 and App. D.3, note 8). The latter practice contradicts the concept of realisation but is permitted because of the growing tendency to reflect current values in accounts.

The use of concepts of value other than original cost might be thought to be justified because they give a 'better' picture of the current position of the firm. The users of financial information would be the judges of what constitutes 'better' in this context and they will assess this on the basis of the relevance of the information to their particular situation. However, the criterion of relevance to the needs of users may conflict with the concept of objectivity.

5.3   Depreciation

We can consider fixed assets as a stock of benefits which will be used up over time. Thus they fall in value over time and this is termed 'depreciation'.[3] In order to calculate depreciation it is necessary to measure this fall in value. Since the value of an asset could differ with the application of alternative valuation concepts, so the calculation of depreciation could also differ. In Chapter 1 the profit of an accounting period was defined as the change in value during that period. If a fixed asset reduces in value during an accounting period this fall in value, or depreciation, represents a reduction in profit and will be an expense matched against the revenues in the profit statement (see Sect. 3.5).

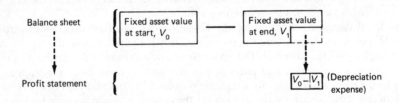

Figure 5.1   The process of depreciation

Fig. 5.1 shows depreciation to be a by-product of the process of measuring the value of fixed assets at the beginning and end of an accounting period.

Ex. 5.1 gives a further illustration of this process.

Example 5.1
In 19X0 the Elton Co. Ltd makes cash sales of £5000 and incurs expenses of £3000 which are paid in cash. Other than cash, the firm's only assets were a machine and a car, their values being:

	V_0 1 January 19X0	V_1 31 December 19X0	V_0-V_1 Depreciation expense
Machine	£1000	£900	£100
Car	£ 500	£425	£ 75

The profit statement for 19X0 would be:

Profit Statement for year ended 31 December 19X0

	£
Sales revenue	5000
Less depreciation expense	

	£	
machine	100	
car	75	
Other expenses	3000	
		3175
Net profit		£1825

The fixed assets in the balance sheets would be shown thus:

	1 January 19X0	*31 December 19X0*
	£	£
Fixed Assets	1500	1325
Cash	—	2000
	£1500	£3325

Since the depreciation expense is the change in value in the year and, since each fixed asset is valued annually, the measure of depreciation is a direct result of the valuations. If in any particular year a fixed asset does not decrease in value, or if it actually appreciates, then there appears to be no depreciation expense. In the latter case there may be an additional revenue but its treatment in practice will be subject to the application of the accounting concepts. An example of this in practice is when an increase in value of land is shown as 'revaluation profit' in the owners' equity (e.g. see App. D.3).

5.4 Depreciation using original cost

Since original cost is the concept of valuation used most frequently by firms when preparing financial statements we will concentrate on measuring depreciation using this concept. Usually residual value, e.g. the sale proceeds, will be lower than original cost and if no interim adjustments are made to the assets value, the value of the firm appear to drop suddenly when the asset was sold. It is usual to recognise this by means of depreciation calculations made during an asset's life. Depreciation using original cost allocates the total fall in value, i.e. the original cost less residual value, over each of the accounting periods during the asset's life. This periodic allocation is treated as an expense in the profit statement and thus it is matched against the firm's revenues arising during the asset's life. This process of matching the depreciation expense against the revenues arising in each accounting period is not one of annual valuation (using one of the concepts discussed in Chapter 1) as it would be with other valuation concepts, but one of cost allocation to the relevant periods. It should be noted that it is unlikely that the revenue arising from the use of an individual asset could be identified as being produced by that asset.

To examine the difficulties of allocating the cost of a fixed asset to the accounting periods during its life we will consider three elements in the calculation, i.e. the life of the asset, its residual value and the method of cost allocation.

The Life of an Asset

An asset will have a physical life during which it will be able to function for its intended purpose. If sufficient resources are committed to it, this physical life may be a very long time, e.g. if repairs are continuously carried out without regard to cost. However, an asset will have an economic life span with a particular firm which should end when its additional costs exceed the additional revenue it generates (see Sect. 11.2 for a decision-making analysis using marginal costs and revenues).

In Fig. 5.2 the total costs curve of the asset reflects the cumulative cost of the asset including its purchase cost, interest charges and maintenance. The total revenues include the sales revenues from the benefits produced by the asset and its potential residual value at the end of each year. The cost and revenue curves represent cash forecasts for possible alternative life spans and it can be seen that life OA is the optimum because with this life the revenues exceed the costs by the maximum possible amount.

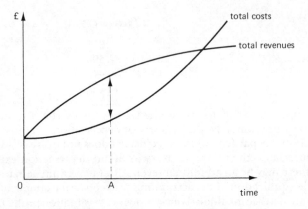

Figure 5.2   Optimum economic life of an asset

The firm will take a decision when it purchases a fixed asset on how long it intends to keep it (we will call a firm's estimate of the optimum economic life the asset's 'forecast life'). The decision may be reviewed later, particularly if unforeseen obsolescence justifies earlier replacement. 'Obsolescence' is a term used when an asset falls in value due to factors other than its use, or the passage of time. This may mean, for example, earning capacity has been affected by changes in demand for the benefits produced by the asset.

The Residual Value of the Asset

To calculate the expense that has to be matched against the revenues arising over an asset's life the estimated residual value must be deducted from the original cost. In most cases this will be positive, but in certain circumstances the residual value could be negative, e.g. the disposal costs may exceed the sale proceeds, and should, in this event, be added to the original cost.

The Method of Cost Allocation

The difference between the original cost and the residual value has to be allocated over the useful life of the asset. The options open to the firm can be summarised in diagrammatic form as in Fig. 5.3, which shows three alternative possibilities for cost allocations. The curves in the figure show the original cost less accumulated depreciation (termed the 'net book value') at particular points in the life of the asset. All the curves start at the original cost and end at the residual value. Points on the curve represent interim valuations of the asset. Curve A allocates more depreciation expense to the early years of the asset's life. Curve C represents an increasing depreciation expense over the life of the asset. This is developed further in other texts.[4] Curve B is straight, illustrating an equal allocation each year. The curves illustrate different results of the methods (commonly called 'depreciation bases') of allocating the asset's fall in value over its life. In practice there are three bases that are commonly used and these are examined below.

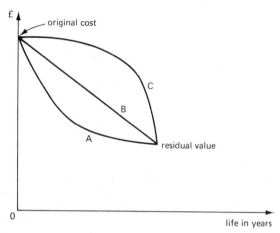

Figure 5.3   Alternative depreciation patterns

(a) The Straight-line Basis

This allocates the difference between original cost and residual value (which we shall call the 'asset's total expense') equally over each year of the asset's forecast life (as in curve B in Fig. 5.3). The formula is:

$$\text{Annual depreciation expense} = \frac{\text{Asset's total expense}}{\text{Forecast life}}$$

The effect of this is to produce an even depreciation expense in the profit statement each year as Fig. 5.4 shows.

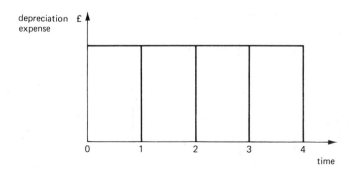

Figure 5.4   Straight-line depreciation

Example 5.2

Mr East operates a mobile grocery store and for this purpose has a van which cost him £1600 on 1 January 19X0. He decides to keep it for two years, at the end of which time he estimates he will be able to sell it for £900.

On a straight-line basis his depreciation expense each year will be

$$\frac{£1600 - £900}{2} = £350$$

In his profit statement in 19X0 and 19X1 there will be a depreciation expense of £350. The balance sheet value for the van at the end of each year will be shown as:

	31 December 19X0	31 December 19X1
	£	£
Van at cost	1600	1600
Less accumulated depreciation	350	700
	£1250	£ 900

The accumulated depreciation, sometimes termed a depreciation provision, is that part of the cost which has been treated as an expense to date.

(b)   Reducing-charge Basis

This basis, sometimes known as the reducing-balance method, produces a decreasing annual depreciation expense during the asset's life (as in curve A in Fig. 5.3). One common way of calculating the annual depreciation expense is to apply a constant percentage to the balance of the original cost less accumulated depreciation, each accounting period. The constant percentage (Y) can be calculated from:

$$Y = 100 \left(1 - n\sqrt{\frac{RV}{C}} \right)$$

where n is the forecast life, RV is the estimated residual value and C is the original cost.

This method of calculating the expense will mean that when the asset is sold the original cost less the accumulated depreciation is equal to the estimated residual value. There are other ways of calculating the depreciation expense, using this basis, which are not discussed here.[5] Fig. 5.5 shows the pattern of the depreciation expense over the asset's life.

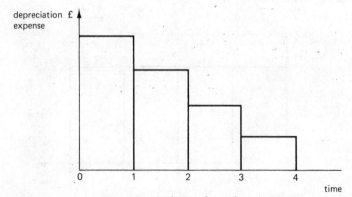

Figure 5.5   Reducing-charge depreciation

Example 5.3

Using the same data as Ex. 5.2, the constant percentage would be 25%, i.e.

$$100 \left(1 - \sqrt{\frac{900}{1600}}\right).$$

The depreciation expense each year is:

Year 1. $\dfrac{25}{100} \times (1600 - 0) = £400$

Year 2. $\dfrac{25}{100} \times (1600 - 400) = £300$

These amounts will be shown as the depreciation expense in the profit statement each year. The balance sheet values for the van at the end of each year will be:

	31 December 19X0	31 December 19X1
	£	£
Van at Cost	1600	1600
Less Accumulated Depreciation	400	700
	£1200	£ 900

(c) Usage Basis

This basis relates the depreciation expense in each year to the use made of the asset. The use can be measured in many ways; for a lorry it may be miles travelled; for a plane, hours of flying time; for a machine, hours of production. The depreciation expense is calculated as an amount per unit of use. The formula is:

$$\text{Depreciation expense per unit of use} = \frac{\text{Asset's total expense}}{\text{Forecast life in units of use}}$$

The depreciation expense each year will be the rate calculated above multiplied by the use made of the asset in that year. This could produce a curve similar to A, B or C in Fig. 5.3 depending on the circumstances.

Example 5.4

Using the same data as Ex. 5.2 and in addition the knowledge that Mr East estimates he will use the van for 7000 miles in the 2 years, when it will sell for £900. He uses the van for 2500 miles in the first year and 4500 in the second year.

$$\text{Depreciation expense per mile travelled} = \frac{£700}{7000} = £0.10 \text{ per mile}$$

Therefore £250 (2500 × 0.10) is the depreciation expense in the first year and £450 in the next year. The balance-sheet values for the van at the end of each year will be:

	31 December 19X0	31 December 19X1
	£	£
Van at Cost	1600	1600
Less Accumulated Depreciation	250	700
	£1350	£ 900

An Assessment of the Bases

When original cost is the valuation concept used, depreciation aims to spread the cost of the asset, less its residual value, over its forecast life. There are several possible criteria for deciding how much of this cost should be matched against the revenues arising each year.

One is to try and relate the depreciation expense with the fall in selling value of the asset each year. The justification for this criterion is that assets with finite lives will eventually be sold or scrapped. Because the forecast lives may be uncertain the firm may wish to keep the net book value of the asset at the end of each year, as near as possible to the residual value of the asset if sold. This will mean that if the asset is disposed of, the book value will be as near as possible to the proceeds from the disposal. This criterion for choosing a depreciation basis could be viewed as an abandonment of the original cost-valuation base and the going-concern concept because the firm would virtually be using the selling price of the asset each year for balance sheet purposes. Using this criterion the usage basis may be most appropriate where the selling value of the asset falls due to use. If the asset falls in selling value evenly over time then it might be considered that the straight-line basis is more appropriate. However, most assets do not fall into such convenient categories. A car's bodywork wears out due to the lapse of time (rust would attack it, whether or not it was used) but its tyres probably wear out through use only. Thus an asset may be a combination of different categories and the use of a single depreciation basis must necessarily be a compromise.

Another criterion that could be used is to apply the matching concept to ensure that the revenues recognised in a period are matched with the expense incurred in earning them. If we assume revenues are constant then the costs associated with the asset should be constant. One interpretation of this is the use of the straight-line basis when original cost is the only cost of the asset considered. Another interpretation is the use of the reducing-balance method when costs such as repairs and maintenance are considered in addition to the initial cost of the asset.

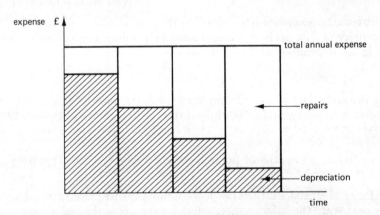

Figure 5.6   Depreciation and repair expenses of an asset

If we cannot assume that revenues are constant each year we could relate the annual expense to the production of the firm using the usage basis. In this way an equal expense per unit of production would be calculated if only the initial cost is considered.

The alternative depreciation bases result in different depreciation expenses each year. The data from Exs 5.2, 5.3 and 5.4 are summarised below:

	Straight line	Reducing charge	Usage
19X0	£350	£400	£250
19X1	£350	£300	£450

Each basis will have produced different profit measures for each year, even though the performance of the firm is the same. Over the total life of the asset the total depreciation expense will be the same, e.g. in the illustration above all the depreciation expenses total £700, but the yearly allocation to the expenses in the profit statement will be different.

Each basis produces different profit figures from the same information and this illustrates the importance of a firm using the same depreciation basis each year if the profits of one year are to be compared with another year. If shareholders are to make profit comparisons between firms, the effect of different depreciation bases being used needs to be quantified to make the comparisons meaningful. Annual profit figures are important as an indicator of a firm's performance. If annual profit figures were not required, then neither would annual cost allocations (the same applies to the residual value and considerations about an asset's life).

The three bases considered above are, as already noted, not the only methods of arriving at the depreciation expense. There are two other bases used in practice that we must mention. The first is that of treating the asset as an expense in the accounting period in which it is purchased. This method is used, for example, for assets whose value is considered immaterial in relation to the other numbers in the profit statement. An example is a firm treating its pencil-sharpeners as an immediate expense at the time of purchase. The second basis calculates depreciation at the time of replacement. This involves treating the original cost as the value of the fixed asset at the end of each accounting period after purchase, and treating all costs arising from replacing the asset (or replacing its replacement, etc.) as depreciation. The advantage of this method is that in periods after the initial purchase, when the replacement occurs, the expense in the profit statement will be equivalent to the current outflow of resources from the firm and will also be nearer the asset's replacement cost. This is most suitable where a firm makes regular annual replacements otherwise the depreciation expense will be very irregular from year to year. This is also suitable for a firm that owns a lot of similar assets and does not want to record each individual assets cost and depreciation, e.g. trailers in a transport firm. However, the balance-sheet value (based on the original cost of the first asset) becomes progressively out of date.

Errors in Estimates

In our discussion of depreciation using original cost, various areas have been examined, i.e. the asset's life and residual value, and the method of cost allocation. In order to calculate the depreciation expense in each accounting period the asset's life and residual value have to be forecast. This implies that errors can arise. In calculating the depreciation expense a base has to be chosen and this also means that an error could arise from choosing the wrong base. We will now consider each of these sources of error.

Life of an Asset. A firm will normally review its forecast of an asset's life regularly. The effect of changing the forecast life is illustrated in Ex. 5.5.

Example 5.5

The Elf Co. Ltd purchases a machine for £1200 and forecasts its life will be five years. At the end of the fifth year it is estimated that the asset will be worthless.

However, after only three years the firm finds demand conditions have changed and it cannot sell the goods produced. At this time the machine is scrapped and has no residual value.

During each year revenues are £1000 and expenses of £500 are incurred. Various possible profit statements are shown for the third year below on the assumption that:

(a) the life is five years (this was the original forecast life);
(b) the life is three years (this would have been the forecast life if the change in demand had been foreseen);
(c) the calculations are adjusted in the third year from the initial forecast life of five years to three years.

Profit Statements for the Third Year

	(a)	(b)	(c)
	5-year forecast	3-year forecast	5-year forecast and adjustment
	£	£	£
Sales Revenues	1000	1000	1000
Less: Depreciation expense	240	400	400
Other Expenses	500	500	500
Additional depreciation (2 × (400 − 240))			320
Net Profit	£260	£100	£220 (loss)

In the case of profit statement (c) there is an adjustment for the under-depreciation in the first two years. For each of the first two years the depreciation was £240 and, if the fall in demand had been known, the depreciation would have been £400. The annual depreciation expense in (a) was calculated as £1200 ÷ 5. In (b) and (c) it was calculated as £1200 ÷ 3.

The residual value of the asset. If forecasts of the residual value are found to be incorrect this will lead to an under- or over-estimate of profits as in Ex. 5.6.

Example 5.6
The East Co. Ltd purchases a machine for £2000 and estimates its residual value as £200 if it retains it for five years. Thus, over the five years it will match £1800 of depreciation expense against the firm's revenues. At the end of the fifth year it sells the asset for £500. Only £1500 (£2000 − £500) should have been matched against the revenues during the five-year period, the depreciation expense was overestimated by £300, and therefore the profits in the first four years understated.

The depreciation base. We have examined some of the criteria used to decide on a depreciation base for a fixed asset. Whatever the criterion used the asset may not fall in value in the manner expected thus suggesting that another base should have been used. Profit measurement will thus be affected. This source of error should not arise as frequently as the first two sources because experience will show the most appropriate base for each type of asset.

5.5 Recording depreciation information

Following the rules in Chapter 4 the entries in the accounts will appear as set out in Ex. 5.7.

Example 5.7

The Eal Co. Ltd purchases a fixed asset for £2000 cash on 1 January 19X0 (TR1) and calculates the depreciation expense to be £200 in 19X0 (AD1) and £300 in 19X1 (AD2). This will be recorded thus:

Fixed Asset		Accumulated Depreciation	
TR1 2000			200 AD1
			300 AD2

Cash		Depreciation Expense	
	2000 TR1	AD1 200	200 To P & L a/c (19X0)
		AD2 300	300 To P & L a/c (19X1)

In Ex. 5.7 £200 will be shown as an expense in the 19X0 profit statement and £300 in 19X1. In the balance sheet at the end of each year the fixed asset will be shown as:

	31 December 19X0	31 December 19X1
	£	£
Fixed Asset at Cost	2000	2000
Less Accumulated Depreciation	200	500
	£1800	£1500

On disposal of the fixed asset a disposal of fixed assets account should be created to eliminate the cost and accumulated depreciation from the accounts and to deal with the sale proceeds. The purpose of this disposal account is to show the profit or loss on the disposal of the fixed asset. This profit or loss is transferred to the profit (and loss) account. This is illustrated in Example 5.8.

Example 5.8

This example continues using Ex. 5.7. On 2 January 19X2 the asset was sold for £1400 cash (TR2). The cost (AD3) and the accumulated depreciation (AD4) are eliminated from their respective accounts. The entries would be:

Fixed Assets		Accumulated Depreciation	
BAL 2000	2000 AD3	AD4 560	500 BAL

Cash		Disposal of Fixed Assets	
TR2 1400		AD3 2000	1400 TR2
			500 AD4
			100 AD5
		£2000	£2000

Profit (and Loss) Account 19 × 2	
AD5 100	

On the disposal of the fixed asset in Ex. 5.8, where the depreciation calculations were based on estimates the proceeds were different from the cost less the accumulated depreciation. This resulted in a balance of £100 in the disposal of fixed assets account. This balance was transferred to the profit (and loss) account (AD5). This balance is a loss resulting from the depreciation expense being insufficient in earlier years. The term 'loss' may be confusing, as the sum could be interpreted as an extra expense this year to make up for an under-expense in previous years. The converse would be true if the sale had shown a profit. The treatment of the balance depends on its materiality. If it is not material, it will probably be shown in the profit statement as a reduction of or an increase in the current year's depreciation expense. If it is material, it could be described in the profit statement as a prior year adjustment, shown separately because it is not a normal trading item.[6]

5.6 Depreciation and replacement

To the extent that a depreciation expense reduces profits and the amount available for cash dividends to the owners, it will help to conserve cash within the firm (see Sect. 7.11). However, the process of depreciating a fixed asset does not necessarily mean that cash is available to replace it because: (*a*) the cash retained in the firm may have been used for other purposes, e.g. increasing inventory or buying other assets; and (*b*) the price of the replacement may be higher than the original cost of the asset.

Example 5.9
On 1 January 19X0 the Endymion Company purchases a van for £500 and depreciates it on a straight-line basis at £250 per year. The year-end balance sheets are:

	31 December 19X0	*31 December 19X1*
Fixed Asset	£	£
Van at Cost	500	500
Less Accumulated Depreciation	250	500
	250	—
Current Assets		
Inventory	1000	1450
Cash	450	150
	£1700	£1600
Financed by		
Owners' Equity		
Capital	£1200	£1600
Loan	500	—
	£1700	£1600

It can be seen from these balance sheets that the company has only £150 cash at the end of 19X1 even though it has depreciated the asset. The reason is that the cash retained in the business has been used to purchase additional inventories and redeem the loan. However, even if the firm had £500 cash, the replacement price could well have risen, making it impossible to replace the asset without obtaining additional resources.

5.7 Non-physical fixed assets

At the beginning of this chapter various types of fixed assets were considered and in this section we consider non-physical fixed assets in more detail. Non-physical assets, using the terminology of Chapter 1, are useful qualities of a firm which are expected to yield benefits in the future. Examples of this type of asset are research and development, advertising, staff training, patents and a firm's labour force.[7] If a non-physical asset is created by the firm it can usually be measured by cost, but sometimes the cost may be more difficult to define, e.g. the cost of a monopoly or staff morale.

The benefits of non-physical assets are usually more difficult to define than the benefits from other assets. In addition there is unlikely to be a market for buying and selling such assets.

The concepts of conservatism and objective evidence mean that non-physical assets rarely appear in the balance sheet (but see Sect. 9.3). Any costs of the assets will appear in the profit statement as an expense of the period in which the costs were incurred. In this latter case there will therefore be no attempt to match relevant costs to the revenues generated by the assets.

There may be difficulties in comparing firms if they treat non-physical fixed assets in different ways. Where the asset has costs, if one firm treats the costs as an asset while the other treats them as an expense the balance sheets and profit statements could not be meaningfully compared. It is now generally accepted that firms should disclose their accounting policies in relation to these assets[8] but special treatment is now recommended for research and development.[9]

5.8 Summary

Fixed assets could be valued using any of the four concepts of value discussed in Chapter 1. However, original cost is the concept most often used in practice. When a fixed asset falls in value this is known as depreciation. In the case of the original cost valuation concept the total depreciation over its life is measured by the difference between the original cost and residual value. The profit of a firm needs to be measured periodically and thus the total depreciation has to be allocated as an expense to the accounting periods over an asset's life. Depreciation can be viewed as an attempt to match costs to revenues during each accounting period, or as an attempt to represent the fall in selling value of the asset. In practice three bases of allocation are commonly used – the straight-line, reducing-charge, and usage basis. Whichever basis is used depreciation is calculated for profit measurement purposes, and is not directly related to the replacement of the asset concerned. However, the ability of a firm to replace its fixed assets is important and is given further consideration in Chapter 7.

Notes and References

1. *Survey of Published Accounts 1973–74* (General Educational Trust of the Institute of Chartered Accountants in England and Wales, 1974).
2. General Educational Trust of the Institute of Chartered Accountants in England and Wales, *Guide to the Accountancy Disclosure Requirements of the Companies Acts 1948–1967* (London, Gee, 1967).
3. Accounting Standards Steering Committee, *ED 15 Accounting for Depreciation* (Institute of Chartered Accountants in England and Wales, 1975).
4. W. T. Baxter, *Depreciation* (London, Sweet & Maxwell, 1971) Ch. 7, where the effects of cost of finance are considered.

5. H. Bierman and A. Drebin, *Financial Accounting: An Introduction* (London, Macmillan, 1970) pp. 218–21.
6. Accounting Standards Steering Committee, *S.S.A.P. 6 Extraordinary Items and Prior Year adjustments* (Institute of Chartered Accountants in England and Wales, 1974).
7. W. J. Giles and D. F. Robinson, *Human Asset Accountancy* (Institute of Cost and Management Accountants, 1972).
8. Accounting Standards Steering Committee, *S.S.A.P. 2 Disclosure of Accounting Policies* (Institute of Chartered Accountants in England and Wales, 1971).
9. Accounting Standards Steering Committee, *ED 17 Accounting for Research and Development* (Institute of Chartered Accountants in England and Wales, 1976).

Further Reading

P. Garner and K. Berg, *Readings in Accounting Theory* (Boston, Mass., Houghton, Mifflin, 1966).
W. T. Baxter, *Depreciation* (London, Sweet & Maxwell, 1971).
E. Hendrikson and B. Budge, *Contemporary Thoughts in Accounting* (Belmont, Calif., Dickenson, 1974).
T. Keller and S. Zeff, *Financial Accounting Theory II; Issues and Controversies* (New York, N.Y., McGraw-Hill, 1969).
International Accounting Standards Committee, *ED 4 Depreciation Accounting* (Institute of Chartered Accountants in England and Wales, 1975).

Questions and Problems

5.1 What do you understand by the following terminology:

Fixed asset	Optimum economic life
Original cost	Forecast life
Depreciation	Physical life
Accumulated depreciation	Straight-line basis
Depreciation provision	Reducing-charge basis
Residual value	Usage basis
Net book value	Obsolescence
Sale of fixed asset account	

5.2 How would you prove that the following are assets of a firm: a ship, a lorry, an oil field, a good name, a patent, good employee relations.

5.3 The Ealing Co. Ltd installs a new machine in its factory. The following are some of the costs incurred by the firm during the first year of operation of the machine; should any of these be treated as part of the machine's original cost?

(a) The cash price was £100,000.

(b) An old machine was removed to make way for the new one and this removal cost £2000.

(c) £55 was paid for delivery of the new machine.

(d) The firm's own labour force was used to install the machine, the relevant wages were £4000.

(e) A new air-conditioning unit (cost £1500) was installed because of extra heat generated by the new machine. It was estimated that the existing air-conditioning unit would have had to be renewed next year even if the machine had not been installed.

(f) The Managing Director, who is paid £8 per hour, spent two hours examining the new machine.

(g) The Chief Accountant is paid £5 per hour and he spent one hour processing the new machine's invoice as it contained some mistakes.

(h) Repair costs of £200 were incurred in the first year.

5.4 Edgar purchased a car in kit form for £200 and proceeded to assemble it himself. The following information was obtained:

(a) £50 of special tools had to be purchased to construct the car.

(b) His garage was used for the work and this was normally kept empty, but £1.00 per week rent could have been obtained for it if let.

(c) The construction time was two weeks, one week being Edgar's holiday, the other week a special unpaid week off work (he earns £100 per week).

(d) When constructed, the car could have been sold for £300.

(e) The car will save Edgar £325 over its life in travelling expenses, etc.

What value would you assign to Edgar's car?

5.5 When measuring the depreciation of a fixed asset what accounting concepts are important and why?

5.6 What are the arguments for and against an organisation such as the Government or the accounting profession specifying the depreciation basis to be used by all firms.

5.7 Explain how the usage method of depreciation could take account of repair costs for a fixed asset so that there is an appropriate expense in the profit statement during the life of an asset.

5.8 Elkington Traders Ltd purchases a machine for £2000, and estimates its optimal life to be five years and residual value to be £400. It is estimated that the sales, less expenses (other than depreciation), arising from the machine will be £3000 each year. Show the estimated profit over the five-year period, using (a) the straight-line, and (b) the reducing-charge bases.

5.9 Egg Eaters Ltd purchased a ship for £25,000 on 1 January 19X0, and decided to depreciate it at £2500 each year. At the end of 19X3, it was sold for £18,000. Show the entries for these transactions in the accounts. How would the ship have been valued in the firm's balance sheet at the end of 19X2?

5.10 A car rental firm is considering how long it should keep a car which cost £1000. It constructs the following cash forecast for the first five years of the car's life:

Possible life (in years)

	0	1	2	3	4	5
	£	£	£	£	£	£
Rental income p.a.	—	1500	1500	1000	1500	1000
Repairs p.a.	—	—	200	400	800	1000
Residual value	1000	650	600	550	500	400

(a) Make whatever assumptions you consider necessary and explain the length of time you would recommend the firm to keep the car.

(b) Explain and justify the assumptions you made.

6
Costing and Inventory

6.1 Introduction

This chapter is concerned with the valuation of the resources used in a firm's operations, e.g. in manufacturing a product, operating a department, or providing a service. In addition we are concerned with valuing the units of production remaining at the end of a period and recorded as an asset (i.e. inventory) of the firm in the balance sheet. As with fixed assets discussed in Chapter 5, the valuation of inventory can have a significant effect on a firm's valuation and therefore its profit.

Firms may find this valuation information useful because they may be able to assess, for example, the profitability of their sales by matching a valuation of resources used up with the relevant sales revenue. In addition they may wish to compare their performance with other firms, or the efficiency of one department with another within the firm. These valuations may also be considered in determining the selling price of a firm's product (see Sect. 11.4).

Chapter 1 introduced alternative approaches to valuation, i.e. replacement cost, selling price, future utility and original cost. Because of the necessity to conform to the accounting concepts in preparing information for published financial statements the valuation concept used in conventional accounting statements will normally be original cost. In addition to published statements there is also a need for information when preparing reports to internal management, e.g. for control or decision-making purposes. In these latter reports the firm can choose the valuation concepts most useful to it. We will see in Sect. 10.8 that original cost valuations may not be appropriate for planning and decision-making purposes. However, this chapter bases its analysis of the value of a firm's use of resources on original cost. The Sandilands report reviewed this approach.[1]

Costing is the process of classifying, recording and analysing expenditure for the determination of the cost of resources used in producing sales revenue. In the first part of this chapter we consider cost classifications and cost systems. We then consider problems relating to inventory.

The model in Fig. 6.1 illustrates a typical flow of resources used up in the firm's operations. The production process referred to in Fig. 6.1 depicts any type of operation, e.g. oil exploration, manufacturing cars, selling goods in a department store, providing a service as a travel agency. The relationship in this figure between the inputs and outputs is what economists would normally refer to as a firm's production function. The work in progress is that part of inventory which has not completed the production process. The finished goods are those assets which have completed the production process but are not yet sold. When the assets are sold their cost is treated as an expense and matched against the appropriate revenues in the period's profit calculation.

Before we consider the cost classifications and cost systems which may be used to ascertain a firm's costs of production, we will consider an example of a complex costing problem which illustrates some of the difficulties that may arise. An oil company may wish to know the cost of producing North Sea Oil. It may, for example, need this for valuing the unsold oil, for determining a selling price, or to see whether it cost more or less than oil from the Celtic Sea. Examples of some of the possible costs to be considered are:

Wages of oil rig operators
Maintenance of oil rigs
Cost of raising finance (including interest)
Exploration licences
Research into better exploration methods
Office administration
Exploration of non-productive wells
Pipelines and refining

It should be clear from the list of possible costs that the calculation of, for example, a cost per barrel of oil or cost per oil well, is likely to be very difficult. The discussion of cost classifications and cost systems that follows will help in the analysis of this and other problems.

6.2 Cost classifications

In this section we will examine direct and indirect costs, fixed and variable costs, product and period costs, including in the latter the principles of absorption and variable costing.

(1) DIRECT AND INDIRECT COSTS

All costs can be classified into direct and indirect according to which unit of the firm's activities they are identified with. Costs that can be identified with a unit of a firm's activities are termed 'direct', all others are termed 'indirect' costs. This latter classification of indirect costs is usually termed 'overhead'. When related to the firm as a whole all costs incurred by the firm are direct. When related to a subdivision of the firm, e.g. a department or a product, some costs are direct and others indirect. (Subdivisions of the firm for which costs are ascertained are often called 'cost centres'. To be meaningful the use of the term 'direct' or 'indirect' costs

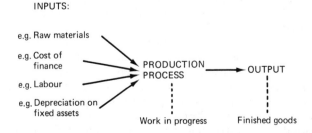

Figure 6.1   Flow of resources in a firm

should be qualified by their relationship to the subdivision (or unit) of the firm's activity with which the costs are to be identified.

The label of direct or indirect is often pragmatic because there are many costs which could conceivably be identified with the unit of activity but where to do so would be too inconvenient or costly. An illustration of a classification of costs into direct and indirect is shown below, using wage costs. A similar analysis could be applied to a firm's other costs.

Sub-divisions of firm	Direct wages	Indirect wages
Firm	Central administrators Factory supervisors Production department supervisors Production operatives	None
Factory	Factory supervisors Production department supervisors Production operatives	Central administrators
Production Department	Production department supervisors Production operatives	Central administrators Factory supervisors
Individual units of production	Production operatives	Central administrators Factory supervisors Production department supervisors

This classification of costs provides useful information in identifying the responsibility for costs (see Sect. 14.2). As the unit of activity becomes larger, e.g. from department to factory, the direct costs for which the unit could be considered responsible increase.

(2)   FIXED AND VARIABLE COSTS

The distinction between fixed and variable costs relates to the changes in total costs in relation to changes in levels of activity, e.g. units produced. It is often useful to make assumptions about how costs vary over a particular range of activity, e.g. the range between 1000 and 2000 units of production. If the range defined is large enough, most costs will vary, but within a restricted range some costs will vary whilst others remain fixed. For most firms the rate of change of variable costs will not be constant over a wide range of activity. In practice, however, the rate of change is often assumed to be constant because this facilitates the costing of production. Unit costs are calculated by assuming that the unit variable costs are the same over all levels of activity, and thus the cost of alternative levels of production can be predicted.

As with direct and indirect costs, the distinction between fixed and variable is often pragmatic and if, for example, the variation of change over a range of activity was sufficiently small the cost may be assumed to be fixed. In Fig. 6.2, which illustrates this pragmatic approach, two wage costs (X and Y) are ascertained for each level of activity and plotted on a graph as a series of dots. The series is then joined by the best fitting line. The cost (X) would be assumed to be variable within the range considered (from output of A units to output of B units), i.e. the relevant range. The cost (Y) would be assumed to be fixed.

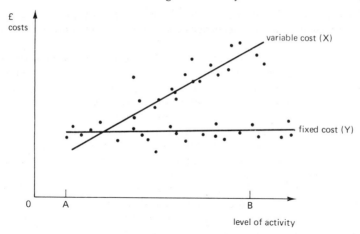

Figure 6.2   Examples of cost behaviour

There may be costs that do not fall easily into either classification, and these are often termed 'semi-variable', e.g. electricity costs. In this case some element of the cost is fixed and some variable. Fig. 6.3 illustrates the fixed, variable and semi-variable classifications:

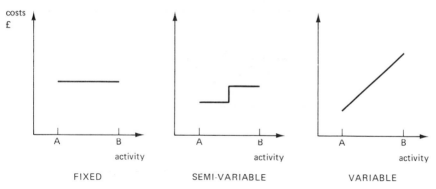

Figure 6.3   Cost behaviour patterns

All three groups show the cost in relation to a particular range (A to B) of activity of the firm. The assumptions about classifications may not hold outside the particular range (see Sect. 11.3). During the course of this chapter some costs will be described in accordance with common practice as variable overheads. It seems incorrect to classify overhead costs, i.e. indirect costs, as variable because variable costs will normally be traceable to the unit of production and therefore be direct. However, some variable costs may be classified as indirect, e.g. electricity in a machine shop. They could be traced to the product because they are variable, but the identification with the units of production may be too costly. Consequently we might assume that their cost behaviour is very similar to a more easily measured factor, e.g. labour costs.

(3) PRODUCT AND PERIOD COSTS

Those items of expenditure defined as part of the cost of a unit of production are termed 'product costs'. These costs are classified as expenses in the accounting period in which the relevant product is sold. All other costs are treated as period costs and are usually classified as expenses in the accounting period in which they are incurred.

The cost of production can be defined as that expenditure which has been incurred in producing the product or service.[2] Most of the items of expenditure incurred by a firm could come within this definition with the exception of costs incurred after production, such as salesmen's salaries. However, in practice not all items of expenditure are treated as costs of production.

Fig. 6.4 illustrates the flow of costs through a firm and the difference of treatment of product and period costs. It shows the payments and accruals, i.e. costs of a firm, being treated in one of three ways. Firstly, as a period cost (A), e.g. office salaries, when they are treated as an expense immediately. Secondly, as a cost of a fixed asset, e.g. machinery, from which the related depreciation could be either a period expense (B[1]) or a product cost (B[2]). Thirdly, as a product cost (C), e.g. raw materials, flowing through work in progress and finished goods, being treated as an expense (cost of goods sold) when sold. The product costs that relate to unsold production will form the value of the inventory of the firm.

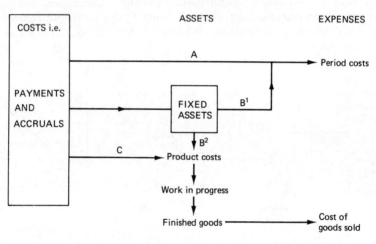

Figure 6.4   Flow of costs

Where a firm calculates its product costs using *variable* (or direct) *costing* then only the variable production costs are classified as product costs. Where all the variable production costs and the fixed production costs are classified as product costs this is known as *absorption costing*. In Sect. 6.4 (iii) we discuss these two types of costing in more detail. Fig. 6.5 illustrates the distinction between the two methods.

Costs	Absorption costing	Variable costing
Direct materials (variable)		
Direct labour (variable)		Product
Variable indirect production costs	Product	
Fixed indirect production costs		Period
Fixed indirect administrative costs	Period	Period
Variable indirect selling costs		

Figure 6.5   Absorption and variable costing

The effect of the two types of costing on profit measurement and valuation is illustrated in Ex. 6.1.

Example 6.1
The Fifty Co. Ltd has the following balances extracted from its trial balance at 31 December 19X0:

Extract from Trial Balance at 31 December 19X0

	£	£
Sales revenue		5000
Raw materials, 1 January 19X0	500	
Raw materials, purchases	1000	
Work in progress, 1 January 19X0	—	
Finished goods, 1 January 19X0	—	
Direct labour	1500	
Power	400	
Depreciation of machinery	600	
Factory rent and rates, etc.	800	
Supervision of production	100	
General administration expenses	200	
Selling expenses	900	

During 19X0 two-thirds of the completed production was sold. The inventory details at 31 December 19X0 were:

Raw materials, £700
Work in progress (this has been assumed at nil for simplicity)
Finished goods ($\frac{1}{3}$ of goods completed in year remain unsold).

To calculate the profit or loss from the relevant trial balance information we need to prepare: (*a*) a statement of the cost of completed production (sometimes termed a 'manufacturing account') and (*b*) a profit statement.

(*a*)   *Cost of Completed Production, year ending 31 December 19X0*

	Variable		Absorption	
	£	£	£	£
Raw materials at 1.1.X0	500		500	
Purchases	1000		1000	
	1500		1500	
Less: raw materials at 31.12.19X0	700		700	
Cost of raw materials used		800		800
Direct labour		1500		1500
Power		400		400
Depreciation of machinery		—	600	
Factory rent and rates, etc.		—	800	
Supervision of production		—	100	1500
		2700		4200
Add: work in progress 1.1.X0		—		—
		2700		4200
Less: work in progress 31.12.X0		—		—
Cost of Completed Production		£2700		£4200

(b) *Profit Statement for year ending 31 December 19X0*

		Variable		Absorption
	£	£	£	£
Sales revenue		5000		5000
Less: cost of goods sold:				
Finished goods 1.1.19X0	—		—	
Cost of completed production	2700		4200	
	2700		4200	
Finished goods 31.12.19X0	900		1400	
		1800		2800
Gross profit		3200		2200
Less: other expenses				
Depreciation of machinery	600		—	
Factory rent, rates, etc.	800		—	
Supervision of production	100	1500	—	
General administration expense		200		200
Selling expenses		900		900
Net profit		£600		£1100

Inventory valuation at 31 December 19X0			
Raw materials		700	700
Work in progress		—	—
Finished goods		900	1400
		£1600	£2100

The difference in profit of £500 under the two systems is created by one-third of the fixed costs of £1500 being included in the balance sheet as inventory using absorption costing, but as a period expense using variable costing. In this example we have assumed that depreciation, rent, and supervision are fixed costs.

6.3 Cost systems

In Chapter 4 we considered accounting information systems and their importance to internal and external users. Fig. 4.6 illustrated an information system, showing data collection, processing and communication which can be applied to cost accounting. Such a system can produce information for control, enabling costs to be monitored for control purposes, or simply for profit measurement by valuing period-end inventory. It is possible for data to be collected separately for each purpose, but in practice most firms use one system to provide both types of information. This implies that costs will be collected for control, then reclassified to produce costing information. It is normal for the firm to collect the data for control first because of the necessity to obtain timely information for effective control.

In the case of direct product costs the firm will normally deal with them initially by allocating them to the product. This gives information for costing and control purposes and thus no reclassification is necessary.

For purposes of control the indirect costs of the product are originally identified within areas of the organisation, i.e. cost centres, where they are incurred. The criterion for choosing these cost centres is the need to reflect the responsibilities defined by the firm's management structure because if control is to be successful, costs must be identified with the managers responsible for them. As a consequence, the cost centre may be very large, e.g. a whole factory, or very small, e.g. the maintenance team for a factory. Cost information is required for determination of selling price of products (considered in Chapter 11). Absorption costing (full cost) systems are commonly used in this context.

In costing the product the indirect costs (i.e. overheads) are absorbed to the product from these cost centres. There are some cost centres not directly related to production, e.g. a factory canteen, which are known as 'service cost centres'.

Fig. 6.6 shows the direct costs allocated to the product while the overheads are allocated first to cost centres and then identified with the product. The dashed lines show, firstly, the process of apportioning overheads among cost centres on some suitable base, secondly the re-apportionment of service cost centre costs to production cost centres, and thirdly, the absorption of costs to the product. From the production cost centres the costs are absorbed to the products (P_1 and P_2) flowing through the production process.

It could be that some direct product costs, e.g. labour in Ex. 6.2, are allocated to cost centres before being reallocated to the product. (This is not shown in Fig. 6.6.)

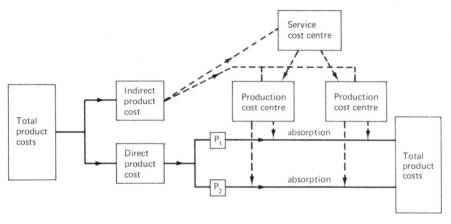

Figure 6.6   Product Costing

We know from our previous discussion that indirect product costs cannot be directly identified with the unit of production. The process of absorption relates the indirect costs using more or less arbitrary assumptions about the indirect costs associated with the production of a particular unit. This is an attempt to relate the costs of capacity to the product (Sect. 11.6). A common assumption is to identify the level of indirect costs with the level of production activity. This can be done using a number of bases:

Direct labour hours
Machine hours
Units of production
Direct labour costs
Cost of material used

At the beginning of an accounting period the indirect product costs (or overheads) and the level of production activity will be estimated. From this an overhead absorption rate can be calculated:

$$\text{Rate} = \frac{\text{Estimated overhead cost}}{\text{Estimated level of production activity}}$$

During the year the overhead costs will be absorbed to the product by measuring the level of activity for each product, e.g. machine hours per product, and multiplying by the overhead rate. At the end of the year it is likely that there will be an under- or over-absorbed overhead cost because the rate is based on estimates. The under- or over-absorbed indirect cost can either be treated as a period cost if not material or, if material, all the products can be recosted based on the actual production data.

The choice of the level of production activity could be determined by the major element in the overhead cost, e.g. the indirect costs of a department with mainly machinery costs could be absorbed on the basis of machine hours.

Example 6.2

A component manufacturer, who makes two products (components 1 and 2) both of which use the paint-spraying department (cost centre A) and the assembly department (cost centre B), wishes to calculate its product costs. The information and calculations were:

(1) UNIT COST AND HOURS

	Component 1	Component 2
	£	£
Direct costs per unit of product		
Material	4.00	3.00
Labour (£1 per hour)		
in cost centre A	4.00	1.00
in cost centre B	5.00	0.50
	13.00	4.50
	hours	*hours*
Machine hours – cost centre A	1	5
– cost centre B	2	3
Labour hours – cost centre A	4	1
– cost centre B	5	$\frac{1}{2}$

(2) FIXED OVERHEAD COSTS AND HOURS

	Cost centre A	Cost centre B
	£	£
Fixed overheads		
Depreciation	8,000	1,000
Indirect labour	2,000	7,000
	£10,000	£8,000
Basis of absorption:	Machine hours	Labour hours

Note:–

The paint-spraying department (A) uses automatic machinery with little labour input, while in the assembly department (B) the work is mainly done by hand. Hence machine hours are used for (A) and labour hours for (B).

Hours of production activity of
   absorption bases:

Machine	10,000	
Labour		16,000

(3) FIXED OVERHEAD RATES CALCULATION

The overhead rates can be calculated:

	Cost centre A	*Cost centre B*
Fixed overhead rate	$\dfrac{£10,000}{£10,000} = £1.00$ per machine hour	$\dfrac{£8,000}{£16,000} = 0.50$ per labour hour

(4) PRODUCT COST CALCULATED PER UNIT

The product cost per unit can be calculated:

	Component 1	*Component 2*
	£	£
Direct material	4.00	3.00
Direct labour – Cost centre A	4.00	1.00
– Cost centre B	5.00	0.50
Fixed overhead – A (hours × rates)	1.00	5.00
– B (hours × rates)	2.50	0.25
Total product cost	£16.50	£9.75

Component 1 absorbs less indirect costs than component 2 from cost centre (i.e. department) A because it requires less use of cost centre A's machines to produce the product than component 2. In cost centre B component 1 requires more labour and therefore it absorbs more indirect cost from that cost centre than component 2.

Levels of production activity vary from period to period and if the indirect product costs remain constant each year this will produce different absorption rates for different periods. To avoid this a firm may use the same normal level of activity each period to calculate the rate. The normal level of activity may be based, for example, on what the firm achieved in the past or what it expects to achieve in the future. The basis will usually remain static over a number of years once the assumption has been made.

In our examination of cost systems we have looked at general principles. We will now examine two particular systems, job costing and process costing, which are designed to produce product costs in different circumstances.

Job-costing Systems

This system is used if a cost for each individual job is required. A job is usually a unit of production but may also be a batch of units. In this system the direct product costs will be allocated to the job and the indirect product costs absorbed on a basis appropriate to the job. Firms that wish to produce this product-cost information could be, for example, a painting business which requires information about the cost for painting a house, or a ship-building business which requires information about the cost per ship.

A job-costing system is illustrated in Ex. 6.3.

Example 6.3
The total production costs of the First Jobbing Co. Ltd for May 19X0 are as follows:

	£
Direct material – variable	1200
Direct labour – variable	2400
Overhead – fixed	1600

The firm makes generators to order for customers. The normal level of activity for a month is 3200 machine hours. The cost details for job number K600, which requires 16 machine hours, £10.00 of direct material and £12.00 of direct labour, are:

Source of information

	£	
Direct material	10.00	From inventory issue records
Direct labour	12.00	From time records
Fixed overhead		
(16 hours @ £0.50 per hr)	8.00	Time records and overhead rate
Total job cost	£30.00	

Process-costing systems
When a firm does not require or cannot accumulate cost information individually for each unit of production, it may use a system that calculates an average unit cost rather than an individual cost. The system should only be used when the units produced are the same or very similar to each other, e.g. mass production of milk bottles. As an average cost is required, the costs of production are not accumulated on a unit basis (as in job costing) but on a process or departmental basis. The system accumulates all the costs of the process and divides the total costs by the number of units produced to give an average unit cost. At the end of the period the total costs will include those of unfinished as well as finished goods. The finished goods can be counted but assumptions will have to be made about the extent of the completion of unfinished goods in order to calculate an equivalent production of finished goods.

A process-costing system is illustrated in Ex. 6.4.

Example 6.4
The Flat Co. Ltd manufactures a single product which passes through two production processes. Production costs for June 19X0 were:

	Process A	*Process B*
	£	£
Direct labour	1000	1300
Direct material	500	1200
Fixed overhead cost	750	500
	£2250	£3000

There is no inventory at the beginning of June. During June completed production was 600 units in process A and 600 units in process B. There were 300 half-completed units in each process that were unsold at the end of the month. All completed production was sold. Flat Co. uses absorption costing for calculating its product costs.

The equivalent completed units of production (for each process) were

$$600 + \frac{300}{2} = 750.$$

The costs per unit were thus:

	Process A	*Process B*
Cost per unit	$\frac{£2250}{750} = £3.00$	$\frac{£3000}{750} = £4.00$

The total cost of the process is divided by the equivalent production to obtain the cost per unit. The cost of inventory at the end of June is:

$$£1050, \text{ i.e. } (300 \times £1.50 + 300 \times £2.00)$$

Standard Costing Systems

Both the examples above used actual costs as their basis of computation. Some firms find it an advantage to use pre-determined (or standard) costs as the basis of their product-costing systems with any deviations, commonly called variances, between actual and the standard being highlighted. This is known as a standard costing system. The reasons for using such a system are:

(*a*)   the costs of inefficiencies, i.e. actual cost deviating from standard cost, need not be included as a cost of production;

(*b*)   the ease of recording the information. The unit cost of production is predetermined and therefore known without the need to wait for the collection of any cost data;

(*c*)   to set prices. The standard unit cost of production is known before the product is produced;

(*d*)   to set standards may help in the planning and control process (see Chapters 10 and 13).

There are various alternative methods of computing a standard cost. For example, it could be the lowest possible cost, or the cost attainable under normal conditions. Some of the benefits from a standard costing system are shown in Ex. 6.5.

Example 6.5

Firefighters Ltd uses a standard costing system, with absorption costing. The following data for 19X0 is available at the end of the year:

	Standard Cost per unit	*Total standard Cost*	*Total actual Cost*	*Variance*
	£	£	£	£
Material	2.00	6,000	5,400	+600
Labour	1.50	4,500	4,800	−300
Fixed overhead cost	1.00	3,000	3,000	—
	£4.50	£13,500	£13,200	£+300

The actual and estimated production in 19X0 was 3000 units, with 2000 sold and 1000 in inventory at the end of the year. The standard cost of inventory would therefore be £4500 at the end of 19X0, i.e. (1000 × £4.50).

The managers will be able to use the variances in helping them control their business, e.g. the adverse labour variance of £300 might have been due to inefficient use of labour or the incorrect operative being used for the job. Chapter 15 explores in more detail the use of variance analysis.

6.4 Inventory valuation and profit measurement

In this section we examine the implications for profit measurement arising from the cost classifications and systems described above. We will examine the problems of (i) variations in product costs over a period of time, (ii) the assessment of the physical data on inventory, and (iii) the implications of absorption and variable costing systems.

(i) PRODUCT COST VARIATIONS OVER TIME

It is common for a firm to find that its purchase of materials over a period are at different costs. We examine here three bases for dealing with these variations so that profit can be determined and inventory valued.

First in first out (FIFO)
This basis assumes that the first goods purchased are the first sold. The basis is assumed and need not be chosen to coincide with the physical flow. Fig. 6.7 illustrates this using the numbers in Ex. 6.6.

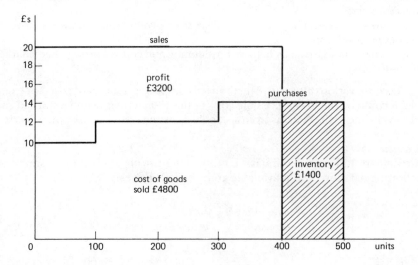

Figure 6.7   FIFO costs and revenues

The shaded area will be the unsold units in inventory at the end of the year.

Example 6.6

The Fearless Co. Ltd purchases and sells the following goods in 19X0:

		Cost	Sales
		£	£
1 Jan. X0	100 units at £10	1000	
31 Mar. X0	200 units at £12	2400	
30 June X0	200 units at £14	2800	
31 Dec. X0	400 units at £20		8000

The firm assumes a FIFO flow of costs.

Profit Statement for year ending 31 December 19X0

	£	£
Sales Revenue		8000
Less: Cost of Goods Sold		
100 at £10	1000	
200 at £12	2400	
100 at £14	1400	4800
Gross Profit		£3200

The inventory valuation at the end of 19X0 will be £1400 (100 units at £14).

Last in First Out (LIFO)

This assumption is that the goods purchased last are the first to be sold, and is thus the opposite of FIFO. Fig. 6.8 illustrates this using the numbers in Ex. 6.7.

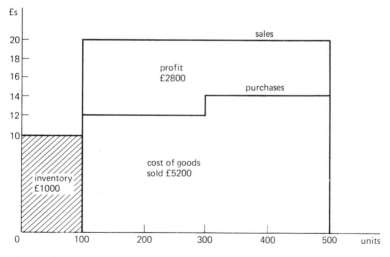

Figure 6.8   LIFO costs and revenues

Example 6.7

Assume the same facts as Ex. 6.6, but that the firm assumes a LIFO flow of costs.

Profit Statement for year ending 31 December 19X0

	£	£
Sales Revenue		8000
Less: Cost of Goods Sold		
200 at £14	2800	
200 at £12	2400	5200
Gross Profit		£2800

The inventory valuation at the end of 19X0 will be £1000 (100 units at £10).

Average Cost
A compromise between LIFO and FIFO is the average cost basis. The cost of goods sold and the year-end inventory are calculated at the average cost during the accounting period. The average cost is found by adding the cost of a purchase to the existing inventory and dividing by the number of units involved.

Example 6.8
Assume the same facts as Ex. 6.6, but that the firm uses average cost for its calculations.

Profit Statement for the year ended 31 December 19X0

	£
Sales Revenue	8000
Less: Cost of Goods Sold	
400 at £12.40	4960
Gross Profit	£3040

The inventory valuation at the end of 19X0 will be £1240 (100 units at £12.40). The average cost per unit is £12.40

$$\left(\text{i.e.} \quad \frac{\text{total cost}}{\text{no. of units}} = \frac{1000 + 2400 + 2800}{100 + 200 + 200} \right)$$

Implications of LIFO, FIFO and Average Cost Bases
A different measure of profit was produced with the same information using each of these bases. In addition they produced a different valuation for closing inventory.

	FIFO	LIFO	Average
	£	£	£
Profit in 19X0	3200	2800	3040
Inventory valuation			
at 31 December 19X0	1400	1000	1240

The price of materials produced was rising in 19X0 and thus FIFO gives a higher profit than LIFO, with the average basis being between them. The LIFO profit would have been greater than FIFO if prices had gone down in 19X0.

Whatever basis a firm chooses they should apply it consistently each year. There are certain implications that should be considered when making the choice of basis. The LIFO method calculates the cost of goods sold by assuming the most recent purchases are used first. This cost may be considered to be nearer the replacement cost of selling the inventory than the cost produced by the FIFO or average bases because it is more up to date. The profit of any selling transaction can be divided into two parts:

(A) Selling price less current replacement cost
(B) Current replacement cost less original cost

Whether LIFO, FIFO or average is used, the conventional profit will be selling price less the original cost. Because the firm has to replace the inventory it may be considered that (A) would give a better measure of profit and LIFO is a better approximation to (A) than FIFO. The distinction between these two parts of a profit is considered further in Sect. 8.3.[1,3]

There is the possibility that the cost of the early purchases will never be used to calculate the cost of goods sold if LIFO is used. This would occur where the firm had a minimum level of inventory (sometimes called a 'base stock'). In a case like this the value of inventory at the end of each accounting period will gradually become more unrealistic if costs rise over time. If this happens and in some future period the base stock is used, because, for example, the firm has difficulties with supplies, it will result in an abnormally high profit in the period when this happens because of the out-of-date cost of the base stock.

In the U.K. FIFO and average cost are the two bases used most frequently.

(ii) PHYSICAL INVENTORY DATA

It is necessary for firms to assess the physical quantities of inventory that they own at certain points in time, either to measure the profit or to provide a check on the financial records. Fig. 6.9 illustrates the connection between the physical quantities and the financial records.

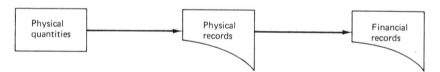

Figure 6.9   Inventory records

Records of the physical quantities normally form the basis of the financial records kept by the firm. This applies to raw materials, work in progress and finished goods. Where firms do not regularly keep up-to-date physical and financial records they will have to count the physical quantities at the end of each accounting period. This is needed in order to calculate the period-end inventory and to calculate the cost of goods sold. Firms may prefer to count inventory rather than keep the records where they consider the costs outweigh the benefits, e.g. firms such as department stores, with a large turnover of small items. Some firms will keep continuous up-dated physical records that always reflect the physical quantities but will not keep continuous up-dated financial records. At the end of each accounting period the firm will value the physical quantities as shown by the physical records. Other firms will keep both types of records on a continuous basis always up-dating them whenever physical quantities change. This last method is described as a 'perpetual inventory system', while the other two methods can be described as 'periodic inventory systems'.

The physical records will consist of a record for each type of inventory showing quantities received and used. The financial records will be similar but will record the receipts and usages in financial terms. A major benefit of continuous physical records is the extra control this gives over the physical quantities. This benefit has to be compared to the cost of maintaining the records. The major benefit of maintaining continuous financial records is that the value of inventory can be calculated without specially counting or valuing inventory. Again, this benefit must be compared with the extra costs of maintaining the system.

Another benefit of keeping continuous physical records is that losses of inventory, not caused by sales – e.g. theft, physical deterioration, mistakes in counting receipts and usages – can be identified. This is done by comparing the physical record with a count of the inventory (often called 'taking stock'). These differences can be valued and reported to management. If no physical records are kept any such losses cannot be identified. This is because the inventory usage is determined by deducting from the opening inventory and purchases the closing inventory ascertained by a physical count. Therefore no inventory losses can be identified but are included in the overall total of the inventory usage.

It may be difficult for a firm to determine the physical quantities of inventory, either for valuation purposes, or as a check of the physical records. For example, 500 tons of coal may look similar to 600 tons. Another difficulty in valuing inventory is found when work in progress has to be valued. It may be difficult to assess the degree of completion of a product and hence its value.

(iii) THE PROFIT IMPLICATIONS OF ABSORPTION AND VARIABLE COSTING

Earlier it was explained that absorption costing treats the fixed costs as part of the cost of a unit of production whilst variable costing treats these costs as an expense of the period in which it is incurred. This has implications for profit measurement which Ex. 6.9 and 6.10 demonstrate.

Example 6.9
The Fasteners Co. commences business on 1 January 19X0. Its cost and revenue data for 19X0–X2 is:

(a) Sales and Production Figures:

Year	Sales (in units)	Production (in units)
19X0	500	800
19X1	1000	800
19X2	900	800
	2400	2400

(b) normal activity is 800 units (i.e. production is normally 800 units)
(c) selling price £12
(d) administrative indirect cost (fixed) £500 p.a., Production Overhead cost £4000 p.a. (fixed)
(e) direct material and direct labour cost per unit is £2.00 (variable).

From the above we can calculate the overhead cost absorption rate as

$$\pounds \frac{4000}{800} = \pounds5.00 \text{ per unit.}$$

The cost per unit can then be calculated:

	Absorption	Variable
	£	£
Direct material and labour	2.00	2.00
Fixed indirect product costs	5.00	—
	£7.00	£2.00

The alternative profit statements are:

(a) *Using absorption costing*

	19X0	19X1	19X2	Total profit
	£	£	£	£
Sales Revenue	6,000	12,000	10,800	
Less: Cost of Goods Sold	3,500	7,000	6,300	
Gross Profit	2,500	5,000	4,500	
Less: Expenses				
Administrative Costs	500	500	500	
Net Profit	£2,000	£ 4,500	£ 4,000	£10,500

(b) *Using variable costing*

	19X0	19X1	19X2	Total profit
	£	£	£	£
Sales Revenue	6,000	12,000	10,800	
Less: Cost of Goods Sold	1,000	2,000	1,800	
Gross Profit	5,000	10,000	9,000	
Less: Expenses				
Production Overhead Cost	4,000	4,000	4,000	
Administrative Cost	500	500	500	
Net Profit	£ 500	£ 5,500	£ 4,500	£10,500

Though the total profit for the three years is the same, the profit each year is different under absorption and variable costing. Where production exceeds sales absorption costing gives a higher profit; where sales exceed production variable costing gives a higher profit. With both absorption and variable costing, the gross profit varies in proportion to changes in sales, but this relationship is weaker in relation to net profits.

Example 6.10
The same facts as Ex. 6.9, except that the sales and production details are:

Year	Sales (in units)	Production (in units)
19X0	800	1000
19X1	800	900
19X2	800	500
	2400	2400

Since the normal production is 800 units there will be an under- or over-absorbed overhead cost each year.

Year	Production (in units)	Normal production (in units)	Variance from normal production under (−) over (+) (in units)	Capacity* variance under (−) over (+)
				£
19X0	1000	800	+ 200	+ 1,000
19X1	900	800	+ 100	+ 500
19X2	500	800	− 300	− 1,500

* This is a multiplication of the physical production variance by the absorption rate of £5.00 per unit. This variance is the difference between the fixed overhead costs absorbed to production in a year and the actual indirect costs in that year (see Sect. 15.5)

The alternative profit statements are:

(a)　*Using absorption costing*

	19X0	19X1	19X2	Total profit
	£	£	£	£
Sales Revenue	9,600	9,600	9,600	
Less: Cost of Goods Sold	5,600	5,600	5,600	
Gross Profit	4,000	4,000	4,000	
Less: Expenses				
Capacity Variance	+ 1,000	+ 500	− 1,500	
Administrative Cost	500	500	500	
Net Profit	£4,500	£4,000	£2,000	£10,500

(b)　*Using variable costing*

	19X0	19X1	19X2	Total profit
	£	£	£	£
Sales Revenue	9,600	9,600	9,600	
Less: Cost of Goods Sold	1,600	1,600	1,600	
Gross Profit	8,000	8,000	8,000	
Less: Expenses				
Indirect Product Cost	4,000	4,000	4,000	
Administrative Cost	500	500	500	
Net Profit	£3,500	£3,500	£3,500	£10,500

The capacity variance is positive (−) if production is below normal production, meaning that some of the overhead cost is not absorbed to the product and has to be treated as an expense of the period in which it was incurred.

In Ex. 6.10 the sales remained the same each year and production varied. The net profit produced by absorption costing varies, though sales are constant. However, variable costing reflects the constant sales with constant profits.

The arguments for and against the use of absorption and variable costing can be summarised as follows:

(1)   Profits calculated under variable costing are more responsive to changes in the level of sales, while profits under absorption costing are more responsive to changes in the level of production. These factors should be considered when using profit information for decision-making purposes (see Sect. 11.5).

(2)   The cost of capacity (see Sect. 11.6) should be reflected in the product cost. Fixed production costs could be interpreted as a proxy for the cost of capacity. Variable costs contain no cost of capacity and therefore understate the cost of the product. This indicates an advantage for including a cost of capacity.

(3)   Because fixed costs do not vary with production they could be identified more with a period of time than with the production of units. This seems to suggest that they should be treated as an expense when they are incurred which is the treatment given them by variable costing.

(4)   Many modern firms are highly mechanised with high fixed costs. The variable cost element in a product may be so small that the firm should include fixed production costs as product costs as in absorption costing, so as to evaluate properly the cost of the product.

(5)   Absorption costing relies on arbitrary costing assumptions about apportionment and absorption of overhead costs.

6.5   Inventory obsolescence

A list of inventory may include items that cannot be sold at the initially expected selling price. This may need to be reflected in the valuation of inventory if the current expected selling price falls below original cost. This is an application of the accounting concept of conservatism. Obsolescence is a fall in selling value caused by physical factors or a change in demand conditions. The selling value can fall to zero in which case the inventory is completely obsolete. The effect of obsolescence on profit measurement is illustrated by Ex. 6.11.

Example 6.11
The Freedom Co. commences business as a wholesaler on 1 January 19X0. During 19X0 it purchases £4000 of inventory and sells half of this for £8000. It incurs £3000 administrative overhead costs. At the end of 19X0 it ascertains the physical quantity of inventory and finds inventory that cost £500 is worthless because of deterioration due to bad storage. Its profit statement will be:

Profit Statement for year ending 31 December 19X0

	£
Sales Revenue	8000
Less: Cost of Goods Sold	2000
Gross Profit	6000
Less: Expenses	
Administration Overhead Costs	4000
Obsolete Inventory	500
	£1500

This example shows the effect of obsolete inventory on profit. The valuation of inventory would be £1500 at the end of 19X0 rather than £2000 because the net realisable value of inventory costing £500 is zero.

6.6 Summary

This chapter has considered the valuation of the resources used in a firm's operations, and the valuation of the units of production remaining unsold at the end of an accounting period. This information is required for profit measurement, and for other reasons, such as the pricing of products. It is obtained by classifying, recording and analysing expenditure incurred by the firm in various ways. In discussing this, we have examined various cost systems and classifications.

These systems and classifications enable information about a firm's production costs to be ascertained. The costs can be fixed or variable, direct or indirect, product or period. Whatever their classification the method by which they are recorded and produced for information purposes, e.g. variable costing or absorption costing, will also affect the cost of production.

For external users of this information the objective is to obtain a measure of the period's profit; for internal users the objectives are varied but will include the control of the firm's costs.

Notes and References

1. Sandilands, *Inflation Accounting*—report of the Inflation Accounting Committee. Cmnd 6225 (1975).
2. Accounting Standards Sterring Committee, *ED 6 Stocks and Work in Progress* (Institute of Chartered Accountants in England and Wales, 1973) and International Accounting Standards Committee, *IAS 2 Valuation and Presentation of Inventories in the Context of the Historical Cost System* (Institute of Chartered Accountants in England and Wales, 1975).
3. See also a debate in the press between Messrs Merrett & Sykes and Messrs Godley & Wood. The articles were:

Financial Times	30 September 1974 (M & S)
The Times	1 November 1974 (G & W)
The Times	7 November 1974 (M & S)
The Times	12 November 1974 (G & W)

Further Reading

P. Garner and K. Berg, *Readings in Accounting Theory* (Boston, Mass., Houghton Mifflin, 1966) pp. 284–335.

D. Solomons, *Studies in Cost Analysis* (London, Sweet & Maxwell, 1968). (See section on Concepts of Cost.

C. T. Horngren, *Cost Accounting – a Managerial Emphasis* (Englewood Cliffs, N.J., Prentice-Hall International, 1972).

Institute of Cost and Management Accountants, *Terminology of Cost Accounting* (London, 1966).

G. Shillinglaw, *Cost Accounting: Analysis and Control* (Homewood, Ill., Irwin, 1972).

Questions and Problems

6.1   What do you understand by the following terminology?

Inventory	Allocation and apportionment of costs
Costing	Normal level of activity
Raw materials	Job-costing system
Work in progress	Process-costing system
Finished goods	Standard costing system

Direct and indirect costs   FIFO basis
Overheads   LIFO basis
Fixed and variable costs   Average basis
Product and period costs   Perpetual and periodic system
Variable costing   Capacity variance
Direct costing   Obsolescence
Absorption costing   Cost centres

6.2 What is the point of distinguishing between direct and indirect costs when considering the costs of production?

6.3 Why should there be a difference between the selling price and replacement cost of inventory? Is the future utility measure of value always the same as the selling price measure of value in the case of inventories?

6.4 Why might it be difficult to determine the value of work in progress?

6.5 Discuss possible interpretations of the phrase 'the original cost of inventory'.

6.6 A firm commences business on 1 January 19X0. It buys and sells silver pots. The following information is available about its purchases and sales in 19X0:

		Purchases	Sales
		£	£
1/1/X0	100 units at £3.00	300	
1/2/X0	200 units at £3.50	700	
1/6/X0	200 units at £20.00		4000
8/6/X0	300 units at £4.00	1200	
30/9/X0	200 units at £25.00		5000

The only other costs incurred by the firm in 19X0 are £500 of administrative non-product costs.

Calculate alternative measures of profit for 19X0. Choose the one you think gives the best measure and justify your choice.

6.7 When valuing inventory why is market value considered if lower than original cost and ignored if higher?

6.8 What problems would be met in assessing the physical quantities of inventory and calculating an appropriate valuation for the following firms:

(a) a general store
(b) a diamond dealer
(c) an oil company
(d) a gold-mining company

6.9 The estimated production data of the Fitful Co. Ltd for April are as follows:

Direct materials	£1200
Direct labour	£2400
Factory overhead	£1600
Labour hours	4000
Machine hours	3200

Required:
   (1) Compute the factory overhead absorption rate, using three different levels of activity, and state briefly the merits of each method.

(2) Apply each of the three rates ascertained to the following job and show the
     resulting profit in each case assuming the sale price of the job is £40.00:

     Actual costs and time for Job No. 62.

Direct materials	£10
Direct labour	£12
Labour hours	18
Machine hours	15

7
Owners' Equity, Liabilities and Working Capital

7.1 Introduction

This chapter continues the initial analysis of the balance sheet of the firm by analysing the relationship between the firm, its owners and others who provide its finance. We consider how a firm obtains its finance through the use of owners' equity and by incurring liabilities, and how the requirement for working capital affects its overall financial resources. We examine the major factors which contribute to the firm's financing decisions and provide a framework for the analysis of financing problems. Long-term and short-term finance and the concepts of equity and debt are analysed. No consideration is given to the finance markets which constitute the contemporary sources of finance for business,[1] but emphasis is laid on the conceptual distinctions between various financial sources. The importance of liquidity is examined as a special problem in the financing of a firm's overall asset requirements.

7.2 Financial structure

The pattern of a firm's finances is termed its 'financial structure' (sometimes termed 'capital structure'). An extract from the balance sheet of Greenwich Ltd, which illustrates its financial structure, is shown below. This example will serve as the basis for much of the analysis in the later sections of this chapter.

Greenwich Ltd extract from Balance Sheet

	at	*31 December 19X1*	
		£000	£000
Owners' Equity			
Ordinary shares 200,000 £1 nominal value		200	
Share premium		20	
Retained profit		40	
			260
8% Preference shares 40,000 £1 nominal value			40
			300
Long-term liabilities			
6% Debentures (1990/1995)			65
Deferred liabilities (see note 1)			
Deferred taxation			25

Current liabilities

Trade creditors	20	
Bank overdrafts	15	
Dividends payable	25	60
		£450

Note (1): The only item which usually appears in this classification is deferred taxation, which is considered as a long-term liability (see App. B).

The legal form of the firm will constrain the way in which finance can be raised (see App. A.1). Rather than concentrating on this type of limitation which will depend on contemporary business law, we will concentrate on an analysis of the conceptual differences between the various sources of finance available. The effect of various types of economic activity on financial structures will be a major theme running through the analysis.

A firm will require finance to enable it to undertake economic activity which necessitates the purchase of assets the returns from which are not immediate. This finance can be provided by owners or lenders. Before examining the way in which the choice between these sources is made, consideration must be given to the type of returns they will require to persuade them to give up their resources to the firm's use.

Providers of finance to a firm require returns to compensate them for the loss of alternative opportunities for their cash. The loss of opportunities is normally referred to as an opportunity cost imposed on the provider of finance. It arises from:

(1) Loss of consumption because the cash provided to the firm is no longer available for the provider's expenditure.
(2) Loss of returns caused by the loss of opportunities to invest the cash elsewhere.
(3) Increase in payments such as interest which may be required to restore consumption and investment possibilities in (1) and (2), e.g. by personal borrowing.

In an uncertain world providers of finance will also assess the amount of returns they require in relation to the possible uncertainty of those returns. Uncertainty could be measured by potential variability in the future returns, e.g. by their standard deviation. Providers of finance may be prepared to accept low returns if the possibility of variability is small, whereas high returns may be required if possibility of variability is high. This will depend on their attitudes towards uncertainty. In a firm's financial structure it may thus be necessary to arrange the finances in a way to satisfy the varying objectives of the providers of finance. Consideration of the security of the repayment may also influence the returns required. These factors are the basis of what is normally termed the 'time value of money' (see App. C.1).

As there will be many possible outcomes from a firm's use of finances in business activities the firm will give consideration in decisions about its financial structure to:

(1) The permanency of finance and the requirement to repay at some time the amount of finance obtained, along with the penalties associated with non-compliance.
(2) The ability to provide the providers of finance with the periodic returns they require.
(3) The possibility of repaying at short notice any finances which the firm finds

are in excess of requirements, or providing for unforeseen requirements.
(4) Minimising the cost of finance in the context of an optimal financial structure.[2]

The problems of finance are those of determining which is the optimal financial structure consistent with the objectives of the firm and its owners. The pattern ultimately chosen will depend on the firm's assessment of the relative importance of the factors above. The firm must produce an appropriate financial structure with long-term and short-term finances, and a mixed ownership and lender interests in the firm. Much of this chapter is concerned with this problem.

Long-term finances are characterised by arrangements which are considered as perhaps almost permanent, or at very least not rearrangeable at short notice, e.g. ordinary shares and debentures. Finance is considered as long-term when neither the firm nor the source can demand that the arrangement is terminated at short notice without mutual agreement. Where these characteristics are absent finance is short-term and is normally classified under current liabilities, e.g. trade creditors.

It may be appealing to suggest that the firm uses its long-term finances to provide fixed assets, and uses its short-term finances to provide current (short-term) assets. If we analyse a firm's activities we will find that the provision of current assets, such as inventory or debtors, is as important to the success of a firm as are its fixed (long-lived) assets. Although individual items within current assets are continuously changing, a firm will require a minimum level of current assets, e.g. cash, on a permanent basis. Furthermore we may find that many firms use finances such as bank overdrafts which are classified as current liabilities to acquire fixed assets. They may effectively be a long-term source of finance because the bank allows the time for termination of the agreement to be continuously moved forward. In Sect. 7.7 we examine the reasons behind the need for short-term finance. We will now examine two concepts, the concept of equity and the concept of debt, which are central in the analysis of financial structure.

7.3 The Concepts of Equity and Debt

The concepts of equity and debt identify the relationship between the firm, its owners and lenders.

CONCEPT OF EQUITY

The shareholders of a company are in an ownership relationship as are the partners in a partnership, but the partners are also more likely to be concerned in a partnership's management. In a company the owners are likely to be different persons from the managers (see App. A).

Equity financing has the following important characteristics.

(a) Relationship with the Firm
The interests of owners in the firm can only cease with cessation of the firm. Ownership of a part of a firm can be transferred through the sale of the specific interest to another party, e.g. when a shareholder in a company sells his shares. Owners of a firm can, of course, have other relationships with the firm and could be, for example, managers, lenders, customers or employees.

(b) Participation in Profits
If the firm earns a profit the owners have a right to all of the profits. This is, of

course, subject to current law, e.g. legislation on profit limits may be operating. The size of an individual owner's share depends on the extent of his ownership. The owners' share includes profits distributed as dividends (termed 'drawings' in a partnership) and those retained within the firm. The firm's management may decide on its owners' behalf to retain some of the dividends for use within the firm, e.g. for providing new assets, with the expectation of paying higher future dividends.

(c)   Participation in Residual Assets
In the event of cessation of the firm, normally termed its liquidation, any assets that exist after all liabilities of the firm have been repaid, belong to the owners (see App. A.5).

(d)   Control
The owners have rights to control the policies of the firm through the appointment of managers or directors; the particular type of arrangement will depend on the type of firm, e.g. a partnership or a company.

(e)   Duration of Relationship
The owners' capital (see Sect. 3.4) cannot normally be returned to the owners except in liquidation. Retained profits, though part of the owners' equity, can be returned to the owners as dividends.

CONCEPT OF DEBT

Debt finance is distinct from equity finance and has the following important characteristics:

(1)   *Relationship with the firm*
The relationship between the firm and the source is of borrower and lender. There is no ownership relationship.

(2)   *Participation in profits*
The lender will be entitled to receive periodic interest payments which are expenses of the firm, independent of the level of profit. These would be contractually determined. This requirement is of course ultimately subject to the power of the lender to enforce the claim, if necessary, in the courts as a creditor.

(3)   *Participation in residual assets*
As a lender, the claim against the firm in the event of cessation is limited to the full amount of the loan. It is normal for the lender to have a prior claim to the assets to that of the owners (see App. A.5).

(4)   *Control*
Provided that the firm satisfies its contractual obligations to lenders with respect to interest payments and return of the amount borrowed, the lenders do not usually participate in the management of the firm. A lender may of course also be a shareholder. The firm will recognise, however, that if it is unable to satisfy these obligations, the firm may then go into liquidation, or alternatively control may be passed to the lenders. The possibility of control imposed by debt finance may thus be an indirect influence on the policy of the firm, so as to avoid these events.

(5) *Duration of relationship*

The firm must repay the amount borrowed when it is due, and thus it is not considered as a permanent source. The arrangements are usually for a fixed duration. In practice many firms will merely arrange a further loan to replace the former loan as it comes to maturity.

7.4 Equity Finance

We will now examine how we can apply the concept of equity in the analysis of sources of finance.[2] In Greenwich Ltd, the equity finance is classified as owners' equity. We can see that a distinction is made between the ordinary shareholders' interests, which are pure equity, and preference shares, which are a hybrid form of finance.

Once the company has decided the total finances required to begin operations and also the mix between debt and equity, it will issue sufficient shares to raise the amount of equity finance that it requires. The shares that it issues will have a face or 'nominal' value, but they may be issued at a premium by requiring more cash from the purchaser of the share than their face value. Thus if Greenwich Ltd wishes to raise £200,000 it may issue any combination of number of shares and nominal value as necessary, e.g. 40,000 shares of £5 nominal value, or 200,000 of £1 nominal value. If 200,000 shares of £1 nominal value were issued, but the prospective owners were required to subscribe £1.10 per share,[9] premium of £0.10 per share would be created. This example is based on the information in the balance sheet of Greenwich Ltd. The value to the shareholder of the shares after issue will not necessarily bear any relationship to the nominal value and share premium. This is the value at the time of issue – an original valuation. To avoid confusion for the shareholder, it has been suggested that firms are allowed to issue shares which have no nominal value, so as not to suggest that the nominal value is an indicator of value. However, a company is not allowed by the Companies Acts to issue shares of no nominal value though this is legitimate in other countries, e.g. U.S.A.

In the course of its operations the firm may decide to obtain further new equity share finance. It can effect this in two ways, either by issuing further shares to its current shareholders (termed a 'rights issue') or otherwise to new shareholders.

As the 'share capital' of a company is not returnable it is thus long-term finance. Retained profits can be considered as either long- or short-term equity as they could be distributed as dividends, but in practice a large part of retained profits are effectively permanent finance. Apart from retained profits, there is no other form of short-term equity finance in the U.K.

The firm's management, on behalf of the shareholders, can retain all or part of the profit that has been earned in the past. Sect. 3.4 showed how retained profits became part of the owners' equity. A useful distinction can be made between equity financing through the new issues of shares and the internal generation of resources by retention of profits. The process of profit retention is identical in its effect to a dividend payment, followed by a rights issue to obtain from the shareholder the amount just received in dividend. Thus profit retention is a preemptive rights issue, but with none of the expenses associated with such a issue.

Assuming that cash is available the maximum dividend distribution in a year is limited to the amount of retained profits carried forward from previous years, plus the profit from the current year (see App. A.7). It is thus not necessary for a company to earn a profit in a particular year for it to pay a dividend in that year. A dividend can always be proposed provided that the total value of the owners' equity does not fall below the value of the firm's capital, i.e. share capital and share premium.

Distribution of profits as dividends need not necessarily use the firm's cash resources. There may be circumstances where a firm has insufficient cash resources to pay a cash dividend or where perhaps for shareholders' personal taxation reasons shareholders do not wish to receive a cash dividend. A dividend of shares, in place of cash, is termed a bonus issue and will involve the 'capitalisation of retained profits'. This is a reclassification of its retained profits as issued share capital. This reclassification and further issue of bonus shares (sometimes termed a 'scrip issue') has no associated cash flow, but results in the shareholder having more shares to represent his interest in the company than he had before the bonus issue. It also has the effect of converting the amount of retained profit into permanent owner's equity, and it is no longer available for distribution. The total market value of a shareholding should be unaffected by the changes, though it is argued in favour of bonus issues that the more shares that are issued, and hence the lower the market price of each share, the more marketable the share is. This increased marketability arises as less must be invested in a company by a prospective shareholder to acquire the same number of shares, and with more shares being available, the greater is the size of the potential market. This may lead to a rise in the total market value of the company's shares after the capitalisation of retained profits.

Using the data from Greenwich Ltd, if we assume that the ordinary shares have a market value of £2.40, the overall market value of the ordinary shares will be £480,000. If all the retained profits are then capitalised the company will make a bonus issue of 40 ordinary shares for every 200 ordinary shares formerly held. After the capitalisation, the relevant section of the owner's equity in the balance sheet of Greenwich Ltd would be:

		£000	£000
Owners' equity			
Ordinary shares	240,000 £1 nominal value	240	
Share premium		20	
Retained profit		—	
			260

The shareholders will have received 40,000 £1 ordinary shares in proportion to their original holdings. Subject to the assumptions outlined above the market value of the ordinary shares will still be £480,000; the new market value per share will thus be £2.00 compared to £2.40 previously.

Preference shares are a special category of share. The dividend entitlement is fixed at a predetermined level. They have a rate of return like debt, but the returns are dividends. Their security, in the event of a liquidation, is one of participating in any residual assets (i.e. similar to equity, though usually preference shareholders have a claim prior to ordinary shareholders). As shareholders, there is no entitlement to a dividend, but if dividends are to be paid, the claim of the preference shareholders dividend is prior to that of the ordinary shareholders. Most preference shares have an accumulative dividend entitlement and no ordinary dividend can be paid until arrears of preference dividends are paid. They do not fall conveniently into our equity/debt classification, but are normally shown as part of owners' equity in the balance sheet.

7.5   Debt finance

Debt finance has many possible variations as we can see by inspection of the balance sheet of Greenwich Ltd. Debt finance covers all kinds of borrowing including fixed-interest long-term loans, deferred liabilities, and formally arranged short-term borrowing such as bank overdrafts. It will also include incidental borrowing or liabilities to trade creditors or to shareholders for dividends which have been declared, but not paid.

Fixed-interest long-term loans are normally termed 'debentures'. The conditions of debentures represent a contract between the borrower and the lender. In the Greenwich Ltd balance sheet we can see that the interest rate, which was fixed at the time of borrowing, was 6%,, and that the repayment date at the company's discretion is between 1900 and 1995.

The safety of a loan and interest for a lender arises from the legal obligation of the firm to return the amount borrowed and any associated interest in accordance with the debt contract. If the firm is unable to discharge this obligation the lenders can make a claim against the assets of the firm through the courts. The priority of the lenders' claim against the assets in liquidation, though higher than equity, is examined in App. A. 5. Lenders can improve their safety by increasing their priority through converting an unsecured loan into a loan secured against the potential proceeds from sale of particular assets. A prior claim established against the firm's assets in general is termed a 'floating charge'. When secured against a specific asset it is a fixed charge – often termed a 'mortgage' – such that the firm cannot dispose of the asset without the lenders' consent. If a firm is forced to sell charged assets any surplus after the secured creditors have been repaid belongs to the firm, though if the proceeds are insufficient the remainder of the outstanding loan reverts to an unsecured loan. As an alternative, lenders may seek personal guarantees from owners or directors as a means of securing their loan against persons with unlimited liability.

In deciding on its financing policy the firm will consider whether it can offer additional safety to its lenders as the rate of return required may be less for secured than unsecured loans. The ability of a firm to offer loan security will depend on the range of its economic activities. A firm such as a property company, with fixed assets about which a selling price valuation can be reasonably established, will be able to offer substantial loan security. On the other hand, a firm engaged in research activities or perhaps prospecting for minerals may have few assets which could be sold in the event of an enforced liquidation. In this case, little loan security can be offered, and debt financing may be less possible. Security also arises from the knowledge that a firm has the backing of government or another reputable firm, or is itself reputable. This information is a proxy for estimating the likelihood of repayment.

While a firm which falls into arrears with its interest payments to lenders will normally have what is effectively an additional loan secured in the same way as the initial loan, the security of periodic interest receipts by lenders has a close relationship with the firm's profitability. Lenders' interest security also arises from their claim, prior to shareholders, against the firm's profits which ensures that shareholders receive the residue of profits only after all other claims have been satisfied.

7.6 Financial risk

The most important implication for the firm and hence the owners of the firm, through the use of debt financing, is that with the introduction of debt into the financial structure, the firm undertakes an additional form of risk, which is termed 'financial risk'. This arises from the possibility that the firm may be unable to satisfy the conditions attached to the borrowing. It can be distinguished from 'business risk' which relates to the possible variability of returns on the use of finance in the firm and which arises from uncertainties inherent in business.

The payment of interest to lenders is an expense that the firm must meet and allow for in the calculation of profit. Debt-financing introduces a claim prior to dividends against the profits of the firm and a claim against the assets. If the interest or the loan itself is not repaid when due the lenders may use their legal powers against the firm, perhaps through an enforced liquidation – equity it should be recalled has no similar rights.

Once debt-financing is undertaken, the policies of a firm must always recognise that a new set of obligations exist, and the decisions about its future activities will necessarily be influenced by these new obligations.

If a firm does not earn a profit in any one year, or a series of years, this will not necessarily lead to a firm's inability to make interest payments, no more than it would be unable to make other payments such as wages. Interest payments use cash resources; it is neither necessary nor sufficient that a firm earns a profit for it to be able to satisfy its creditors for interest payments (see Sect. 3.9). However, over a period of years recurrent losses will mean that the shareholders will no longer receive their dividends and they or other prospective shareholders may be unwilling to provide further finance. The cash resources of the firm will decline until no further cash is available to make interest payments, and the firm may be unable to repay any of its loans. On the other hand profitability will not necessarily ensure in the short term a sufficiency of cash, and the introduction of debt-financing will increase the monetary claims against the firm's cash resources.

It is argued that debt-financing can benefit the owners of a firm. The idea on which this proposition is based is that the firm may be able to borrow at a known, certain rate of interest from those who consider that security of loan and security of periodic payment is important, and use these finances to generate a series of profit flows that are greater than the additional interest payments required. This is normally termed 'gearing' or 'leverage'. Chapter 8 examines the possible benefits from borrowing during periods of changing price levels and App. B.3 explains the taxation advantages of debt. Ex. 7.1 provides an illustration of the use of gearing. In the example the effect of company or personal taxation is ignored, as are the effects of changing price levels.

Example 7.1

Goat Ltd has 5000 £1 shares issued and earns £8000 per annum in profits which are all distributed as dividends. The shareholders expect that the firm will continue to earn that level of profits and pay the same dividends in the foreseeable future. Goat Ltd has an opportunity to undertake expenditure of £5000 which it is forecast will return about £450 per annum in cash for twenty years, and a further £5000 in cash in twenty years time when the project finishes. The firm can borrow money on a long-term basis at an interest rate of 8% per annum.

Assuming Goat Ltd borrows £5000 repayable in twenty years time at 8% interest per annum, the forecast annual profit for Goat Ltd after it has undertaken this project would be:

Goat Ltd – Forecast Annual Profits for next twenty years

	£
From current activities	8000
From proposed project	450
Profit before interest	8450

Less

Interest payments	400
Profit available for distribution	£8050

£8050 is available for distribution to shareholders, whereas only £8000 was available previously, increasing the prospective dividends per share from £1.60 to £1.61. This has been achieved by using finance with an expense less than the associated anticipated revenue. This additional return or profit is attributable to the shareholders alone.

In Ex. 7.1 it can be seen that the ordinary shareholders take most of the risks related to the new project, and should the project fail the interest payments will continue to be borne by the firm as a whole. The issue of a long-term loan gives the lenders a claim against profits which were formerly solely available as dividends for the ordinary shareholders. Furthermore the liability to repay £5000 is a further claim against the assets of Goat Ltd as a whole.

It may appear that this projected increase in dividends is an improvement for the shareholders, assuming the firm continues to distribute all its profits as dividends. Alternatively it can be argued that this increase in the potential dividends of the shareholders does not necessarily mean an increase in their wellbeing. Associated with this projected increase in their dividends is the possibility that the project may not come to fruition and that the firm may become insolvent, or that dividends per share may fall if the project fails to return its projected profits. If we could say with certainty that the project would yield the forecast returns we could say with certainty that the shareholders are better off. Whether in practice the potential extra dividend compensates them for their increased risk depends on the attitudes of the individual shareholders towards risk.

MEASUREMENT OF FINANCIAL RISK – USING BALANCE SHEET DATA

It will be clear that the degree of financial risk will relate to the amount of debt in the financial structure, and of course the terms of the contracts relating to the borrowing.

It will be useful for the firm, shareholders and the current or potential lenders to be able to make an assessment of the extent of a firm's financial risk. For the firm and the shareholders the importance lies in attaining the maximum benefits from gearing, i.e. minimising the overall cost of finance to the firm, consistent with the attitudes of current and potential shareholders to the increased risk. For the potential and existing shareholders and lenders an assessment of financial risk will be important in assessing their own personal financial risks.

It is only possible to comment fully on financial risk by examining a firm's future plans. Those will show its future cash availability, its future projects and expectations. Discussion of this follows in Parts II and III. With lesser information, a conventional measurement of financial risk is the debt/equity ratio. Problems arise in deciding which data is appropriate for this purpose. To gauge financial risk at a particular point in time we could use the ratio of all debt to equity, but as the amount of short-term debt may fluctuate we may prefer to use a ratio of long-term debt to equity. The classification of preference shares and convertible debentures may also be open to question. Furthermore as the balance sheet is likely to reflect historical values rather than current values we could use either book value or market values.

Using the data from the Greenwich Ltd balance sheet, as shown in Sect. 7.2:

$$\text{all debt/equity ratio} \qquad \frac{\text{all debt}}{\text{equity}} = \frac{150}{300} = \qquad 0.5$$

$$\text{long-term debt/equity ratio} \qquad \frac{\text{long-term debt}}{\text{equity}} = \frac{90}{300} = \qquad 0.3$$

but if we reclassified preference shares as long-term debt:

$$\text{all debt/equity ratio} \qquad \frac{\text{all debt}}{\text{equity}} = \frac{190}{260} = \qquad 0.7$$

$$\text{long-term debt/equity ratio} \qquad \frac{\text{long-term debt}}{\text{equity}} = \frac{130}{260} = \qquad 0.5$$

As can be seen from the ratios the measurement of the degree of financial risk depends on the ratios that are chosen. They may be useful for comparison of financial risk for the same firm through time or in comparison between firms which have similar assets and business risks. The ratios are useful as relative measures for inter- or intra-firm comparison in ranking the relative extent of gearing but as absolute measures they mean little.

The notion of a gearing limit, measured in terms of a maximum debt/equity ratio, is a traditional approach to the problem of determining the maximum gearing possible. However, the extent to which a firm can gear itself to increase the returns of the shareholder will depend on the types of economic activities in which it is involved, the attitudes of management and investors to financial risks, and the institutional financial environment.

Another measure of financial risk and security of loans could be to examine the extent to which the total debts of the firm can be covered by the realisable assets of the firm. The notion of cover is based on the relationship between claims and the size of the pool from which they are to be satisfied. This form of analysis will not be so easily applicable where assets are charged as security for a loan, as the secured loan is not competing for repayment with other unsecured loans.

A suitable measure for loan safety is debt cover:

$$\frac{\text{Realisation (selling price) value of assets}}{\text{Total liabilities}}$$

If the realisation value of assets covers the total liabilities the ratio will be greater than 1 and show that the firm would, if necessary, be able to satisfy all its lenders. Using the data from Greenwich Ltd; the net book value of assets would be £450,000 as a going concern. However, the realisation value, if assets are sold individually, is estimated as £90,000. The relevant data is the realisation value, giving a ratio of

$$\frac{£90,000}{£150,000} = 0.60$$

This shows that if Greenwich Ltd tried to repay all its liabilities they would receive 60p per £ owing. However, as many of the liabilities are not current liabilities and are thus not due for repayment now, the company *may* be in a position to repay in the future. A more appropriate asset valuation basis against which to measure all liabilities would have been future utility using a going concern assumption.

It will be difficult to obtain data to adopt this approach to the measurement of gearing, as data to be found in published company balance sheets is based on going concern and other cost concepts. As seen in previous chapters realisation values do not necessarily have any relationship with the book values shown in balance sheets.

As a further surrogate for the measurement of financial risk we could analyse the security of interest and dividend payments by examining the extent to which the revenues of a period cover its expenses and dividends. It must be recalled that expenses and dividends are paid from cash, not revenues, but that if a firm is to be able to continue in existence it must ultimately cover its interest expenses and pay dividends to satisfy the shareholders. Fig. 7.1 analyses the claims against the revenues of a hypothetical firm with revenue of 100.

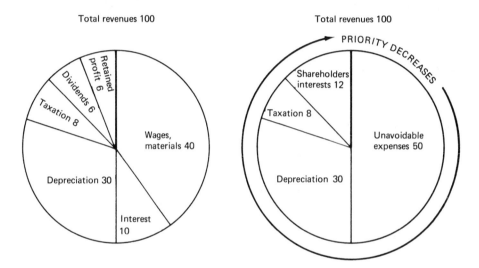

Figure 7.1   Claims against revenues of a firm   *Figure 7.2   Type and priority of claims against revenues of a firm*

The data of Fig. 7.1 can be reclassified as in Fig. 7.2 to give an indication of the possible type and priority of claims against revenues. In Fig. 7.2 we can see that some of the firm's expenses are unavoidable commitments, such as wages, salaries and interest. The expenses that could be classified as unavoidable depend on the time-scale, e.g. debenture interest has a long-term commitment and wages could be avoided by reducing the labour force. While depreciation does not use up a firm's revenues, if over many periods there are insufficient revenues to cover both unavoidable expenses and depreciation there may be insufficient resources to enable the firm to replace the assets it is using up, or to repay the finances it used to acquire the assets. Taxation claims against a firm's revenues only occur when a firm's revenues exceed all its expenses. In Fig. 7.2 we can see that if revenues fall by 20% that there will be no tax liability, but that all expenses are covered. Fig. 7.2 also illustrates the residual claim of equity.

This kind of analysis is useful in gauging security and financial risk as it can give an indication of the effect of variability in a firm's revenues on its ability to meet its expenses and pay dividends. We could calculate the extent to which revenues would have to fall to effect dividends, expenses, etc. A complementary exercise is to calculate the cover for various claims against revenues and profit. We will do this using the data in Figs 7.1 and 7.2. The unavoidable expenses cover is:

$$\frac{\text{Revenues from operations}}{\text{unavoidable expenses}} = \frac{100}{50} = 2 \text{ times}$$

As this data is difficult to obtain from published company statements many financial analysts use what is known as interest cover:

$$\frac{\text{Net profit before tax and interest}}{\text{Interest payments}} = \frac{12 + 8 + 10}{10} = \frac{30}{10} = 3 \text{ times}$$

The former calculation indicates that all the unavoidable expenses are covered twice, and the latter that interest is covered three times. The latter calculation is not very satisfactory as the coverage does not arise from net profits before tax and interest but from revenues, and even if the net profits before tax and interest were zero interest would be covered.

The application of coverage can be further applied:

Preference dividend cover:

$$\frac{\text{Net Profit after tax}}{\text{Total preference dividends}}$$

Ordinary dividend cover:

$$\frac{\text{Net profit after tax and preference dividends}}{\text{Total ordinary dividends}}$$

To illustrate the calculation of coverage ratios we can consider Ex. 7.2.

Example 7.2
The following is an extract from the profit statement from Gorgon Ltd:

		£
Net profit before tax and interest		20
Interest expense (on debentures)		4
Net profit before tax		16
Corporation tax at 50%		8
Net profit after tax		12
Preference share dividend	4	
Ordinary share dividend	6	
		10
Retained profits		£2

The cover for the sources of finance:

Interest cover $\dfrac{20}{4} = 5 \text{ times}$

Preference dividend cover $\dfrac{12}{4} = 3 \text{ times}$

Ordinary dividend cover $\dfrac{12 - 4}{6} = \dfrac{8}{6} = 1\tfrac{1}{3} \text{ times}$

Corporation tax is simplified in this example for ease of explanation, and personal taxation is ignored. For a fuller explanation see App. B.

7.7 Short- and long-term finances

In the process of budgeting cash requirements a firm will need to select a combination of long-term and short-term finances for its financial structure. This combination is required because the total amount of assets and hence finances that a firm may require will probably fluctuate over time. In Fig. 7.3 we show the cumulative amount of cash that a firm might require from debt or equity sources from its inception, over a period of time – say one year. The external cash, as opposed to cash from cash sales or collection of debros, could be required to acquire fixed assets, current assets such as inventory, or to repay liabilities. Large increases in cash requirement may perhaps be associated with the acquisition of fixed assets, and decreases with the reduction of current assets, e.g. inventories or debtors. The cumulative cash requirements of firms with cyclical or seasonal activities will be variable with both increases and decreases over time.

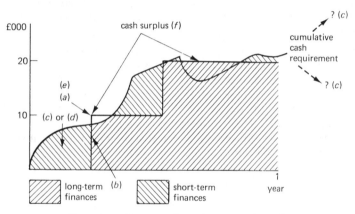

Figure 7.3   Forecast cash requirements and supply

We have illustrated a possible pattern of financing which uses both short- and long-term finances. It shows the selection of a particular financial structure which changes through time. Initially it is all short term and it changes to various mixes of short and long term. The letters in brackets can be related to the optimality considerations explained in (a) to (f) below. Whilst an extensive discussion of the procedures is outside the scope of this book[3] the following are the major considerations:

(a)   The relative returns required by providers of short- and long-term finances;

(b)   the greater reliability of supply of long-term as opposed to short-term finances for the firm;

(c)   uncertainty about the future because of potential variability in future returns, and cost of finance may not justify the entering into a fixed long-term commitment;

(d)   the availability of both long- and short-term finances, e.g. small firms may not have long-term finances available to them due to the imperfections of the capital markets;

(*e*)   indivisibilities: the firm may be able to borrow long term in large fixed amounts which are not divisible, e.g. £10,000 units as shown in Fig. 7.3;

(*f*)   variability in cash requirements: a firm with variable cash requirements through time may find that it will have excess cash if it has obtained its maximum requirement through the use of long-term sources. Unless the firm has use of this excess such as short-term lending or purchase of marketable securities, it will be incurring costs of finance for cash it is not using, and a combination of short-term and long-term finances may be preferable.

7.8   Cost of finance

The firm should be able to measure its cost of finance because it is important in its choice of financial structure and in making decisions about its use. By choosing between possible financial structures the firm may be able to reduce its overall cost of finance. As explained in Sect. 7.2 the cost of finance to the firm is the opportunity cost arising from the alternative use of cash.

The cost of equity finance is the rate of return required by owners to compensate them for their opportunity costs (see Sect. 7.2). As compensation they receive returns in dividends and the proceeds from disposal of their shares. There are several approaches to the problem of measurement of the shareholders' opportunity cost:

(*a*)   In a small firm it may be possible to ask the owners directly.

(*b*)   An estimate could be made of the historical rate of return received by owners, or by owners of similar shares.[4]

(*c*)   An average cost of finance for the economy as a whole could be calculated and adjusted by a premium or discount for risk of the particular firm.

(*d*)   Use of an empirical valuation model using information about the market value of the firm's shares.[5] If we assume that shareholders value their shares using both their future expectations of returns and their opportunity cost in the valuation process by assuming a relationship we could calculate the opportunity cost using market data about share price and market expectations. Sect. 9.5 examines such a model.

The cost of debt is the rate of return required by lenders, which could be expressed in terms of a required interest rate. In some cases the original rate of interest may not be a true indication of the cost of debt. If the amount borrowed is different (excluding interest) from the amount to be paid back, e.g. debentures issued at a discount, or if interest rates change and the firm still pays the original rate. Although the firm still pays the original cost in most cases, the opportunity cost of finance becomes the amount the firm could get by lending at the new rate of interest.

It is unlikely that the attitudes of equity or debt finance holders will be unaffected by the issue of new finances. One major criticism of measuring costs of individual sources is that it assumes that individual source costs are independent. The introduction or increase of financial risk by, for example, the issue of debentures may cause the rate of return required by equity to rise and thus the full cost of debt will be the rate of return required by debt plus the increased return required by equity. Measurement of the cost of finance is discussed fully in other books (see Further Reading) and Chapter 12 considers its application in decision-making. Example B.3 considers the taxation implications.

7.9   Liquidity and solvency

A firm will require cash to enable it to commence or continue its business activities.

The ability of a firm to provide sufficient cash for its activities is termed its 'liquidity'. The concept of liquidity relates to the balance between the demands for and supply of cash resources over a period of time in the future. We can develop a notion of short-term and long-term liquidity according to our horizon in time. For example, a firm may be unable to pay a creditor on demand because it has insufficient cash in the bank. The firm would be illiquid in the very short term if it was, for example, unable to borrow the necessary cash from the bank, and it would be illiquid in the long term if it was unable to obtain further cash from any source at that time, or at any time in the future. A firm must plan its sources and applications of cash if it is to attain its objectives and maintain an appropriate level of liquidity.

The concept of solvency is closely related to liquidity.[6] A firm would be considered solvent if at a moment in time its assets if realised would exceed its liabilities. This is related to debt cover discussed in Sect. 7.6. However, a short-term illiquid firm may be forced to sell its assets quickly, i.e. not as a going concern and may become insolvent, although if it had been allowed to continue as a going concern it may have been long-term liquid and thus be solvent. It is only possible to comment on a firm's long-term liquidity by analysing the demand and supply for cash in the firm's future plans. A guide to short-term liquidity can be obtained from its working capital position.

7.10   Working Capital

The cash flowing through the firm can be seen illustrated in Fig. 7.4 in the cash cycle. The working capital cycle is a flow within the overall cash cycle of the firm. The importance of working capital is that it identifies a relationship between current assets and current liabilities. Current liabilities are closely related to the

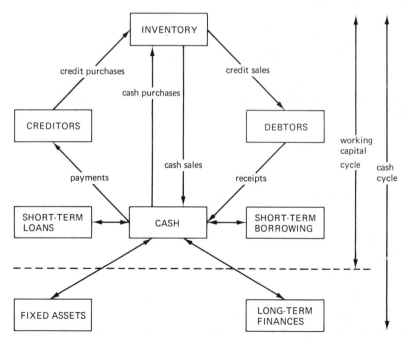

Figure 7.4   Cash and working capital cycle

financing of current assets, and an increase in current liabilities can often be thought of as a source of finance. For example, a firm may acquire its inventory on credit and hence it is effectively financing its current assets through current liabilities. However, fixed assets may be acquired using credit which would be classified as current liabilities.

The overall rate at which current assets and current liabilities change is termed the 'rate of working capital turnover'. We can analyse the rate of turnover of individual current assets and current liabilities:

cash turnover depends on the amount of cash the firm holds on average per day in relation to its daily usage;

creditors' turnover depends on the time between the purchase of resources on credit, and payment to creditors and the amount of creditors;

inventory turnover depends on the time between purchase and use of inventory, and the amount of inventory held;

debtors' turnover depends on the time between credit sale and the collection of cash, and the amount of credit allowed.

Turnover can be measured as the number of times per year an item of working capital changes. It can be calculated as:

$$\frac{\text{average amount of } z \text{ held}}{\text{average daily usage of } z} = \text{average number of days } z \text{ held}$$

$$\frac{\text{number of working days in a year}}{\text{average number of days } z \text{ held}} = \text{turnover of } z \text{ per annum}$$

where z is an item of working capital.

Limitations from this analysis arise from the reliance on averages in our calculations, especially when published data is being used. If an average is being calculated from the balance sheet it must be representative.

Example 7.3
Glasgow Ltd holds £20,000 of inventory on average throughout the year. Its average daily usage is £500. There are 240 working days in the year.

$$\text{The number of days inventory held is } \frac{£20,000}{£500} = 40 \text{ days}$$

$$\text{The inventory turnover is } \frac{240}{40} = 6 \text{ times per annum}$$

We can measure the rate of the working capital turnover by adding the number of days we hold current assets and deducting the number of days for current liabilities.

Example 7.4
Glasgow Ltd holds its inventory for 40 days before it is sold on credit. It obtains 60 days' credit on its purchases and gives 50 days' credit on its sales. Therefore the total time that the company's cash is tied up is $40 + 50 - 60 = 30$ days. This can be shown:

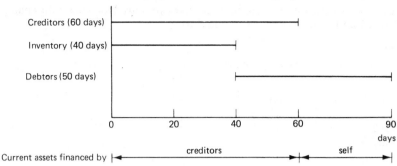

Figure 7.5

The working capital cycle of 90 days is financed by the creditors for the first 60 days and by the firm's cash for the last 30 days.

The importance of the analysis of the working capital cycle is that a firm can control the amount of working capital, and hence finance required, by increasing net current asset turnover, e.g. holding less inventory, or same inventory for less time and by increasing its short-term finance, e.g. current liabilities. It can also influence its liquidity by speeding up the conversion into cash and by increasing current liabilities.

The choice of an appropriate level of working capital depends on an evaluation of the cost of finance and costs of not having sufficient working capital, e.g. shortage of short-term liquidity, or inventory when required.

Comparison of rates of working capital turnover between industries becomes difficult because of different technologies and norms, etc. As with the use of debt/equity ratios they may be useful as comparative rather than absolute measures.

Working Capital and Liquidity
Ex. 7.5 illustrates how we could analyse the changes in working capital and use data to measure liquidity.

Example 7.5
Gloucester Ltd wants to analyse the change in working capital during 19X1 and examine its liquidity position. It has prepared a statement of its working capital position extracted from its balance sheets at the end of 19X0 and 19X1.

Working Capital Summary: Gloucester Ltd
(extract from balance sheets) at:

	31 December 19X0		31 December 19X1	
Current Assets	£	£	£	£
Inventory	3,500		7,000	
Debtors	7,500		8,000	
Marketable Securities (see note 1)	2,500		500	
Cash	1,500		1,000	
		15,000		16,500
Current Liabilities				
Trade Creditors	5,000		3,000	
Interest Payable			500	
Dividends Payable	2,000		1,000	
		7,000		4,500
Working Capital		£ 8,000		£12,000

Note: (1) Short-term investments.

From the data the following statement can be prepared to explain the change in working capital from £8000 to £12,000 during 19X1.

Statement of Changes in Working Capital during 19X1:
Gloucester Ltd

Increases in working capital

	£	£
Increases in current assets		
Inventory	3500	
Debtors	500	
Decreases in current liabilities		
Trade Creditors	2000	
Dividends Payable	1000	
		7000
Less: Decreases in working capital		
Decreases in Current Assets		
Marketable Securities	2000	
Cash	500	
Increases in Current Liabilities		
Interest Payable	500	
		3000
Net Increase in Working Capital		£4000

Before we can meaningfully comment about the significance and relevance of this change we will have to obtain information about how the changes relate to size and activities of the company.

A change of working capital is clearly important for a firm's liquidity. Changes in particular items, such as cash, will influence a firm's very short-term liquidity. Although a firm's working capital could rise its very short-term liquidity could decrease. When examining the time scale we must be careful to define it in terms of the firm's life and not in terms only of the working capital cycle.

We will analyse liquidity in comparative rather than absolute terms, using data in Ex. 7.5:

	19X0	19X1
Very short-term liquidity (known as acid test ratio)		
$\dfrac{\text{Very liquid assets (cash + marketable securities)}}{\text{Current liabilities}}$	$\dfrac{4}{7} = 0.57$	$\dfrac{1.5}{4.5} = 0.33$
Short-term liquidity (known as current ratio)		
$\dfrac{\text{Current assets}}{\text{Current liabilities}}$	$\dfrac{15}{7} = 2.14$	$\dfrac{16.5}{4.5} = 3.66$

As we can see the very short-term liquidity of the company has deteriorated whilst the short-term liquidity is much improved. It is normal to consider a firm's short-term liquidity as satisfactory if the acid test ratio is more than 1, and the current ratio is more than 2. However, this will depend on the industry, and the management's policies. It is necessary to consider the long-term liquidity as well, to gain a complete picture, but this is omitted here.

The use of this form of analysis of liquidity is limited by the data we use.[7,8] Balance sheets do not provide all the relevant data, e.g. an unused overdraft arrangement would normally be excluded, and they provide valuations based on the original cost rather than selling price bases. They do not provide information about rates of working capital turnover, with this information added we could make predictions of cash flows in and out of the firm for future periods in the very short and short run. This would provide a more sophisticated liquidity analysis. The analysis also assumes that the factors determining the ratios will remain constant in the future. However, if these limitations are recognised the ratios may provide crude approximations.

7.11 Flow of funds

An analysis of the causes of historical changes and of the methods of providing for proposed changes in a firm's assets may prove useful to users of financial statements.[9] In relation to Ex. 7.5 we might find it necessary to explain the way in which the increase in working capital was financed. Alternatively, we may wish to analyse how a proposed increase in fixed assets were to be financed. A statement providing such an analysis is termed a statement of source and application of funds. The term 'funds' may be used to refer to cash or working capital.

A convenient starting-point for analysis of flows of working capital or cash, using comparative balance sheets at different points in time, is the fundamental accounting equation which shows that changes in assets will be matched by corresponding changes in other assets, liabilities or owners' equity. The term source of funds will be used to refer to changes which provide the firm's working capital, and application of funds to changes which require the use of working capital. In Fig. 7.6 the effect of these flows is shown in the context of the fundamental equation, using some examples.

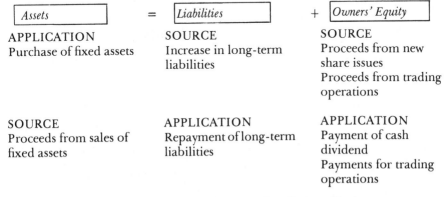

Figure 7.6   Examples of sources and applications of funds

The procedures we could adopt to prepare a statement of source and application of funds could involve a complete analysis of all the accounts of the firm or alternatively we could use aggregate data from the balance sheet and profit statement. For example if we wished to explain a change in a firm's cash position we could analyse its cash account as seen in Sect. 3.9. As this procedure could be time consuming and information may not be available to an external analyst we will examine an alternative procedure which uses data from a balance sheet and profit statement. Ex. 7.6 provides an illustration of the procedure.

Example 7.6

A shareholder of Greig Ltd wishes to explain the way in which the change in the working capital was financed during 19X1. Balance sheet and profit statement data are available.

Balance sheet of Greig Ltd as at 31 December

		19X0	19X1
Fixed Assets		£000	£000
Machinery at Cost		50	70
Less: Accumulated Depreciation		30	45
		20	25
Current Assets			
Inventory	12		8
Debtors	10		28
Cash	8		6
	30		42
Current Liabilities			
Creditors	21		24
Net Current Assets		9	18
		£29	£43
Financed by			
Owners' Equity			
Ordinary shares £1		23	23
Retained profit		6	16
		29	39
Long-term Liabilities			
Debentures 12% (1990)		—	4
		£29	£43

Profit Statement of Greig Ltd for year ended 31 December 19X1

		£000
Sales Revenue		120
Less: Cost of Goods Sold		76
Gross Profit		44
Less: Other expenses		
Clerical	9	
Depreciation	18	
Loss on sale of fixed asset (see note 1)	4	
		31
Net Profit		13
Dividends		3
Increase in retained profits		£10

Note: (1) An item of machinery which cost £12,000 and had a net book value of £9000 was sold for £5000, i.e. a 'loss' of £4000.

The preparation of the statement relies on a systematic analysis of data. Initially we must identify the relevant sources and applications of funds. We could proceed either by examining and listing every change in the balance sheet and identifying how it affects our sources and application of funds as a means of ensuring that all relevant data is included. Alternatively, we could consider ourselves as completing a statement like the solution to Ex. 7.6 found below, and check after preparation that all the relevant data has been included. As the data from which it is prepared is balance sheet data there may be compensating increases and decreases over time which are not reflected separately in the change between two points in time.

The following statement shows the relevant sources and applications of funds to explain the change in the cash position during 19X1.

Sources and Applications of Funds during 19X1: Greig Ltd

	£000	£000	Explanatory Notes
SOURCES			
From trading operations			
Net profit for year	13		(1)
Adjustments			
add non-fund expenses			
depreciation for year	18		
loss on sale of machinery	4		
		35	(2)
Proceeds from sale of machinery		5	
Debenture issue		4	
Decrease in inventory		4	
Increase in creditors		3	
Total sources		£51	
APPLICATIONS			
Purchase of machinery		32	
Payment of dividend		3	
Increase in debtors		18	
Total applications		£53	
Resulting in a decrease in cash of		£ 2	

Notes:

(1)   Rather than show the revenue and expenses as sources and applications respectively in statement, we show the net profit for the year. After adjustments we arrive at the net cash flow from trading operations (£35,000), or more strictly net working capital flow.

(2)   To arrive at the net cash flow from trading operations we will analyse the profit statement and identify the revenues and expenses which require cash flows. As we saw in Sect. 3.9 not all expenses or revenues require cash or working capital and these are termed 'non-fund items'. For example, the depreciation expense of a period does not use working capital as it is an allocation of a cost which was incurred in a previous period when the actual flow occurred. Other items such as the loss or profit on the sale of a fixed asset which are included in the profit statement must also be eliminated as they are adjustments to depreciation. Thus to arrive at the cash or working capital flow in this example we could calculate the sum

of revenues less those expenses which use cash or working capital, or we can make an adjustment to the profit:

The sources from trading operations can be computed as:

Alternative 1

Cash/working capital flow from trading operations

		£	£
IN	Sales revenue		120
OUT	Cost of goods sold	76	
	Clerical	9	85
	Net Cash/Working Capital flow in		£35

Alternative 2 as shown on the previous page is often simpler where there are many revenues and expenses which use working capital or where only net profit and depreciation data are available.

In alternative 2 non-fund expenses or losses are added to make the adjustments, and non-fund revenues and non-trading revenues and profits would be subtracted. Examples of non-fund expenses are depreciation and amortisation of leases, and examples of non-fund revenues are the unrealised profit (or revenue) on revaluation upwards of fixed assets or 'profits' on the sale of fixed assets.

When examining changes in liquidity or in the planning of future liquidity requirements it may be useful to examine the change in liquidity in terms of working capital. The previous statement explained how the change in cash was provided. To explain the change in working capital by £9000 we would eliminate all working capital changes.

From the statement of source and application of funds we can see that the firm has financed its acquisition of fixed assets from retained profits, a debenture issue and from the sale of other fixed assets, and at the same time it has increased its debtors and creditors, and reduced its inventory. Chapter 13 examines a budget framework for preparation of similar statements.

7.12 Valuation of Owners' Equity, Liabilities and Working Capital

Our discussion about the valuation of fixed assets in Chapters 1 and 2, and inventories in Chapters 5 and 6 can be developed and applied to the valuation of owners' equity, liabilities and working capital.

OWNERS' EQUITY

As we explained in Chapter 3, owners' equity consists of capital and retained profit. The capital element is valued on the basis of the amount paid into the firm at the time of the initial receipt. The retained profit element is valued at the time the profit is retained. These valuations do not necessarily reflect the valuations that the owners give to their shares, nor to the selling price of the shares on a stock exchange. This valuation problem is discussed in Chapter 9. In Chapter 8 we consider some of the problems that arise when monetary values from different points in time are added together, as would usually occur with the owners' equity valuations in the balance sheet.

LIABILITIES

The valuation of liabilities is based in practice on the amount of the liability at the time it was incurred. In many transactions of a firm the liability may be expressed in contracts in which the amount is agreed, e.g. on borrowing finance, or on an invoice, and estimation of the amount of the liability is not necessary. In some circumstances, the firm may need to estimate the amount of the liability; for example, if a firm has acquired and used material for which a definite price has not been agreed, it will need to estimate the amount of the liability to calculate the expense of the period. The accounting concepts of conservatism and materiality will guide the valuation. The term 'provision for liability' is used where the exact amount of the liability is not known and we must estimate it. Any under- or over-provision of the liability is an expense or revenue respectively and may be treated as an extraordinary item in the profit statement. If the liability is an amount borrowed, and where the firm will eventually repay an identical sum, the valuation of the liability will be that sum. Where the amount to be repaid differs, e.g. the issue of debentures at a discount, then the usual practice is to value the liability initially at the amount borrowed, and gradually increase the valuation of the liability as the time of repayment approaches. This will show that the present value of the liability is increasing through time.

Valuation of liabilities will become more difficult with uncertainty about future events. A firm may admit liability for damages for an accident, but the amount of compensation has still to be fixed; or there may be doubt about the existence of a liability, e.g. where a court case for damages is being contested. Where the actual existence of a liability is established the assessment of the probabilities will be of importance in establishing a valuation. Where the actual existence of a liability is in some doubt the term 'contingent liability' is used, and it is normal for contingent liabilities to be excluded in the valuation of liabilities in the balance sheet, but a note of their existence is included. In the event of a contingent liability becoming an actual liability, and therefore an expense of the period when the liability was recognised rather than when it was caused, the amount, if material, may be treated as an extra-ordinary item in the profit statement.

The basis of valuation of liabilities normally uses accounting concepts and follows a similar pattern to that for assets, and adheres to an equivalent to original cost. This leads to the situation where equal amounts owed are valued identically in the balance sheet, even when the point in time at which repayment is due is significantly different. For example, if a firm owes £100 payable tomorrow, and £100 repayable in 30 years' time, these have an identical valuation for accounting purposes, despite probably different present values.

WORKING CAPITAL

The valuation of working capital follows similar lines to our previous considerations. Current asset valuations will in most circumstances be based on a cost basis. Current liabilities are valued as discussed in the previous section. In Chapter 6, we considered the special problems of valuing inventories. Other current assets, such as debtors, marketable securities and cash are valued on the basis of original cost, or net realisable value, whichever is the lower.

When there is doubt about valuations of any asset a firm could reduce its value by treating part of the asset as an expense. For example, if a firm wished to reduce the value of its debtors because of doubts about the ability of its debtors to pay, rather than reducing the value of one particular debt, it could make a provision for doubtful debts as shown in Ex. 7.7.

Example 7.7
The valuation of the debtors of Gengis Ltd was £10,000 on 31 December 19X1.

This valuation was considered doubtful as it was estimated that 10% of debtors were unlikely to pay. The abridged balance sheet of Gengis Ltd would show:

Current assets	£	£
Debtors	10,000	
Less: Provision for doubtful debts	1,000	
		9,000

The relevant T accounts for these adjustments would be:

Debtors		Doubtful debts provision		Doubtful debts expense	
Balance 10,000			1,000 AD1	AD1 1,000	Transfer to P & L
31.12.19X1 Balance 10,000			31.12.19X1 1,000 Balance	nil Balance	

Any assets or liabilities about which the valuation is doubtful can be similarly adjusted. Where a provision is against future losses or future liabilities it may be shown in the balance sheet separately under owners' equity or liabilities.

7.13 Summary

This chapter examined the dimensions of a firm's decisions about financing its activities. A firm will need to provide returns to compensate providers of finance for their opportunity costs and for the risks they undertake. It will wish to select an optimal financial structure which may consist of a combination of debt and equity finance, and long- and short-term finance. One of the major objectives of financing decisions is to attain optimal financial structures in the context of financial risk, cost of finance and liquidity considerations. As well as financing fixed assets a firm must maintain its liquidity and provide sufficient working capital. A statement of source and application of funds can be useful in the historical analysis of changes in liquidity, and also in the planning of methods of financing the acquisition of assets in the future.

Notes and References

1. Association of Certified Accountants, *Sources of Capital* (A.C.C.A., 1965).
2. J. Freear, *Financing Decisions in Business* (London, Haymarket, 1973), chaps 4, 5, 6.
3. Ibid., chap. 8.
4. A. J. Merrett and A. Sykes, 'Returns on Equities and Fixed Interest Securities: 1919–66', in *Studies in Optimal Financing*, ed. R. J. Lister (London, Macmillan, 1973).
5. E. Solomons, 'Measuring a Company's Cost of Capital', in R. J. Lister, ibid.
6. M. W. E. Glautier, 'Towards a Reformulation of the Theory of Working Capital', *Journal of Finance* (1970).
7. S. Dev, 'Ratio Analysis and Prediction of Company Failure', *Debits, Credits, Finance and Profits*, ed. H. Edey and B. S. Yamey (London, Sweet & Maxwell, 1974).
8. G. A. Lee, 'Working Capital: Theory of Control', *Accountancy* (July and September 1970).
9. Accounting Standards Steering Committee, *SSAP 10, Statements of Source and Application of Funds* (Institute of Chartered Accountants in England and Wales, July 1975).

Further Reading

J. M. Samuels and F. M. Wilkes *Management of Company Finance* (London, Nelson, 1971).

Questions and Problems

7.1 What do you understand by the following terminology?

Financial structure	Equity finance
Capital structure	Debt finance
Share premium	Bonus issue
Nominal value	Floating and fixed charges
Deferred taxation	Financial risk
Ordinary share	Gearing
Preference share	Liquidity
Debenture	Solvency
Opportunity cost of finance	Working capital turnover
Provisions	Cash cycles
	Flow of funds

7.2 Gault Ltd obtains the following finance during 1974:

(a) borrows £1000 to be repaid in two years time with annual interest of 10%;

(b) borrows £5000 with £5832 to be repaid in two years time, with no annual interest payment.

What is the annual cost of finance in (a) and (b)?

What valuation would be shown in the balance sheet at the time of the borrowing and after one year?

7.3 How would you calculate your personal opportunity cost of finance if you are deciding whether to buy:

(a) a sweepstake ticket for an event in one year's time

(b) a season ticket on British Railways

(c) a car

(d) a house

Explain the differences if any between the costs you calculate.

7.4 The market value of the ordinary shares of Gallic Ltd is £80,000. The shareholders expect to receive £10,000 per year in dividends in the future. What discount rate are the shareholders applying to their expected dividend stream to arrive at the valuation?

7.5 When analysing the accounts of Gen Ltd you discover that the following information has not been considered:

(a) only 90% of the debtors included in the balance sheet at £25,000 are expected to pay even after £500 is spent on legal fees

(b) included in the creditors is £60 owing to an unknown person

(c) the firm is being sued for £50,000 damages from a road accident

How would this affect the profit statement and balance sheet?

7.6 The following are the balance sheet and profit statement of Geranium Ltd:

Balance sheet at 31 December		19X1		19X2
Fixed Assets		£000		£000
Machinery at cost	52		60	
Less: Accumulated Depreciation	20		15	
		32		45
Current Assets				
Inventory	7		2	
Debtors	3		1	
Cash	2		7	
	12		10	

Current Liabilities			
Creditors	3		5
Dividends payable	1		2
	4		7
Net Current Assets		8	3
		£40	£48

Financed by			
Owners' Equity			
Ordinary £1 shares	26		26
Retained profit	6		10
		32	36
8% Preference shares £1		—	4
		32	40
Long-term Liabilities			
10% Debentures 19X6		8	8
		£40	£48

Profit statement for 19X2		£000
Sales revenue	60	
Less: Cost of goods sold	49	
Gross profit	11	
Less: Other expenses		
depreciation	13	
interest – debentures and loans	1	
administration	13	
profit on sale of machinery	(22)	5
Net profit		6
Dividends – ordinary		2
Increase in retained profit		£ 4

Note (1) An item of machinery which cost £42,000 with a net book value of £24,000 was sold for £46,000.

Using the above data and any assumptions you think necessary analyse the following questions:

(a) has the financial risk of the firm changed during 19X2?

(b) what factors would determine whether the optimal financial structure has been maintained?

(c) has the liquidity of the firm improved or deteriorated during 19X2?

(d) to what extent can the debtors and inventory be considered as available to pay off creditors?

(e) prepare a statement which explains the change in working capital during 19X2.

(f) prepare a statement which explains the change in cash during 19X2.

(g) what should be the financial structure if the firm intends to acquire fixed assets as follows

19X3	£50,000
19X4	£20,000

7.7 If you are considering investing £10,000 what criteria would you use in choosing between an investment in ordinary shares, preference shares and debentures?

7.8 At a meeting to discuss the liquidity problems of a firm, the following proposals are made:

(a) an increase in the depreciation expense to conserve more cash in the firm.

(b) a reduction in the credit given on sales from 60 days to 30 days.

(*c*) an increase in the credit taken on purchases to 60 days from 90 days.

(*d*) an increase in the working capital cycle from 40 days to 50 days.

(*e*) an issue of 1000 shares as a scrip issue.

(*f*) an amendment to accounting bases which will result in increased profits in the future.

Comment on these proposals.

8
Value and Profit under Changing Price Levels

8.1 Introduction

Accounting data is measured, recorded and communicated in monetary terms. Values expressed in this way derive their meaning not from the amounts themselves, but from what they can purchase. The purchase price of any asset may change frequently and therefore the value of a monetary amount attributed to the asset may also change. The implications of this, particularly in the area of accounting value and profit, are explored in this chapter.

The concepts of value and profit were introduced in Chapter 1, and their relationship established. The firm's balance sheet and profit statement show respectively the firm's value and how the firm has performed in a period. Together they may also contribute to an assessment of how the firm is likely to perform in the future. The effect of price-level changes on the measurement of value and profit is important because of their effect on accounting statements, and consequently on the users of accounting information. Before examining this further we will consider an example of the effect of price-level changes.

Example 8.1
A house was purchased on 1 January 19X0 for £10,000. On 31 December 19X0 it was sold for £15,000. An index of general price changes rose from 100 to 110 in 19X0 while an index of average house prices rose from 100 to 120. The house in this example was in a location where house prices rose more than the average. Ignoring all other costs and revenues, what profit was made in 19X0? The profit could be:

	V_0	ADJ	$V_0(ADJ)$	V_1	*Profit*
	(1 Jan. 19X0)	£	£	(31 Dec. 19X0)	£
1.	10,000	—	10,000	15,000	5,000
2.	10,000	$\frac{110}{100}$	11,000	15,000	4,000
3.	10,000	$\frac{120}{100}$	12,000	15,000	3,000

The profit is calculated using the model $P = V_1 - V_0$. The adjustments $V_0(ADJ)$ are an attempt to reflect the change in price levels under various assumptions (No. 1 no price change; No. 2 the general price-level change; No. 3 the average house-price change). These adjustments are made to express V_0 as an equivalent in current terms, thus facilitating better comparison with V_1.

In the first measure of profit no adjustment to the numbers is made and the profit is simply the difference between the purchase cost and selling price. This is the profit that would be shown in conventional accounting statements. The second measure makes adjustment for a general price index, which is a measure of the general rise in prices of a wide range of assets. This measure shows that £10,000 at the beginning of 19X0 is equivalent to £11,000 at the end, because the two amounts could purchase the same quantity of assets in general. The profit is the excess value at the end of the year over the £11,000. The third measure makes an adjustment for the rise in the index for average house prices from 100 to 120 and indicates that the only profit is the extra increase in the value of this particular house.

Ex. 8.1, though a relatively straightforward situation, illustrates the difficulty of measuring value and profit when there are price-level changes. These changes were of two kinds, i.e. a general price rise and a rise in the price of a specific type of asset – in this example a house. The former change can be equated to what is known as the rate of inflation. These two categories of price changes are discussed later, but we should note that they were expressed as indices rather than percentage rises. The general price change could have been expressed as 10% and the specific one for the house as 20%. In the rest of this chapter for the ease of exposition we will continue to use indexes rather than percentages.

Our original definition of profit was in terms of a change in value. This could be reinterpreted as profit, being the extra value at the end of a period over and above the starting value. This way of expressing profit is generally termed the profit 'after maintaining value intact'. Where there is no change in price levels the agreement on a satisfactory definition of maintaining value intact may cause problems, but where prices have changed the idea of maintaining the starting value is even more difficult to apply. In the second measure in Ex. 8.1 the £10,000 at the beginning of 19X0 could purchase the same assets in general as £11,000 at the end of 19X0. It was argued that the profit was the excess proceeds over this £10,000 expressed in the year-end amount of £11,000. The profit was thus calculated after maintaining the value of the £10,000 intact at the end of the year (which was £11,000 by the end if 19X0). The third measure showed that the value to be maintained before calculation of the profit was £12,000 – that is, as measured by the ability to buy houses in general rather than assets in general. There are many other possible definitions that could be used, e.g. the ability to buy a house in the same location, which reveals no profit in Ex. 8.1. This idea of 'maintaining value intact' is important and will be discussed further below.

8.2 Maintaining value intact

The profit of a period for an individual has been defined as 'the maximum amount that he could consume and still remain as well off at the end as he was at the beginning'.[1] This definition can be amended to be applicable to a firm's profits for a period: 'the maximum amount that the firm could pay as a dividend and still remain as well off at the end of the period as it was at the beginning'. The interpretation of this definition revolves around the meaning of 'as well off as'. Three possible interpretations of this phrase are: (a) the ownership of assets with the same monetary value (first measure in Ex. 8.1); (b) the capacity to purchase the same quantity of assets in general (second measure in Ex. 8.1); and (c) the capacity to purchase the same quantity of a specific asset (third measure in Ex. 8.1). The expression 'as well off as' is equivalent to the concept of maintaining value intact. The profit of a period is the surplus of the value at the end of the period over the starting value adjusted to maintain initial value intact.

As we have seen above, the interpretation of maintaining value intact may vary.[2] A person's interpretation may be affected by his intended expenditure pattern. As we all have different expenditure patterns a change in prices will affect some people more than others. For example, if two people each have £1000 and one intends buying a particular car with it while the other does not, and the price of the car rises (everything else remaining the same), the former will be less well off while the latter will be unaffected.

There are many users of accounting information relating to the firm, but for the purposes of exposition we can divide them into two groups: those who will look at the information from the point of view of the owners, and those who will look at it from the point of view of the firm (or perhaps the managers of the firm). Owners will be interested primarily in making sure that their investment in the firm, which entailed them sacrificing consumption when the investment was made, enables them, at the minimum, to enjoy the same consumption later. This could only be ascertained accurately by constructing an index for each owner based on his own personal expenditure patterns. If this index increased from 100 to 150 over the investment period, then investment of £100 would have to return at least £150 at the end of the investment period to maintain value intact. If it returned £160 then there could be said to be a profit of £10 to the investor using the formula

$$V - V_0 \times I = \text{Profit}$$

$$160 - 100 \times \frac{150}{100} = £10,$$

where I is the appropriate index of expenditure patterns for the investor.

The other view is that of the firm. An index could be calculated based on its expenditure pattern which would depend on the pattern of the forecast acquisition of assets. Using this in the above formula the firm can calculate its profit after maintaining its value intact.

The government publishes the Consumer Expenditure Deflator (C.E.D.), which measures the effect of price-level changes on the average consumer. It is published annually by the Central Statistical Office. Another similar index is the Index of Retail Prices (R.P.I.) published monthly by the Department of Employment. Both these general price indices could possibly be considered as a proxy for the expenditure patterns of the two groups considered above. Both indexes are based on the average consumer and will not reflect exactly each individual owner's index of his expenditure patterns. While most owners would accept them as a reasonable proxy, the expenditure patterns of most firms will be specific to the firm, being based on the purchases of the specific assets necessary to continue its particular trade. Thus most firms will find that the C.E.D. and R.P.I. are not good proxies for their expenditure.

Firms may thus need to calculate their own specific index in order to calculate whether their value has been maintained intact. The use of such an index may mean that the firm compares its end-of-period value (V_1) with the replacement cost of the components of the starting value. The use of this index is therefore sometimes called a 'replacement cost adjustment'.

It is possible to construct specific indexes for particular assets. This can be done by collecting data from the market, or from information supplied by a trade association or the government. Alternatively it may be a published index, e.g. the Index of House Prices published annually by the Nationwide Building Society.

Specific indexes are more easily constructed when assets are frequently replaced with similar assets, but if technology changes and replacements are not similar it may be difficult to construct such an index.

When examining the information needs of the owners and the managers of a firm it is necessary to consider the objectives of the firm. It is common to assume the objective is to maximise the owners' wealth, i.e. the owner's ability to purchase assets in general, and that the managers of the firm should identify with the objectives of the owners. Thus they should be concerned about the expenditure patterns of the owners as well as those of the firm. As a consequence the general price index (as a proxy for the expenditure patterns of all the owners), and a set of specific price indexes for the expenditure pattern of the firm, could be relevant to the information requirements.

It is possible to use these indexes to make adjustments to the accounting information which is produced using the accounting framework examined in Chapter 2. In this chapter we will concentrate on adjusting this accounting information rather than substituting other valuation bases which may not be acceptable within this framework. To this end we will now examine the effect of price changes on a firm's assets and liabilities and the way this will affect financial reporting.

8.3 Financial reporting

The theme of Chapter 1 was that accounting seeks to assess the health of a firm by measuring its value and profit. The principal financial reports that seek to show this are the balance sheet and the profit statement. There are many other financial reports that firms may prepare, e.g. forecasts and budgets (considered in Parts II and III). These will be affected by price-level changes in the same way as balance sheets and profit statements. The comments in this chapter are relevant to all reports, but we concentrate on the effect on published statements. This analysis of price-level changes continues with a consideration of the particular effects on non-monetary and monetary assets and liabilities.

(i) NON-MONETARY ASSETS AND LIABILITIES

These are assets and liabilities that are not fixed amounts in terms of numbers of pounds, i.e. their prices may change. There are many such assets, e.g. cars, land, inventory, but few liabilities, e.g. an agreement to deliver a specified quantity of inventories at a future date. They may both be affected by the two types of price changes explained earlier, i.e. changes related to the specific asset or liability and general price changes.

Whatever the price changes, two basic views of the profit made by a firm may emerge. This is illustrated in Ex. 8.2.

Example 8.2
The Helix Co. purchases £100 of inventory and three months later sells it for £200. Over this time the specific price index for inventory purchases rose from 100 to 140. Ignoring general price-level changes the value of the firm can be shown as:

	V_0	V_1	*Profit*
	£	£	£
Inventory	100	—	
Cash	—	200	
	£100	£200	£100

The conventional accounting profit would be reported as £100. For the firm to purchase the same quantity of inventory, and thus maintain the same physical level of business, it must have £140 at the end of the three months. If more than £60 is taken out of the firm by the owners, the firm would have to raise new finance to purchase, i.e. replace, the same amount of inventory. The firm could argue that the 'profit' for the period should be calculated thus:

$$V_1 - V_0 \times I_s = \text{Profit (where } I_s \text{ is the specific price index)}$$

$$200 - \left(100 \times \frac{140}{100}\right) = \text{Profit}$$

$$200 - 140 = £60$$

To distinguish this 'profit' from the conventional accounting profit it is termed 'current operating profit' (C.O.P.).

The difference between the accounting profit and the C.O.P. is normally termed a 'holding gain' (in this case £40). This is because it arises through owning or holding assets (in this case the inventory) over a period of rising specific prices. The owners may consider this holding gain as a profit, depending on the general price-level changes, but both groups will find it useful to distinguish it from the accounting profit.

If the general price index had increased from 100 to 130 in the same three-month period the owners would consider £130 at the end to be equivalent to £100 at the beginning. As long as this value was maintained any excess could be regarded as 'profit' thus:

$$V_1 - V_0 \times I_g = \text{Profit (where } I_g \text{ is the general price index)}$$

$$200 - 100 \times \frac{130}{100} = \text{Profit}$$

$$200 - 130 = £70$$

This 'profit' is termed 'adjusted accounting profit' to distinguish it from other profit measures. Using this analysis, £30 of the accounting profit is termed 'illusory' from the owners' point of view because it had to be earned merely to maintain the value of the owners' equity, i.e. increase it from a monetary amount of £100 to £130. The firm would need to have held an asset that increased in value from £100 to £130 to have maintained the firm's value. In the context of this example the £40 holding gain can be split into an illusory and a real part and therefore the accounting profit can be analysed as:

	£	£
Current operating profit (C.O.P.)		60
Real holding gain	10	
Illusory holding gain	30	
Total holding gain		40
Conventional accounting profit		£100

The illusory holding gain is that part of the gain that is 'illusory' from the owners' point of view. We use this terminology in the rest of the chapter. The C.O.P. tells us how much can be withdrawn by the owners while maintaining the firm's (replacement) value intact, while the C.O.P. plus real holding gains (the 'adjusted accounting profit') tells us how much the owner can withdraw while maintaining his view of the firm's value intact (i.e. adjusting for the general price level). The C.O.P. is based on replacement cost which is in many cases an approximation to the concept of deprival value discussed in Chapter 1 and of 'the value to the business' defined in the Sandilands Report.[4]

The C.O.P. is the difference between the sales revenue and the replacement cost at the time of sale of the assets sold. It is the same whatever changes take place in the general price level. This is because it concentrates on the specific price changes of the assets involved as opposed to general price changes. The total holding gain is that gain arising from the specific price rise of the asset involved and can be thought of as the gain from buying in advance of the rise. When there are assets unsold at the end of a period there could be holding gains on these assets which might be ignored because of the concept of realisation. Ex. 8.3 illustrates the above analysis.

Example 8.3
The Halogen Co. purchases a machine for £120 on 1 January 19X0. At this time it has no other assets or liabilities. It is estimated that the machine will last for three years and will be depreciated by £40 each year. Using the machine, the firm provides a service for which it receives £180 in cash at the end of 19X0. No other costs are incurred. The general price index rose from 100 to 110 and the specific index for the machine from 100 to 120 in 19X0.

The profit for 19X0 can be analysed by calculating:

(1) the conventional accounting profit;
(2) the current operating profit;
(3) the adjusted accounting profit;
(4) the holding gains.

(1) The conventional accounting profit
= revenues less expenses
= 180 − 40 = £140

(2) The current operating profit (using I_s, the specific price index)
= revenues − expenses × I_s
$$= 180 - \left(40 \times \frac{120}{100}\right)$$
= 180 − 48 = £132

(3) The adjusted accounting profit (using I_g, the general price index)
= revenues − expenses × I_g
$$= 180 - \left(40 \times \frac{110}{100}\right)$$
= 180 − 44 = £136

(4) The holding gains

Real holding gain	= adjusted accounting profit − C.O.P.
	= 136 − 132 = £4
Illusory holding gain	= conventional accounting profit − adjusted accounting profit
	= 140 − 136 = £4

The conventional accounting profit can thus be analysed as:

	£
Current operating profit	132
Real holding gain	4
Adjusted accounting profit	136
Illusory holding gain	4
Conventional accounting profit	£140

It should be noted in Ex. 8.3 that the firm could be said to have made a holding gain from the part of the machine that had not become an expense in 19X0 but remained in the balance sheet at the end of the year. The gain was £16

$$£80 \times \frac{120}{100} - £80$$

but was unrealised at the end of the year and was therefore not included in the statement above. It follows that the gains calculated in the example were realised holding gains. It should be noted in this context the depreciation expense is interpreted as being the realisation of a proportion of the fixed asset.

(ii) MONETARY ASSETS AND LIABILITIES

These assets and liabilities are fixed in terms of numbers of pounds, e.g. cash, debtors, loans and creditors. The amounts do not change even when changes in specific or general price levels occur, but their value in terms of purchasing power will be affected.

If there is a rise in the price of the specific assets traded by a firm holding monetary assets and no change in the general price level the managers may consider that the firm has made a loss, i.e. not maintained its ability to purchase the specific assets. The owners may consider themselves neither better nor worse off. If there is a rise in the general price level and no change in the price of the specific asset traded by the firm the owners may consider themselves worse off if the firm is holding a monetary asset. The managers may not consider that the value of the firm had changed. If the firm is holding a monetary liability, and there is a specific rise in the price of assets traded by the firm and no change in the general price level, the owners may consider themselves neither better nor worse off as they have to sacrifice the same potential consumption of goods in general at the beginning and end of the period in order to repay the loan. In the case of the managers they may consider the firm better off as they would have to sacrifice a smaller physical quantity of goods (with which the firm trades) at the end than at the beginning in order to repay the loan.

The effect of both specific and general price rises is illustrated in Ex. 8.4.

Example 8.4
The Hard Co. buys and sells assets for which the specific price index increases from 100 to 140 in January 19X0. However, during this month it does not trade, holding £1000 cash and a £200 liability throughout. The general price index increased from 100 to 130 in the month. The values of the firm ignoring price changes, would be shown as:

	V_0	V_1	Conventional accounting profit
	£	£	£
Cash	1000	1000	
Less: Liability	200	200	
	£ 800	£ 800	Nil

It could be considered that the firm has made a loss if the specific index is used to adjust the opening value:

$$V_1 - V_0 \times I_s = \text{Profit}$$

$$800 - 800 \times \frac{140}{100} = \text{Profit}$$

$$800 - 1120 = £320 \text{ (loss)}$$

This is a loss that can be attributed to holding net monetary assets, i.e. monetary assets less monetary liabilities rather than the specific asset traded by the firm. These adjustments reflect the firm's expenditure patterns. If the expenditure patterns of the owners are considered, the loss would be:

$$V_1 - V_0 \times I_g = \text{Profit}$$

$$800 - 800 \times \frac{130}{100} = \text{Profit}$$

$$800 - 1040 = £240 \text{ (loss)}$$

The loss of £320 or £240 could be analysed into a part relating to monetary assets and a part relating to monetary liabilities. We will examine here the analysis of the £240:

Loss on holding monetary assets
$$= V_1 - V_0 \times I_g$$

$$= 1000 - \left(1000 \times \frac{130}{100}\right)$$

$$= 1000 - 1300 = £300 \text{ (loss)}$$

Gain on holding monetary liabilities
$$= V_1 - V_0 \times I_g$$

$$= 200 - \left(200 \times \frac{130}{100}\right)$$

$$= 200 - 260 = £60 \text{ (gain)}$$

Net loss $\qquad\qquad\qquad = £240 \text{ (loss)}$

The interpretation of the £60 gain on holding monetary liabilities is that the firm now owes only £200 whereas the value of its liability at the start of the year expressed in year-end £s is £260. Most firms trade in a number of different assets which may change in price at different rates. Consequently if price-level adjustments are made and monetary assets and liabilities are involved, it is recommended from the point of view of convenience that adjustments are made, using a general price index only as a proxy for the index of the expenditure plans for the firm and the owner rather than an average specific index representing the potential use for monetary assets.

Summary of Section 8.3
In this section we have analysed the effect of price-level changes on particular types of assets and liabilities and we can see how these changes affect the total firm. Attention was focused on the effect on profits and how conventional accounting profit could be adjusted to provide more information. It is useful to separate out

the holding gains on non-monetary assets and liabilities, and to show the effect of holding monetary assets and liabilities. Holding gains from the non-monetary assets and liabilities arise mainly from inventory and fixed assets, as either a realised gain (when the asset is sold or 'used up') or an unrealised gain if the profit is calculated at a time between acquisition and sale. As we have seen, conventional accounting profit ignores unrealised gains, thus a distinction is made between unrealised and realised gains when price-level adjustments are made. This analysis of the gains and losses from monetary assets and liabilities is a controversial view. Many arguments exist for a contrary treatment.[5]

8.4   Comparing financial statements

An important need of users of financial statements is the possibility of making comparisons between firms, and between years. Conventional accounting statements, prepared for periods of changing prices, do not provide a good basis for either type of comparison because firms may have: (a) different proportions of non-monetary and monetary assets and liabilities; (b) different financial structures; and (c) different age structures of assets. Furthermore, items in (a), (b) and (c) may vary from year to year.

(a)   *Different Proportions of Assets and Liabilities*
We have seen the effect that price-level changes have on monetary as opposed to non-monetary assets and liabilities. Unless adjustments are made to allow for firms holding different proportions of these, e.g. a bank holding a lot of cash as compared with a property company holding a lot of land, inter-period and inter-firm comparison will be difficult.

(b)   *Different Financial Structure*
The amount of debt a firm has will influence the way price-level changes affect it. The balance between equity and debt-financing will produce different effects, e.g. the more debt a firm has the more the firm may gain in times of general price-level rises through holding liabilities. Conversely, the more it may lose in time of general price level falls.

(c)   *Different Age Structure of Assets*
The different age structure will also affect comparison. A firm can hold a mixture of non-depreciating fixed assets, depreciating fixed assets and other assets. The holding of non-depreciating fixed assets of different ages means that firms will have differing unrealised holding gains from this source as between firms and years. When different firms hold depreciating fixed assets comparison will be affected by unrealised holding gains and realised holding gains (i.e. the effect of depreciation, see Ex. 8.3). The longer an asset is held before realisation the more out of date will be the depreciation expense in the conventional profit statement. In times of rising prices the realised holding gains will be greater. The holding of other assets will also affect comparison for the same reasons as depreciating fixed assets. Ex. 8.5 illustrates one aspect of this.

Example 8.5
Two firms make sales of an identical product at the same price. In 19X0 their total sales were £10,000 each. Their expenses, excluding depreciation, were £5000. Both produced the product on a similar machine, but one firm purchased its machine thirteen years ago for £15,000, the other two years ago for £30,000. Both machines were depreciated on a straight-line basis assuming no scrap value and a

fifteen-year life. The conventional profit statements for 19X0 are:

	First Firm	Second Firm
	£	£
Sales Revenue	10,000	10,000
Less: Depreciation Expense	1,000	2,000
Other Expense	5,000	5,000
Profit	£ 4,000	£ 3,000

Because the price-level changes in the machinery have been ignored by these conventional profit statements one firm looks more profitable because it purchased its machine earlier than the other. By 19X2 when the first firm replaces its machine the second firm may appear more profitable because the first firm will then have a higher depreciation expense. If adjustments were made to the depreciation expense to show it at the level it would be if the machine had been purchased at current costs the profits would be reported as being the same. The difference between the adjusted expense and the expense shown above would be a holding gain which could be shown separately to the profit statement. Adjustments of this kind to conventional costing data provide useful management and investor information.

So far we have considered the factors that must be adjusted to make comparisons between firms in the same year. There is a special problem when comparing profits over a period of years. This is illustrated in Ex. 8.6.

Example 8.6
Heat Ltd has the following profits in the years 19X0–19X4:

	19X0	19X1	19X2	19X3	19X4
Current operating profit	£12,500	£5,500	£13,000	£11,000	£14,000
Profit adjusted to current year basis	£15,000	£6,285	£14,182	£11,000	£14,000
General price index	100	105	110	120	120

The current operating profit was calculated after adjusting the items in the profit statement by the appropriate price index. It can be seen that these adjustments were not sufficient to facilitate the comparison of the annual profits. It is necessary to adjust all the reported profits to a common base, which in this example we have chosen to be the year 19X4. When this has been done the profit figures are all in price units of the same year and can be compared. It can be seen that, for example, the profit of 19X0 was higher than the profit of 19X4, i.e. if paid out as a dividend it could purchase more assets in general than the profit of 19X4.

The Accounting Standards Steering Committee issued S.S.A.P. No. 7 in 1974 'Accounting for changes in the purchasing power of money.'[6] This document recommended that the profit of a firm should be adjusted by a general price index but did not recommend adjustments for specific price-level changes. An analysis of the estimated effect of these general price-level adjustments on the accounting profits of particular industries is shown below.[7]

Industry	Average decrease (−) or increase (+) in accounting profits after adjustment
Electricals	−174%
Banks	− 31%
Food retailing	− 6%
Breweries	+ 20%
Property	+228%

This table shows the considerable effect that general price-level changes could have on firms in particular industries. The adjustments using the general price-level index, exclude from accounting profit illusory gains from holding non-monetary assets and adjust for the effect on holding monetary assets and liabilities. It is only after adjustments such as these that meaningful comparisons can be made between firms and industries. The reason for the large differences lie in the various factors outlined at the start of this section. For example, property companies gain because they are normally highly geared. They also have land as their major asset and thus may not have a large depreciation expense. Banks hold more monetary assets than liabilities. Electrical firms have large holdings of inventory and depreciating fixed assets consequently part of their conventional profits are illusory holding gains.

8.5 Proposed adjustments to financial statements

The previous analysis showed that there is a need to make adjustments to conventional financial statements. The adjustments dealt with in this section have been discussed widely within the accounting profession and could be implemented within the generally accepted accounting framework discussed in Chapter 2.

In Chapter 1 the balance sheet was explained as a statement that may help in the assessment of a firm's current value, and as a guide to its future value. The profit statement may help to assess how a change in value took place, and act as a guide to future changes in value. The proposals in this section should be judged by their success in helping such assessments. These proposals are illustrated by Ex. 8.7.

Example 8.7
The Hermit Co. Ltd commenced business on 1 January 19X0 by purchasing a machine for £400 and inventory for £500. These were paid for in cash provided by the initial capital of the firm of £500 and a £500 long-term loan. At the end of 19X0 the firm incurred, on credit, expenses of £200 and it sold half the inventory for £1000 in cash. The machine was estimated to have a two-year life and no residual value. The relevant price indexes are:

	General	Specific: Inventory	Specific: Machine
1 Jan. 19X0	100	100	100
31 Dec. 19X0	110	120	150

The balance sheets, using original cost, specific price indexes adjustments (replacement cost adjustment), and adjustments which use a general price index, are shown below:

Balance Sheets of Hermit Co. Ltd at 31 December 19X0

	Original Cost	Specific Price Indexes	General Price Index
	£	£	£
Fixed Assets			
Machine	400	600	440
Less: Accumulated Depreciation	200	300	220
	200	300	220
Current Assets			
Inventory	250	300	275
Cash	1100	1100	1100
	1350	1400	1375
Current Liabilities			
Creditors	200	200	200
Net Current Assets	1150	1200	1175
	£1350	£1500	£1395
Financed by:			
Owners' Equity			
Capital	500	500	550
Retained Profit	350	500	345
	850	1000	895
Loan	500	500	500
	£1350	£1500	£1395

Profit Statement for the year ended 31 December 19X0

	Original Cost	Specific Price Indexes	General Price Index
	£	£	£
Sales Revenue	1000	1000	1000
Less: Cost of Goods Sold	250	300	275
	750	700	725
Less: Depreciation Expense	200	300	220
Other Expenses	200	200	200
Profit — conventional	350		
— current operating		200	
— adjusted accounting			305
Realised holding gain		150	
Unrealised holding gain		150	
Loss from holding monetary asset			(10)
Gain from holding long-term loan			50
Profit — retained	£350	£500	£345

Specific Price Index

A specific price index is used to adjust the original cost to a replacement cost for each non-monetary asset in the balance sheet. In the profit statement all the holding gains (from purchasing assets and holding them before use) are separated out. These are also divided into realised and unrealised holding grants. There is no division between illusory and real gains because the general price index is ignored in this part of the example. For ease of exposition we show the effect of different indexes separately, but it is possible to use a combination of specific price index and general price index to show this (see Ex. 8.3). In the balance sheet the fixed asset and the inventory not used are revalued using the relevant specific index to replacement cost. The increase in value is the unrealised gain:

	£
	£
Fixed asset	100
Inventory	50
Unrealised holding gain	£150

In the profit statement the holding gains are separated out by adjusting the expense of depreciation and cost of goods sold to replacement cost. This reduces the conventional profit by £150 (this realised gain is only the same as the unrealised gain because the fixed asset's life is half over and the inventory half used) and this shows as a realised holding gain:

	£
	£
Fixed asset	100
Inventory	50
Realised holding gain	£150

A £300 holding gain is added to the £200 C.O.P. to give a retained profit in the profit statement of £500. The inclusion of holding gains in the profit statement was not recommended by the Sandilands report.[8]

General Price Index

In the balance sheet the cost of non-monetary assets of the firm are assumed to increase at the same rate as the general price index. The amount of owners' equity is adjusted by the general price index, thus reflecting the gain that the firm has to make merely to maintain the general purchasing power of the owners. The monetary assets and liabilities are not adjusted because they are in current monetary values.

In the profit statement the conventional profit is recalculated by adjusting the cost of goods sold and depreciation expense (the double entry for these adjustments is in the owners' equity adjustment in the balance sheet). The gains or losses from monetary assets and liabilities are calculated and shown in the profit statement. The latter adjustments reflect the fact that the lenders have lost (£50 in this case) and the firm has gained from the loan. The loss suffered by the firm from holding £100 of cash throughout the year is shown as £10.

Assessment of the Adjustments

The general price index adjustments are, in principle, those recommended by the S.S.A.P. no. 7 (in fact this recommends the use of the Retail Price Index). All the illusory gains will be excluded from the conventional accounting profit and the effect of holding monetary assets and liabilities will be shown. This is of interest to the owners because it will show whether or not the firm has maintained its value intact where this is defined as the ability to purchase assets in general. However, it ignores any unrealised gains from assets that have increased in value faster than the general price index. (This is because the general price index ignores any moves in specific prices thus assuming all non-monetary assets increase in value at the same rate as the general price index.) In accordance with the concept of conservatism S.S.A.P. no. 7 recommends that if the selling price of the assets has not increased at the same rate as the general price index the value should be adjusted to the selling price.

The specific index adjustments show the balance sheet with current replacement values. The C.O.P. which is produced will indicate the amount the firm can pay in dividends and tax and still replace the physical quantities of assets used up in the year with similar assets. This will be of particular interest to managers of firms.

Current Developments

There has been considerable debate in the U.K. about accounting for price-level changes. Although the Accounting Standards Steering Committee issued S.S.A.P. no. 7 the government also set up in 1974 the Inflation Accounting Committee (Sandilands Committee) which reported in 1975 with recommendations quite different from S.S.A.P. 7. The Consultative Committee of Accountancy Bodies has published its initial reactions to the Sandilands Report.[9] Following this the Inflation Accounting Steering Group was set up by the profession to study the problems further and make recommendations to the Accounting Standards Committee on a further Statement of Standard Accounting Practice. The fourth draft directive of the E.E.C. Commission issued in 1974 suggested index adjustments to original cost figures in financial statements. The draft directive suggests that authority might be given to countries to introduce other valuation methods based on current values rather than original cost values.

There are other countries where price-level adjustments are made to financial statements (e.g. Chile, Brazil).[10] In the U.S.A. very few firms allow for price-level changes, though the Accounting Principles Board has issued a statement recommending adjustments for price rises.

8.6 Summary

This chapter reviewed the problems that arise in interpreting accounting statements because of price-level changes. The problems affect value and profit measures because of changes in the prices of specific assets, and because of general price-level changes.

Any adjustments made to conventional accounting statements must be judged by the help they give in assessing a firm's current value and past profit as a guide to its future performance. The adjustments discussed in this chapter were based on conventional accounting statements produced in accordance with the concepts outlined in Chapter 2 (except when considering unrealised gains).

The objective of an owner was assumed to be to maximise his wealth by maximising his purchasing power. The managers were assumed also to be concerned about the owners' objectives. Both owners and managers will wish to ensure that the firm is able to purchase the assets necessary to continue at the same level of business activity. This indicates that adjustments for specific price changes will help the firm to maximise its owners' wealth. In addition the owners will wish to ensure that the firm's value expressed in general purchasing power is maintained. The adjustments proposed in this chapter should meet those needs.

Notes and References

1. J. R. Hicks, *Value and Capital,* 2nd edn (Oxford, Clarendon Press, 1946) pp. 171–81.
2. G. Macdonald, *Profit Measurement: Alternatives to Historical Cost* (London, Haymarket: Accounting Age Books, 1974) chap. 6.
3. For a fuller treatment see Sandilands, *Inflation Accounting—Report of the Inflation Accounting Committee,* Cmnd 6225 (1975) chap. 2.
4. Ibid., chap. 6.
5. See note 13, chap. 17.
6. Accounting Standards Steering Committee, S.S.A.P. 7, *Accounting for Changes in the Purchasing Power of Money* (Institute of Chartered Accountants in England and Wales, 1974).
7. R. Cutler and C. Westwick, 'The Impact of Inflation Accounting on the Stock Market', *Accountancy* (March 1973).
8. Sandilands, ibid. (1975) chap. 13.
9. *Accountancy* (December 1975). (Institute of Chartered Accountants.)
10. R. W. Scapens, *The Treatment of Inflation in the Published Accounts of Companies in Overseas Countries* (Research Committee of Institute of Chartered Accountants in England and Wales, 1973).

Further Reading

E. O. Edwards and P. W. Bell, *The Theory and Measurement of Business Income* (Berkeley, Calif., University of California, 1961).

R. H. Parker and G. C. Harcourt, *Readings on the Concept and Measurement of Income* (Cambridge, Cambridge University Press, 1969).

W. T. Baxter, 'Inflation and Accounts', *Investment Analyst No. 4* (1962); reprinted in *Modern Financial Management,* ed. B. V. Carsberg and H. C. Edey (Penguin, 1969).

P. R. A. Kirkman, *Accounting under Inflationary Conditions* (London, Allen & Unwin, 1974).

Accounting Standards Steering Committee, *The Corporate Report* (London, 1975).

Journal of Business Finance and Accounting, vol. 3, no. 1 (Spring 1976).

Questions and Problems

8.1   What do you understand by the following terminology?

General price-level changes	Unrealised holding gain
Specific price-level changes	Realised holding gain
Inflation	Monetary assets and liabilities
Maintaining value intact	Non-monetary assets and liabilities
Consumer expenditure deflator (C.E.D.)	
Index of Retail Prices (R.P.I.)	
Current operating profit (C.O.P.)	
Adjusted accounting profit	
Illusory holding gains	
Real holding gain	

8.2   Discuss whether the effect of price-level changes on value and profit of a firm would be of interest to:

(a) creditors

(b) trade unions

(c) customers

(d) government

8.3   What problems would arise in trying to construct a price-level index for the following:

(a) an individual's consumption

(b) cars

(c) a firm's expenditure pattern.

8.4 Price-level changes tend to reduce the usefulness of financial statements prepared on the basis of original cost transactions. Discuss.

8.5 If financial statements used replacement cost as the basis of value rather than original cost would there be any need to consider other price-level changes when reporting to owners and managers?

8.6 Why is it that price-level changes affect the ability to meaningfully compare the financial statements of one company with another?

8.7 A firm has £1000 in its bank account during March 19X0. It has no transactions affecting the bank account in this month. During the month the index of retail prices rose from 100 to 105, but the specific index relating to the assets normally traded by the firm decreased from 200 to 180. Explain whether the firm is better or worse off. Quantify the amounts involved.

8.8 If both taxation and dividends are paid out of the conventional accounting profit what problems does this raise in times of price-level changes?

8.9 A firm commences business on 1 January 19X0 by purchasing a car for £1000 and inventory for £200 using the initial capital of £1200. On the 30 June 19X0 it sells half the inventory for £300 cash. At the end of 19X1 it sells the rest of the inventory for £600 cash. The firm has no other transactions. The relevant indexes are:

	1 Jan. 19X0	31 Dec. 19X0	31 Dec. 19X1
Inventory	100	100	100
Car	100	105	110
General Price Index	100	100	105

The car is expected to have a ten-year life, with no residual value at the end of its life. It is depreciated on a straight-line basis.

Calculate the profit for 19X0 and 19X1. What problems do you foresee in the reporting of the profit in 19X1? Will the firm be able to replace the car at the end of the tenth year?

9
Review of Value
and Profit

9.1 Introduction

In Chapter 1 the relationship was established between measurement of value and the calculation of profit for a firm. The initial model used in that chapter was:

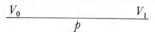

where V_0 is the value at a particular point in time and V_1 the value one period later, and p is the profit. This of course ignores the possibility of the introduction of new capital and distribution of profit (see Sect. 3.4). Various alternative approaches to measurement were considered in Chapter 1, and in Chapter 2 the conceptual framework adopted by accountants in presenting financial statements was discussed. It was stated in these chapters that the objective of presenting accounting information should be to give to interested parties evidence of the economic health of the firm and that the concepts of value and profit may be useful in this context. In Chapters 3–8 we were concerned chiefly with an explanation and analysis of accounting methods of measurement and recording of particular assets and liabilities. In this chapter we return to the problems of the measurement of an overall value of the firm and the needs of the users of this information. The accountants' concept of value based on original cost is reviewed and analysed together with the alternatives, replacement cost, selling price and future utility introduced in Chapter 1.

In Chapter 1 the economic health of a firm was measured in terms of its value and it was explained that there are various situations where such information is required. The manager requires to know how successful he is and the owners wish to know of the success of the firm. The manager may also be required to choose between various available opportunities and he will need to evaluate their effect on the economic health of the firm. The owners need to know the value of their shares in a firm in order to decide whether to sell or retain them. The owners may be asked collectively to sell their shares in a takeover situation and both the potential buyer and the seller need a valuation to form the basis of their bargaining. A valuation may be necessary in a partnership where a partner wishes to retire and be paid his share of the value of the business or where an interest in the business forms part of an estate being valued for capital transfer tax purposes. Thus we may be concerned with the valuation of the firm as a whole or of the owners' share in the firm.

In Sect. 9.2, we consider the balance sheet as a basis for valuing the firm. Balance sheet figures are widely used at least as a starting-point for decisions in many of the situations outlined in the previous paragraph. In Sect. 9.4 we analyse the situation where the firm's shares are traded on a recognised share market and examine whether the share price can be used as an appropriate valuation for the firm. Finally in Sect. 9.5 we outline a valuation model which seems to be most appropriate for decision-making.

9.2 The Balance Sheet as a Valuation Statement?

The balance sheet of a firm records its assets and liabilities and shows the net worth of the firm. The items included and the value placed upon them are determined by the accountant's application of accounting concepts, bases and policies. In general these are founded on a transactions approach in that the inclusion of items in a balance sheet is determined to a great extent by whether the firm acquired the asset or liability as a result of a specific transaction for which there is objective evidence. Thus such things as the degree of product monopoly, efficient management, good customer relationships or harmonious industrial relations are excluded from the balance sheet as assets (or as liabilities if they are bad management or relationships).

An example of a typical balance sheet is given in Fig. 9.1. This balance sheet shows a net worth for the Irwin Company of £300,000 being the total of the owners' equity. It should be clear that only in a restricted sense is this a valuation of the firm as a whole. It is rather the total of a number of individual assets owned by the firm and valued individually using accounting principles. It excludes assets such as those mentioned in the previous paragraph for which it would be difficult to obtain an acceptable valuation. In addition the firm earns its profits by using its assets in conjunction with each other and the value of the firm as an entity is not necessarily the same as the sum of assets valued individually. Thus even if the assets and liabilities in the balance sheet were valued using up-to-date market values instead of the original cost usually adopted, the balance sheet would still not necessarily show an appropriate value for the firm as an entity.

IMPLICATIONS OF THE USE OF ORIGINAL COST

It will be recalled that in Chapter 2 we stated that users of accounting statements need information which will give them an indication of what is going to happen to the firm in the future because this information affects current valuation. However, the application of accounting concepts bases and policies in the preparation of financial statements is more likely to result in information on what has happened to the firm in the past. An appropriate illustration of this would be if the Irwin Company's manager who was earning a salary of £10,000 in 19X0 retired at the beginning of 19X1 and was replaced by a manager who was paid a salary of £25,000 for 19X1. The ability of the new manager is such that he is expected to improve the firm's future performance in excess of the extra £15,000 a year he is being paid. However, it will take time to bring about the improvement and none of the benefits will be apparent by the end of 19X1. The accounting profit for 19X1 will, other things remaining equal, fall by £15,000 as a result of the firm appointing a more efficient manager. Another example would be if Irwin Company had decided to improve the skill of its production workers by embarking on a three-year training programme costing £15,000 per year. It estimates that the resultant increased efficiency will reduce production costs from 19X2 onwards far in excess of the cost of the training programme. Again the current cost would normally be considered as an expense which would cause accounting profit in 19X1 to fall by

£15,000. In either of these examples if the extra expense of the manager's salary or the training cost had not been incurred but had, for example, been left in the bank, then the balance sheet cash figure would be £15,000 higher and the retained profit figure would also be £15,000 higher. This is because the accounting value concept does not recognise these future benefits as assets.

How relevant then is the information in conventional accounting statements to an investor making a decision whether to invest or disinvest in the firm? If the information is to be relevant it should enable the investor to make a reasonable judgement about the firm's future because it is from future returns that he will derive his benefits, i.e. dividends. This judgement can only be based on information relating to estimates of future performance and conventional accounting statements do not satisfy this requirement. It is possible that references may be made in the Chairman's report accompanying the balance sheet to events in the current year such as the development of a new product which may have an effect on future performance but it is rare that these are quantified.

Balance Sheet of Irwin Co. at 31 December 19X1

Fixed Assets	£000s	£000s	*Likely valuation base*
Land – freehold	100		Original cost or realisable value
Buildings	80		Original cost less accumulated depreciation
Machinery	60		,,
Vehicles	40		,,
		280	
Current Assets			
Inventory	70		Lower of cost or realisable value
Debtors	90		,,
Cash	20		
	180		
Current Liabilities			Amount of liability incurred
Creditors	70		
Tax payable	30		,,
Dividend payable	10		,,
	110		
Net Current Assets		70	
		£350	
Financed by:			
Owners' Equity			
Ordinary shares, 60,000 at £1	60		Nominal value
Share premium	40		Excess of issue price over nominal value
Retained profits	200		Profits not paid out as dividends
		300	
Long-term Liabilities			Amount of liability incurred
Debentures 12%		50	
		£350	

Figure 9.1

In Chapter 1 we considered various approaches to valuation and in Chapter 2 it was shown that original cost was the generally accepted accounting approach. Nevertheless there is evidence that relevance to the needs of users is beginning to influence the valuations in the balance sheet.[1] Land and buildings, for example, are increasingly being revalued using current market prices, either annually or at less frequent intervals[2] (see also App. D.3, note 8). The contents of Chapter 8 showed that in the U.K. as in other countries the problems of inflation are giving rise to adjustments to the use of original cost as evidence of value. These adjustments for inflation are a means of improving the approach to the valuation of individual assets or liabilities which have arisen out of transactions and are not an attempt to give an overall revaluation of the firm. The problem of improving published accounting information is considered further in Chapter 17. Some aspects of accounting bases and policies are discussed below and finally we consider alternative approaches to the valuation of the firm.

IMPLICATION OF ALTERNATIVE ACCOUNTING BASES

It has been explained in earlier chapters that one of the criticisms of accounting information is that even within generally accepted accounting principles there are often several acceptable alternative ways of valuing an asset or liability. The following are examples of possibilities that are available.

Land   Valued at cost or a valuation based on an assessment of current market value.

Buildings }
Machinery } Depreciation bases can be, for example, straight-line, reducing-balance or usage method.
Vehicles }

Inventory   Varying assumptions on flow of costs such as treatment of overheads and FIFO, LIFO, etc.

This is not an exhaustive list of the policies available to the firm but clearly the alternatives shown will result in different valuations for the individual asset. One of the ways in which accounting information could be seen to be more reliable would be if the accounting profession standardised the acceptable bases and policies, thus introducing more uniformity by reducing the number of acceptable methods of valuation.[3,4] For example, all firms could be required to adopt FIFO for inventory valuation and a straight-line basis of depreciating fixed assets. This approach would remove many difficulties in comparing different firms' reported results, but firms may feel that they will not then be in a position to reflect adequately their individual situations. An alternative to uniformity is that firms are allowed to use various bases but that they must disclose the bases they have adopted (see App. D.3, note 1). If the effect of using different bases is material it would not be sufficient merely to disclose the bases used, the effect of using the alternative bases on the reported profit should then be quantified.

Another problem area is the interpretation of the going concern concept. Unless the firm is likely to be broken up and sold asset by asset, the user of financial statements is interested in the value of the firm as an entity rather than individual assets. However even where it is not the current intention to break up the firm, useful information may be provided from the values of the individual assets. The balance sheets of most banking firms, for example, include, in the valuation of their fixed assets, branch offices situated on prime sites in town centres. As long as the firm intends to continue operating in the banking business there is some justification for recording these assets at cost. It would, however, be of interest to shareholders to know the value which, say, a retailer was prepared to pay for the sites of the bank's branches. This may, for example, give an indication of the opportunity cost of the firm continuing to apply its resources to banking. As explained earlier, in most situations the balance sheet gives only a partial view of the firm's value. Before we examine alternative approaches to the valuation of a firm, we consider the treatment of goodwill which is an exception to this accounting approach of taking into consideration only individual resources.

9.3   Goodwill

When used in the context of valuing a firm the term goodwill is often used to cover the variety of qualities or assets which contribute to the value of the firm but because of the fundamental accounting concepts are not normally shown in the balance sheet. Some of these qualities and assets have been referred to in previous chapters, e.g. a product monopoly, a long-term government contract, a reputation with customers, relationships with employees, or an efficient management team. Where these assets are such that they give the firm a comparative advantage over other firms in selling its products they are what the economist would define as the source of super-normal profits. In some cases such assets will have been acquired as a result of a firm's strategy and by incurring costs such as research or advertising. In other cases they may be the result of a fortunate situation, e.g. where geographical accident makes the firm's position strong compared with its competitors.

There is a situation where goodwill may appear in a balance sheet. This is when some outside agency, usually another firm, has purchased the goodwill. This normally only occurs when one firm acquires another. Ex. 9.1 shows how this might apply to the Irwin Co.

Example 9.1
The balance sheet shown in Fig. 9.1 records that the value of the owners' equity is £300,000. Suppose that the owners accept an offer of £400,000 from another firm, the Ideal Co., to acquire the Irwin Co. as an entity, including all its assets and liabilities. The Ideal Co. intends to operate the Irwin Co. as a department within its own organisation. In the balance sheet of Ideal Co. the assets and liabilities acquired in the takeover would be added to those it already owned (see Sect. 16.5 for more details of consolidated financial statements). Assuming that the £400,000 was paid in cash then the cash balance in Ideal Co.'s accounts would be reduced by £400,000 but if the assets and liabilities acquired are recorded at the values shown in Irwin's balance sheet, there is a difference of £100,000 which represents the excess of the purchase price over the balance sheet value of the firm. This excess would normally be shown as goodwill in Ideal's balance sheet. However this definition of goodwill, which we will term accounting goodwill may not be identical in concept to the notion of goodwill in the previous paragraph.

There are many reasons why a purchaser may be prepared to pay more than the balance sheet value of the firm being purchased. One is that the selling price or replacement cost of the assets recorded in the balance sheet may be greater than their balance sheet value, so that the takeover price is merely reflecting current market selling or replacement prices. Another is that the purchaser will obtain assets which are not recorded in the balance sheet such as an efficient management team, a monopoly position, or a range of products. There is also the possibility of benefits from synergy where the combination of the purchaser's firm with that being bought provides extra benefits as from vertical and horizontal integration which could not be achieved if the firms operated separately.

There are several points of interest arising out of Ex. 9.1. When the Ideal Co. acquired the Irwin Co. it paid £400,000 for assets and liabilities valued at £300,000 in the balance sheet of the Irwin Co. If the current replacement cost of those assets was say £340,000 then the £100,000 accounting goodwill could be said to be composed of two parts: £40,000 reflecting the undervaluation of assets in the balance sheet and £60,000 which reflects the other qualities and assets mentioned in our original definition of, goodwill at the beginning of this section and which are not normally included in balance sheets. If the goodwill existed before the takeover, then it seems inconsistent to recognise it in the accounts of the Ideal Co. as if it had suddenly materialised. This is highlighted if we consider an identical company to Irwin which had not been taken over and in whose balance sheet the goodwill was not recognised. The argument in defence of these procedures is that it is possible to recognise it in the takeover situation because someone, in this case Ideal Co., has valued and purchased the goodwill. As there has been a transaction a formerly subjective valuation now becomes an objective valuation. There is some justification for this line of argument because the valuation of Irwin Co. by Ideal Co. may be different to that by any other purchaser or even by Irwin's managers. This is particularly true where the benefits of synergy are obtained.

If Ideal Co. had spent £100,000 on training schemes to improve its employees' efficiency, or on improving its competitive position, or on better industrial relations, this would not normally appear as an asset. However, if it purchased a firm which owned these types of assets they could appear in the balance sheet as goodwill. The inclusion of goodwill in some situations but not others illustrates the inconsistency in reporting which, as previously discussed, adds to the problems of the user of financial statements.

VALUING GOODWILL

There are two approaches to the valuation of goodwill. The first is that an attempt is made to measure the value of the assets normally excluded from the balance sheet, e.g. equivalent to the £60,000 in Ex. 9.1. The second approach is to value the firm as an entity and then the accounting goodwill is the difference between this value and the balance-sheet value of the assets. As in Ex. 9.1 we could split the accounting goodwill into two parts. In a takeover situation the second view seems most appropriate in that it is the value of the firm as a whole that the buyer is chiefly interested in and this depends on how the resources of the firm can be combined to produce future benefits (see Sects 9.5 and 12.6 for discussion of how these benefits can be quantified). It is unlikely that a valuation derived from considering overall future benefits can then be attributed to individual assets. If the £400,000 purchase price in Ex. 9.1 is based on the present value of potential future benefits, it would probably be impossible to attribute it to individual assets in Irwin Co.'s balance sheet in Fig. 9.1 by revaluing each asset to show their individual contribution to the firm's profitability.

Including specific goodwill resources as individual assets would not solve the problem because items such as a monopoly position, efficient management or customer relations are usually only valuable in their use in conjunction with other assets. Thus it is unlikely that attempting to value each asset, even including goodwill resources, would add up to the value of the firm as considered by a takeover bidder, but it might be an appropriate starting point in such a valuation. It is apparent from this discussion of goodwill that it may arise from the elements of the firm which are difficult to quantify as individual resources and that the problem is normally not how to value goodwill but how to value the firm as a whole. It is this problem that is now considered further.

9.4   Valuation of the Firm by means of Share Prices

The firm's shares represent the owners' equity of a firm, and, where there is a share market, the market price of the shares gives a market value for the firm. Shares are bought and sold either privately, where a buyer finds a specific shareholder willing to sell, or through a recognised Stock Exchange.[5] The prices at which shares are bought and sold depend on the supply and demand for those shares. If in Fig. 9.1 the current stock exchange price of the Irwin Co. ordinary shares was £6.50 each then the total market value of the firm appears to be £390,000. A valuation for the firm arrived at in this way must be treated with caution. The daily market price of a share represents a marginal value based on the current supply and demand. It may not be representative of the price were a large block of shares to be supplied or demanded. Thus an owner of say 20,000 shares in Irwin Co. may say that his holding is worth £130,000 but if he tried to sell them all at the same time he might not be able to obtain the current market price of £6.50 each. Nevertheless the stock exchange price is a guide to overall valuation. A takeover bidder, for example, would normally have to offer at least this market value to persuade a shareholder to sell his shares. There are now three valuations of the Irwin Co.: the balance sheet value of £300,000, the takeover price of £400,000 and the £390,000 based on current market share prices. Assuming the share market does not know of the takeover bid then the current share prices may differ from the takeover bidder's price because of the latter's assessment of the firm's value to him. If the takeover bid is known to the market then the share price may rise until it is close to the takeover price of £6.67 per share (i.e. £400,000 ÷ 60,000 shares). It may even move higher than £6.67 if the market's opinion is that the bidder will eventually have to pay a higher price than £400,000 for all the shares.

This section has been concerned with the use of the market prices of shares to value the firm as a whole. This procedure does not help where there is not a market for a firm's shares, nor does it provide a criterion for judging whether this valuation of the firm is satisfactory. To arrive at such a criterion we would need to know much more about how the supply and demand for a share is generated and thus how the share price is arrived at. In fact we are back to the question posed in Chapter 1, i.e. what is value?

9.5   Basis of Valuation for Decision-making

The need for an acceptable model of value for the firm has been well rehearsed throughout the first part of the book. Value is the basis for profit measurement and thus for the most commonly accepted means of assessing performance. The external users of financial information require an appropriate measure of value and profit on which to base decisions in relation to their involvement with the firm. The management of the firm must also know what basis of valuation these external users use so that they can take it into consideration when choosing among alternative courses of action. Original cost, which is the valuation base for most balance-sheet items, is a market price but related to the time of the original transaction. Replacement cost and selling price are market prices relevant at the time of making the valuation. Future utility appears to be an alternative not relying on market prices but considering and assessing the qualities inherent in the asset or firm to be valued.

The problems of using market prices whether they are original or current have been discussed in earlier chapters with regard to individual assets and in this chapter in relation to the firm as a whole. One of the major problems in both cases is the difficulty of assessing a market price where the asset or firm is not frequently bought and sold; for example, a production line which is specific to the firm, or assets which do not normally appear in the balance sheet such as quality of the product or reputation with customers. For the firm as a whole the problem is more obvious in that there is not a market for firms in the normal sense of the term. There is the possibility of a market for the firm's shares if they happen to be quoted on a stock exchange.

In attempting to value a firm it seems necessary to have some form of valuation model.[6] It should be noted that even if there is an existing recognised market such as for share prices, it may still be useful to have such a model. It would, for example, be useful to anyone deciding whether to buy or sell shares to have a model which assessed the value of shares independently of the market price. Similarly, anyone considering acquiring a firm must assess whether the market share price is a fair value or whether it is worth while to pay more than the market value. It will also be important for a manager of a firm to be able to assess the effect on the value of the firm of his choice between alternative courses of action. Another situation is where a firm having been privately owned wishes to raise finance by selling shares to the public. In fixing the initial price at which the shares will be offered, it is necessary to place a value on the firm. We must now attempt to identify the components of a valuation model suitable for making such decisions.

A Valuation Model

In assessing the health of an individual, one is concerned with the length and quality of his life in the future. In valuing a firm similarly one is concerned with the benefits to be received by the firm in the future. Therefore a simple valuation model could be:

$$V = f(a, r, n)$$

where V = value, and is a function of a (future expected benefits), r (method of transforming future into present values (see App. C), and n (future life of the firm).

The model describes the value of the firm as being dependent on a, the benefits receivable over n, the remaining life of the firm and includes r, an adjustment to allow for the timing of the benefits. The relationship between the variables could be expressed mathematically as:

$$V = \frac{a_0}{(1 + r)^0} + \frac{a_1}{(1 + r)^1} \cdots \frac{a_n}{(1 + r)^n}$$

which can be summarised as:

$$V = \sum_{t=0}^{n} \frac{a_t}{(1 + r)^t}$$

and where $a_0, a_1, a_2, \ldots a_n$ refer to benefits in period 0, 1, 2 etc., and n is the number of periods in the future life of the firm.

Example 9.2

A simple example of the operation of the model would be where a firm is set up to last only three years and is expected to receive £1000 at the end of each of the three years. The total benefits are £3000, which after adjustment at 10% show that the present value is £2487, i.e.

$$\frac{1000}{(1.10)^1} + \frac{1000}{(1.10)^2} + \frac{1000}{(1.10)^3} = £2487 \text{ (App. C explains methods of calculation)}$$

The model may enable us to identify the factors determining value but may be difficult to use in practical situations because of difficulties in forecasting values for the variables. When applied to the valuation of the firm the future benefits should refer to cash flows to the firm as a result of its activities. As was shown in Sect. 3.9 this would not be the same as accounting profits.

The model could also be applied to the valuation of a share where the variables in the model could be: V, the share value to be assessed; d, the future benefits which to a shareholder are the dividends he will receive while he holds the share, and a final benefit of the selling price when he sells it; r, the shareholders' cost of finance (see Sect. 7.8), and n, the length of time the shareholder intends to hold the share.

The relationship between the variables is expressed as:

$$V = \sum_{t=0}^{n} \frac{d_t}{(1 + r)^t}$$

The use of this share valuation model is the basis for much of our analysis of planning decisions in Part II. If we assume the objective of shareholders is to maximise their wealth, managers taking decisions on behalf of shareholders must understand the effect of their decisions on the shareholders' wealth. The way in which the decisions of the firm effect the shareholders' wealth is through changes in their future dividends and we would expect the firm to attempt to maximise the present value of expected future dividends. In terms of this model this means maximising the current share value. As we can see the term 'profit' has not been used when talking about the objectives of the firm but as the objectives of the shareholder is to maximise the change in value of their shares any change in value could be termed the 'shareholders' profit'. However difficult the problem of forecasting future values of the variables it will be necessary to forecast in making decisions affecting the future. The investor in shares is only concerned with what the investment will yield in the future. He may use past data as a guide but his decision inevitably requires a forecast of future returns. Similarly a takeover bidder is interested in the future benefits he can expect from the purchase of a firm and this could be the estimated extra cash flows he could earn as a result of the takeover. The assessment of the performance of a firm in, say, the past year implies an analysis of the future because if the objective is to improve value by increasing profit then according to our definitions of value and profit the profit in one year is dependent on value at the beginning and end of the year. Therefore to properly assess last year's profit requires a measurement of the value of the firm at the end of the year, which according to our model requires estimates of the future benefits.

The assessment and valuation of the future benefits and hence the value of the firm may well differ, depending on who is making the assessment. This will occur for several reasons. One is that the level of information and expertise will differ from person to person. Another occurs in a takeover situation where synergy is present. In addition the valuation will differ because of the attitude to the risk implied in the forecasts. For example, an investor with a gambling streak may put a higher value on a set of predicted dividends than a more conservative investor, even though the predictions are made by a third, independent party.

The analysis of future benefits will inevitably imply a degree of subjective judgement. We have seen that a major influence on the nature of published accounting information is the emphasis placed on the importance of objective evidence. This emphasis has resulted in reliance on historical information. There may thus be a dichotemy between accounting information for published financial statements and that for internal decision-making. Because investors or lenders do not normally have access to internal management information they will normally rely on information published by the firm. This is discussed further in Chapter 17.

9.6 Example of Alternative Approaches to Valuation

To conclude this chapter and Part I we give an example which illustrates the different profit figures which could result from using the alternative approaches to valuation introduced in Chapter 1 and discussed throughout Part I.

Example 9.3
Mr Illingworth starts a firm with £1600 cash on January 1 19X1. The cash was withdrawn from his building society where the current return is 8% per annum. He buys a removals van, at a cost of £1600, which he intends to hire out. He estimates that he will keep the van for nine years at which time it could be sold for £700 and that the firm's annual net cash flows (i.e. hire charges less expenses) from hiring will be £200. During 19X1 the firm does earn a net cash flow of £200 and at the end of the year the estimated replacement cost of a similar one-year-old van is £1550 and the estimated selling price is £1450. From this data we will calculate alternative profit measurements for 19X1 using: (*a*) original cost, i.e. conventional accounting profit; (*b*) replacement cost; (*c*) selling price; and (*d*) future utility.

The above calculations will be made for each of the following three alternative assumptions, made on the 31 December 19X1. Throughout the calculations assume a stable monetary unit.

(1) Mr Illingworth's initial estimates are appropriate.
(2) He has managed to obtain a contract for eight years which he estimates will increase his annual net cash flow to £250.
(3) He fears increased competition will reduce his future annual cash flows to £150.

Assumption 1—Initial estimates appropriate

	V_0 Value at 1/1/X1 £	V_1 Value at 31/12/X1 £	$V_1 - V_0$ Profit £
(*a*) Original Cost			
Van	1600 (Note 1)	1600	
Accumulated depreciation	—	100	
		1500	
Cash	—	200	
	1600	1700	100

(Depreciation is calculated using a straight-line basis.)

			$V_1 - V_0$
(b) *Replacement cost*			Profit
Van	1600	1550	
	(Note 1)		
Cash	—	200	
	1600	1750	150
(c) *Selling Price*			
Van	1600	1450	
	(Note 1)		
Cash	—	200	
	1600	1650	50
(d) *Future Utility*			
Van	1600	1528	
	(Note 2)	(Note 2)	
Cash	—	200	
	1600	1728	128

Notes: (1) It is assumed that at the precise time of purchase the original cost, replacement cost and selling price are identical. (2) The calculation of the value of the van to the firm using future utility with a discount rate of 8% which is Mr Illingworth's cost of finance:

At 1 January 19X1:

Present value of £200 each year for 9 years	£1250
Present value of resale value of £700 at end of 9 years	350
	£1600

At 31 December 19X1:

Present value of £200 each year for further 8 years	£1150
Present value of resale value of £700 at end of 8 years	378
	£1528

Assumption 2—Contract obtained

		$V_1 - V_0$ Profit
		£
(a)	Original cost – as for (1)	100
(b)	Replacement cost – as for (1)	150
(c)	Selling price – as for (1)	50
	(Assuming that obtaining the contract has no effect on estimate of market selling price of the van)	

(d) Future utility

	V_0	V_1	
Van	1600	1815	
		(Note 3)	
Cash	—	200	
	1600	2015	415

Note: (3) Present value of £250 per year for a further 8 years   £1437

Present value of resale value of £700 at end of 8 years   378

£1815

Assumption 3—Increased competition

		$V_1 - V_0$ Profit £
(a) Original cost – as for (1) and (2)		100
(b) Replacement cost – as for (1) and (2)		150
(c) Selling price – as for (1) and (2)		50
(d) Future utility:		

	V_0	V_1	
Van	1600	1241	
		(Note 4)	
Cash	—	200	
	1600	1441	−159

Note: (4) Present value of £150 per year for a further 8 years	£863
Present value of £700 at end of 8 years	378
	£1241

Comments on Example 9.3

The purpose of this example is to illustrate how value and profit would be calculated under the alternative approaches introduced in Chapter 1 and to illustrate the effect on the calculations of changes in future conditions. The table below summarises the alternative profit calculations for 19X1.

	Original cost	Replacement cost	Selling price	Future utility
Assumption 1	£100	£150	£50	£128
Assumption 2	100	150	50	415
Assumption 3	100	150	50	−159

The paragraphs which follow highlight a number of significant points which arise out of Ex. 9.3:

The value and profit calculated under original cost, replacement cost and selling price do not vary despite the alternative assumptions described in (1), (2) and (3). The value and profit figures under the future utility calculation reflect the improved position in (2) and the worse position in (3). This occurs because the first three approaches measure the value of only some of the individual assets using past and current market figures, e.g. in (2) the contract is not included as an asset. The future utility values not the assets themselves but the present value of their overall future contribution to the firm. For example, it is not the value of the van which increases when he obtains the contract under assumption (2) but the value of the firm which consists of the van plus the contract.

The future utility approach may provide better information on which to base decisions. The increase of profit under future utility from £128 in (1) to £415 in (2) is a measure of the extra value of the contract to the firm, i.e. £287 (£415–£128). This would give an indication of how much the firm might be prepared to pay to buy such a contract if it could be purchased. On the other hand in (3) the revision of future prospects indicates a loss of £159 for 19X1. This suggests that it may not be worth while to continue the business. This suggestion is confirmed by a comparison of the value in (3) (*d*) of £1241, with that under (3) (*c*) which shows a current selling price of £1450. In these circumstances using financial criteria only it would be better to sell the van and go into some other business.

Future utility may also provide better information for purposes of control. If we wish to appraise the performance of a manager – e.g. in terms of obtaining new contracts – we would expect the profit to reflect how well he has done during a period of time. It is only the future utility approach under assumption (2), which reflects his success in obtaining the contract and in (3) his failure to maintain the potential future benefits of the firm. The use of profit for Planning and Control is discussed in Parts II and III.

It is not true to say that the original cost relies entirely on past data. The depreciation calculation is based on an estimate of useful life for the asset and its selling price at the end of that life. Thus changes in these estimates will affect current profit as they will change the depreciation expense. In Ex. 9.3 these estimates did not change as it was the estimate of net cash flows into the firm which changed.

The cost of finance of the owner is said to be 8%. None of the approaches as illustrated adequately allows for the opportunity cost of the finance used in this firm.[7] At 8% this can be calculated as £128 in 19X1, i.e. 8% of £1600 the sum which was introduced to start the firm. The future utility calculation in (1) (*d*) discounting at 8% showed V_0 to be £1600. This means that if Mr Illingworth's estimates are correct the firm will yield 8% each year, hence the profit of £128 for 19X1 in (1) (*d*). Although the calculations show a profit under each alternative the fact that the firm could be earning £128 elsewhere in 19X1 using the value of the asset tied up in the firm, shows that it is dangerous to evaluate a firm out of the context of the alternative opportunities for its finance. An economist's analysis might show that Mr Illingworth has not made a profit but that he had earned a normal return on his capital. Alternatively, if the firm had borrowed the £1600 at 8% from the bank then the cost of finance would appear in the profit statement as bank interest. The effect of this on the profit figures in (1) would be:

	Original cost	Replacement cost	Selling price	Future utility
	£	£	£	£
Profit in (1)	100	150	50	128
Cost of finance	128	128	128	128
Profit	− 28	22	− 78	—

The future utility calculation of a nil profit shows that the owner is no better off than if he had left the money in the building society. One of the reasons why the cost of the owner's finance is not included as an expense of the firm whereas the cost of borrowing is included in the profit statement is the application of the entity concept (see Sect. 2.5). This recognises only costs incurred by the firm and not those incurred by the owners on the firm's behalf.

Given the variety of results shown in Ex. 9.3 it may seem important to be able to say which is the best approach to measurement of value and profit. It is appropriate to quote here some of the comments made at the beginning of Sect. 1.2 on the 'Objectives of measurement':

The question of what information accounting attempts to measure is perhaps best illustrated by reference to the needs of users of the information

and

It is likely that the different users will be interested in different aspects of the accounting information

and

If accounting is to provide an adequate service then accounting measurement . . . should be concerned with the needs of these users.

Thus the decision on the best measure must be related to the objectives of the users of the information. These objectives will vary and so will the choice of the best measure. The strength and the weakness of the future utility approach is that it considers the future performance of the firm. This makes it appropriate for decisions concerning future activities such as buying or selling shares in the firm. It also means that the figures are subjective and difficult to corroborate and where this is of great importance, say in assessing taxes, then an alternative measure may be preferred.

9.7 Summary

This chapter continued the analysis of value and profit by considering possible measures of the overall value of the firm. The possibilities of using accounting balance sheets or share prices as a basis for valuation were considered. The section on a valuation model for decision-making concluded that the most appropriate model would be based on estimates of future costs and benefits. However, as we have seen throughout Part I the emphasis on objective evidence results in accounting information for external users being largely of a historical nature. In Parts II and III, which are concerned with the analysis of decisions for planning and control, we shall explore further the appropriateness of historical data for decision-making.

Notes and References

1. Sandilands, *Inflation Accounting—Report of the Inflation Accounting Committee*, Cmnd 6225 (H.M.S.O., 1975) chap. 8.
2. *Survey of Published Accounts 1973–74* (General Educational Trust of the Institute of Chartered Accountants in England and Wales 1974).
3. P. Bird, *Accountability: Standards in Financial Reporting* (London, Haymarket, 1973).
4. P. Bird, 'Standard Accounting Practice', in *Debits, Credits, Finance and Profits*, ed. H. C. Edey and B. S. Yamey (London, Sweet & Maxwell, 1974).
5. For a description of stock market operations see J. Freear, *Financing Decisions in Business* (London, Haymarket, 1973).
6. B. Carsberg, *Analysis for Investment Decisions* (London, Haymarket, 1974). B. Carsberg, 'The Role of the Valuation Model in the Analysis of Investment Decisions' in H. C. Edey and B. S. Yamey (eds), op. cit.
7. W. T. Baxter, *Depreciation* (London, Sweet & Maxwell, 1971) chap. 8.

Further Reading

H. C. Edey, 'The Nature of Profit', *Accounting and Business Research* no. 1 (Winter 1970).
E. Stamp and C. Marley, *Accounting Principles and the City Code: The Case for Reform* (London, Butterworth, 1970).
E. O. Edwards and P. W. Bell, *The Theory and Measurement of Business Income* (Berkeley, Calif., University of California, 1961).
H. C. Edey, 'Accounting Principles and Business Reality', *Accountancy* (July 1963), reprinted in *Modern Financial Management*, ed. B. V. Carsberg and H. C. Edey (Penguin Books, 1969).
Arthur Andersen & Co., *Objectives of Financial Statements for Business Enterprises* (Chicago, Arthur Andersen & Co., 1972).

R. H. Parker and G. C. Harcourt, *Readings in the Concept and Measurement of Income* (Cambridge, Cambridge University Press, 1969).

H. C. Edey, 'The True and Fair View', *Accountancy* (August 1971).

T. A. Lee, 'Goodwill, an Example of Will o' the Wisp Accounting', *Accounting and Business Research* (Autumn 1971).

G. Macdonald, *Profit Measurement: Alternatives to Historical Cost* (London, Haymarket, 1974).

T. A. Lee, *Income and Value Measurement: Theory and Practice* (London, Nelson, 1974).

Accounting Standards Steering Committee, *The Corporate Report* (Accounting Standards Steering Committee, 1975).

Questions and Problems

9.1   What do you understand by the following terminology?

Accounting concepts	Goodwill
Accounting bases	Accounting goodwill
Accounting policies	Synergy
Takeover	Valuation model
	Cost of finance
	Normal return

9.2   What would be the most appropriate procedures for valuing the following as individual assets?

   (a)   a monopoly
   (b)   good customer relationships
   (c)   efficient management
   (d)   harmonious industrial relations

9.3   What are the advantages and disadvantages of the use of original cost as a measure of value and profit?

9.4   Shown below is the balance sheet of the Ironside Co. at 31 December 19X1 after its first year of operation as a producer of aero-engines. The columns A and B represent alternative balance-sheet figures. Both A and B are calculated using generally accepted accounting principles.

		A		B
Fixed Assets	£000s	£000s	£000s	£000s
Research and development	30		—	
Land	50		40	
Machinery	60		50	
Vehicles	15		10	
		155		100
Current Assets				
Raw materials	20		18	
Work in progress	33		20	
Finished goods	15		12	
Debtors	22		20	
Cash	30		30	
	120		100	
Current Liabilities				
Creditors	15		20	
Net Current Assets		105		80
		£260		£180

Financed by:		
Owners' Equity		
Ordinary Shares	200	200
Profit	60	
Loss	—	20
	£260	£180

Give an explanation of how the difference in the figures in A and B might have arisen. Can both give a true and fair view of the company's position?

9.5 Shown below are the summarised balance sheets of the Imperial Co. and the Iota Co. at 31 December 19X1:

	Imperial Co.	Iota Co.
	£000s	£000s
Fixed assets	140	110
Net current assets	220	30
	360	140
Ordinary shares	300	100
Retained profits	60	40
	360	140

On 1 January 19X2 Imperial Co. acquired the whole of the Iota Co. for £200,000 cash which was paid to the ordinary shareholders of the Iota Co. Show the balance sheet of the Imperial Co. immediately after the acquisition.

9.6 Share prices often fluctuate daily. Is it possible to justify the use of share prices to value a firm?

Part II

PLANNING

10
Concepts of Planning

10.1 Introduction

In Chapter 1 we established that the chief objective of accounting is to provide a measurement process for the firm. Part I was mainly concerned with the measurement of past performance especially for the presentation of financial statements. In Part II we are concerned with problems of measurement of information as a basis for planning decisions.

According to the dictionary, to plan is to 'arrange beforehand'. When applied to a business this does not mean it can arrange the future but that it can arrange beforehand what it intends to do. The concept of planning used in this book is that the planning process will involve the determination of objectives, the identification and measurement of the effects of alternatives and a decision to choose between alternatives. Part II of the book is concerned with an analysis of this explanation of planning. The planning process is illustrated in Fig. 10.1 and the elements of the diagram form the basis for the chapters in Part II. This chapter considers several general planning issues such as objectives, strategies and data for planning. In Chapter 11 the important decision-making areas of pricing and output are analysed and in Chapter 12 we consider the long-term investment of resources. Chapter 13 deals with the overall effect of decisions from Chapters 10, 11 and 12 expressed in the form of budgets as a means of detailed planning for the total firm, as opposed to sectional decision-making.

Also included in Fig. 10.1 is a reference to control processes. A simple definition of 'control' is that it is the process of checking to see how plans are being carried out and how far the objectives are being achieved. There are close links between planning and control and in practice it may be difficult to distinguish one process from the other. It is merely for ease of exposition that we have separated the two topics and devoted Part III to the general subject of control. The relevance of these aspects of business to accounting is that most plans use accounting information as their data base and the design and implementation of systems of control is usually one of the functions of the accountant. In Chapter 4 the design of accounting systems was seen in the context of the need for information for measurement and the need for planning information is also an influence on design of the system.

The planning process adopted will differ from business to business but set out in Fig. 10.1 is what might be considered to be acceptable generalised elements of the process.

In order to illustrate the application of Fig. 10.1 and its terminology, it may be useful to consider a simple and familiar example of a planning decision before going on to look at the components of the process in more detail. Let us examine

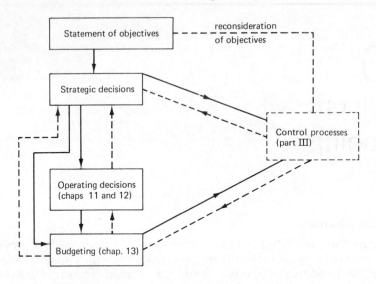

Figure 10.1   The planning process

the attendance at an interview in Newcastle by a man who lives in London. The words in italics in the following explanation relate to particular elements of Fig. 10.1. Assuming the *objective* is to improve the man's prospects and the new job is the means of achieving it. There are different levels of decision to be taken in connection with achieving objectives. The *strategic decision* to change jobs (rather than, say, attempting to be promoted by his present employer), is of more significance than, say, the decision of how to get to Newcastle. The latter is an *operating decision*, i.e. whether to take the car or travel by public transport. The man does not want to drive so a further decision between bus and train has to be made. The bus is cheaper but takes longer so he decides to go by train. The journey has to be planned in detail so that he knows which station to go to, what time the train leaves, and what changes if any have to be made. This is equivalent to the *budgeting* stage in a firm. If everything goes smoothly he will arrive in Newcastle and at the interview at the planned time. However, things may go wrong; for example, the taxi to the station may be held up in traffic, the times of the trains may have altered, or the train may be slowed up because of fog. The *process of control* is the activity of checking what is actually happening with what was planned and the feeding back of information to the decision-maker so that he can amend his plans if necessary. The dashed lines in Fig. 10.1 represent the feedback of control information to enable replanning to take place. This replanning may mean simply switching to a different train, or more seriously, going on a different day or even cancelling the journey altogether. This in turn may lead to a reconsideration of strategy if the job is given to someone else because our man did not arrive for his interview.

In the situation discussed above, it would have been possible to go to the interview without explicitly going through the process in Fig. 10.1. The man could have applied for the job in Newcastle without considering his objectives for doing so and he could have set out without considering how to get there. This could clearly have been an unfortunate experience if, for example, he went to the wrong station or to the wrong train. We have illustrated the benefits for an individual from planning and it is the benefits for a firm that are now considered further.

10.2 Benefits from Planning

In Chapter 1 it was stated that the current health or value of an individual or a firm was determined as much by what was going to happen as to what had already happened. Efficient planning will not only improve future performance, it may also be reflected in current values.

The alternatives open to a firm are not necessarily planning or no planning but rather a formal planning process as outlined in Fig. 10.1 or *ad hoc* planning on a day-to-day basis. One answer to the question of why should a firm plan, is that it is better for the firm to have some idea of where it is going. This argument has an intuitive appeal but it is very difficult to prove that a firm has benefited from planning because of the many variables which affect the firm's environment and its success or failure.

There is evidence[1] that a firm which survives successfully over a long period is one which adapts to changing circumstances. Those which stay with the same products or markets tend not to survive and those which are successful over long periods are often vastly different firms as regards products and markets at the end of such periods.

A firm which regularly reviews its long-term strategy will be more likely to see that it must change direction to succeed. There are numerous examples of declining industries, in the U.K., for example, cotton textiles or shipbuilding, and of relatively new industries, such as computers, nylon textiles or North Sea oil exploration; and examples of declining products, such as gas-lighting or valve radio sets, and new products, such as micro-electronics or domestic deep freezers. Many firms which did not realise they were in declining industries or selling declining products have gone out of business. There is no way a firm can accurately foretell the future, but it may be able to adapt more quickly to changes if it is part of its planning process to attempt to look for and identify such changes.

In addition there are benefits from short-term planning. Detailed short-term planning is usually called budgeting. This may highlight, for example, production bottlenecks, the need for extra credit facilities or the existence of unused capacity. These benefits are considered further in Chapter 13.

10.3 Statement of Objectives

In Fig. 10.1 the first step in the planning process was to state objectives. This seems to be an obvious starting-point and yet it is one which is often neglected. It may also seem at first sight to be an easy thing to do, but we shall see that it can be a complex problem. The absence of a stated objective means that the firm has no criterion against which to evaluate its success or failure or to use in the process of choosing between alternative activities.

One of the problems in stating objectives for a firm is that only people involved with the firm can have objectives, not the firm itself. If this is accepted, then it is obviously possible that there is more than one relevant objective. In a one-man business the objective is determined by the one man. Even here, it may not be clear cut if he sees possible alternative objectives; for example, maximising profit, security for his family or fair play for the customers. The problem is compounded in a larger organisation if these alternative objectives belong to different individuals or groups. There is not necessarily any reason to suppose that the objectives of owners, managers and workers should be the same. There is also a growing acceptance that company objectives should not be determined without regard to the interests of society.

The most commonly stated objectives are those formulated in terms of profits. Maximised profits, increased profits or satisfactory profits are alternative versions of this objective. It should be made clear whether reference is being made to conventional accounting profit or to profit calculated as the change in the present value of future utility. If accounting profits are used, then this could refer to short-term or long-term profits. It may be necessary to accept reduced accounting profits in the short term to obtain higher profits later. It is because the measurement of accounting profit excludes prospective but unrealised gains from the calculation that the distinction between short term and long term is valid. A measurement of profit using concepts of future utility would include the present value of unrealised benefits so that the distinction between short- and long-term profit is not valid. Ex. 9.3 illustrated the importance of the difference between conventional accounting profit and profits based on future utility. It is obviously of great importance that the firm should have a clear definition of such terms as profit where they are used in its statement of objectives.

A further complication arises when we consider the relationship of the owners of the firm to the firm as an entity. In a one-man business it may be possible to regard the firm's accounting profit as synonymous with earnings which the owner could withdraw and spend on his own consumption. Where ownership is represented by shares held in a company there are normally two ways in which the owner or shareholder can realise his earnings in the company. The first is by means of the dividend paid by the company and the second is by selling some or all of his shares. As discussed in Chapter 9, there will clearly be some relationship between the amount of dividends paid, the market value of the shares, and the performance of the company. Thus an alternative objective for a company could be to maximise (or increase) the size of the dividends and/or the market value of the owners' shares. In either case the shareholder could benefit because he has the cash from the dividend to consume or to invest and he can convert the shares into cash if he wishes. If maximising dividends is considered to be a major objective then in the analysis of planning and decisions the firm should be aware of the effect of the decision on the future dividend stream rather than on accounting profits. By this criterion any decision which increases the present value of the dividend stream is a good decision. It was shown in Chapter 9 that there may be no close relationship between the balance-sheet value of the company and the market valuation as shown by share prices. If the objective is to influence share prices it is obviously necessary to understand the factors affecting the movement of these prices.

Other possible objectives of the firm may be to minimise variations in annual profit. This may lead to decisions to avoid taking risks which in turn may put an upper limit on the firm's present value. If it were left to management and employees to determine the firm's objectives, then the survival of the firm might be given a higher priority than the present value of the firm. There is here the potential for conflict of interests between owners and management and employees whose prime objectives are likely to be high wages and job security.

There are also possible non-economic objectives, such as job satisfaction, power and influence. For example, the owner of an organisation may seek influence with government and industry. Similarly, owners or managers may seek the power that comes with running a large organisation. Clearly personal objectives will be related to motivation as to why people work.

These are some of the possible objectives open to a firm. There are others, but sufficient examples have been given to show that stating objectives can be a complex problem. Inevitably there will be a range of objectives within an organisation and the planner can consider this problem in several ways. For example, he can take profit maximisation over the long-run as his principal objective and see conflicting objectives as constraints on his actions, or he can try to strike an intuitive (as opposed to a quantified) balance between conflicting objectives in making decisions. It is easy to confuse means and ends in this discussion. If profit is the objective chosen, then it is possible to see security of employment, high wages, high dividends, good working conditions, customer satisfaction, as means to that end in the long term, even though they may appear to increase costs and thus reduce profit in the short term. One of the major problems is that many of the possible objectives are extremely difficult to quantify – e.g. employee and customer satisfaction, security, power – so that there is the danger of basing plans, which have to be quantified as budgets, solely on those objectives which are more easily quantified, e.g. profits. In the public sector these problems are even greater because of the increased difficulties of defining benefits and cost related to objectives.[2]

10.4 Strategic and operating Decisions

In Fig. 10.1 decisions have been divided into strategic and operating. Strategic decisions are here defined as those which affect the policy of the organisation and may change its whole orientation. An example of a strategic decision in practice is the Cunard Steam Ship Company's decision in the 1950s to reduce their reliance on shipping and extend their range of activities to include hotels and off-shore drilling equipment. Then in 1971 the Trafalgar House Investments property company expanded its range of activities by taking over Cunard. Both companies had also extended their markets in recent years by involvement in Europe, Africa and the West Indies.

Operating decisions are concerned with making the best use of the business's resources once the strategic decisions have been taken. Thus they are concerned for example with pricing of products, methods of production, raising finance or purchase of machinery. In Chapters 11 and 12 a distinction is also made between short- and long-term decisions. This is chiefly for purposes of explanation as there are particular analytical problems involved in long-term decisions. In practice it may be difficult to distinguish a business's short- or long-term decisions.

It may also be difficult in some situations to distinguish strategic and operating considerations. A strategic decision to open a branch of a firm in Europe may result in operating decisions which show that the project is not feasible. For example, there may not be adequate skilled labour available. Is a decision to build an extension to a factory an operating or a strategic decision? If the company is considering such a step, provided they are aware of all the implications, it does not matter what label is put on the decision. However, the advantage of making the distinction is that it emphasises the importance of strategic decisions. It is possible for a business to go on from year to year without consciously considering objectives or strategy. The decisions made are those which are required by current operations and are essentially operating decisions. It should therefore be a part of planning process to consider at regular intervals the strategic possibilities open to the firm. The very fact that these often imply a change of direction or a different range of products or markets mean that they may not be brought to management's attention in the normal course of events. It is important to recognise that in analysing planning and decision-making that doing nothing or going on as before are decisions. It is also important that the planning process should include a revision of the ongoing effects of past decisions.

One of the major problems in planning is the collection and proper use of relevant data. We are now going to consider four aspects of this problem, forecasting, search methods, motivation and relevant cost concepts.

10.5   Data for Planning – Forecasting

It is stating the obvious to say that planning is concerned with making decisions about what to do in the future. This cannot be done without forecasting events. Even with a certain knowledge of the future it would be possible to make wrong decisions by incorrect analysis but if the forecasts are inaccurate then plans based on them are less likely to yield the required results. The use of the term accurate does not imply absolute precision but the acceptable margin of error depends on the importance of the forecast in the decision.

All forecasting is, to some extent, the application of past experience to future events. However, this covers a wide variety of situations. At one extreme is the actuary, an expert in the application of statistics, especially in the insurance industry. He can predict with great accuracy, for example, the number of births, deaths, thefts or fires that will take place in a given period. This is possible because of two factors: first, there is a vast amount of past evidence to use and, second, because the nature of the events makes it unlikely that the pattern will change unexpectedly in the future. At the other extreme is, for example, the business man trying to predict the demand for a luxury product never previously marketed. There is no past evidence for the product and the future pattern depends on a variety of factors including people's tastes, which are untested. Even here it is unlikely that the business man is working completely in the dark. He may have launched similar products or carried out market surveys to collect evidence on possible demand.

There are various techniques to assist the forecaster, the detailed description of which is beyond the scope of this book.[3] These include the application of statistical time series, regression analysis and simulation models to accumulated data in order to predict future events. However there is no way to ensure that forecasting will be accurate and no amount of sophisticated techniques is any use without intelligent application.

10.6   Data for Planning – Search Methods

The previous section emphasised the importance of accurate information for planning decisions. It is perhaps more important that the right sort of information is estimated. To take a rather obvious example, there is little point having accurate forecasts of the cost of building a factory in Durham if it would in practice be cheaper to build it in Cornwall. The methods by which the firm decides on what information is relevant are of great importance. The process of discovering opportunities to be considered is often called 'Search'.

The concept of opportunity cost is important in the analysis of search methods. Opportunity cost defines the cost of an action as the benefits forgone from not undertaking an alternative action. If the benefits from the action chosen are higher than any opportunity cost, then it is the best action. The term opportunity cost is often restricted to the benefits forgone from not taking the next best alternative. The usefulness of this concept in decision-making is that it highlights the importance of alternative courses of action which might otherwise not be considered.

Where economic theory assumes perfect knowledge this can be interpreted as having knowledge of all possible available alternatives when making a decision.

The decision-maker will have an incomplete knowledge of all possible alternatives and thus there is the danger of taking a course which provides benefits but where there are better though unknown alternatives. The search for information on possible alternatives is not cost-free and thus there is a trade-off between the cost of the search and the potential loss from not finding the best alternative. It is important, especially for strategic decisions, to direct the search at the proper targets and at the right level. For example, if a firm retailing groceries wishes to expand, it may decide to search for new grocery products to market and it may spend time and money evaluating alternative products and finally decide on what appear to be best. However, it may be that a better alternative would be to extend their range of products to include toilet goods or garden equipment. The way in which a search is carried out will often determine the result. If this firm asked their existing store managers for suggestions and if their experience has been solely in the grocery business, it is likely that proposals would be for extending the range of groceries. An expert in retailing might on the other hand suggest the toilet goods or garden equipment. However, someone with an entirely different background might look at the firm and suggest that they sell the valuable sites of their stores and retire, or go into the property business and develop the sites as office space. Successful decision-making relies not only on accurate forecasts of events, but on forecasting in the appropriate area. Successful application depends on how the individual perceives the problem. The results of search procedures may also be influenced by the nature of the data collection and retrieval system used by the firm (see Sect. 4.7.).

10.7   Data for planning – Motivation

The purpose of this section is to emphasise that firms are organised by individuals. This is often ignored in preparing accounting information. In recent years the topic has been given increasing attention under the general heading of the behavioural aspects of accounting.[4] The particular aspect discussed here is motivation, and it will be illustrated by an example from each of three areas of planning: decision-making, budgeting and control.

It has already been stated that decision-makers should consider the objectives of the firm. In discussing objectives it was recognised that the motivation of various individuals and groups may be different and may indeed be in conflict. Profit maximisation for the firm might describe the motivation of the owners whereas a large salary, job security or a desire to exercise authority might be a better description for managers. Strategic or operating plans which fail to recognise these possible conflicts are likely to run into problems.

It was explained earlier that the budget is the firm's operating plan and within each budget there are various types of targets. These may be targets for volume of sales, efficiency in production, or other levels of performance. A target may be set at a level which is easily achieved or it may not be achievable but designed to motivate those involved to try harder. How people will respond to targets is a complex problem. For example, research has shown that certain levels of management may react favourably to the 'carrot' approach whereas others may not.[5] The firm's budgets may be more appropriate if such questions of motivation are taken into consideration.

A control process is a method of monitoring a plan. Feedback about the operation of the plan will be generated at all levels of the organisation and it is important that people at each level are motivated to make the system work. If they are not it is possible that vital information will not be obtained. Understanding the motivation of the operators of the system is thus of great importance to the design of an efficient control system.

It is not suggested here that the motivation of individuals or groups involved in an organisation can be changed or suppressed. However, by identifying such motivation it may be possible to make decisions and construct systems of budgeting and control which are more efficient in achieving the firm's objectives.

10.8   Data for Planning – Relevant Costs

In Part I we were concerned with the measurement of a firm's position and performance, concentrating on the methods currently employed in accounting. One of the main aims of this measurement was to provide information for users other than the internal management of the firm. In general the information provided was based on what had happened to the firm rather than what was going to happen and as has been stated earlier in this chapter, planning and decision-making are concerned with the future. It follows that information based on the conceptual framework introduced in Chapter 2 may not be adequate for the purposes of internal management in planning for the firm. However, we shall see that the concept of deprival value introduced in Sect. 1.4 is relevant to our analysis. We discuss here, and further in Chapters 11 and 12, the differences of approach to valuation between conventional accounting information and that relevant for decision-making. It is important to understand fully these differences and the reasoning behind them because much of the basic data in a firm available to the decision-maker will be the output from the accounting system and will have been prepared using the accounting concepts bases and policies.

The planner is concerned with considering alternative courses of action available to the firm in the future and selecting those which provide the greatest benefits consistent with the firm's objectives. The major weaknesses of conventional accounting information for planning are:

(*a*)   that its valuations are based largely on original costs (see Ex. 10.1);

(*b*)   it records actual events and ignores possible alternatives (see Ex. 10.2);

(*c*)   calculations of accounting profit are prepared using concepts such as matching, which although it may produce a true and fair view of profit within the accounting framework disguises the firm's cash flow (see Ex. 10.3).

It will be seen from the examples that one way to overcome these weaknesses is to concentrate on the changes in cash flows arising from the planning decision rather than less precise terms such as cost, revenue or profit.

Example 10.1
A firm is considering replacing an existing machine with a more expensive model. The existing machine cost £10,000 six years ago and is being depreciated on a straight-line basis over its useful life of ten years. A new machine would have a cash price of £14,000, a useful life of four years and reduce cash outlays on running costs from £9000 to £5000 per year. Neither machine will have any resale value.

An initial reaction might be to reject the new machine because the old one has a book value of £4000 and to scrap it now would mean a loss of £4000. However, the cost of £10,000 was incurred six years ago and depreciation merely represents an allocation of this original cost. It can be seen from the following cash flow statement that the book value is irrelevant to the decision. It does not appear in the statement because it cannot affect the cash flows arising from the decision.

	Alternatives	
	Replacing the old machine	Keeping the old machine
	£	£
Initial cost of new machine	14,000	—
Annual running costs: 4 × 9000		36,000
4 × 5000	20,000	
Total cash flow out	£34,000	£36,000

The information in the statement shows that there is a saving of £2000 if the new machine is bought to replace the old. In this example, by adding the four years cost savings we have of course ignored the time value of money (see App. C). The lack of significance of the book value may be emphasised if we consider what would be the situation if the original machine had cost not £10,000 but £100,000 six years ago, again assuming that the scrap value is zero. The answer is that it would not make any difference to the solution. This example illustrates the possible dangers in the use of original costs in decision-making.

Example 10.2
A firm owns a stock of 100 tons of material A which originally cost £15 per ton and which could now be sold for £25 per ton. As an alternative to sale, material A may be changed into 100 tons of material B at an additional cash cost for processing of £20 per ton. Material B has a selling price of £42 per ton. Using conventional accounting the figures relating to the possible sale of Material B would show:

Forecast Profit Statement

		£
Sale of Material B £42 × 100 tons		4200
Expense – purchase cost	£15	
process cost	20	
	35 × 100 tons	3500
Profit		£ 700

This statement, however, ignores the alternative use of Material A. It ignores its opportunity cost, the value of the rejected alternative. If we assume initially that Material A could not be replaced, the opportunity cost of using Material A to produce B is not £15 but the £25 per ton which could have been received if it had been sold. On this basis the total cost is £45 per ton which then makes the selling of Material B unprofitable. It is better to realise the £25 from selling Material A than the extra £22 (£42 – 20) from processing it further. The following statement shows the cash flows resulting from the decision.

Forecast Cash-flow Statement

	Alternatives	
	Selling Material A	Processing further and selling as Material B
Cash in	£	£
Selling price – £25 × 100	2500	
– £42 × 100		4200
Cash out		
Process cost £20 × 100		2000
Net cash flow in	£2500	£2200

The original cost of Material A is excluded from the statement because it is cash already spent and not affected by the decision. We can now see clearly that selling Material A is the better alternative.

Using this example we will alter the details, and drop the initial assumption of impossibility of replacement, to show how it is possible to envisage several alternative situations and the related relevant (or opportunity) costs for Material A, i.e. the cash the firm would be deprived of if they use Material A to produce Material B. There may of course be other opportunities which at the time of making the decisions the firm does not know about. The 'true' opportunity cost can only be ascertained with complete information. As it is never possible to obtain complete information an operational definition is based on the level of information about alternatives which the firm has or could reasonably be expected to be informed about.

Detail of situation	*Relevant cost*
If Material A was already purchased at £15 but now had no alternative use.	£ 0
The original cost figure may still be used as a guide if the material is useful but its current replacement or selling price is not known.	£15
Where selling price has risen to £25.	£25
If replacement cost of material has doubled and material is in common use in the firm, its use will result in firm having to pay £30 to replace it.	£30
If the material cannot be replaced or sold but could be used as a substitute for another material costing £45.	£45

It can be seen from this example that what is relevant information depends on the deprival value (opportunity cost) which can only be measured by reference to the context in which a decision is being taken. However, the accounting system because it records original cost will usually show only a single figure.

Example 10.3
A firm is considering a three-year project which will have an initial cost of £1800 for the purchase of a machine. Annual cash sales are estimated as £1000 and annual running cost as £300. The profit statements for the three years shown in conventional form could be:

Forecast Profit Statement

	Year 1	Year 2	Year 3	Total
	£	£	£	£
Sales Revenue	1000	1000	1000	3000
Less: Expenses – Running costs	300	300	300	900
– Depreciation of machinery	600	600	600	1800
Profit	£ 100	£ 100	£ 100	£ 300

Although the figure of £100 each year may give a 'true and fair view' of the profit for that year in accordance with the accounting framework, it obscures the cash flow of the firm which is:

Forecast Cash-flow Statement

Beginning of Year 1	*Year 1*	*Year 2*	*Year 3*	*Total*
£	£	£	£	£
(1800)	700	700	700	300

It should be noted that the net totals for the three years are both £300 but the pattern of profits and cash flow are very different. The decision maker is essentially interested in this cash flow because this may have an effect on the firm's dividends or share value, and because of the time value of money. Using accounting profit as a basis for decision will obscure the cash flow. In this simple example the effect of allocating depreciation can be clearly seen but in a normal profit statement there are many such items, e.g. several types of depreciation, research and development cost, bad debt provisions and all other accruals and prepayments which are there because of the matching concept and do not represent actual cash flow (see Sect. 7.11). This matter and the timing of cash flow, is considered further in Chapter 12 and App. C.

It is important to re-emphasise that accounting cost and profit calculations are usually made to compute the past year's profits whereas we are concerned in this chapter with decisions affecting the future.

10.9 Budgeting and Control

The remaining aspects of Fig. 10.1 are budgeting and control. Budgets are the means by which a firm expresses its plans in quantified and operational terms. They show the expected results of the strategic and operational decisions. As strategic decisions are usually concerned with broad policy it is usually operating decisions which have a direct relationship with budgets. Budgets and the budgeting process are dealt with in detail in Chapter 13 but it must be emphasised at this stage that there is a two-way flow of information between strategic and operating decisions and budgeting. Clearly the decisions made will determine what goes into the budgets but probably less clear is the fact that the preparation of detailed budgets may lead to changes in the decisions themselves. For example, a company may have narrowed its strategic decisions down to expansion in either France or Germany. Its market survey leads it to narrow its considerations and then operational decisions are made, for example, on a site for the factory, on finance and on supplies of materials and labour. In preparing the detailed budgets for the first year of operations problems arise in scheduling of resources of finance, materials and labour at the required times. This leads to a revision of the cost of the site chosen and results in consideration of another site in France and the reconsideration of the one previously considered in Germany. The arrows in Fig. 10.1 flow in both directions emphasising this two-way flow of information.

Budgeting is detailed planning of operating decisions and control processes are methods of monitoring the plans as they are put into operation. The simplest way of doing this is to compare what actually happens with what the budgets said would happen. It should be clear that again there is a two-way process, i.e. that in controlling in this way it is possible that information is discovered which leads to a change in decisions made. The subject of control is dealt with further in Part III.

10.10 Summary

This chapter introduced Part II of the book with an analysis of the concepts of planning. Fig. 10.1 illustrated the important elements in the planning process. These were the formulation of objectives, which are translated into a programme of action by means of decisions, analysed for the purposes of explanation into strategic and operating decisions. A significant factor in proper planning is an understanding of and an ability to obtain relevant data. This was discussed under the headings of forecasting, search methods, motivation and relevant costs. Plans and decisions are expressed in operational terms as budgets. The analysis of decisions is considered further in Chapters 11 and 12 and budgeting in Chapter 13. The monitoring of the planning process by means of control processes is considered in Part III.

Notes and References

1. H. I. Ansoff, 'Strategies for Diversification', *Harvard Business Review* (Autumn 1967).
2. D. W. Pearce, *Cost–Benefit Analysis* (London, Macmillan, 1971).
3. C. Robinson, *Business Forecasting* (London, Nelson, 1971).
4. A. Hopwood, *Accounting and Human Behaviour* (London, Haymarket, 1974).
5. S. W. Becker and D. Green, 'Budgeting and Employee Behaviour', in *Accounting and its Behavioral Implications*, ed. W. T. Bruns and D. T. De Coster (New York, N.Y., McGraw-Hill, 1969).

Further Reading

W. T. Bruns and D. T. De Coster (eds), *Accounting and its Behavioral Implications* (New York, N.Y., McGraw-Hill, 1969).

R. H. Coase, 'The Nature of Costs', in *Studies in Cost Analysis*, 2nd ed. (ed. D. Solomons) (London, Sweet & Maxwell, 1968).

H. Igor Ansoff, *Corporate Strategy* (New York, N.Y., McGraw-Hill, 1965; Harmondsworth, Penguin Books, 1968).

R. M. Cyert and J. G. March, *A Behavioral Theory of the Firm* (Englewood Cliffs, N.J., Prentice-Hall, 1963).

R. F. J. Dewhurst, *Business Cost–benefit Analysis* (London, McGraw-Hill, 1972).

J. R. Gould, 'The Economist's Cost Concept and Business Problems', in *Studies in Accounting Theory*, ed. W. T. Baxter and S. Davidson (London, Sweet & Maxwell, 1962).

J. T. S. Porterfield, *Investment Decisions and Capital Costs* (Englewood Cliffs, N.J., Prentice-Hall, 1965), ch. 5.

B. Carsberg, 'The Role of the Valuation Model in the Analysis of Investment Decisions', in H. C. Edey and B. S. Yamey (eds), *Debits, Credits, Finance and Profits* (London, Sweet & Maxwell, 1974).

Questions and Problems

10.1   What do you understand by the following terminology?

Planning	Budgeting	Opportunity cost
Control	Cost-benefit analysis	Feedback
Strategic decisions	Search methods	Relevant costs
Operating decisions		Deprival value

10.2   Firms are often said to have a vector of objectives. Explain what this means. What are the problems in implementing a vector of objectives?

10.3   What is the point of distinguishing between strategic and operating decisions?

10.4   How can a knowledge of statistical probability be used in forecasting?

10.5   'Deprival value, opportunity cost and relevant cost are synonymous concepts'. Discuss.

11
Pricing and Output Decisions

11.1 Introduction

This chapter provides a framework for the analysis of a firm's decisions about prices for its products and about its level of output. The procedures and techniques examined are appropriate to the analysis of decision-making, irrespective of the length of time over which the decisions will have effect. Chapter 12 considers the additional dimensions to problems which arise when long-term effects are taken into consideration. Many of the analytical tools developed in this chapter are the basis for long-term decision-making and the two chapters on decision-making should be considered together. In previous chapters the importance of determining the objectives of the firm and the relevant costs of decision-making was emphasised and the problems examined here will illustrate the importance of this.

The chapter begins by analysing decision-making procedures on the assumption that complete information is available about demand and costs. Then we examine the ways in which we can develop decision-making models and procedures which may be useful in the normal situations of limited information being available.

11.2 Profit–Volume Analysis with Complete Information

Firms take important decisions which relate to the prices of their products and the level of output of those products. Our analysis is about a firm's revenues and costs at various levels of output, conventionally termed by accountants the 'profit–volume relationship'. As a starting-point we will assume that a firm is able to obtain information about possible future prices for its products and the future costs of manufacturing them. Later in this chapter we shall examine different ways in which a firm may establish a price if it is unable to obtain complete market information about the prices at which it will be able to sell its products.

We shall, for simplicity, assume that a firm produces only one product and firstly we shall consider information about the demand for its product. This information will show the amount of the product demanded in relation to the price charged and can be expressed in the form of a demand curve shown in Fig. 11.1.

The curve is the locus of forecast combinations of prices and quantities demanded, and it shows that the higher the price the lower the quantity demanded. The slope of the demand curve will depend on the type of product and the competitive position of the firm. From data about prices and quantities we could construct a curve showing the total revenue for various levels of sales (see Fig. 11.2). The most important information shown is the elasticity of demand.

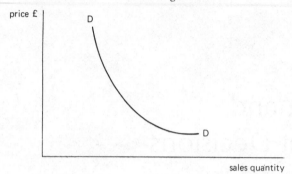

Figure 11.1   An example of a demand curve for a product

Different patterns of cost behaviour were introduced in Chapter 6, in relation to costs of production and inventory valuation. We will assume for convenience that the firm can obtain the information necessary to forecast the total costs associated with any level of output.

A firm may use actual cost data as a basis for its cost forecasts. Cost data which relates cost to a level of production could be shown as in Fig. 6.2. For purposes of prediction a simplifying classification of costs into fixed and variable may be made, as examined in Sect. 6.2. Care must be taken in use of the term 'cost' in this context as for decision-making purposes we are interested in opportunity costs rather than costs already incurred (see Sect. 10.8). If the firm finds that it must purchase the resources used in production the opportunity costs and the original costs will be the same. However, if the firm already has resources, for example, raw material inventory, the original cost may not be a good guide to the opportunity cost as the firm may not intend to replace them or it may have other uses for the inventory. Similarly fixed costs must represent the opportunity costs of providing the capacity to produce the products and this may not be the fixed costs allocated to a particular product through allocation and apportionment of fixed overheads. Calculation of the cost of capacity is discussed in Sect. 11.6.

Ex. 11.1 provides the information which is subsequently used to illustrate the use of graphical procedures to choose the optimal combination of selling price and quantity produced (output).

Example 11.1
Kafka Ltd produces one product and wishes to select its optimal levels of output and selling price. It holds no inventories. It has estimated the following relationships:

DEMAND

Sales Quantity	Selling Price	Sales Revenue
	£	£
0	20	—
100	18	1800
200	16	3200
300	14	4200
400	12	4800
500	10	5000
600	8	4800

TOTAL COSTS

Production Quantity	Total Costs
	£
0	1000
100	1450
200	2000
300	2650
400	3400
500	4250
600	5200

This demand and cost information is presented in Fig. 11.2. Although we have only information about discrete points on these curves we have joined them up with a continuous curve on the assumption that there is some underlying relationship. If we were required to produce a curve this could be achieved, for example, by a regression analysis.

If we wish to maximise profits (see Sect. 10.3) we will select the level of output and sales where total revenues exceed total costs by the maximum amount (see Fig. 11.2). The optimal level of output will be 320 units. The profit will be £1560 (total revenues £4352 less total costs £2792). The price at this level of sales will be

$$\frac{£4352}{320 \text{ units}} = £13.60.$$

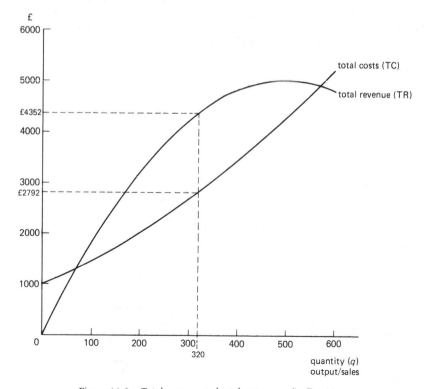

Figure 11.2   Total revenue and total cost curves for Ex. 11.1

Because we are often interested in the additional effects of decisions on the ongoing activities of the firm, e.g. changes in levels of output or sales, we will often find it more convenient to examine the marginal implications of changes. This is provided by an approach to determining the optimal level of output which analyses the *marginal revenue* or *marginal cost* that is associated with changes in levels of sales and output. The term 'marginal' can often be equated with accountant's term 'variable'. The term 'incremental' is also used to describe the change in total revenue or costs resulting from a decision. In relation to sales revenue, marginal revenue (MR) will be the increase or decrease in total revenue which results from an increase in sales quantity by one unit or a small number of units. Thus by producing a table of sales quantities and their associated selling prices, and sales revenue we could calculate the associated marginal revenue per unit. An identical procedure can be adopted for the calculation of marginal cost per unit (MC) which will show the increase or decrease in total cost.[1]

The significance of marginal cost and marginal revenue calculations is that if the firm can calculate this information, it will be able to calculate the level of output where marginal revenue equals marginal cost and profits will be maximised. Profits will be maximised, because at levels of output lower than the optimum, by increasing levels of output and sales, the increase in total revenue will exceed the increase in total costs, i.e. MR > MC. The firm should select higher levels of output and sales until the point is reached where the increase in total revenue equals the increase in total cost, i.e. MR = MC, as after this point the total profits will decrease, i.e. MC > MR.

Fig. 11.3 shows marginal revenue and marginal cost data from Ex. 11.1 and the demand curve for the product. As we can see the profit-maximising level of output is as previously indicated 320 units, and the relevant price determined from the demand curve is £13.60. The use of marginal revenue and marginal cost analysis lends itself to a mathematical treatment through the use of calculus.[2] We could

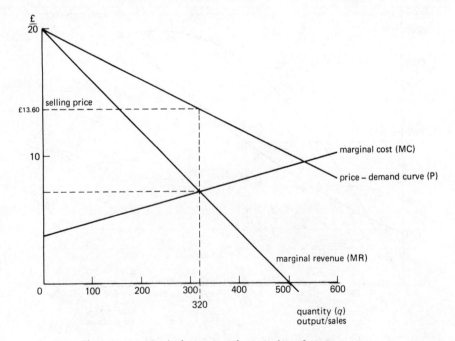

Figure 11.3   Marginal revenue and marginal cost from Ex. 11.1

calculate a solution given the following mathematical expressions of demand and cost functions in Ex. 11.1.

$$\text{Price} = 20 - 0.02q \qquad \text{Demand function}$$
$$\text{Revenue} = 20q - 0.02q^2 \qquad \text{Revenue function}$$
$$\text{Costs} = 1000 + 4q + 0.005q^2 \qquad \text{Cost function}$$

The need to assume that demand and cost data is available may prove a major obstacle to the use of the procedures outlined. Where firms operate in highly competitive markets their prices may be set for them and there is little data to collect about demand. However, in most circumstances a firm will have some influence over the prices it can charge for its products, and it may be able to influence demand through its advertising and marketing policies. Where firms accept a price as given as in a highly competitive situation they will be left with a decision about the level of output, whereas with uncertain demand data, a decision about both price and quantity must be made. One solution to the problem is to consider price and output decisions separately. While they are clearly not independent decisions because of demand elasticity, over certain ranges of output and price, either price or output could be considered as fixed. We will now develop some further analytical techniques which may assist our examination of decision-making in situations of incomplete information.

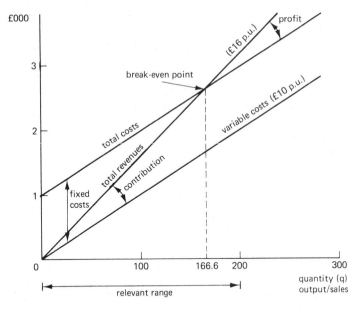

Figure 11.4   Linear profit–volume chart

11.3   Profit–volume analysis with limited information

In situations where full information is not available it may be necessary to make assumptions about demand and costs. Firstly, we may only have information about a few discrete points on the revenue and cost functions. Secondly, we may need to make simplifying assumptions about their shape, e.g. linearity. To illustrate a method of analysis we have used the situation found in Ex. 11.1, but assumed that only limited data is available. The profit–volume chart shown in Fig. 11.4 represents the data from Ex. 11.1 in the range of output and sales from zero to

200 units. We could see by inspecting Fig. 11.2 that the curve for TR and TC is approximately linear in this range. To construct the profit–volume chart we have assumed our only information is that for the range of 0–200 units the selling price is £16 per unit and fixed costs are £1000 and variable costs £10 per unit.

The range of output and sales volume over which a profit–volume chart is considered a realistic approximation is termed the 'relevant range' (in our example 0–200 units). Outside the relevant range (in our example above 200 units) the linearity assumptions cannot be assumed to hold and price and variable cost per unit may be affected by levels of sales and output, e.g. we can see from Fig. 11.3 that in the range 200 to 400 units the price is lower. The relevant range may also be determined by such factors as production or finance constraints. Decision-making using linear profit–volume charts is clearly limited by the restriction of relevant range, but if necessary we could construct a series of charts for various ranges if data were available so that linearity assumptions could be approximately correct in each chart, e.g. 200–400, 400–600. The selection of the optimum price and output would be shown on the profit–volume chart which indicated the largest profit. Although we are making decisions with crude analytical tools and limited data the use of linear profit–volume charts may provide a close approximation to profit maximisation.

Profit–volume charts are sometimes termed 'break-even charts' as they show some important relationships including the break-even level of sales and output. The important terms in Fig. 11.4 are:

1. Contribution   = Total Revenue *less* Total Variable Costs
2. Profit   = Total Revenue *less* Total Fixed + Total Variable Costs
   or
   Profit   = Contribution *less* Total Fixed Costs
3. Break-even point: level of output and sales where:

   Total Revenue   = Total Fixed + Total Variable Costs
   or Contribution   = Total Fixed Costs
   or Profit   = Zero

The break-even output can be calculated as:

$$\frac{\text{Total Fixed Costs}}{\text{Contribution per unit}}$$

The above analysis shows that the excess of total revenue over total variable costs can be considered as making a contribution towards the payment of fixed costs. Once the break-even level of sales has been attained all fixed costs will have been covered and the contribution then increases the profit of the firm. We can see from Fig. 11.4 that a contribution to fixed costs and profit begins once a unit is sold at a price greater than variable cost.

Fig. 11.4 shows that in using this model forecast profit would be at a maximum when we produce and sell 200 units of our product at a price of £16, which is at the upper limit of the relevant range. If our data is correct this will give a profit of £200. To check whether this is optimal we could collect data for other levels of sales and output. If we considered that the data in Fig. 11.4 suggests a suboptimal decision, we could construct and inspect profit–volume charts for different relevant ranges to see which chart indicates the highest total profit. The final decision will also be affected by the reliability of the forecast cost and demand data.

11.4 Full-cost Analysis for Pricing

In situations where data about demand is incomplete it may be necessary to develop techniques for determining prices using minimal market information. Incomplete information about demand may relate to uncertainty about the range of possible prices for a given level of sales, or uncertainty about the level of sales for a given price. One approach to pricing which has been a practical response to this problem is based on full cost (sometimes termed 'cost plus', or 'absorption cost plus' profit). Full-cost pricing is an attempt to ensure that the firm's total revenues from its sales are sufficient to cover the variable and fixed costs of the firm and to provide a required amount of profit. The required profit mark-up may be determined by such factors as the need to earn a minimum profit on finance employed, on government profit limitations or on the practices of a particular industry.

If a firm selects a level of output for its products and calculates its total costs and required profit it could then establish a selling price which would provide sufficient contribution, if sales resulted, to cover all its fixed costs and provide the required profit. As a pricing strategy it relies on the levels of output chosen for products being realised into sales. The level of profit chosen will depend on the firm's objectives. Because of the way in which required profit levels may be calculated this approach to pricing may lead to decisions which are suboptimal.

The use of full cost may also arise where a firm is attempting to calculate a possible price where there is no question of choosing a level of output, i.e. it is a special contract, for example, in a tender to supply a ship. Another use is where a firm may calculate a series of prices based on different levels of output which could be used as a trial price (a first approximation) to see if it would be saleable at that price. The use of profit-volume charts may be useful in this process.

Full-cost pricing is illustrated in Ex. 11.2.

Example 11.2

Kite Ltd is considering producing a new product, the Kombat, and it forecasts that it can sell at least 250 units, but no more than 600 units. The relevant costs relating to this new product have been calculated as follows:

Forecast Costs of producing Kombats

Variable Costs per Unit	£
Direct Labour	3
Direct Materials	4
Variable Overheads: electricity	2
	£9

Relevant Fixed Costs (Considered as attributable to Kombats)

Rental and rates of additional factory space for production of Kombats:	£4000

We can calculate a price based on a variety of assumptions

Alternative assumptions

Sales Volume	250	250	500	500
Required Profit	Nil	£1000	Nil	£1000

Selling Price Calculation

	£	£	£	£
Total costs – variable	2250	2250	4500	4500
– fixed	4000	4000	4000	4000
Required profit	Nil	1000	Nil	1000
Total Cost and Required Profit	6250	7250	8500	9500
Required Selling Price	£25	£29	£17	£19

From our calculations we can see that the required selling price will depend on the proposed sales volume level, total costs and required profit. Reference could now be made to the elasticity of demand.

Comments of full-cost Pricing

Because a whole range of output levels is often possible a corresponding range of prices can be calculated. There must therefore be some mechanism for choosing the appropriate level of output on which to determine price and this may be arbitrary. A process of comparison with crude market data may be appropriate.

The determination of which costs are to be included in the pricing decision is difficult. In some cases, as in Ex. 11.2, the 'relevant costs' will be incremental costs and thus readily identifiable, e.g. costs of additional capacity. In a firm which already has capacity for production, the fixed costs may already be committed, and hence not incremental. To ensure that the firm makes an overall profit, the firm must still have sufficient contribution from all its products to cover its total fixed costs. In a firm which manufactures several products, the decision as to which fixed costs are attributable to a product will be arbitrary in many cases as was seen in Sect. 6.3. Further consideration of problems of fixed costs and the costs of capacity are given in Sect. 11.6.

By pricing a product at a figure much above cost, the firm's total contribution may be reduced from selling a lower volume of its products or none at all, rather than selling more at a lower contribution per unit. This problem is discussed in Sect. 11.5. This situation occurs when the demand for the production is elastic.

The use of full cost is often criticised on the grounds that no reference is made to the market for price guidance. This criticism oversimplifies the problem as the context in which it is used is in the absence of complete market data. It has been shown that many firms use this approach to pricing as a guide to price setting, particularly minimum prices, and it would be naïve to assume that the final price is fixed without any reference to the demand situation. Full cost could be used as a starting-point and adjustments made to the profit required to reflect the market conditions applicable to the product.[3]

The use of full-cost pricing, which includes a profit element, could be misinterpreted as a means of guarantee of profitability because profit is often included in the calculation. The volume of production is an important assumption as selling one unit at the required price does not necessarily produce an overall profit if these are unsold units.

11.5   Variable cost and cash-flow analysis

In this section we will examine how we can analyse decisions by concentrating on changes in the contribution to fixed costs and profits arising from alternative courses of action. Full-cost pricing was criticised in Sect. 11.4 because it may fail to recognise the incremental revenues and costs in decision-making. Variable-cost analysis (sometimes termed 'direct cost', 'marginal' or 'contribution analysis') concentrates on the changes in contribution which arise from selling products or selecting a particular course of action. It avoids the problem of overhead absorption, but does not help directly in solving the pricing problem.

We will now analyse Ex. 11.3 below to illustrate the use of variable-cost analysis and contrast it with full-cost analysis and cash-flow analysis. We shall show how variable-cost analysis is likely to be more useful to the decision-maker than full-cost analysis. However, it will be preferable to analyse the effects of decisions in terms of cash flows (see Sect. 10.8). The data is analysed in the following sequence: (*a*) using full-cost analysis; (*b*) using variable-cost analysis; and (*c*) using forecast cash-flow analysis.

Example 11.3

Konti Ltd has a special machine which is normally used to make Kogs. The firm plans to sell 500 Kogs per year in a market where competition is fierce; the current price is £20 per Kog. The firm has been asked to provide 250 Togs, a product which is in no way similar to Kogs but which has been found can be made on the same machine using its unused capacity. The price per Tog that has been offered is £7. The estimated costs of production are:

Variable Costs (per unit)		Kog £		Tog £
Direct Materials		4		3
Direct Labour	2 hours	2	1 hour	1
Variable Overheads: Electricity		3		2
		£9		£6

No additional (incremental) fixed costs will be incurred by production of Togs. Fixed overhead costs of £2500 are allocated to the machinery for depreciation and factory overheads. Konti Ltd has to decide whether the additional production of 250 Togs is in the company's interest.

(a) Full-cost analysis

The calculation of the unit product cost on a full-cost basis in this example is identical with the absorption-cost basis described in Sect. 6.3 although full cost could include costs and profit nor normally absorbed. We will assume that fixed overhead costs are absorbed on the basis of forecast labour hours. We will calculate the unit cost under the two alternatives.

Alternatives

Forecast Product Cost per Unit	Produce and sell 500 Kogs		Produce and sell 500 Kogs and 250 Togs	
	£		£	£
Variable Costs	9		9	6
Fixed Overhead Costs				
2 hours @ £2.50	5	2 hours @ £2	4	1 hour 2
	£14		£13	£8

The fixed overhead absorption rate is calculated:

(i) Fixed Overhead Costs	£2500			£2500	
(ii) Forecast Labour Hours	1000	(1000 + 250)		1250	
(iii) Overhead Absorption Rate (per labour hour)	£2.50			£2.00	

Forecast Profit Statements	Produce and sell 500 Kogs	Produce and sell		
		500 Kogs	and	250 Togs
	£		£	£
Sales Revenue @ £20	10,000	@ £20	10,000	@ £7 1,750
Less: Cost of Goods Sold @ £14	7,000	@ £13	6,500	@ £8 2,000
Profit	£ 3,000		£ 3,500	−£ 250 (loss)

Comparison of the profit in total indicates that the firm should produce an additional 250 Togs because the total profit from Kogs and Togs of £3250 is greater than from Kogs alone of £3000. However, the individual profit statements for joint Kogs and Togs production shows Togs making a loss. This is because fixed costs have been absorbed by Togs even though the production of Togs has not increased fixed costs. The profit (or loss) which either Kogs or Togs makes depends on the way in which the fixed costs are allocated to the machine and absorbed by the products.

The use of full costing may cause problems for decision-making because different signals are given about acceptance or rejection of the proposal according to the data which is inspected. The overall change in profitability correctly shows an increase, but the individual profitability of Togs shows a loss of £250. The signals appear to be inconsistent, the former indicating that the selling price of £7 is in the best interests of company profitability, and the latter that a selling price of £7 is less than the forecast product cost per unit of £8.

Although it may appear that we could always resolve this problem by determining the overall position, as we can see clearly in this example, this may not always be possible particularly in a multi-product firm. In most decision-making situations we would like to be able to appraise marginal decisions independently of the rest of the firm. If an absorption cost system for calculating product cost was used a decision-maker would find, on requesting the cost of Togs, that this was stated at £8. This cost information could lead to the rejection of a profitable opportunity.

(b) Variable cost analysis
Our starting-point will be to prepare forecast profit statements using variable costing to calculate the product cost (see also Sect. 6.4 (iii).

Forecast Profit Statements	Produce and sell 500 Kogs	*Alternatives*		*Produce and sell*	
		500 Kogs	and	250 Togs	
					Total
	£		£	£	£
Sales Revenue @ £20	10,000	@ £20	10,000	@ £7 1750	
Less: Cost of Goods Sold @ £9	4,500	@ £9	4,500	@ £6 1,500	
Total Contribution	5,500		5,500	250	5,750
Fixed Overheads	2,500				2,500
Profit	£ 3,000				£3,250

From the forecast profit statements we can see that production and sales of Togs is in the best interests of the company as the total profit increases by £250 from £3000 to £3250. The production of Togs when considered separately shows an additional contribution of £250. The signals given by examining the total profit and individual product contribution are identical. The major advantage of this form of analysis is that we could prepare an individual profit statement for the Togs proposal independently of the rest of the company and use it for decision-making purposes.

The use of variable-cost analysis must include all incremental costs which arise because of the proposal under consideration. However, in many circumstances, as in Ex. 11.2, additional costs may be incurred which would be classified as fixed, but which would be direct costs in relation to a proposal, e.g. acquiring new machinery. Where there are direct fixed costs the definition of contribution as revenues less variable costs may not be appropriate for decision-making. In this situation any other direct costs should be deducted from the 'gross' contribution to arrive at the 'net' contribution.

(c) Forecast Cash-flow Analysis

The conventional profit statement relies for its calculations on accounting concepts. For decision-making purposes we are concerned not with the original cost of resources but rather their opportunity cost. Rather than relying on profit calculation it is often more convenient and less ambiguous to prepare a forecast cash-flow statement (see Ex. 10.2). As we are concerned with the future, cash flows are important because all future costs and benefits will affect cash. Furthermore, improvements in cash flows can be seen to correlate to the owners' interests by affecting his potential dividends.

A forecast cash-flow statement identifies the potential cash flows from a proposal. To illustrate the way in which cash-flow analysis could improve our decision-making procedure let us assume that the opportunity cost of Togs is £8 per unit, perhaps arising from replacement considerations rather than £6 per unit original cost used in the profit calculation.

Forecast Cash-flow Statement	*Produce and sell 250 Togs*
	£
Cash in	
From Sales Revenue @ £7	1750
Cash out	
Variable Costs @ £8	2000
Net Cash-flow Out	—£ 250

The cash-flow statement reflects the cash-flow out from the company assuming replacement material at £5 per unit (i.e. an additional £2 per unit for 250 units). When the additional £500 is included in the cash-flow statement as cash out the net cash-flow out is −£250. This would indicate that the proposal should be rejected. Thus unless a profit statement includes the opportunity cost of resources used, e.g. the material cost at £5, it would incorrectly indicate that the proposal should be accepted. In the following section on measuring the cost of capacity cash-flow analysis will also assist our decision-making.

11.6   Costs of capacity

In our analysis so far we have assumed that the firm has resources available to carry out its proposals. In many situations the resources of a firm may be fixed at least in the short term and this leads to problems of restrictions which might be imposed on a firm's plans by shortage of capacity. The term 'capacity' can be used in a very broad sense to include, for example, physical manufacturing capacity, finance, labour or management. Where there is a shortage of capacity this implies that the firm will be unable to carry out all its proposals and must select between them.

In decision-making we should therefore include in our calculations the opportunity costs of capacity. Where there are no capacity limits, as in Ex. 11.3, the opportunity cost of capacity will be nil and no capacity costs are included in the calculations. However, where a firm has to make payments for capacity, e.g. as seen in Ex. 11.2, or forgoes receipts, e.g. by not selling a machine, it incurs costs of capacity. Costs of capacity also arise where a firm cannot accept two proposals because they are made mutually exclusive because of capacity considerations. The opportunity cost of capacity in this case is the contribution lost from the rejected proposal. Illustrations of decision-making procedures using costs of capacity are analysed in Exs 11.4 (no capacity limit), 11.5 (one item of capacity limited) and 11.6 (two items of capacity limited). We will assume in these examples that revenues and costs are expressed in opportunity-cost terms. It was explained in the previous section that the term 'contribution' was commonly used in variable cost profit statements. We will continue using the concept in cash-flow analysis.

Example 11.4
Konti Ltd has to decide which one of two mutually exclusive products to produce and sell. The following selling prices and variable costs have been estimated for amounts up to an estimated maximum demand of 200 units.

| | *Products* | |
	X	Y
	£	£
Selling price	20	27
Variable cost	13	17

Capacity to manufacture the products is available within the firm's factory and it has no alternative use.

From this data we can prepare the following cash-flow statements:

| | *Alternatives* | |
Forecast Cash-flow Statements	200 X	200 Y
	£	£
Cash in		
From Sales Revenue	4000	5400
Cash out		
Variable Costs	2600	3400
Net Cash-flow In (contribution)	£1400	£2000

Konti Ltd would choose to produce 200 Y as it has the higher net cash inflow.

Example 11.5

Using the data from Ex. 11.4, except that Konti Ltd has a limit of 240 hours' manufacturing capacity. The hours necessary to manufacture one unit are: X, 2 hours; Y, 4 hours. As capacity is now limited it is necessary to measure the effective use of capacity. This can be seen if the contribution per hour of capacity used is calculated:

	X	Y
Contribution per unit	£7	£10
Manufacturing hours required per unit	2	4
Contribution per hour of capacity	£3.50	£2.50

This indicates that the company should produce X in preference to Y, because the contribution per hour of capacity for X is higher than for Y.

The contributions from X and Y will be:

	X	Y
Units produced	120	60
Contribution	£840	£600

This approach to the problems of limited capacity is termed 'limiting-factor analysis' and is appropriate to the solution of problems where there is only one constraint.

Costs of capacity in Ex. 11.5

It would be useful to be able to calculate the cost of capacity because a product cost should include the opportunity cost of capacity required to produce it. To appraise any proposal we would include the cost of capacity in the product cost and thus simplify the process of comparison between projects. This would be useful in a large company where many activities were being undertaken simultaneously.

Having arrived at our optimal plan in Ex. 11.5 we will be producing 120 units of X. For every hour of additional capacity the company can acquire it will be able to produce an additional ½ unit of X (up to a limit of an additional 80 units) 200 units being the maximum demand. This will yield a contribution of £3.50 per hour. To use current capacity for the manufacture of products other than X will lose the company a contribution of £3.50 per hour and this is thus the opportunity cost of capacity. Suppose that at a later stage when X was being sold, a new proposal to produce 60 Y was made at a time when the firm had no spare capacity. We could then prepare a forecast cash-flow statement, assuming that production of Y would replace X.

	Production of 60 Y	
Forecast Cash-flow Statement	*per unit*	*60 units*
	£	£
Cash in		
From Sales Revenue	27	1620
Cash out		
Variable Costs	17	1020
Capacity Cost 4 hrs @ £3.50 per hour	14	840
Net cash-flow out	−£ 4	−£ 240

The forecast cash-flow statement shows that the production of Y would lead to a net cash outflow of £240. This arises because the firm would lose a contribution of £840, from the change in the use of its capacity, and gain only a contribution of £600 (£1620–£1020) in return.

It is sometimes argued in favour of full-cost pricing that the fixed overheads absorbed by a product is a charge for use of the capacity. As we have seen the charge for the use of capacity relates to its alternative uses. If it has no alternative use there will be no opportunity cost. Fixed costs absorbed are often apportionment of fixed costs, e.g. depreciation on machinery, buildings, rates, rent. There is no reason to suppose that the amounts of fixed costs absorbed should bear any relationship to the opportunity cost. The opportunity costs will change over time as different opportunities for use of capacity arise and different production plans are agreed.

The use of a limiting-factor analysis illustrated in Ex. 11.5 is normally only appropriate if there is only one factor limiting the output decision and we will now examine Ex. 11.6 where two factors, termed 'constraints' in the latter context, limit the output.

Example 11.6
Kelvin Ltd is considering the production plan for two products, Alpha and Beta. Both products can be sold simultaneously and their markets are not related. The company considers that it will accept the ruling market price. The only relationship between the products is that they both use the services of the company's assembly and painting departments. During the time that these products will be manufactured these departments will manufacture no products other than

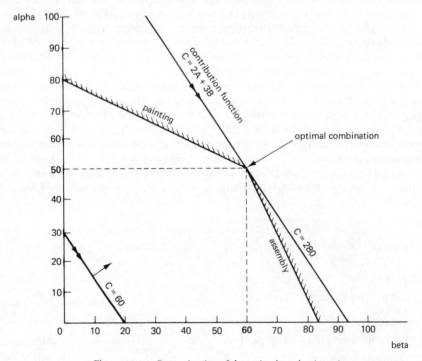

Figure 11.5   Determination of the optimal production mix

Alpha or Beta. The variable costs, selling prices and production times are outlined below:

Cash-flow Data (per unit)		Alpha	Beta
		£	£
Selling Price		10	14
	£	£	
Variable Costs: material	3	6	
labour	4	2	
overheads	1	3	
	8	11	
Contribution per Unit	£ 2	£ 3	

Use of Production Capacity per unit	hours	hours
Assembly	1	2
Painting	2	1

The hours of production capacity available are:

Assembly   170 hours
Painting   160 hours

We could use the procedures of limiting-factor analysis to give an initial insight into the problem.

Contribution per Hour of Capacity	Alpha	Beta
Department	£	£
Assembly	2.00	1.50
Painting	1.00	3.00

The contribution per hour indicates that in the assembly department the production of Alpha yields the highest contribution per hour, while in the painting department the production of Beta is most effective. Limiting-factor analysis cannot necessarily help us solve problems of more than one constraint. If one department indicated a higher contribution using both criteria, limiting-factor analysis could be applied. In this example we will use a linear programming formulation to provide a solution. The graphical method shown below can be replaced by using the Simplex method.[4]

In Fig. 11.5 the constraints and objective function from Ex. 11.6 are shown. The graph shows that the optimal combination is the production of 50 units of Alpha and 60 units of Beta.

It is possible that we might have arrived at this combination of Alpha and Beta by a process of trial and error. The solution to problems by trial and error is a relatively simple procedure when the number of possible combinations is small. With problems where numerous combinations are feasible, the use of an analytical method is necessary. Graphical methods are suitable where two products are under consideration, but with more than two a mathematical solution is normally necessary. The following information shows the total contribution from the proposed output levels and that the capacity constraints have been satisfied.

	Alpha	Beta			
Output Units	50	60			

	Hours used			*Total*	*Spare capacity*
Capacity:					
Assembly	50	120		170	nil
Painting	100	60		160	nil

	£	£		£
Contribution function	2A	+3B	=	C
Total	100	+180	=	280

We could calculate the opportunity cost of capacity by solution of the dual, or by seeing how much the total contribution changed when a marginal change was made in capacity available, but this is outside the scope of this book.[4]

11.7 Summary

In this chapter we have analysed some of the major factors which contribute to the firm's decisions about prices and output. When complete information is available we can determine levels of output and price simultaneously. In the absence of complete demand and cost information we may have to analyse price and output decisions separately. We have developed several tools which are useful in decision-making. The profit–volume chart, full-cost pricing and variable-cost analysis will improve the quality of our analysis. The use of forecast cash-flow statements rather than profit statements is useful to clarify relevant costs and benefits.

The importance of attempting to quantify opportunity costs plays a central role in decision-making. To begin to quantify the opportunity costs of capacity will be very useful for the firm if it is considering any additional proposals. The firm will examine the contribution and the opportunity cost to the firm in terms of using scarce capacity before making its final decision. In Chapter 12 we consider the additional dimensions of decision-making imposed when the results are spread over a long period of time in the future.

Notes and References

1. For an illustration of this calculation see R. G. Lipsey, *An Introduction to Positive Economics* (London, Weidenfeld & Nicolson, 1971), or most elementary micro-economics texts.
2. For a full explanation of the application of calculus to optimisation problems see G. C. Archibald and R. G. Lipsey, *An Introduction to a Mathematical Treatment of Economics* (London Weidenfeld & Nicolson, 1967).
3. W. T. Baxter and A. R. Oxenfeldt, 'Approaches to Pricing: Economist v. Accountant', *Studies in Cost Analysis*, 2nd ed., D. Solomons (ed.) (London, Sweet & Maxwell, 1968).
4. For an explanation of the mechanics of linear programming, see B. V. Carsberg, *Introduction to Mathematical Programming for Accountants* (London, Allen & Unwin, 1969).

Further Reading

J. Arnold, *Pricing and Output Decisions* (London, Haymarket, 1973).
R. H. Coase, 'The Nature of Costs', *Studies in Cost Analysis*, ibid.
H. Anton and R. Firmin (eds), *Contemporary Issues in Cost Accounting* (Boston, Houghton Mifflin, 1966) parts 4 and 5.

Questions and Problems

11.1 What do you understand by the following terminology?

Fixed cost	Demand function	Contribution
Variable cost	Cost function	Full-cost pricing
Regression analysis	Profit–volume chart	Relevant cost
Marginal cost	Relevant range	Incremental cost
Marginal revenue	Break-even point	Linear programming
Cash-flow analysis	Cost of capacity	Direct cost
Limiting-factor analysis	Elasticity of demand	

11.2 The Kongo Company estimates the following relationships between price, total costs and quantities of sales and output for production:

Quantity	Total revenue	Price	Total costs
000	£000	£	£000
0	—	—	40
10	52	5.2	50
30	108	3.6	70
50	100	2.0	90
70	28	0.4	110

(a) Construct a graph showing total revenue and total costs.
b) What is the level of output and sales at which profit is maximised? What is the amount of profit?
(c) Show how it would be possible to construct profit–volume charts, using linear assumptions to calculate the optimum price–output combination.
(d) Explain why the demand and cost functions have their particular shape.

11.3 A firm is considering the sale of product Z produced two months ago. The accountant has drawn up the following statement:

Forecast profit statement for sale of product Z

	£
Sales revenue 100 units @ £2 per unit	200
Less	
Cost of goods sold 100 units @ £3 per unit	300
	£100 *Loss*

He concludes from analysis that an offer of £2 per unit for 100 units in the firm's inventory is unacceptable. Do you agree? State clearly any assumptions that you make.

11.4 The Kendo Co. uses machinery in its manufacturing processes. You have been asked to calculate the costs to the firm of the use of various machines during the next month:

Machine A
(i) Net book value: now £100, after one month: £70;
(ii) Resale value: now £ nil, after one month: £ nil;
(iii) Subcontracting the use of the machine to another firm would yield a contribution of £25;
(iv) Use for a special order yielding a contribution of £22.

Machine B
(i) Net book value: now £500; after one month: £200;
(ii) Resale value: now and in one month's time: £50 less dismantling costs of £200.
(iii) Modify machine during month for £120 and save replacing by another machine which would cost £200.

Machine C
 (i) Completely depreciated three years ago;
 (ii) Resale value now and in one month: £ nil;
 (iii) Dismantle for spares with a selling price of £50, or replacement cost of £250. This is possible only this month;
 (iv) Cost of hiring a similar machine: £200 per month.

11.5 The Katto Co. is considering its production plan for the next month for two products, X and Y. B'th products use some of the firm's manufacturing and bottling capacity which would otherwise be unused. The forecast contributions per unit of X and Y for sales up to 1000 units each are £1.50 and £2.00 respectively. The production requirements of X and Y and the capacity of the relevant manufacturing and bottling plant is as follows:

Plant	Hours required per unit		Total capacity
	X	Y	Hours
Manufacturing	3	5	1500
Bottling	6	2	1000

Product Y requires special quality control and a maximum production limit of 270 unit of Y has been established by the company's manager.

(a) Calculate the production plan for quantities of X and Y for the next month which maximises the contribution from the products. What is the contribution?

(b) The company is considering sub-contracting the bottling of X and Y. What is the maximum the company should be prepared to pay for an additional (i) 1 hour, (ii) 10 hours, (iii) 100 hours of bottling capacity? Explain the differences, if any, between the hourly prices.

(c) The company is considering increasing the price of Y by £0.25 per unit, and it expects that the maximum sales will fall to about 700 units. Should the proposal be accepted, and if so what amount of X and Y should be produced next month?

12
Long-term Decisions

12.1 Introduction

Chapter 11 provided a framework for the analysis of decisions on pricing and output which play an important part in the planning process. In this chapter we extend the analysis, concentrating on decisions where there is the additional dimension of results which are spread over a long period. It is convenient for purposes of analysis and exposition to consider the content of Chapter 11 as relevant to short-term decision-making and the content of this chapter as relevant to long-term decisions. However, it should be understood that this is an over-simplification because the content of Chapter 11 is relevant for the analysis of the problems discussed in this chapter, and the conditions described below as being present in long-term investment decisions may be found in many pricing and output decisions.

The decisions discussed in this chapter are concerned with the investment of resources, e.g. what type of assets to purchase and what type of projects to undertake. An investment may be defined as the exchange of present resources for an uncertain amount of future resources. The decision may be concerned with acquiring land, building a new factory and buying new machinery, with replacing existing facilities which are wearing out, or with the provision of long-term finances. We will analyse the criteria and techniques for choosing between the alternative use of resources and their commitment for long periods. The related problem of providing finance was considered in Chapter 7 and it will be briefly referred to again later in this chapter. It is important to make correct decisions on the commitment of any resources, but this is accentuated in the context of long-term investment decisions by two factors. The first is where the required resources are significant in relation to the firm's overall size and the second is that the costs and benefits are spread over a long period. For example, the liner *Queen Elizabeth 2* was built in 1968 for the Cunard Shipping Co. Ltd at a cost of almost £30m at a time when the total net assets of the company were £73m. An illustration of the possible time periods involved can be seen from the building of the London underground Victoria line.[1] This was started in 1959, took over six years to build and the economic working life is assumed to be fifty years. The Victoria line is an example of a public sector investment and although we are mainly concerned with investment by firms, the methods of analysis discussed are relevant to other organisations, e.g. public corporations and local authorities. There are, however, particular problems in public expenditure of identifying costs and benefits.[2] We could also be concerned with an individual's decision, for example, to buy a house or to invest in shares or an insurance policy. A common factor in the first two examples is that there is a heavy initial cost with the returns or benefits spread over a number of years. With an insurance policy the position is reversed as the payments of the premiums are spread over a number of years with the return being a single receipt at the end of the policy.

12.2   Analysis for Investment Decisions

The quality of investment decisions will depend on many factors, two of which are the quality of the analysis and the quality of the information. Although they are discussed separately in the following sections it should be recognised that in many situations it may not be possible to distinguish which factor is involved. For example, a company considering whether to invest in a large advertising campaign must decide whether the expenditure is worth while. The major problem is identifying and enumerating the benefits, and this includes problems of analysis and of information. The basic analysis in investment decisions is one of measuring and comparing the costs and benefits arising from the decision and we have seen in Chapter 1 some of the difficulties of identifying and measuring costs and benefits.

The term 'project' is often used in connection with investment decisions. A project can be considered as an activity that a firm is considering. In order to present information about the project it may be necessary to assume that its effects can be considered as separate from the other activities of the firm. One of the major problems lies in identifying the nature of the project and its implications for other existing or prospective projects. If a project is independent of the rest of the firm it can be assessed without reference to other projects or aspects of the firm's operations. Some projects may be mutually exclusive where their acceptance would exclude the possibility of doing another project. For example, if a firm has a single plot of land then its use to build a new canteen may rule out all other possibilities of factory extensions, new offices, etc. In practice it is unusual for a project to be completely independent as it usually has some effect on the rest of the firm through its implications for the firm's cash flow, risk and strategy. The problem of aggregating individual projects into an overall budget for the firm is considered in Chapter 13.

Relation to Objectives

It was state in Chapter 10 that without known objectives the firm has no criteria against which to measure success or failure. Similarly it is not possible to identify properly the costs and benefits arising from a decision without relating them to the objectives of the firm. In Chapter 10 several possible objectives were considered, e.g. returns for the owner in terms of profits, dividends, share prices, or returns for the employees, customers or society which could be expressed in various forms, such as high wages, good quality products or pollution-free air. A simple example of a possible decision will illustrate the difficulty of the identification. A project to undertake open-cast mining in an area of natural beauty using low-paid labour working in unpleasant conditions is an example where the definition and measurement of the costs and benefits of the project can vary depending on the firm's objectives.

A firm could define benefits as proceeds from sales of the coal and define costs simply as the extraction costs of mining which together results in higher dividends while ignoring the cost to the worker of low wages and bad working conditions and the social costs of losing attractive scenery. It is, however, possible to adopt a more sophisticated definition of costs. For example, we could add to the cost of the wage paid to labour the cost of occasional strikes resulting from bad conditions or low wages. In addition pressure may force the firm into restoring the countryside when the mining is complete or to paying a financial penalty. This approach may be seen as either changing the objectives of the firm or as recognising the objectives of others as constraints which might impose costs on the firm.

12.3 Allowing for the Timing of the Costs and Benefits

It has been stated that the decisions under consideration are those where the costs and benefits are likely to be spread over a long period. We will now consider how we can incorporate the problem of the timing of the costs and benefits into the analysis. For example, if a firm has the opportunity of buying an asset for £10,000 and reselling it five years later for £12,000, does this seem an acceptable project? If the choice is between £1000 per year for five years or £6000 at the end of five years, which seems the better proposition? There is no obvious answer to these questions. A simple comparison in the first example between costs of £10,000 and benefits of £12,000, and in the second between benefits of £5000 or £6000 is not satisfactory. The reason is that in general we prefer to receive benefits sooner rather than later and similarly prefer to defer costs. It is thus necessary to give different weight to costs and benefits arising in different periods.

The weighting is determined by the strength of this preference, which is usually termed 'time preference' (explained more fully in App. C). Time preference in financial models is usually expressed by the opportunity cost of having benefits later rather than now. In general this is represented by the rate of interest in financial markets which is the collective assessment of individual time preference (see also Sect. 7.2 for explanation of this opportunity cost).[3]

The appropriate rate for a firm is that which it would have to pay to raise finance to undertake its projects. It will be apparent from Chapter 7 that a firm can raise its finance from various sources or by using a combination of sources. The measurement of the cost of finance of a firm was discussed in Sect. 7.8. It is this cost-of-finance concept which we we will use in the rest of the chapter as the rate of interest in discounted cash-flow calculations.

12.4 Discounted Cash Flow

Sect. 12.3 established the need to allow for the timing of costs and benefits in investment decisions. The methods adopted to achieve this are commonly termed discounted cash-flow techniques (see App. C). In this section we concentrate on two of these, the net present value (N.P.V.) and yield methods.

Example 12.1
Lea Valley Ltd are considering a project which will involve a cash payment of £10,000 now and give a cash benefit of £7000 at the end of year one and another £7000 at the end of year two. Total returns are £14,000 compared with a cost of £10,000 but this simple comparison is inadequate to assess the project.

Assuming the relevant rate of interest is 10% we could calculate the present value of the benefits (see App. C for explanation of calculations):

Present Value of Benefits
$$= \frac{A_1}{(1+r)^1} + \frac{A_2}{(1+r)^2}$$
$$= £7000 \times 0.9091 + £7000 \times 0.8264$$
$$= £6364 + £5785$$
$$= £12,149$$

The future cash flows have been reduced to a form where they can be compared with the initial cost of £10,000 which does not itself require adjustment because it is already in present value terms. The net present value (N.P.V.) of the project is thus:

$$\text{N.P.V.} = £12,149 - £10,000$$
$$= £\ 2,149$$

How does the N.P.V. value analysis relate to the valuation model introduced in Sect. 9.5? In effect the N.P.V. tells us (assuming the estimates are correct) that as a result of taking a decision to undertake the project the present value of the firm has increased by £2149. This means, whereas before the decision £10,000 was available for payment as dividends, as a result of the decision the firm will have available dividends of £14,000 in the future. The present value of these dividends is £12,149. This shows that the use of N.P.V. analysis is consistent with maximising shareholders' value.

As an alternative to N.P.V. we could also assess the project by compounding the £10,000 forward for two years and the first £7000 forward for one year and compare costs and benefits in equivalent terms for two years hence. This shows that the net terminal value of the project is £2600. It can be seen that this is the same result as that obtained by the present value two years earlier, i.e. £2600 × 0.8264 = £2149 which is the net present value of the project. Although this gives the same end result as the present-value calculation it is not commonly used because of the problem of comparing projects with different lives.

One of the difficulties in understanding the computation using N.P.V. in Ex. 12.1 is that apparently no interest charge has been included in the cost of the project. If the firm has to borrow the £10,000 would this give a different result? The answer is that it does not matter whether the firm has the cash or whether it has to borrow, provided it can borrow at 10% or, if it uses £10,000 it already has, it incurs an opportunity cost, i.e. earning 10% elsewhere. Ex. 12.2 should clarify this explanation.

Example 12.2
Compare the cash flows where the firm undertakes the project in Ex. 12.1 and (a) has £10,000 available or (b) it borrows £10,000 for two years at an interest rate of 10% and repays the £10,000 at the end of two years.

Forecast Cash-flow Statements	*Beginning of Year 1*	*End of Year 1*	*End of Year 2*
	£	£	£
(a) Project (costs) and Benefits			
– internally financed	(10,000)	7,000	7,000

(b)	Project (costs) and Benefits	(10,000)	7,000	7,000
	– financed by borrowing			
	Loan (and interest)	10,000	(1,000)	(1,000)
	Loan (repayment)			(10,000)
	Net Cash Flow	—	£6,000	(£4,000)

We know from Ex. 12.1 that the present value of (a) is £2149. The net present value of (b) is:

or

$$(£6000 \times 0.9091) - (£4000 \times 0.8264)$$

$$£5455 \qquad -£3306 \qquad = £2149$$

Thus, provided the rate of interest on the loan is the same as the rate of discount to be used, the existence of the loan, interest and repayment can be ignored in the net present-value calculations because they will automatically be included by the discounting process.

Referring back to Ex. 12.1 it can be seen that the present value of the £7000 receivable in Year 2 is less than the present value of that receivable in Year 1. This is the effect of two years' discounting as opposed to one and of course the longer the period that elapses before the benefit is due, the smaller will be the present value. This effect will be even more noticeable with a higher rate of discount than 10% and correspondingly less severe with a smaller rate. This is illustrated in Fig. 12.1. (N.B. The curves in Figs 12.1 and 12.2 have for simplicity been depicted as straight lines. If drawn accurately they would be slightly concave to the origin.)

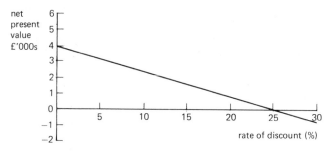

Figure 12.1   Graphical presentation of Ex. 12.1

At a rate of discount of 10% the N.P.V. is £2149. At a rate of 5% the N.P.V. rises to £3015 but at 20% it falls to £694. Two points on the graph of particular significance are where the N.P.V. is £4000 and where it is £0. The N.P.V. is £4000 where the rate of discount is 0%. This would be the case if there was no cost of finance and the firm was indifferent between amounts receivable now and in the future. Thus the £7000 in Years 1 and 2 would be as valuable as £7000 receivable now and the N.P.V. is simply the sum of cash receipts less cash payments, i.e. £14,000 less £10,000. The N.P.V. is £0 at approximately 26%. This means that if the cost of finance was 26% the project would be on the margin between acceptance and rejection because the present value of the benefits would be equal to the present value of the costs and at a rate of discount above 26% the project would have a negative N.P.V. The rate of discount at which N.P.V. is zero is known as the Yield (or internal rate of return) for that project.

The decision rules relating to the N.P.V. and yield methods of analysis can best be summarised by reference to the general arithmetical expression for the discounting calculation:

$$\text{N.P.V.} = \frac{a_0}{(1 + r)^0} + \frac{a_1}{(1 + r)^1} + \frac{a_2}{(1 + r)^2} \cdots \frac{a_n}{(1 + r)^n}$$

where a is the cash flow in a particular period (and may be negative in the early years of initial payments), r is the discount rate and n the number of periods. The rules are applied as follows:

Net Present Value Method. Discount the annual cash flow using the relevant cost of finance. If the N.P.V. is positive then the project should be accepted. This decision is, of course, based only on the numbers in the calculation and there may be other non-quantified factors which will be of importance to the decision-maker.

Yield Methods. The yield is the rate of discount which reduces the net present value of the cash flows to zero. If the yield of the project exceeds the cost of finance the project should be accepted subject to the qualifications below.

Comparisons of N.P.V. and Yield Methods
These two methods of applying discounted cash-flow techniques to decision-making are alternative approaches to the problem of timing and in general will suggest similar decisions. For example, in Fig. 12.1 if the cost of finance were between 0 and 26% the N.P.V. of the project would be positive. Using the N.P.V. criterion the project will be acceptable. A comparison of the yield of 26% with a cost of finance between 0 and 26% will also result in the project being accepted. If the cost of finance was over 26% then the project would be rejected using either the N.P.V. or the yield approach.

In this type of situation, when a project is independent and is being accepted or rejected by comparison with a criterion such as the cost of finance then the two methods will give the same decisions. There are situations where the yield method could be confusing, e.g. by showing more than one yield for a project or even when it is not possible to calculate a yield.[4] Where projects are mutually exclusive or it is necessary to compare projects with each other, care must be taken in interpreting the results of yield calculations.

Example 12.3
If the project in Ex. 12.1 which is identified below as Project A is compared with a Project B:

Forecast Cash-flow Statement

	Year 0	Year 1	Year 2	N.P.V.	Yield
	£	£	£	at 10%	%
Project A	(10,000)	7,000	7,000	2,149	26
Project B	(10,000)	1,000	14,000	2,479	23

Using the N.P.V. or the yield method and comparing the projects with a cost of finance of 10% clearly shows that both projects are acceptable. Comparing them with each other would be necessary if they were mutually exclusive, e.g. if they represented alternative uses for a single plot of land and it is then not clear which is the better. The N.P.V. of B using a discount rate of 10% is greater than A but the yield of A is greater than B. The two methods appear to give different signals. The explanation of this situation is best expressed by means of a diagram similar to Fig. 12.1. In Fig. 12.2 the results of Project B are included together with those for Project A as they were shown in Fig. 12.1.

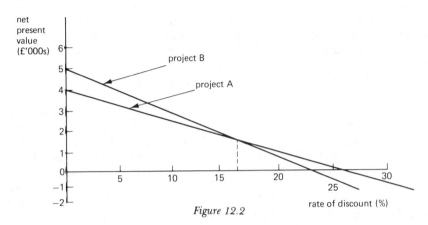

Figure 12.2

Fig. 12.2 shows that for discount rates up to approximately 17%, Project B has the higher N.P.V. but Project A has the higher N.P.V. for rates above 17%. The reason for this situation is the different pattern of cash flows in the two projects. As the discount rate should represent an opportunity cost, the higher this rate is, the more importance is placed on early rather than late cash inflows. Thus at low rates of discount the fact that Project B has the greater proportion of its returns in the second year is less significant, but this changes as the rate increases and the comparative weighting of Project A's earlier inflows increases, until at 17% they exactly compensate for the extra overall £1000 inflow in Project B. Care must be taken when using the yield method that the opportunity cost is considered. In most situations this will be done merely by comparing the yield with the cost of finance and accepting projects with yields in excess of it. Comparing the yields of projects does not always give the same result as considering the opportunity cost, as is shown by the above example. It is incorrect to say that Project A with a yield of 26% is better than Project B with 23% without considering the firm's opportunity cost of finance. With an opportunity cost of 10%, Project B should be preferred.

12.5 Payback and Return on Investment

These are two methods of analysis of investment projects which do not explicitly allow for the timing of the cost and benefits. They are, however, in common use and it is important to understand their strengths and limitations.

Payback is concerned with the length of time that elapses before the project covers its initial outlay.

Example 12.4

Forecast Cash-flow Statement

	0	1	2	3	4	Payback period
			Year			
Project X	(£20,000)	8,000	6,000	6,000	6,000	3 years
Project Y	(£20,000)	11,000	9,000	2,000		2 years

A firm is usually concerned with minimising the payback period and it could use a decision rule which states that no projects with payback above a maximum number of years is considered. The arguments in favour of this method are that it is easy to understand and to apply, it operates as a regulator of liquidity by concentrating attention on projects with earlier cash returns, and it offers an approach to the problem of risk by concentrating on short-term projects. It has obvious disadvantages if used as a sole criterion because it excludes from the analysis performance after the payback period and thus fails to measure the overall financial result. In Ex. 12.4, although Y has the shorter period of payback it is possible that X is more attractive; the payback calculation ignored cash flows beyond the payback period.

Although the payback method seems a very blunt instrument it might have the advantage of highlighting potential liquidity problem areas. Liquidity is an obviously important area and there is a danger in applying only discounted cash-flow methods that it is overlooked because the usual assumption made in discounted cash-flow calculations is that a firm can borrow at the market rate of interest. If this is so then liquidity should never be a problem. However, firms cannot always obtain finance to undertake all their projects. This may be because at a particular time a firm's reputation in the finance market is not good or perhaps the firm does not want to issue more shares or to incur further debts. In these conditions, known as capital rationing, the payback approach with its emphasis on early returns may have more justification.

Return on investment (also commonly known as the accounting rate of return) is a very common accounting ratio which compares the overall returns from an investment with its initial cost. It is a ratio frequently used by firms and by financial analysts to assess a firm's performance by taking profit as a percentage of assets employed by the firm. It can also be applied where the returns are expressed as cash flows rather than profits.

Example 12.5

Project Y in Ex. 12.4 had the following results:

Forecast Cash-flow Statement

Year				Total
0	1	2	3	
(20,000)	11,000	9,000	2,000	£22,000

This shows a net return of £2000 on an investment of £20,000, an overall return on investment of 10% or as the project lasts for three years an average annual return of $3\frac{1}{3}\%$. The disadvantage of using this method of analysis is that the timing of the cash flows is not considered. In Ex. 12.5 the return on investment would be the same if the pattern of cash inflows had been £1000, £1000, £20,000 or £20,000, £1000, £1000.

It was stated earlier that this ratio of return on investment is a key ratio in financial analysis of a firm's performance so that it should not be dismissed lightly. However, the essential difference between using it to assess a firm's past performance and using it to analyse decisions about the future is the importance of timing the returns in the latter. The use of return on investment is considered further in Sect. 16.3.

We have considered four methods of analysing investment projects; net present value, yield, payback and return on investment, the first two being discounting methods which allow for the timing of cash flows and the last two which ignore timing. It is important to re-emphasise here that in assessing decisions we are concerned with future performance and that the data should be in the form of cash flows rather than accounting profits. In Ex. 12.6 the methods are applied to three projects.

Example 12.6

Forecast Cash-flow Statements

				Year			Total
	0	1	2	3	4	5	1–5
	£	£	£	£	£	£	£
Projects: D	(£20,000)	6,000	6,000	6,000	6,000	6,000	30,000
E	(£20,000)	10,000	8,000	5,000	5,000		28,000
F	(£20,000)	12,000	12,000				24,000

From this data the following analysis can be made:

	D	E	F
Payback—years	4 (3)	3 (2)	2 (1)
Return on Investment—%			
– Overall	50 (1)	40 (2)	20 (3)
– Average Annual	10 (1)	10 (1)	10 (1)
Net Present Value	£1630 (2)	£2046 (1)	£280 (3)
Yield—%	15 (2)	18 (1)	13 (3)

The figures in brackets represent the project's ranking in the order of preference shown by use of the various methods. The significant point here is the different ranking shown by different methods, especially the difference between payback and return on investment and the similarity between net present value and yield.

12.6 Quality of the Information in Investment Decisions

In the previous sections stress was laid on the importance of using proper methods of analysis in investment decisions. While it is true that an incorrect method of analysis may impair decision-making, the information input to the analysis is at least of equal importance. In this section we concentrate on two aspects of the quality of information; (a) the problem of identifying relevant information and (b) the uncertainty implicit in forecasts.

(a) IDENTIFYING RELEVANT INFORMATION

The problem of relevant information was discussed in Chapters 10 and 11 where the conclusion reached was that relevant information for decision-making should be estimates of future costs and benefits. In addition emphasis was placed on the concept of opportunity cost as a means of ensuring that alternative courses of action are given proper consideration when decisions are made. These conclusions give general guidance on the problem of relevant information, and we consider below more specific aspects in relation to investment decisions.

In Sect. 12.2 the problem of identifying the parameters of a project was introduced. This is an important stage in the identification of relevant information, particularly with a large investment project affecting many aspects of a firm's organisation. Consider, for example, a firm's decision to market a new product. There are the more obvious costs, such as advertising, production and distribution but there may be others less obvious and more difficult to identify, e.g. the cost of increases in inventory, debtors and creditors, the possible adverse effect on the production and distribution of other products sold by the firm caused by overstretched capacity, or the effect of the extra burden on the management organisation. In addition there are considerations such as the effect of the new product on the firm's image, on employee morale or as a benefit to the consumer. Whether these last-named factors are considered relevant may depend on the agreed set of objectives for the firm in question.

The effects of an investment decision may thus be difficult to identify and in most cases will be difficult to quantify in monetary terms. The analysis discussed in the earlier part of this chapter and in Chapter 11, in general assumed that the information on which decisions are based would be quantified information. How should the factors mentioned above be included in the analysis of investment decision? The first and perhaps the most obvious way is to provide the decision-maker with the quantitative data, for example, the net present value, plus relevant but not quantified information and allow him to use his judgement. The key issue is how much of the data must necessarily remain unquantified. The more information that cannot be expressed in monetary terms which the decision-maker has to handle, the more difficult will it be for him to arrive at a reliable decision.

It may be more satisfactory to make a rigorous attempt to quantify some of these apparently qualitative factors. Take for example a situation where a manager states that a piece of equipment is so necessary to the firm that it must be purchased. A possible approach would be to consider the alternatives if the equipment is not replaced, e.g. what benefits would be lost. If it is said, that a generator in a factory needs replacing no matter what it costs, the implication is that probably the benefits forgone if it is not replaced will exceed the replacement cost. It may be that the benefits are the entire profits of the factory which could not operate without power. Much of the research into quantifying such costs and benefits has been done in connection with projects in the public sector. The reason for this is that for such projects, e.g. airports, roads, irrigation, there is a large amount of public money involved and many of the costs and benefits are very difficult to quantify. One such project which was referred to earlier in the chapter is the Victoria Line. The benefits considered, apart from the fares received, included the time saved by commuters and the relief on other parts of the transport system. These could have been regarded as qualitative benefits but in fact were quantified in the analysis of the project. It may not be possible to quantify all aspects of business decisions, but it is important that the attempt be made because it is extremely difficult to choose between competing projects where resources are limited if large elements of the data remain unquantified.

(b) UNCERTAINTY IMPLICIT IN FORECASTS

The importance of the problem of uncertainty in the forecast results of long-term investments is that decisions once taken may be costly to reverse. One of the elements in the analysis of the Victoria Line project which had an estimated cost of £55m was a discount rate of 6%. Since the time of the analysis and the decision to go ahead rates of interest have doubled. However, by the time the scale of the upward trend of interest rates was known it was too late to decide against the continuation of the project.

It was stated in Chapter 10 that all decisions are concerned with what is to be done in the future and thus will be based on estimates. These estimates must to some extent be subject to the errors inherent in all forecasting. The potential size of the dispersion of actual results are an indication of the risk or uncertainty involved in the decision. A distinction is sometimes made between a risk situation where there is statistical evidence of the parameters of likely events, for example, fires, theft or death, where data is collected by insurance firms, and an uncertainty situation such as a one-off project where there is no reliable evidence on which to estimate future events. Most business decisions, however, fall in between these extremes and thus in this context the terms are used interchangeably.

It may be possible to improve the forecast of the potential dispersion of results. This can be attempted, for example, by greater time spent on analysis of past performance and its relation to the future; by constructing more sophisticated predictive models; and by testing these models, e.g. by simulated production runs or by market research. These are examples of how forecasts may be made more reliable but they cannot eliminate uncertainty and in addition they involve costs which must be assessed in relation to the improved quality of the estimates.

The amount of risk which can be identified in a situation by more accurate forecasting varies between decisions, firms and industries. If there were no such differences then there would be a tendency for all returns from investments to be the same. The reasons why returns in some industries are favourable compared with others may be that the risks involved are considered to be high. Therefore if the aim of the investor was simply to minimise risk he may find he had also minimised the return on the investment. The analysis of risk and uncertainty is thus not concerned with its elimination but rather with its identification and measurement.

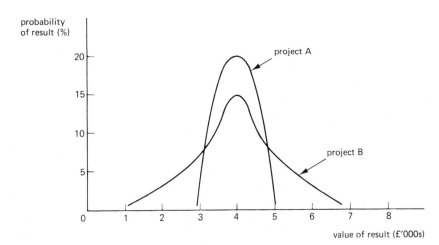

Figure 12.3

The most satisfactory method of measuring risk is by means of probability concepts. If riskiness is defined as the possibility of variation in predicted results then the likely outcome of results from two investments can be depicted as in Fig. 12.3.

The probability distribution for project A shows that almost all the predicted outcomes lie between £3000 and £5000 whereas for B they lie between £1000 and £7000. The most likely result in either investment is £4000 but whereas in Project A there is a 20% probability of it being £4000 in B the probability is only 15%. A may therefore be said to be the less risky investment because the estimates show that there is more chance of achieving the most likely result and that possible variation from £4000 will be plus or minus £1000, whereas for B the variation is plus or minus £3000. This variation or dispersion of results can be depicted using the statistical measure of standard deviation, higher values of this measure denoting greater risk.

It should be remembered that we are concerned here with the quality of information for making investment decisions. The approach described above is based on the assumption that a single predicted result is not adequate information in that the decision-maker does not know with what level of certainty (or conversely what level of risk) the estimate has been made and also what the possible variation from it might be.

The single-value estimates could represent an optimistic or pessimistic forecast by a manager or his estimation of the mean, median or modal value. It is important to understand the approach adopted by those presenting such information. It was stated above that the presentation of forecasts in terms of probability distribution may be superior to single-value forecasts. An interesting aspect of this argument is whether an individual who estimates a single value for a particular aspect of a project, e.g. sales volume, actually used an internalised probability distribution based on his experience to arrive at the single value. If he does then the single value may be the weighted average of the underlying distribution. The important aspect of asking for explicit information or the possible dispersion of results is that it makes the presenter of the information state his assumptions and enables the decision-maker to improve his understanding of the data he must use for his decision.

Knowledge of the dispersion of possible results adds information but this is still liable to errors in prediction. An everyday example is the prediction of the weather for the day of a picnic. The predicted average temperature for the day might be 65°F. It would be useful to know what level of confidence can be placed on the prediction. For example, a professional weatherman might be able to forecast with 80% confidence that the temperature will be within 5° of his predicted average. He might also be able to say with 99% confidence that the range of temperature on that day would be 55° to 80°. All this information would make one better able to select the right day for the picnic. Similarly in business investment decisions the quality of information is improved if the parameters of the risks can be specified.

The possibility of such specification will vary for different decisions. It has been stated earlier that in certain industries actuarial calculations based on a large volume of statistics can be used to depict the parameters with a high degree of accuracy. A company involved in life insurance can confidently predict the numbers of deaths in a given year, and the subsequent cost of claims. A company drilling for oil can predict successful drills and the subsequent volume of oil found with much less confidence, partly because it does not have the large volume of relevant statistics available to the life insurer. Prospecting for oil would usually be thought to be more risky than providing life insurance but the returns from the former would be expected to be higher as a reward for the extra risk. For example the returns might be:

	% Predicted Yield	Confidence Level	Possible Range of % Returns
Oil prospecting	40	20%	0–150
Life insurance	15	70%	12– 18

Looking only at the percentage predicted yield would clearly not be adequate for an investment decision. Which of these two investment possibilities seems more attractive will depend on the attitude of the investor – whether a firm or an individual – to risk taking. With proper information it is possible to know what risks are being taken and thus investments undertaken are more likely to be consistent with the objectives of the firm. This will only be true, of course, where the decision-taker within the firm adopts the attitude to risk which his shareholders would wish. In practice there will often be a divergence between the attitudes of owners and managers.

Sensitivity Analysis
A further means of improving the interpretation of the information available to decision-makers is by sensitivity analysis. This type of analysis is an attempt to identify the more critical variables in a decision by showing how sensitive the overall result is to changes in these variables. This can be done by showing how much the actual values of the variables would have to differ from the predicted values in order to make a significant difference to the overall result, e.g. sufficient to change an overall gain into a loss.

Example 12.7
Using the project depicted in Ex. 12.1 as the basis for the example, the details of which were:

Initial cost	£10,000
Cash benefits each year	£7,000
Length of project	2 years
Rate of discount	10%
N.P.V.	£2,149

In this example there are four variables, which are combined together to calculate the net present value. The decision criterion discussed earlier in this chapter was that a project should be accepted where the N.P.V. is positive. Thus it would be interesting for the decision-maker to know what variations from the predicted values for the variables would reduce the net present value of £2149 to zero.

Before the analysis is taken any further it must be emphasised that the examples are deliberately simplified so that we can concentrate on the principles involved. For example, assuming a short life of two years makes calculation easy but may not be typical of investment projects. Also the single figure of cash benefits could be the net result of several component variables such as:

Sales volume and sales price
Manufacturing costs; labour, materials and overheads
Taxation charges on profits earned by the project
Tax allowances or government grants for capital expenditure

However, taking the values of the variables as they stand, the following calculation could be made to show how much each would have to change to make the project break-even with a zero net present value.

Initial Cost – £10,000
Initial cost of £10,000 would have to increase to £12,149, a rise of

$$\frac{2,149}{10,000} \text{ or } 21.49\%$$

Annual Receipts – £7000
Using Table B in App. C we can see that the factor for converting £1 per year for two years at 10% to a present value is 1.7355 and thus the annual receipt which would have a present value of £10,000 must be

$$\frac{£10,000}{1.7355}$$

or £5762. This is a fall of

$$\frac{1238}{7000} \text{ or } 17.7\%.$$

Length of Project – 2 years
The factor which will convert the £7000 annual receipt to a present value of £10,000 must be

$$\frac{10,000}{7,000} \text{ or } 1.428.$$

Using Table B in App. C we can see that at a rate of discount of 10% a factor of 1.428 falls between 1 and 2 years at approximately 1.6 years. This would be a fall of

$$\frac{.4}{2} \text{ or } 20\%.$$

As previously mentioned in a short-life project, this sort of analysis may not be appropriate but the principle should be clear.

Rate of Discount – 10%
The same factor of 1.428 applies but in using Table B, instead of holding the rate of discount constant as in the previous calculation, the life of two years is assumed and the appropriate rate of discount is found to be approximately 26%. This would be a rise of

$$\frac{16}{10} \text{ or } 160\%.$$

This shows that the cost of finance could rise to 26% before the project becomes unacceptable. The figure of 26% is the yield of the project shown in Fig. 12.1.

The additional information that this analysis gives is an indication of the sensitivity of the overall result, in this case the N.P.V. to changes in the value of variables. For all except the rate of discount it shows that it would take an adverse change of around 20% in the predicted value to eliminate the positive net present value. Using the concepts of probability discussed earlier it might then be possible to say what the chances are of a variation of as much as 20%. With this information the decision-maker has a better idea of how confidently he can expect a positive benefit from the project.

It is important that anyone using such information as described above should understand the methods used in its preparation and be aware of its limitations. For example, it was assumed that the variables are independent by holding all constant apart from the one under consideration. In practice it is likely that all variables will change from the predicted values. This can be partially met by means of a more sophisticated analysis, perhaps using a computer-based simulation model where the effect of a combination of changes in values of variables can be considered.

Another aspect is where a single variable represents several separate elements and by considering only the single figure some element of sensitivity may be missed. For example, it was calculated that the figure of £7000 for annual receipts would have to fall by 17.7% before the net present value became zero. If, however, the £7000 represented a sales figure of £107,000 less costs of £100,000, then the picture is considerably altered. The sales revenue would only have to fall by

$$\frac{1,238}{107,000} \text{ or } 1.16\%$$

and costs rise by

$$\frac{1,238}{100,000} \text{ or } 1.24\%$$

to reduce the annual receipts to £5762 and thus make the net present value zero. Such low percentage changes are likely to have a high possibility of occurring and thus the confidence in the project expressed earlier may be much reduced.

Adjusting the Discount Rate

A method of handling the problem of risk and uncertainty which has the initial attraction of being simple to operate is that of adjusting the rate of discount to allow a safety margin for the possible risk involved. For example, in the project discussed earlier, this approach might suggest using a discount rate of 20% instead of 10%. The justification for this approach is that by adopting the higher criterion of say 20% in selecting projects an allowance is made to cover the possibility of the project going wrong. If 10% represents the firm's cost of finance or the return it could earn on another similar project, then by raising the rate of discount above 10% the firm is, however, in danger of rejecting viable projects.

This method of allowing for the possible risk involved in undertaking an investment project is a widely used approach[5] but there are possible disadvantages which it is important to understand. The first of these is that if the same rate of discount adjusted by the addition of a risk premium is used for all the projects the firm is considering then all projects are being treated alike as regards their risk possibilities. However, it would be unusual if all a firm's projects had the same inherent risk. What might happen is, for example, if the firm adopted a 20% discount rate instead of the cost of finance of, say, 10%, then some very safe project with returns between 10% and 20% may be rejected whereas those with possible returns above 20% but very risky would be accepted. This result may be acceptable to the firm if it fits their objectives but using solely a risk-adjusted discount rate approach to the problem of risk may not identify the problem illustrated here. This can be overcome by using variable discount rates, that is, higher for the more risky and lower for the less risky. This, if acceptable, requires some criterion for defining more or less risky and identifying how much higher the rate should be for the former. This seems to bring us back to the use of probability.

The result of increasing the discount rate is that a greater emphasis is placed on early returns because the later returns are obviously more affected in terms of present value. This is appropriate if it is felt that the longer a project goes on the more uncertain are the predictions. In many cases this is valid because the firm is likely to be more confident about its estimates for, say, next year than it is for results in ten years' time. However, there are cases where this may not be valid, with the greatest uncertainty in the early years. An example of this is in the provision of electricity from nuclear power, where the greatest uncertainty is the cost and efficiency of the construction of the power station which must take place at the beginning of the project, whereas the demand element for electricity could be calculated with much more certainty. In this case adjusting the discount rate over the life of the project would not have been an appropriate method of allowing for the risk involved.

It has also been assumed that the appropriate discount rate is the firm's cost of finance. This will already include an allowance for risk reflected in the rate of return required by lenders and investors. Thus an additional adjustment may result in an element of double-counting.

It should be emphasised with regard to the treatment of risk and uncertainty in project analysis that because of the nature of the problem there is no ideal method for handling a situation which is uncertain. Each of the methods suggested provides information which may help in selecting the sort of risk situation in which the firm wishes to operate. This selection is part of the planning process. Taken individually each method has disadvantages which it is important to understand. The most appropriate form of analysis is probably to use some or all of the methods in conjunction with each other.

12.7   Summary

This chapter has been concerned with the particular problem of assessing long-term investments. The analysis developed in Chapters 10 and 11 has general applicability in decision-making. The additional problem areas dealt with in the chapter relate to the development of appropriate methods of allowing for the timing of forecast cash flows and the computation and presentation of the information on which decisions are based, in particular the problems of the treatment of risk and uncertainty. Investment decisions were discussed in terms of individual projects; in Chapter 13 we consider how projects are aggregated within a budget to represent the overall planning decisions of the firm.

Notes and References

1. Ministry of Transport and Civil Aviation, *The Victoria Line* (H.M.S.O., 1959).
2. D. W. Pearce, *Cost-Benefit Analysis* (London, Macmillan, 1971).
3. B. Carsberg, *Analysis for Investment Decisions* (London, Haymarket, 1974).
4. H. Bierman Jr and S. Smidt, *The Capital Budgeting Decision*, 3rd edn (London, Collier–Macmillan, 1971).
5. N.E.D.O., *Investment Appraisal* (H.M.S.O., 1971).

Further Reading

S. H. Archer and C. A. D'Ambrosio, *Business Finance, Theory and Management* (New York, Macmillan, 1966).

J. T. S. Porterfield, *Investment Decisions and Capital Costs* (Englewood Cliffs, N.J., Prentice-Hall, 1965).

W. J. Baumol, *Economic Theory and Operations Analysis* (Englewood Cliffs, N.J., Prentice-Hall, 1965).

M. Bromwich, 'Capital Budgeting – A Survey', *Journal of Business Finance* (Autumn 1970).

E. Solomons (ed.), *The Management of Corporate Capital* (New York, N.Y., Free Press, 1959).

T. H. Naylor *et al.*, *Computer Simulation Techniques* (New York, N.Y., John Wiley & Sons, 1966).

David B. Hertz, 'Risk Analysis in Capital Investment', in *Harvard Business Review*, vol. 42, no. 1 (January–February 1964).

R. A. Fawthrop, 'Underlying Problems in Discounted Cash Flow Appraisal', *Accounting and Business Research* (Summer 1971).

R. M. Adelson, 'Discounted Cash Flow – Can We Discount it? A Critical Examination', *Journal of Business Finance* (Summer 1970).

R. O. Swalm, 'Utility Theory – Insights into Risk-taking', *Harvard Business Review* (Nov.–Dec. 1966).

C. J. Grayson, 'The Use of Statistical Techniques in Capital Budgeting', in *Financial Research and Management Decisions*, ed. A. A. Robichek (New York, N.Y., John Wiley & Sons, 1967).

R. J. Lister (ed.), *Studies in Optimal Financing* (London, Macmillan, 1973).

R. F. J. Dewhurst, *Business Cost-benefit Analysis* (London, McGraw-Hill, 1972).

Questions and Problems

12.1 What do you understand by the following terminology?

Investment project	Yield
Independent projects	Rate of discount
Mutually exclusive projects	Cost of finance
Time preference	Payback
Discounted cash flow	Return on investment
Cost–benefit analysis	Uncertainty
Net present value	Risk
Net terminal value	Sensitivity analysis

12.1 Is it possible to distinguish between short-term and long-term decisions?

12.3 Discuss the problems of identifying and quantifying the costs and benefits of:

(a) the purchase of shares in a company
(b) the purchase of a whole firm
(c) a firm's purchase of additional factory space
(d) the purchase of a reserve generator for use in an emergency
(e) an advertising campaign
(f) a new hospital
(g) a new motorway.

12.4 A firm requires a return of 12% on investments and is considering whether to invest £18,000 in new equipment with an expected economic life of four years. Cash inflows are expected to be £7000 in each of the first two years and £6000 in each of the last two years. Would you advise the firm to invest in this equipment?

12.5 In 1952 the Lawther Co. Ltd issued 4% Debentures (1982). Mr Little bought some of these Debentures in 1973 at 60p each when they had nine years to go to redemption and when similar Debentures were being issued with a yield of 10%. Do you consider Mr Little made a good investment?

12.6   Discuss the major risks that might be met in:

   (a)   the marketing of a new product
   (b)   the purchase of a computer
   (c)   the production and marketing of nuclear power.

12.7   The Latham Co. Ltd, which has an annual sales turnover of £1 million, is considering buying a new machine at a cost of £5000. It is expected that the machine would reduce production costs by £1000 during each year of its useful life at the end of which the machine would have no scrap value.
   The company can obtain finance at a cost of 8%.

   (a)   Assuming the expected life of the machine is seven years would you advise the company to purchase?
   (b)   What would your advice be if after a survey of 200 similar machines you discover that the years of useful life varied thus:

Years of useful life	Number of machines
2	10
5	10
6	60
7	50
8	50
9	20

   (c)   If the machine had cost £500,000 and the annual cost reduction £100,000 would this affect your advice in (a) or (b).
   (d)   If there was no statistical evidence of the likely useful life of the machine but from your experience you would have expected the life pattern to be the same as in (b), would this have affected your decision?

13
Budgeting for the
Total Firm

13.1 Introduction

In the previous chapters we have examined how the firm could evaluate and choose between various courses of action. As we saw in Chapter 10 strategic decisions are usually concerned with broad policy, and it is normally operating decisions which are reflected in detail in the budgets. A central part of the process of decision-making is the forecast of costs and benefits of the alternatives. The alternatives chosen will form the basis of the set of budgets for the total firm which will present the implications of aggregating the forecast costs and benefits of all the decisions taken by the management of the firm. The budgets provide a useful method of control by acting as criteria against which to measure actual performance. The forecasting and the control aspects of budgets cannot be completely separated, but for expositional purposes this chapter examines the process of budgeting and in Chapter 15 we examine budgetary control.

The plans of a firm will project the future of the firm over the period up to its planning horizon. The point in time that a firm should consider as its planning horizon cannot be laid down as a rule. Its selection will involve evaluating the costs and benefits of varying horizons. For example, a too close horizon excludes useful information about the future, and benefits from examining plans with distant horizons. This includes motivations to develop a long-term vision of the firm. The rate of change in a firm's environment may also have an important influence, as uncertainties may make a particular set of plans for the distant future meaningless. The firm may, however, have several sets of plans for various time horizons. As time passes the firm will probably roll its planning horizon forward and update its information. Budgets are detailed plans and often considered as relating to a period of one year only. The period over which it is useful to prepare detailed information is influenced by considerations similar to those of determining the planning horizon.

A typical set of budgets for a firm will reflect its activities and organisation. Fig. 13.1 illustrates a possible set of budgets for a manufacturing firm. The form of organisation structure illustrated is one divided up according to its separate activity functions. Different organisational structures will require different sets of budgets.

As we shall see, the budgets of a firm are not independent of each other, and their interrelationship is a major consideration in their preparation. The data in budgets will normally relate to revenues and costs, and other physical measures, e.g. production quantity, and manpower. The extent of detailed budgeting will

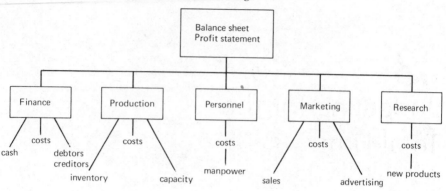

Figure 13.1   Set of budgets for a manufacturing firm

depend on the various uses for which budgets are prepared and also the costs of preparing reliable data.

13.2   Decisions and Budgets

As we saw in the previous two chapters it was necessary to draw up a forecast for every project under consideration to provide a satisfactory decision-making procedure. Those projects chosen will become part of the overall activities of the firm. It is unlikely, except perhaps in a small or new firm, that it will have only one project. The preparation of the set of budgets will involve aggregation of the effect of decisions recently taken and the continuing effects (revised if necessary) of projects undertaken in previous periods.

Individual projects often cut across the administrative (i.e. functional) boundaries of a firm. Functional managers will normally have responsibility for the activities within their areas, e.g. marketing, production, finance. If in the preparation of the budgets we merely aggregated the individual forecasts of past and current projects, we fail to recognise that several projects may jointly use the same resources. For example, a company making separate decisions about manufacturing many different products may have to share the use of its packaging and warehousing facilities between its products. It would also be unlikely that it would have a separate management or debt collection organisation for each product.

As we can see from Fig. 13.2 the projects cut across functional boundaries and problems may arise in the definition of responsibility as the project becomes absorbed into the firm's overall activities. The projects may have been considered separately for decision-making purposes, but once they have been undertaken, separate responsibility for them may not exist.

Function	Project 1 *Production and sale of Togs*	Project 2 *Retailing of product Q*	Project 3 *Repayment of debt and new share issue*
Production	x		
Marketing	x	x	
Finance	x	x	x
Purchasing	x	x	

Figure 13.2   Interrelationships between projects and functions

The budgets will usually be concerned with identifying what the effect of the aggregate of all project forecasts are for the firm's organisation and resources. In Fig. 13.2 we could see that the budgeting operation may have at least two dimensions. The forecasts for the resources required by the projects must ultimately equal the resources under the control of the functions. The process of budgeting will involve the reconciliation of any differences between individual budgets.

There are clear advantages to be gained from considering projects in the context of the total firm. The firm may be able to use its resources more efficiently, for example, through attaining production economies of scale or through bulk buying. Furthermore, the individual projects may not fit into an overall strategy for the firm and this may only become clear when all the forecasts for the various activities are aggregated. This process will be important if a firm's policy is to minimise the overall risk from its business activities.

In the process of budgeting overall resources of the firm it may become clear that because of joint use of resources among projects imbalances between demand and supply may arise. For example, the shortage of manufacturing capacity or cash could lead to suboptimal results. This may be avoided by budgeting, which should ensure that functional managers know about the demands likely to be made on their resources. The requirement to budget resources also arises from the time and cost incurred in acquiring further resources. For example, if a firm runs out of raw materials immediate delivery may not be possible. If the firm had prepared a budget for its raw material it may have been able to predict the future shortage and place an early order. The lead time for most resources may be influenced by physical factors, e.g. oil in transit in a tanker, or by price, e.g. paying a premium for immediate delivery of inventory.

13.3 Participation in budgeting

The way in which the members of an organisation participate in the budgeting process can have effects on their behaviour and attitudes.[1] Understanding the importance of participation can be an important element in successful administration. Budgeting for the firm as a whole may be successful in stimulating functional managers to view their own departments in the context of the total firm rather than as an isolated unit. It may also provide a check on the congruence of their goals and those of the firm. They may also begin to understand the difficulties which other departments face. The involvement in budgeting may prevent managers of functions becoming so absorbed in the solution of their own departmental problems that the overall business context of their activities becomes a secondary consideration. Members of different levels of the organisation may also become more familiar with problems arising at different levels of the firm. Thus participation in the budgeting activity may stimulate new ideas and improve the communication of information within the firm.

Participation in the budgeting process through the establishment of targets or forecasts is also of considerable importance in assisting the development of the identification of individuals with the firm. This participation could be carried out on a democratic basis and managers and other employees could play a major part in the preparation of their budgets which may later be used as criteria for gauging their performance. However, it could be considered that this may be no more than a process of pseudo-participation where the appearance is of participation but where no effective decisions about the future budgets can be made by the participants. Clearly the way in which the numbers in budgets are chosen either through participation or through being assigned as targets could influence the way in which the managers and other employees view the budget. They may find it acceptable or they may be antogonistic towards the whole budgeting operation.

The budgets could be an important determinant of future organisational behaviour if they were considered as targets rather than simply as an expression of the effect of past or current decisions. For example, a firm may establish that for budgeting purposes its objective will be to increase sales by 50% per annum over the next three years, without knowing how this could be achieved at the time of stating the objective. The purpose of this would be to stimulate managers into the search for opportunities. The way the numbers in budgets are expressed in terms of the motivational assumptions are thus important.

13.4   Preparation of budgets

In the previous section we examined the effects of participation of the organisation in budgeting. We cannot make any definitive statement about who should be involved in budgeting unless assumptions are made about the desirability of participation. Our analysis will proceed using the premise that participation is desirable. In addition, budgeting offers a useful opportunity to remind the individual managers of parts of a firm of their responsibility for the activities under their control. Responsibility needs to be established so that actual results can be attributed as the responsibility of particular individuals and reported to them when they occur. In the budgeting process, assumptions will be made about future events which will affect the firm and which will to a varying extent be under the firms control. In Chapter 15 we discuss the importance of a careful definition of responsibility in the context of budgetary control.

The group of budgeters should be selected after consideration of the importance of motivation and responsibility. It will probably consist of functional and project managers who will need to co-operate with each other to produce an overall set of budgets for the firm. Information about projects and resources will be available to them. Budgeting may require a substantial period of time and use substantial management and data-processing resources in collecting the relevant data and assembling it in a suitable form for analysis. In Figs. 13.1 and 13.2 we could see that individual budgets within the overall set of budgets for the organisation may be closely related. This interrelationship, particularly in the area of financing the business, can be seen in Fig. 7.4, where all those many factors which affect cash can be seen.

As budgeting involves reconciliation of requirements of projects and functions it is unlikely that the budgets which are prepared initially will be acceptable to all those concerned. For example, it may become clear that insufficient cash is available to continue with the projects which have been accepted in the past and that new decisions have to be taken to revise the former forecasts. The problem of reconciliation arises because of inter-budget relationships where changes in one budget may have effects on other budgets. We will examine two approaches to the solution of this problem.

Firstly, we may identify some factors and consider them as fixed and develop our budgets within a framework of constraints, e.g. that cash or factory capacity is limited. This approach to the problem is clearly open to the criticism that selection of these critical factors may be difficult or arbitrary and that it is rare for limitations to be absolutely fixed. The extent to which factors in budgeting are considered fixed will vary between firms. For example, an objective to increase sales by 20% may be amended because of a limit to factory capacity. More resources may be made available if the firm is prepared to raise further finance. Certain factors may, however, be considered as fixed for the budget period, for example if a firm is completely unable to raise further finance or if its objectives are considered as beyond alteration.

The other approach to the process of reconciliation may be an iterative process in which different combinations of objectives, resources and project plans are considered until a preferred set of budgets is established and agreed. It may represent a suboptimal set of budgets in the context of what the firm could have achieved with full information and limitless data collection and processing facilities, but it may result in the best approximation to optimality that was possible. The development of computer-based simulation models of the firm offers the greatest hope of improvement of iterative methods of reconciliation.[2]

The classifications used in the budgets for control should reflect the division of responsibility within the firm (see Sect, 14.2). In Fig. 13.1 we showed an outline of the budgets that could be prepared for a functionally organised manufacturing firm. The budgets selected and prepared by any firm will reflect the needs of users of budget information who will require information for forecasting and control purposes.

As budgets are quantitative statements about the future it is important to understand the significance of the numbers incorporated in them. The firm could produce a variety of budgets based on different assumptions. Alternative sets of budgets could be produced which had an assumed probability of 0.4, 0.6, or 0.9 chance of being attained. As a further alternative it could produce budgets using optimistic, pessimistic or conservative assumptions if probabilities could not be quantified. Consistency and knowledge of the assumptions used are a prerequisite if the numbers in budgets are to be meaningful. For example, if a budget were to be used to avoid shortages of resources, the firm may use conservative assumptions, while optimistic assumptions may be more appropriate for motivation.

Once budgets have been prepared they will provide useful statements about the future of the firm and be used for planning and control within the firm. In Chapter 15 we will examine how useful budgets can be in helping to control the firm.

13.5 Example of budget preparation

Ex. 13.1 provides an illustration of the preparation of a set of budgets. We are considering for simplicity a new firm, because to attempt to simulate all the aspects of interrelationships through an example is too complicated. We will prepare all relevant budgets except a profit statement and balance sheet.[3] The decision to undertake the project has already been taken and forecasts would normally exist, but may not provide data in operational detail. The budgets are prepared both for purposes of planning the business's future and for control.

Example 13.1
Mr Mata decided to commence business on 1 January 19X1 to produce Metas. He has arranged an overdraft limit of £170,000 for the first year. He will not withdraw any amount from the business for his own use during the first year. The forecast

effect of his decisions for the first three months are:

1.   Commence sales of Metas in January 19X1 with 4000 units increasing by 2000 units per month for the first 6 months. The selling price will be £20 per unit. Customers will normally pay two months after receipt of the goods.

2.   Purchase machinery costing £40,000 on 1 January 19X1 which will be paid for during the first month. The capacity of the machinery is 20,000 units per month.

3.   Production will be 8000 units per month for the first 3 months and 16,000 units per month thereafter.

4.   The production of one Meta will require:

(i) 3 man hours of direct labour; each man will work 160 hours per month at monthly pay of £80.

(ii) 5 units of material X, which costs £2 per unit.

5.   An initial stock of 15,000 units of material X will be delivered on 1 January 19X1; thereafter sufficient amounts of material X will be purchased regularly to ensure that half the following month's requirements will be held in stock at the end of a month. Materials purchased in a month will be paid for in the following month.

6.   Supervisers will be engaged at a total cost of £1000 per month.

7.   Production overheads will require payment of £30,000 per month.

Mr Mata wishes to know month by month for the first three months how much he must pay into the firm's bank account to keep within its overdraft limit. The bank manager, who has agreed to the overdraft, wishes to inspect the firm's budgets to see if the limit is realistic and to use the data as a means of monitoring the firm's progress during the first three months. Mr Mata also wishes to use the budgets for purposes of controlling the firm during the first three months.

Set of Budgets

Commencing 1 January 19X1

		January	February	March	April
1. Sales budget					
quantities	'000	4	6	8	10
revenue: price £20	£'000	80	120	160	200
2. Debtors' Budget	£'000				
opening debtors		—	80	200	
sales on credit		80	120	160	
		80	200	360	
receipts		—	—	80	
closing debtors		80	200	280	
3. Production Budget					
A. *Finished Products(physical)* '000					
opening inventory			4	6	6
production		8	8	8	16
		8	12	14	22
sales		4	6	8	10
closing inventory		4	6	6	12

B. Direct Labour					
hours	'000	24	24	24	48
men		150	150	150	300
cost	£'000	12	12	12	24
C. Production Overheads	£'000				
supervisors		1	1	1	1
overheads		30	30	30	30
		31	31	31	31
D. Direct Material X (physical) '000					
opening inventory		—	20	20	40
purchases initial		15	—	—	—
regular		45	40	60	80
		60	60	80	120
usage		40	40	40	80
closing inventory		20	20	40	40
E. Direct Material X (cost)	£'000				
opening inventory		—	40	40	80
purchases initial		30	—	—	—
regular		90	80	120	160
		120	120	160	240
usage		80	80	80	160
closing inventory		40	40	80	80
F. Production Cost	£'000				
variable – materials		80	80	80	160
— labour		12	12	12	24
fixed – overheads		31	31	31	31
Total standard cost		123	123	123	215
4. Creditors' budget	£'000				
opening creditors		—	120	80	120
credit purchases		120	80	120	160
		120	200	200	280
payments		—	120	80	120
closing creditors		120	80	120	160
5. Fixed assets budget	£'000				
Acquisitions – machinery		40	—	—	
Disposals		—	—	—	—
6. Cash Budget	£'000				
Sources					
from debtors		—	—	80	
total cash inflow		—	—	80	
Applications					
payments to creditors		—	120	80	
direct labour		12	12	12	
production overheads		31	31	31	
fixed asset aquisitions		40	—	—	

total cash outflow	83	163	3
Net Cash Flow	—83	—163	—43
To be provided by			
Bank Overdraft	83	87	—
Mr Mata payments into bank	—	76	43
cumulative bank overdraft	83	170	170

The budgets for April are prepared in some cases, as the budgets for March are affected by events which will occur in April, e.g. purchase a inventory in March for use in April.

Comments on the Set of Budgets
The budgets reveal information not previously shown by the individual forecasts from which the budgets were calculated. The cash budget (6) shows that Mr Mata must pay £76,000 in February and £43,000 in March into the firm's bank account. In addition we can see, for example, the following useful information:

1. Production Budget (3A & B): the amount the firm needs to produce month by month and the number of men he must employ. It shows that the firm must plan to engage 150 new men in March.

2. Production Budget (3D): the amount of raw material the firm must purchase month by month is increasing. As well as requiring extra cash resources the increased inventory will place demands on storage capacity.

3. Cash Budget (6): the effect on the total cash flow of the firm's policy on debtors, inventory and creditors.

4. Production Cost Budget (3F) can be used for cost control during the first four months. The budgets can also be seen to be incomplete as they have omitted interests expenses from the bank overdraft. There is no statement about the reliability of the forecast data. We can clearly see the interrelationships between the budgets. Also we can see that if Mr Mata was, for example, only able to provide £50,000 for each of the first two months he would have to re-examine each budget to see the cash-flow implications of changes, e.g. he may adopt different policies on working capital by offering discounts to debtors for early payment, holding less inventory, etc.

13.6   Summary

The set of overall budgets of the firm summarises the aggregate forecast implications of the various decisions taken by the firm. The set of budgets can be used for various purposes including communication of objectives within the firm, co-ordination of resources, and elimination of inconsistencies of objectives and forecasts within the organisation of the firm.

Budgets and budgeting have effects on the motivation of managers and others in the firm, and the use of budgets and budgeting for planning purposes cannot be completely divorced from control. The interrelationships between budgets may often require the use of iterative methods in the process of reconciliation of objectives and resources within the firm. The budgets can be used for control purposes as a basis against which to compare actual results. This is discussed in Chapter 15.

Notes and References

1. S. W. Becker and D. Green, 'Budgeting and Employee Behaviour', *Accounting and its Behavioral Implications,* W. T. Bruns and D. T. De Coster (eds) (New York, N.Y., McGraw-Hill, 1971); A. C. Stedry, 'Budgeting and Employee Behavior: A Reply', in W. T. Bruns and D. T. De Coster (eds), ibid.; S. W. Becker and D. Green, 'Budgeting and Employee Behaviour: A Rejoinder to a Reply', W. T. Bruns and D. T. De Coster (eds) ibid.; C. Agyris, 'Human Problems with Budgets', *Studies in Cost Analysis*, 2nd ed., D. Solomons (ed.) (London, Sweet & Maxwell, 1968); C. I. Hughes, 'Why Budgets go Wrong', *Studies in Cost Analysis*, ibid.
2. J. Flower, *Computer Models for Accountants* (London, Haymarket, 1974).
3. For a detailed examination of types of budgets and possible pro-formas for budgets, see H. C. Edey, *Business Budgets and Accounts* (London, Hutchinson, 1966).

Further Reading

G. H. Hofstede, *The Game of Budget Control* (London, Tavistock, 1968).
A. Hopwood, *Accounting and Human Behaviour* (London, Haymarket, 1974).

Questions and Problems

13.1   What do you understand by the following terminology?

Planning horizon	Budgeting
Plans	Relevant data
Budgets	Simulation models
Functions	Participation
Projects	
Goal congruence	
Targets and forecasts	

13.2   What are the objectives of budgeting? Explain any difficulties which may arise in attaining these objectives.

13.3   What problems do you foresee in budgeting for:

(a)   direct labour and direct materials
(b)   heating and lighting
(c)   rent and rates
(d)   cash
(e)   research and development
(f)   sales

13.4   What problems do you foresee in budgeting in the following types of organisations:

(a)   a steel-manufacturing company
(b)   a market research agency
(c)   a polytechnic
(d)   a local authority
(e)   a greengrocer

13.5   How would you overcome the problems of inflation in the budget data?

13.6   'All forecasts are speculative and thus budgeting in an uncertain world is pointless?' Do you agree? How can budget data be made useful if the underlying data is unreliable?

13.7   'Budgeting in cyclical or seasonal industries poses severe problems.' What are these problems?

13.8 'Participation in budgeting is a genuine attempt at democratisation of a firm's organisation.' Do you agree?

13.9 A sales manager plans to launch a new product next month, but he is informed by the production manager that as it is not in the firm's budget that it is not possible. How would you resolve this conflict? Can any general statements about the objectives and problems of budgeting be abstracted from this problem?

13.10 Is last year's budget of any use in the preparation of the current budget?

Part III
CONTROL

14
Concepts of Control

14.1 Introduction

Part I was concerned with measurement, especially for the presentation of past performance by means of financial statements. Parts II and III are concerned with measurement of information for purposes of planning and control decisions. Part II was concerned with planning and methods of analysis for planning decisions and we now turn to a consideration of control systems. A system of control is necessary because the actual results of planning decisions will almost always differ from the planned result because of variation from the expected levels of performance, and in addition it will often be possible with hindsight to see that the plans contained errors and omissions. This is due to the uncertainty inherent in business, the imperfect knowledge available at the time the decisions are made, and to human fallibility. In Chapter 10 control was defined as the activity of checking what actually happens with what was planned and feeding back information to the decision-maker so that he can take whatever action seems necessary. An analogy is often made with mechanical control systems. An example would be a thermostatically controlled cooker which can be planned to operate at a specific temperature and where any deviation from that temperature results in the heating being automatically switched on or off as required.

In Part III we consider the internal and external systems of control operating on the firm. In general we will be concerned with financial control systems. A firm may also have other systems, e.g. production control or quality control, which also provide management with information to help them in decision-making. In Chapter 15 we examine budgetary control, which is the major financial control system operating within many firms. Fig. 10.1 showed the planning process of comparing budgets with actual results and acting on any revealed differences. This method of control is usually only available to management, as it is rare for a firm to reveal its budgets outside the firm even to the shareholders who are its owners.[1] Another means of control is by an analysis and interpretation of financial statements and comparing the results with criteria other than budgets, e.g. with other firms. This is examined further in Chapter 16. This form of analysis is available to those external to the firm because of the availability of published financial statements, to shareholders, creditors or trade unions, as well as management. Nevertheless the scope and content of such published statements is limited and management has better information for producing a proper analysis on which to make decisions than has the external user. 'External' is used here to distinguish those using published information from internal management. The controversial problem of what is the desirable level and quality of published information is taken up in Chapter 17.

The content of Chapters 16 and 17 provides the basis for several aspects of control. The individual investor who uses published financial information to make his own planning decisions may also use it to control those decisions, i.e. to control his own performance. He may decide to buy or sell shares in a firm on the basis of a comparison of a firm's actual performance with what he anticipated when he bought the shares. Other controls operate on the firm itself. If the firm makes higher profits than planned it may be subject to trade union pressure for better wages and conditions, or to government action on prices, or to monopoly control. Conversely, if it makes lower profits than planned or declares lower dividends it may be subject to pressure when its shareholders feedback their discontent by selling their shares or by protest at shareholders' meetings. It is for these reasons that we have felt it appropriate to include Chapters 16 and 17 in the part of the book devoted to systems of control.

The accounting systems of processing data as described in Chapters 3 and 4 will usually have built-in control procedures. These are to provide a check that the system is operating as planned. Examples of these procedures are control accounts, trial balances and the double-entry system which is itself a method of control over the firms book-keeping. Another control procedure which was referred to in Chapter 2 is auditing. This can be an internal audit which consists of checking the firm's accounting procedures and is performed by employees of the firm. External audit is a legal requirement where auditors are acting on behalf of the shareholders to whom they report on the financial statements in the form of a published audit report. A further analysis of auditing is beyond the scope of this book.[2]

14.2 Nature and objectives of control

The first part of this chapter included examples of different types of control associated with the firm. All the examples involved a comparison of what actually happens against some form of desirable criterion or plan. The process by which the planner is kept informed of the results of such comparisons is referred to as feedback. The planner is defined here as the person with the responsibility for the planning decision and for the operation of the plan. Fig. 14.1 gives a simple illustration of the process.

Using the previous analogy with the cooker in conjunction with Fig. 14.1, the predetermined criterion or plan is the planned temperature needed for cooking a particular dish. If a comparison with the actual heat of the cooker shows that the temperature is too low, this information is fed back and activates the heating element. Similarly if the cooker is too hot, the heat will be automatically switched off. The action taken as a result of feedback information is a simple mechanical system such as this is invariably one which affects performance (i.e. Type B). Another important feature of a simple mechanical system is that the action taken in response to the comparison is predictable and can therefore be programmed to operate automatically. Most systems of planning and control involve human operators and the action cannot be programmed to respond automatically to feedback. They require the data for an analysis of the reasons for the deviation before remedial action can be taken.

The desirable planned criteria used as a basis for the comparison varies according to the type of control being exercised. In budgetary control the criteria are in

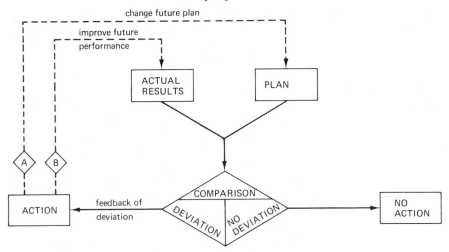

Figure 14.1   Control process using feedback

the budget which sets out the standards of performance. These criteria are determined by the firm's management and can be designed to achieve its overall objectives. Instead of budgets, an analysis of financial statements can be used as a means of control by external users and the firm's management. The actual results can be compared with, for example, the results of previous periods for the same firm, for other firms, or with an accepted norm for the industry. The action that can result from this comparison will depend on the position and objectives of the operator of the system. The firm's management can take either action A or B illustrated in Fig. 14.1. The external user cannot directly control the firm's performance as a result of the comparison, but can influence it; for example, if he is a shareholder, by voting at a shareholders' meeting or by selling his shares, buying or not buying shares if he is an investor, or pressing for a wage increase if it is a trade union. This distinction between control by the internal and external user should not necessarily be interpreted as being different in importance, with internal management always having more influence. A large institutional shareholder with power to appoint and dismiss directors may have more direct control than internal management.

The examples of control appear to provide a form of *ex post* control by looking back at what has happened, but it is important to recognise that it is not possible to control what has already happened. The only virtue in performing this *ex post* exercise is that it should result in action which will affect *future* planning and performance. The objective should be to minimise deviations of future performance from plans. Feedback information about past deviations can be used either to amend future plans (Type A) if past performance has shown up possibilities of improving them, or to improve future performance (Type B) to achieve the objectives set out in the plans. This distinction is important because it determines the action to be taken. Deviation from planned criteria can be the result of plans or performance and there is no point in adjusting one if the problem is caused by the other. For example, a change in world prices may affect raw materials costs which result in cost variations. This is a case for reconsidering plans, as the environment of the firm has changed. On the other hand, if the cost variations result from buying the wrong raw material then it is the performance of the purchasing function that needs to be improved. It is thus important that if possible the actual performance should be compared with an amended plan which shows what was possible given the changed circumstances.[3]

It was suggested in Chapter 10 that planning and control are closely related topics. In our original definition, control consists of comparing plans with actual performance and in Fig. 14.1 the Type A action resulting from feedback of control information is to change future plans. It is debatable whether the act of replanning is a planning or a control process. Some actions which in everyday language would be termed control procedures, e.g. the installation of locks and alarm bells to prevent pilfering of raw material, can take place before any actual performance occurs and thus may be considered as planning. Examples of a similar nature in the area of external control of a firm would arise from legislation on resale price maintenance, equal pay for women or pollution control. These appear to be different from *ex post* control which consists of comparing deviations from plans and acting on them. They are a form of *ex ante* control (control before the event). Another example would be a system of controlling employees' performance by setting them targets with rewards for achieving them. *Ex ante* control can either be called planning or it can be brought within our definition of control, which consists of comparing plans with actual performance, by assuming that *ex ante* measures are taken because of foreseen potential deviations, for example, if the locks and alarm bells are not installed material usage will be more than planned because some would be stolen or if the law is broken penalties will be incurred. It should be part of the planning process to consider these *ex ante* control measures because if successful they may go some way to achieving the objective of control which we said was to minimise deviations of future performance from plans.

When interpreting control information which reveals a need for improvement in plans, a distinction should be made if possible between (a) inadequacies in plans caused by the changes in the environment and outside the control of the planner, i.e. non-controllable (e.g. unforeseen government action or movements in prices), and (b) those caused by inefficient planning, i.e. controllable (e.g. a failure to properly co-ordinate the timing of raw material purchases with the production process or the over-estimation of demand for a product). The use of this last example highlights the difficulty of making such a distinction because errors in demand forecasts may be a combination of forecasting errors and changes in demand conditions. The reason for making this distinction is that as the success of an organisation is dependent on efficient planning then control information on how well the planning function is being performed is at least as important as information of the performance of those operating the plans.

If the planner is to take appropriate action it is important that he is given proper feedback information at the right time. The possible problem areas in connection with the feedback process and the consequent action are analysed below under three headings. (a) identifying responsibility, (b) delay and (c) distortion.

IDENTIFYING RESPONSIBILITY

An axiom of a good control process is that when an action in a particular area can only be taken by the person responsible for that area, information on deviations from plans must be fed back to that person. Part of the planning or budgeting process should be clearly to delineate responsibilites for each part of the plan or budget. There will be a hierarchy of responsibility in most firms, the areas attributable to an individual being greater as one works up through the hierarchy. Fig. 14.2 provides an illustration of this.

From Fig. 14.2 we can see that the managing director is responsible for the whole firm and thus could take action on any deviations from plans. However it may not be practical to provide him with all information, for example, on the performance of each machine in each workshop in each department. At the other end of the hierarchy an individual responsible for a particular machine cannot be expected to take action to affect the performance or plans of any area outside his level of responsibility. It may be that the firm wishes to provide employees with information about areas for which they are not responsible for reasons other than control, e.g. in an attempt to generate motivation by giving a feeling of participation and involvement.

A useful distinction can be made between those aspects of operations which are controllable and those which are not. Controllability used in this context, means that it would have been possible if the proper action had been taken to have avoided or reduced the deviation from the plan. Non-controllability can arise where the events which led to the deviation were outside the control of the firm, e.g. a government devaluation of the currency or a strike in a supplier's factory. A further example of non-controllability is that relating to a specific area of responsibility within the firm. For example, in Fig. 14.2 if the manager of Department A is inefficient and purchases raw material that is more expensive than planned, the cost of Workshop X may increase but the foreman in charge cannot be held responsible. Thus the cost of raw materials in this example is controllable at one level of responsibility but not at another. The concept of controllability must therefore be seen in the context of the analysis of responsibility. This analysis has assumed a time period equivalent to the budget period. If a longer period is considered, the definition of what is controllable may also change. Responsibilities within the firm may change; it may be possible to influence external factors which are not controllable in the

LEVELS OF RESPONSIBILITY

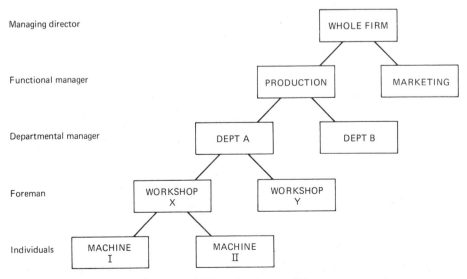

Figure 14.2   Hierarchy of responsibility

short term or it may be possible to select an alternative plan. For example, in the case of a strike at the suppliers, it may be possible to switch to a less strike-prone supplier.

DELAY

It is important that feedback of deviations should be made in time for decisions on appropriate action to be taken. The time scale and the nature of the process depicted in Fig. 14.1 will determine what constitutes a delay. For example, a machine registering the heartbeats of a critically ill patient is a control system where the comparison, feedback and action must be possible in minutes or even seconds. The control process within a firm could vary from the *daily* reporting of the usage rates of expensive raw materials, to *monthly* comparisons by managers of profit earned with planned profit, to *annual* reporting of results to shareholders. The determination of what constitutes an appropriate time scale depends on the related costs and benefits. The necessity for a short-time scale is obvious in the example of the patient's heartbeat. The benefits from having a short time-scale in a firm's control system is that where deviations are taking place it is important that action to change the plan or improve the performance is taken promptly. However, data must be collected, processed and communicated, and then those responsible must decide what action is necessary and implement their decisions. The time involved in this process could represent a substantial cost to the firm. The frequency of considering and acting on deviations will be a trade-off between these costs and benefits. For example, if a firm uses gold in its manufacturing process it will probably be desirable to go through the control process daily to ensure that the gold is not being wasted or pilfered. If the same process also uses cheap plastic it may only be necessary to check its usage monthly.

DISTORTION

In Fig. 14.1 the feedback of information on deviation leads to decisions about what action to take. In a simple system the appropriate response to control information may be predictable. In the example of the thermostatically controlled cooker, the response was to switch the heating on if the temperature was too low and off if it was too high. The result of such action is also predictable. However, in complex control systems such as those in a firm the relationship cannot be clearly defined. Thus the information that the deviation signals show may be distorted. One reason for this is that a firm's control systems are seldom self-contained and independent of other systems and are thus affected by changes in the environment, action by other firms, or by action of other systems within the firm. Another reason is that a firm's control systems are usually not mechanical but are carried out by human operators. Thus if a firm's profit deviates from the plan and this information is fed back to the managers, the action he will need to take may not be at all clear. In Sects 14.3 and 14.4 we elaborate on two further specific problems of operating an efficient control system.

14.3 Behavioural aspects of control

The application of ideas of control to systems which include human operatives raises a number of issues relating to the attitudes and motivation of the individuals associated with the system. The designer of a control system must realise that the introduction of such a system may cause a reaction from those involved. It may be perceived as having a purpose which may or may not be the same as that intended. A mechanical system will not react to the mere idea of control but a human system invariably will. The existence of a system of defining responsibilities as discussed in Sect. 14.2 and using it for formal appraisal may affect the performance of those responsible. This is true in budgetary control where employees are in effect set targets based on plans or budgets against which their performance is compared. This may lead to rewards for achieving the target or to penalties for falling short of it. In either case there is likely to be an effect on the behaviour of the members of the firm as a result of the introduction of such a system. In addition, the knowledge that this comparison will take place will affect the attitude of (a) anyone asked to participate in the setting of targets through work-study procedures or preparation of budgets and (b) anyone who is involved in collecting and reporting back information on actual performance.

These behavioural reactions can be observed both in the firm's internal systems of control and in its external relations with users of information about the firm. The firm provides information for external users such as shareholders, trade unions or consumers, chiefly through its financial statements. The firm knows that this information will be used by these groups to make their own decisions about the firm and this may affect the way in which the information is presented. It was shown in earlier chapters that there is much scope for manipulating accounting information while remaining within the law and generally accepted accounting principles. Another example is that a firm's decisions on dividend policy will affect the stock market's attitude towards its share price if it is a quoted company. There may be good economic reasons why a company should not pay a dividend in a particular year but unless investors can be persuaded to look favourably on a cut in dividend it is likely that the share price will fall even though the company's prospects are enhanced by retaining and using the funds instead of paying the dividend. It was stated earlier that legal constraints provide a form of *ex ante* control on a firm's actions. In addition there is the possibility of legal sanctions being imposed if firms behave in a particular manner. Two examples of this are the threat of stock exchange action or government legislation to control the use of inside information in connection with share dealing, and the threat of more legislation on pollution control if firms do not act to minimise environmental pollution in their operations. The importance of social pressure via television, newspapers etc. is also relevant in considering controls on firms' planning decisions.

It is beyond the scope of this book to go into detail on the research findings of behavioural scientists on the attitudes and motivations of people involved in control systems,[4,5,6] but in designing such systems there seem to be two seemingly obvious but often ignored pitfalls. One is to make over-simplified assumptions about behaviour such as: 'People are motivated simply by financial rewards', 'people will strive to reach targets set by managers', or the opposite that, 'people are basically work shy and need to be made to work'. The other is to assume that all individuals will react in a similar fashion or, what is more likely, to ignore the possibility that they might react differently.

14.4 Information relevant for control

Fig. 14.1 showed that control consists of setting up a criterion or plan, comparing it with what actually happens and taking action for the future as a result of the comparison. This general description leaves several unanswered questions about the nature and volume of the information to be used as the basis for the comparison. Many of these questions will be answered in detail in subsequent chapters but we introduce several general points in this section.

It would be possible for management to use a single overall figure as a criterion, for example, profit after tax, and compare actual profit with it. There is clearly little information in this situation on which to base any action. At the other extreme every minute activity of the firm could be analysed, with a standard criterion for each activity and a comparison made with actual performance. There would then be a vast amount of information, especially in a large firm. The following questions might be asked in deciding what information is relevant for control:

(a)   Which type of data is relevant?
(b)   Is it necessary to consider all data?
(c)   What additional data would be useful?

(a)   *Which type of data is relevant?* Control information is used to make replanning decisions, i.e. to change plans or improve performance. Not all data relating to past performance is relevant to the future. It was stated in Sect. 10.8 that as accounting information is largely based on original costs it may not be an adequate guide for current decisions. It follows that data on such costs as depreciation may not be good control information if it gives little indication of current opportunity costs. Similarly, information on costs and revenues which is not controllable (as defined in Sect. 14.2) may be of little use in decision-making.

Data used for control purposes should if possible be free from bias. If an individual's performance is being assessed it is important that the data is not prepared solely by the person being assessed. As was discussed in Sect. 13.4 it is common for sections of budgets to be prepared by the individual most closely connected with the operations being budgeted for, and then of course the budget is used to control that individual's performance. It is difficult in practice to overcome this problem but it may be possible by means of an independent check or internal audit on the preparation of budget information. We have also stressed the need for an opportunity-cost approach to planning and control by assessing planning decisions against the available alternatives and by incorporating into the control analysis the implication of changes in opportunities which have taken place since the plans were made. However, this approach requires a skilled interpretation of the firm's operations and often the only person to give such an interpretation is the individual being assessed. Take, for example, a budgeted sales figure of 10,000 units prepared by the marketing manager where actual sales turned out to be 6000 units. How could a firm explain the deviation of 4000 units? It is likely that the man most expert to assess this is the marketing manager whose performance we are attempting to appraise. In this situation it is very difficult to obtain budgeted data or explanations of deviation which are free from bias.

(b)   *Is it necessary to consider all data?* If the basis of the control process is comparing planned with actual performance, then it would seem initially that management need only be interested in areas where differences occurred. If the plan is being achieved, there is no need to investigate further. This process is known as 'management by exception' as it focusses attention on the areas of deviation from the plans. If there are deviations in every area then the procedure would not seem to have any meaning. In practice, however, while there may be some deviation in most areas, the magnitude of the deviation will differ. It is possible to adopt a procedure of ignoring small deviations, perhaps those differing less than a fixed percentage from the planned figure. This would have the advantage of concentrating attention on the larger differences on the assumption that these are more important. By use of statistical concepts of probability, it is possible to adopt a more sophisticated approach and to select only those deviations which are statistically significant.[7] The advantage of concentrating on large differences is that it saves the time of management who then have to consider only a relatively few areas. The disadvantage is the possible information lost by ignoring small or even nil deviations. Ex. 14.1 illustrates this:

Example 14.1

	Total firm	*Dept X*	*Dept Y*
Budgeted production (units)	1000	600	400
Actual production (units)	990	450	540
Deviation	−10	−150	+140
% Deviation from budget	−1%	−25%	+35%

Clearly in this situation if management were only presented with aggregate data for the firm and decided that the difference was too small to investigate they would have overlooked significant information. This illustrates the danger of singling out particular areas, in order to allow management to concentrate their time, which may result in other important areas being missed. The particular danger of ignoring small variations is that there is the possibility that they are made up of larger but compensating variations as in the example. What information should be communicated to the person responsible is perhaps a matter of intuition and experience. In Ex. 14.1 if information on Dept X and Y was communicated, management could decide whether it was worth investigating. It should be recognised that the system of management by exception is a trade-off between the time saved by minimising the amount of information that management has to consider and the cost of missing important information.

(c)   *What additional data would be useful?* There is a danger that control data is restricted to that which is easily quantified in financial terms. This is partly because control is defined as a comparison of plans with actual performance, and a firm's plans when translated into budgets tend to be expressed in financial terms. In formulating the plans many relevant factors, such as the quality of the products, future benefits from research or advertising, customer relations and employer/employee relations, will have been considered but are rarely included in budgets. Consequently there is no built-in incentive to collect information in those areas. This is not to say that such information is not used, but often not as part of the formal control process so that only certain aspects of the business are being formally controlled.

14.5   Summary

This chapter, introducing Part III which is devoted to control of the planning decisions considered in Part II, attempted to set out the basic principles of control systems which are most relevant to the firm. We paid particular attention to the concept of feedback and to defining responsibility and controllability. The two other areas emphasised were the impact of behavioural responses to control and the importance of selecting the appropriate information. The remainder of Part III is concerned with the analysis of particular aspects of internal and external control systems which affect the firm.

Notes and References

1. There have been suggestions that budgets should be part of required published information. For example see H. C. Edey, 'Accounting Principles and Business Reality', *Accountancy* (July 1963). Also reprinted in *Modern Financial Management*, ed. B. V. Carsberg and H. C. Edey (Harmondsworth, Penguin, 1969).
2. For further discussion of auditing see P. Bird, *Accountability Standards in Financial Reporting* (London, Haymarket, 1973).
3. M. Bromwich, 'Standard Costs for Planning and Control', *The Accountant* (April – May 1969).
4. W. J. Bruns and D. R. De Coster, *Accounting and its Behavioural Implications* (New York, N.Y., McGraw-Hill, 1969).
5. R. Likert and S. E. Seashore, 'Making Cost Control Work', in *Studies in Cost Analysis*, ed. D. Solomons (London Sweet & Maxwell, 1968).
6. A. G. Hopwood, *Accounting and Human Behaviour* (London Haymarket, 1974).
7. Carl E. Noble, 'Calculating Control Limits for Cost Control Data', *Studies in Cost Analysis*, ed. D. Solomons., ibid.

Further Reading

C. T. Horngren, *Cost Accounting, A Managerical Emphasis*, 3rd ed. (Englewood Cliffs, Prentice-Hall, 1972) chap. 6.
C. T. Horngren, *Accounting for Management Control – An Introduction,* 2nd ed. (Englewood Cliffs, N.J., Prentice-Hall, 1970).
H. Anton and R. Firmin (ed.), *Contemporary Issues in Cost Accounting* (Boston, Mass., Houghton Mifflin, 1966).

Questions and Problems

14.1   What to you understand by the following terminology?

Internal control	*Ex post* control	Distortion of feedback
External control	*Ex ante* control	Management by exception
Financial control	Responsibility	
Budgetary control	Controllability	
Feedback	Delay of feedback	

14.2   Using the concepts of control illustrated in this chapter, discuss the systems of control that operate on and by an individual.

14.3   What do you think are the problems of operating financial control in a firm?

14.4   What problems does the difficulty of making accurate forecasts pose for control in a firm?

14.5   What relevance has an understanding of employee motivation in the design of a control system?

15
Budgetary Control

15.1 Introduction

Budgetary control is a system for controlling the activities of a firm through the use of budgets. The concepts of control examined in Chapter 14 are interwoven into a system of budgetary control and in this chapter we shall consider some of the applications of control concepts through the use of budgets. In Chapter 13 we examined how a firm may prepare a set of budgets for its activities which enable it to plan its resources and activities, and we will now examine how control can be effected by comparison of actual results with budgets.

Budgets are normally expressed in quantitive monetary terms and the comparison of what actually happens with a budget will yield a quantitative measure of the effect on the firm of deviations from budgets. In systems of budgetary control deviations are termed 'variances' and a major feature of the system is the use of variance information. Its major use may be as a guide to show which of the firm's activities are not proceeding according to budget. Variance reporting is a central part of the feedback control model represented in Fig. 14.1. The use of such an *ex post* analysis is appropriate in controlling a firm's activities if it ensures that the firm's management can use variance information to identify where, within the firm, decisions need to be taken which will affect future performance. Elements of *ex ante* control also operate where the behaviour of the organisation of a firm or individuals within a firm is influenced by knowledge that there will be a feedback of any future variance information.

15.2 Budgets for comparison

In Chapter 13 we examined how to prepare a set of budgets for a firm. If they are to be used for control purposes the individual budgets that are prepared should reflect the division of responsibility in the firm. The system for collection of data about what actually happens, and for reporting of variances, must also follow this pattern. It is not useful to have budgets for control purposes unless actual data can be collected and variances reported to those responsible for the decisions which led to the variances. The system of variance reporting will have to be aligned with the responsibility structure of the firm and at the same time ensure that information is communicated to all who can learn from it. The correct analysis of variances into those which are controllable or non-controllable (as defined in Sect. 14.2) at various levels of responsibility in the organisation is a major part of the effective use of budgetary control as an aid to management control. Ex. 15.1 illustrates the comparison of budgeted and actual performance.

Example 15.1

Noggin Ltd produces Dings. It operates a system of budgetary control. The profit for January 19X1 is £3000, which is £2700 below the budgeted profit of £5700. A comparison of actual and budgeted profit statements is shown below:

Actual and budgeted Profit Statements January 19X1

	Actual	*Budget*	*Variance*
	£	£	£
Sales Revenue	22,000	26,000	
Less: Cost of Goods Sold	12,870	14,300	
Gross Profit	9,130	11,700	−2,570
Less: Expenses:			
Marketing	4,200	4,000	−200
Administration	1,930	2,000	+70
Net Profit	£3,000	£5,700	−£2,700

The effect of the variance on the profit is shown by the sign. A positive sign indicates an increase in profit, sometimes termed a 'favourable variance', and a negative sign a reduction in profit, termed an 'adverse variance'.

The elements of the feedback control system which are operating in Ex. 15.1 are that criteria for comparison are available in the form of a budget, and that actual data is available. What is missing in our analysis is the process of comparison and variance calculation from which actions can result which influence the future. To translate the feedback information into effective action the firm must provide a means of analysing variances so that the underlying causes of variances can be identified. It is this underlying *causal* information rather than the knowledge that a variance exists (which is solely *evidence* for non-budgeted events) which is useful for replanning. The way in which variance information is analysed is frequently organised into a routine basis within the accounting function.

It is often difficult for routine analysis procedures to identify the causes of variances. However, it may be able to give *indications* as to where the cause of variances lies and thus save administrative resources by this preliminary analysis.

In Fig. 15.1 we have produced an analysis of variances into indicative and causal parts to illustrate a detailed variance analysis based on the data from example 15.1. The details of these calculations are considered in Sect. 15.5.

Effective feedback control systems of budgetary control thus have three major problems to overcome if they are to operate effectively.

(a)   Identification

The firm must be able to identify where within its organisation a variance is occurring and identify the cause. In Ex. 15.1 we have a breakdown of the net profit variance, showing how variances on gross profit, marketing and administration expenses contributed. Further analysis of the net profit variance in Fig. 15.1 is provided by a more detailed comparison of items in the budget with actual events, e.g. a breakdown of actual and budget production costs item by item, is seen on page 241. A detailed indicative analysis could normally be carried out by accountants, based on information about actual expenditure obtained from the accoun-

Analysis of Profit Variance – Summary for January 19X1

	Indicative £	use of lower skilled labour £	rates reduction negotiated £	clerical vacancy not filled £	low-quality material purchased £	devaluation of £ £	machine breakdown £	price change in response to competition £
				Causal				
Favourable Variances (+)								
Production Cost: labour wage rate	220	+220						
fixed overhead expenditure	170		+170					
Sales Revenue: selling price	2000							+2000
Other expenses: administration	70			+70				
total favourable	£2460							
Adverse variances (−)								
Production Cost: material price	550				+40	−590		
material usage	500	−300			−200			
labour efficiency	200	−100			−100			
variable overhead expenditure	110						−110	
variable overhead efficiency	150	−75			−75			
fixed overhead capacity	500						−500	
fixed overhead efficiency	250	−125			−125			
Sales Revenue: sales volume	2700							−2700
Other Expenses: marketing	200							−200
total adverse	£5160							
total net profit variance	−£2700	−380	+170	+70	−460	−590	−610	−900

Figure 15.1   Indicative and Causal Analysis of Net Profit Variance based on Example 15.1

ting information system. However, an indicative analysis as carried out in Fig. 15.1 will rarely lead to information about why the variance occurred. Identification of causes as shown in causal analysis is the central factor in the process of control for unless causes of variances are known action of type A or type B shown in Fig. 14.1 cannot be taken.

(b) Learning

The firm must learn from variance information in so far as it desires to avoid the recurrence of variances by replanning its future activities. The reporting of variances cannot solve underlying problems unless it is followed by decisions about the future. In the learning process the firm's management will be required to assess the probability of recurrence of past causes. As the learning process involves collection and analysis of data by management it is unlikely to be cost free.

The benefits from identification of the causes of variances lie in the potential savings from replanning. A decision on whether investigation is going to be worth while has to be made, by comparing the cost and prospective benefits, both of which factors are unknown until investigations are complete. The cost of investigations may be zero if the firm already has unused managerial resources. In estimating the potential savings, difficulties arise from determining whether a variance is likely to be significant, as until a variance is investigated the firm may not know if it is the 'tip of an iceberg' or the result of a non-recurring event (see Section 14.4).

The communication of variances in an organisation is also important as a learning process, as it may provide a means of reminding individuals of their responsibility for decisions and control. It also provides a monitoring device for managers to evaluate the decisions taken at lower levels of the organisation.

(c) Replanning

The process of replanning in the period after a variance has occurred will involve reappraisal of the original plan which may no longer be optimal in the light of the new, though non-budgeted events. Feedback information is often thought of as leading to remedial action which rectifies the effects of previous deviations from plan. As explained in Chapter 14, past events cannot be altered though their effects may be negated by replanning the firm's future activities to achieve the original budget if it is still considered as optimal. As shown in Fig. 14.1 replanning can result in alteration of future actions, or reappraisal of original objectives set out in budgets.

15.3   Operation of budgetary control

The considerations of the previous section appear to place a large burden on a budgetary control system. Budgetary control cannot, however, carry out all a firm's control activities. As a control system which measures variances in financial terms, it may reflect the financial implications of deviations from plans which have previously been discovered by other control systems. In some areas of a firm's organisation budgetary control may operate as a primary system, e.g. in administrative expenditure, but it may be of secondary importance in areas where other systems operate, e.g. production, where there may be physical material control as well as standard costing. It is not only through the comparison of actual events with budgets that managers and others obtain information about problems which are their responsibility. Individuals within an organisation may be continuously monitoring their own progress or the progress of others through comparison with criteria which are not found in the firm's budgets e.g. ensuring that all employees turn up to work on the days when they are required.

The use of intuition by managers who feel that 'things aren't quite right' is an example of an informal system of deviation reporting which does not rely on budgets. However, as managers become more remote from individual problems of the firm or as its organisations grow in size, it may be necessary to augment the informal system by use of budgetary control and formal variance reporting. Rather than relying on periodic checking using personal contacts, budgetary control will provide an overall control system of the whole firm. Variance reporting would normally be formalised and routine and provide automatic reporting on problem areas of the firm, and act as a reminder to lower management of their responsibilities.

When operating as a secondary system it is not of vital importance that variances are reported when they occur as the other control systems should already have reported the problem. As more reliance is placed on variance reporting in budgetary control where other control systems are absent or deficient, the timeliness of reporting becomes of paramount importance.

A comprehensive budgeting system for a firm will prepare budgets for all the firm's activities, e.g. sales, production, manpower, but some firms may produce budgets for only a limited range of its activities, e.g. sales. The more comprehensive the set of budgets the greater the potential control of the management through the feedback of information on a routine basis. Thus in some firms deviations from plans may occur because the plans are not sufficiently comprehensive as control systems and hence no deviations are reported in the firm.

The interval between deviations occurring and the reporting of variances, and consequent managerial action, is important in determining the effectiveness of the systems. Clearly large variances could occur and remain undetected if the delay period is long. As budgetary control systems are closely associated with accounting systems for calculating costs and periodic profit, the time scale that is used for reporting of variances is often determined by the accounting period rather than the sales, production or expenditure cycle of the firm. This may mean that the collection of data through the accounting system makes the variance reports inappropriate for replanning purposes. Accounting periods may be inappropriate for primary control, but still provide useful data as a secondary control and for reminding management of their responsibilities. For example, the reporting cycle for the production of batches of goods should be determined by the frequency of the batches rather than the calendar period.

The process of reporting variances will also depend on the extent to which the process of variance analysis itself is routinised and geared to the accounting period, which may reduce the system's flexibility to respond quickly to large problems indicated by variances.

Our final consideration in this section is whether the arithmetic of sign of a variance is important in its interpretation, analysis and informational content. Should we investigate only adverse variances? Though it may seem implicit in our analysis that only negative variances were our concern, positive variances are of equal importance for the information they can give about areas for tightening the budgets and about cutting corners. In terms of our feedback model both kinds of variances are important because irrespective of the sign there should be replanning activity. If the original budget is still optimal, a positive variance cannot be considered as favourable, e.g. a saving on labour in a product may not be in the firm's best interests in terms of product quality. Thus both positive and negative variances will be adverse under this situation though it is probable that a positive variance merely reflects the suboptimality of the budget.

15.4   Interpretation of variances

The major problem of the use of budgetary control is in the interpretation of variance information. Managers of a firm wish to know when events occur and decisions are taken which are not consistent with the objectives of the firm, i.e. they are suboptimal. Any economic event of this type is a deviation from the objectives of the firm, and clearly a perfect system of feedback in budgetary control would always provide managers with signals of deviation as they occur. This can be shown diagrammatically as:

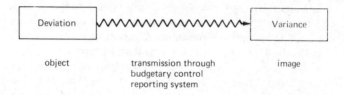

What we would wish to achieve would be a system where the image was totally consistent with the object. In terms of budgetary control this would mean that variances signals should not be given when no *real* variance has occurred and also conversely. Such misrepresentations will clearly occur where budgets are inappropriate as criteria, where actual data is incorrect, or where there are faults in the communication system which introduce distortions.

A central assumption of the feedback model is that the criterion for comparison is valid. This is important for two reasons; firstly in budgetary control the budgets are normative statements against which to evaluate actual results; secondly they act as a statement of the firm's objectives for current planning decisions. Budgetary control uses the budget as both a norm and a target, which is of particular importance in replanning after variances have occurred. It is critical that the budget is expressed in terms of the optimal plan for the firm. If the budget is suboptimal, variances from it may be shown as favourable but which are adverse in relation to the optimal budget. For replanning purposes decisions taken to achieve a suboptimal budget in the future will not be in the best interests of the firm.[1]

When the planning assumptions underlying the budget are proved incorrect by actual events the original budget should be revised as these changes in planning assumptions become apparent. It is often the practical problems of recomputing new budgets with its associated expense which forecloses this opportunity. If the changes are sufficiently large to discredit the whole process of budgeting, recomputation may occur, e.g. petrol prices doubling for a transport firm. As we saw in Chapter 13 the process of budget preparation is both a time- and resource-consuming exercise and it may be with some reluctance that outdated budgets are revised and new budgets prepared.

One practical approach to introducing a limited amount of flexibility into the system is through the use of flexible budgets and standard costs, or the preparation of several budgets based on alternative assumptions. Flexible budgets are related to the costs of a firm and postulate a relationship between the costs of the firm and the level of its activities, i.e. they provide information about the production and cost functions of the firm. Thus when the actual level of business activity is known the amount of costs appropriate to that level of activity can be calculated, e.g. for the costs of administration, marketing, production. Clearly some of these costs will be fixed, variable or semi-variable and if the process of variance calculation is to be meaningful the budgets should include the most appropriate cost. The use of standard costs is a further example of flexible budgeting except that normally standard costs are only used for costs of production and a total standard cost for the actual level of production would be used as the cost budget for production. The use of standard costing is illustrated in Sect. 15.5. A degree of suboptimality is inherent in any system which relies on forecasts, but if the budget is significantly different from the optimal budget this has serious implications both for the use of a feedback model, and also for the way in which those affected by the system perceive it.

Budgets influence behaviour both in the budgeting stage and in the control application. The motivational assumptions underlying the budgets will have an important influence on the incidence of variances. Variances may, for example, be entirely due to the efficiency criterion incorporated into the initial budget, e.g. 'tight target'. In this sense it may be that variances are expected because of the underlying assumptions about motivation. There is thus an element of budgeted variance.[2] In Chapter 13 budgets were used for planning. There is in some sense a conflict between the use of the same budgets both for planning and for control which arises from a need in some aspects of planning for conservative estimates, e.g. to avoid shortages of raw materials, and perhaps elsewhere optimistic plans to encourage high levels of efficiency. These conflicts may give rise to elements in variances which reflect the different uses for the same data.[3]

Variances which occur may also be attributed to incorrect planning. When actual events turn out different from the budget this may be due not only to the absence of control within the firm but also because the forecasts incorporated in the initial budget were incorrect. This may be due partially to changes in the firm's environment which could not be foreseen, but it may also be due to the failure of the planner to collect or interpret data correctly. As planning is an important managerial activity it would seem important to be able to appraise the success of the planner and to establish the degree of his reliability. Any analysis would of course depend for its success on establishing the extent to which the planner could have been expected to foresee future events and to have allowed for these in his forecasts. To illustrate these important distinctions we could possibly analyse variances in, for example, a sales budget which was proved incorrect *ex post*, partly because the planner ignored or omitted certain important information, i.e. bad planning and part because of completely unforeseen events, e.g. a devaluation of the pound. Although in practice it will be difficult to carry out such an *ex post* analysis it is important to recognise those parts of variances due to bad planning and those arising from charges in the firm's environment.[1, 4]

Some problems of variance analysis lie in the data about actual events, such as for example the time it takes a man to tighten a nut, which will, if observed, form a frequency distribution of varying times. Using some assumptions about the normality of the distribution it is possible to establish a budgeted mean and standard deviation. Using this type of budget we could then compare any actual events with the probabilistic budget and establish through the use of significance tests whether any variance from the mean was due to chance, and hence an acceptable variance, or due to systematic reasons which require investigation. This is a further example of the difficulty in determining whether variances are significant.[5]

The way in which variances are measured and communicated in budgetary control is based on a particular system of valuation implicit in our variance calculation.[6] In Part I we explored the problem of measurement in accounting and saw that valuation depended on the definition of the spectrum of items to be included in the measurement, and the basis of valuation chosen. Variances may thus arise because the basis of measurement used for budgets and actual events which is normally based on accounting concepts,has failed to reflect the underlying economic reality of the firm. This could occur in various ways. The firm could take decisions during a budget period which result in adverse variances, but which are consistent with the firm's long-term objectives, e.g. an unexpected adverse variance with a positive net present value, but which causes short-term adverse performance when measured in conventional accounting terms (see page 142 onwards).

Similarly decisions may be taken whose benefits are not separately reflected on the accounts. An example of both these problems would be where a manager responds to high labour turnover by introducing a training scheme for manual workers where benefits are spread over several years. These problems arise because budgets and variance analysis normally cover only one period of time in a firm's overall plans, though its objectives will probably be expressed in terms of a more distant planning horizon.

Variance analysis is usually carried out at the end of a budget period (or at intervals within it) and is essentially an historical exercise, in so far as it compares actual results of the past period with the budget. It does not compare future expectations as seen at the end of the budget period with the longer-term plans of the firm originally expressed at the beginning of the budget period. If this latter analysis was available we would have two types of variances available, those relating to past periods and those relating to future periods which would together reflect the effects of decisions taken in the budget period of performance in the budget period and forecast performance in the future.

If budgetary control systems are to be used to appraise performance of managers in achievement of the firm's objectives it is important that the system of variance analysis shows the long-term effect of decisions rather than merely the short-term implications.[4]

If budgets are optimal, variances should reflect the opportunity cost to the firm of deviations from plan. Thus if we consider Ex. 15.1 and Fig. 15.1 this would be interpreted to mean that the cost to the firm of the deviation from budget was £2700, i.e. the profit should have been £2700 more. This conclusion is only valid if the original budget is still optimal and if the actual and budget data reflects the opportunity costs of resources used and received. This information may be important in decisions relating to investigation of variances, or in measuring the extent of the success or failure of managers in terms of their opportunity cost to the firm.

To provide a valid budget for these purposes it may be necessary to calculate an *ex post* budget based on all the information that would have been available if the budgeter had improved knowledge. In Ex. 15.1 this may reveal an optimal profit of say £4000, which differs from the original by £1700 because of factors in the firm's external environment, e.g. devaluation of the pound.

15.5 Variance analysis and reports

Variance reports are produced to show whether replanning is necessary and if it is, whether, such action is being taken. Traditionally they are limited to analysis of historical variances, rather than explanation of future variances, and we will illustrate only historical analysis. Future analysis would differ in so far as it would require explanations of the need for replanning the future.

For replanning purposes the variance reports must give a clear indication of where the variances have occurred, and when used as a feedback device they must show where responsibility for taking action lies. For the latter purposes the reporting system will again follow the responsibility pattern of the organisation. If variance reports are to be useful they must be constructed in the recognition of the hierarchy of responsibility discussed in Sect. 14.2 and identify variances which are controllable at different levels of the organisation as well as containing the necessary information to facilitate investigations.

The analysis of variances illustrated in Ex. 15.1 by comparison of actual and budgeted profit statements fails to satisfy all criteria for a useful variance report. There is no indication to show if the variances are controllable, if they are significant, nor do they give a clear guide to areas where useful investigation could be concentrated due to the absence of detailed analysis. To resolve these latter problems we could provide a further more detailed analysis of variances as shown in Fig. 15.2 though as there are many objectives of reporting variances it is doubtful whether one statement could incorporate all the necessary data.

Variances in profits can be attributed either to revenues or expenses. Variances in revenues normally relate to selling a firm's products and would arise from changes in the selling price or sales volume of particular products. In a multi-product firm this may be due to changes in the volume of sales for particular products with different selling prices.

Although expenses are matched against revenues in the profit calculation a firm will wish to control its costs rather than expenses. This is because some costs become expenses at a point far removed from the possibility of control, e.g. cost of fixed assets becoming depreciation expense. Clearly many costs may simultaneously be expenses, but use of the term 'cost control' rather than 'expense control' is terminologically more correct. Thus a firm will wish to analyse its total production cost variance and any other expense variances.

To enable us to provide a detailed analysis we will provide more data for Ex. 15.1 and explain the calculations of indicative variances shown in Fig. 15.1.

Example 15.1 (continued)
The following data relates to the budget for January 19X1:

Budget January 19X1

Sales and production quantities			1300 units
	per unit		
	£	£	£
Selling revenue per unit and total		20	26,000
Standard cost			
Material, 10 kilos of A @ £0.50 per kilo	5		
Labour, 2 hours @ £1.00 per hour	2		
Variable overheads, 2 hours @ £0.75 per hour	1.50		
Total variable cost	8.50		

Fixed overheads 2 hours @ £1.25 per hour   2.50

	11	14,300
Gross profit	9	11,700
Other expenses: marketing		4,000
administration		2,000
Net profit £5,700		

The budgeted variable and fixed overheads per unit, which were calculated as follows, are absorbed using labour hours as the basis for absorption:

	Overhead	Labour Hours	Rate per hour
	£		£
Variable Overhead	1950	2600	0.75
Fixed Overhead	3250	2600	1.25

The actual revenue, costs and expenses for January 19X1 were:

Actual January 19X1

Sales and Production quantity   1000 units

	£	£
Sales Revenue per unit and total	22	22,000
Cost of Goods Sold and Cost of Production		
Material 11,000 kilos of A @ £0.55 per kilo	6,050	
Labour 2200 hours @ £0.90 per hour	1,980	
Variable Overhead	1,760	
Fixed Overheads	3,080	
		12,870
Gross Profit		9,130
Other Expenses: marketing		4,200
administration		1,930
Net profit £3,000		

The variable and fixed overheads shown are based on the actual expense incurred. We will analyse the net profit variance of £2,700 in three stages: (1) due to changes in sales revenue; (2) due to changes in production costs; and (3) due to changes in other expenses. The effect of analysis of variances was shown in total in Fig. 15.1

(1) SALES REVENUE VARIANCES   total   +£700

This analysis measures the effect on the gross (and net) profit of the firm of changes in sales revenue; it can be conveniently split into two parts:

(a) Selling-price Variance
This is the amount of the variance which arises from changes in selling price. It is assumed that there is no relationship between the selling price and quantity sold as

otherwise the effect of changes in selling prices would be difficult to separate from the volume effect.[7] The variance can be calculated as:

Actual sales quantity × (actual selling price − budgeted selling price)

$$= 1000 \times (£22 - £20)$$
$$= +£2000$$

(b)   Sales Volume
This variance measures the change in gross profit due to changes in the sales volume, limited by the assumptions of the selling-price variance. It is calculated:

(Actual sales quantity − budgeted sales quantity) × budgeted gross profit per unit

$$= (1000 - 1300) \times £9$$
$$= -£2700$$

In a multi-product firm total sales revenue may be affected by change in the mix of products sold, which will also affect gross profit if the margins of profit for each product are different.

Using a variable costing system budgeted gross profit per unit would be £11.50 and sales volume variance £3,450.

(b)   PRODUCTION-COST VARIANCES   total   —£1870

The correct criterion against which to judge the actual production costs is the *total standard cost for the actual level of production*. The total production-cost variance can be analysed into parts for all the individual costs in the standard cost specification.

	Standard per unit	Standard 1000 units	Actual	Variance
	£	£	£	£
(a) Material A	5	5,000	6,050	−1,050
(b) Labour	2	2,000	1,980	+20
(c) Variable overhead	1.50	1,500	1,760	−260
(d) Fixed overhead	2.50	2,500	3,080	−580
	£11.00	£11,000	£12,870	—£1,870

If required these variances can be further sub-analysed as shown below to show the effect of deviations in the prices of resources and the quantity used.

(a)   Material Variance   total   −£1050
Fig. 15.2 provides a graphical representation of the total standard and actual costs of material A.
The total standard material cost is represented by the area ABCO and the total actual material cost by the area A′B′C′O′, the variance being the difference between these two areas is shaded and subdivided into three sectors. Sector I indicates the amount of the total variance solely due to the difference between the actual and standard price. Sector II is the amount of total variance solely due to the difference between the actual and the standard quantities. Sector III is a joint variance due to

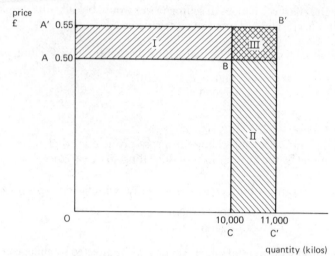

Figure 15.2   Graphical representation of total standard and actual cost

both the price and quantity effects. The monetary value of these sectors is:

		£	*Responsibility*
Sector I price	10,000 kilos × £0.05	500	Purchasing managers
Sector II quantity	1,000 kilos × £0.50	500	Production manager
Sector III joint	1,000 kilos × £0.05	50	Joint —
		£1050	

This threefold analysis is important for purposes of determining responsibility for variances. The traditional analysis uses a two-variance system and adds the joint variance to the price variance, i.e. Sector I and Sector III become the overall price variance.

Thus traditional price and usage variances are:

(i) *Price variance.* Actual quantity used × (standard cost per unit − actual cost per unit)

$$= 11,000 \text{ kilos} \times (£0.50 - £0.55)$$
$$= -£550$$

(ii) *Usage variance.* (Standard total usage less actual total usage) evaluated at the standard cost per kilo

$$(10,000 \text{ kilos} - 11,000 \text{ kilos}) \times £0.50 = -£500$$

(b)   *Labour Variance*   total $\boxed{+£20}$

The approach to analysing the labour variance is identical to the material variance; both price and quantity variables are operating except that in this case the variances are termed wage rate and efficiency respectively. The variances are thus:

(i) *Wage rate.* Actual hours worked × (standard cost per hour − actual cost per hour)

$$2200 \text{ hours} \times (£1.00 - £0.90) = +£220$$

(ii) *Labour efficiency*. (total Standard hours − actual total hours) evaluated at the standard labour cost per hour:

$$(2000 \text{ hours} - 2200 \text{ hours}) \times £1.00 = -£200$$

It is possible with more information to provide a further analysis of both the material and labour variances to refine the procedure. In the case of materials they may be yield variances arising from special production processes; in the case of labour they may separate the efficiency variance into losses of efficiency due to waiting time of operators, idle time, breakdown of equipment, etc.

(c) *Variable Overhead Variance*   total $\boxed{-£260}$

The variable overhead cost also has a price and quantity aspect, although it is not clear as in material and labour.
(i) *Variable overhead expenditure variance*. This term is normally used for the amount of the total variable overheads used in excess of the amount expected to be incurred for the actual level of production. In the budget it was assumed that, for purposes of overhead absorption, variable overheads were directly related to labour hours. For 2200 hours of actual labour hours the budgeted variable overheads would be 2200 × £0.75 per hour or £1650, assuming that £0.75 is the correct rate at which variable overheads are incurred. Further, to be valid the overhead would actually have to vary in proportion to labour hours. It may be correct, e.g. lighting or power, but it is an assumption in the budget which may not even be a good approximation. The variance is thus:

Standard variable overheads for actual activity − actual variable overhead

$$(2200 \times £0.75 \text{ per hour}) - 1760$$
$$£1650 - £1760 = -£110$$

(ii) *Variable overhead efficiency*. This variance measures the effect of the changes in the amount of variable production overheads absorbed per unit which are due to changes in the volume of activity on which overheads are absorbed. In this example the standard time to produce one unit is 2 labour hours, but the actual time is 2200 hours for 1000 units, i.e. 2.2 labour hours per unit. The difference in the time (labour efficiency) is assumed to result in more variable overheads being incurred, and this variance measures the cost:

(Total standard hours − total actual hours) × standard variable overhead rate
$$(2000 \qquad - 2200) \times £0.75 = -£150$$

(d) *Fixed overhead variances*   total − $\boxed{+£580}$

These variances measure the effect of changes in the fixed overhead per unit produced. In simple terms they arise because the average fixed costs per unit produced differs from the budget. When using a variable costing system only the fixed overhead expenditure variance occurs, and then as an expense variance. Using absorption costing, the result of this can be analysed in three separate parts:
(i) *Fixed overhead expenditure*. These are due to changes in the fixed overhead to be absorbed by the products which arises from the amount of fixed overhead incurred during the budget period.
(ii) *Fixed overhead efficiency*. These are changes in the amount of fixed overheads to be absorbed due to variations in the level of activity per unit of production on

which overheads are absorbed. The principle is identical with the variable overhead efficiency variance.

(iii) *Fixed overhead capacity*. These are changes in the capacity measured in terms of the basis on which overheads are absorbed, e.g. man hours (see Sect. 6.4 (iii)).

The latter two variances arise only when a system of absorption costing is used and a direct result of the absorption process which shares the fixed costs between units of production. The average fixed costs per unit will change (I) if the total fixed costs change, (II) if the number of units produced is affected by changes in efficiency which change the fixed costs per unit, or (III) if the actual capacity of the factory changes and is different from the budgeted capacity, which again changes the fixed costs per unit. The only variance which reflects real changes in resources used is (I) as the others arise from the averaging process of absorption costing, i.e. fixed costs are treated as if they were variable. The individual variances are calculated as follows:

(i) *Fixed overhead expenditure variance*. As with the previous overhead expenditure variance, this variance measures the difference between the actual level of expenditure incurred and the amount of expenditure that would have been expected given the revised levels of production. But this category of expenditure is classified as fixed and it is axiomatic that there will be no anticipated change in the level of expenditure over the relevant range of the firm's activity. The variance is:

$$\text{budgeted fixed overhead} - \text{actual fixed overhead}$$
$$£3250 - £3080 = + £170$$

(ii) *Fixed overhead efficiency variance*. This variance arises in a similar way to the variable overhead efficiency variance and reflects the change in unit cost arising from changes in the numbers of hours of fixed overheads allocated to the product. The variance is:

(Total standard hours − total actual hours) evaluated at standard fixed overhead rate:
$$(2000 - 2200) \times £1.25 = - £250$$

(iii) *Fixed overhead capacity variance*. This variance measures the effect on the fixed overhead allocated per unit of production which arises from any changes in the firm's level of activity. It will be clear that an increase in the output passing through a department will be reflected in a reduction in the average fixed cost per unit. The converse is of course correct. The effect is measured by comparing the actual and budgeted levels of the firm's activity (measured in whatever units the original absorption rate was calculated) and evaluating the difference at the budgeted fixed overhead rate. The variance is:

(Budgeted capacity − actual capacity) × budgeted fixed overhead rate
$$(2600 \text{ hours} - 2200 \text{ hours}) \times £1.25 = -$$

This variance is considered as adverse as it implies that there were 400 hours of unused capacity available to the firm; if it had been utilised this would have led to a reduction in the unit cost.

(3)   OTHER EXPENSE VARIANCES

No further analysis of these variances has been completed because it could only involve a subdivision of individual items within the overall classification – e.g. marketing could probably be subdivided into selling, advertising, etc. Using variable costing, production overheads would produce an expense variance of £170.

Commentary on Fig. 15.1

The variances were summarised in Fig. 15.1. The left side of the figure shows the variances classified into indicative variances following the pattern of analysis of Sect. 15.2. The data shown would be a useful indication of where variances have been incurred, perhaps where control is lacking, but they do not show the causes for the variances nor identify the responsibility. If this data were to be used in a management report some preliminary division would be made between variances which were controllable by the person for whom the report were designed. For example, the purchasing manager may only be interested in variances related to purchase price and quality. The right side of Fig. 15.1 has analysed the variances into causes. This could probably only be completed after the analysis and investigation of causes had been completed. A full classification into controllable and non-controllable variances at different levels of the organisation would then be possible. Variance reports which show causes and responsibility would then be useful in appraising the performance of a manager.

In the causal variance report we can see that the indicative variances are allocated into several causal headings. This allocation, based on the results of investigation, illustrates that in some cases indicative variances can be clearly identified with one event and are under the control of some particular person, e.g. rates reduction under control of the manager of factory site, whereas in other cases the control and responsibility are difficult to establish, e.g. use of skilled labour affects many indicative variances and the responsibility may lie with the factory manager, or personnel manager, or the cause may be due to factors external to the firm. This provides a useful illustration of some of the problems which may arise from the implementation of a system of variance reporting. Although responsibility and control should be clearly defined within any organisation, there will be many areas where responsibility, blame or praise cannot be equitably allocated.

Finally it may be useful to comment briefly again on the numbers in variances by using Ex. 15.1 and talking two illustrations.[1] The material price variance is £0.05 per kilo arising from £0.55 actual and £0.50 standard, and shows the cost to the firm of £550. If on investigation it was found that the firm could have acquired the material for £0.40 per kilo the opportunity cost to the firm would be £0.15 per kilo, £1650 in total. The only situation in which a variance report would reflect the opportunity cost would be if the standards were continuously updated.

In Sect. 11.5 the opportunity cost of capacity was examined. The fixed overhead capacity and efficiency variances reflect changes in average costs, but do not reflect the opportunity cost of use or failure to use capacity. The signal that costs may be incurred through failure to use capacity is useful to management but it is doubtful if the numbers calculated on page 244 can accurately reflect this. The limitations of these particular variances may lead to the adoption of a variable costing reporting system (see Sect. 6.4 (iii), and separate reporting or capacity utilisation.

15.6 Summary

In this chapter we have examined the ways in which the concepts of control are applied in a budgetary control system. A budgetary control system is one of the major control systems which operate in many firms. As organisations, grow in size and complexity it is often necessary to augment the other formal and informal control systems in the firm with a planning and control system which uses budgets. The link between budgets for planning and control is important as plans can be used as a guide to check performance provided that they are updated to reflect changes in the firm's environment.

A system of variance analysis can be used either as an aid in determining the causes of variances or as a means of summarising the effects of decisions which were not budgeted. Although the signal that a variance has occurred is a useful guide to action, care must be taken in establishing its significance and in interpreting any numerical value given to it. As budgets normally relate only to one period it is important to study the extent to which the achievement of budgets targets in the short term is consistent with the long-term objectives of the firm.

Notes and References

1. M. Bromwich, 'Standard Costs for Planning and Control', *The Accountant* (April – May 1969).
2. See notes and references for Chapter 13, note 1.
3. R. G. Morriss, 'Budgetary Control is Obsolete', *Management Accounting* (August 1968).
4. M. Bromwich, 'Measurement of Divisional Performance in the Long Run', *Debits, Credits, Finance and Profits,* ed. H. Edey and B. S. Yamey (London, Sweet & Maxwell, 1974).
5. E. Noble, 'Calculating Control Limits for Cost Control Data', *Studies in Cost Analysis*, 2nd ed., D. Solomons (ed.) (London, Sweet & Maxwell, 1968).
6. J. Demski, 'Variance Analysis Using a Constrained Linear Model', *Studies in Cost Analysis*, ibid.
7. D. Solomons, 'The Analysis of Standard Cost Variances', in *Studies in Cost Analysis*, ibid.

Further Reading

H. C. Edey, 'The Principles and Aims of Budgetary Control', paper presented to PERA symposium (May 1967).
G. H. Hofstede, *The Game of Budget Control* (London, Tavistock, 1968).
A. Hopwood, *Accounting and Human Behaviour* (London, Haymarket, 1974).

Questions and Problems

15.1   What do you understand by the following terminology?

Budgetary control	Variance	Adverse variance
Ex post control	Responsibility structure	Causal variance
Ex ante control	Variance analysis	Replanning
Indicative variance	Flexible budgets	Variable costing
Standard cost	Favourable variance	Absorption costing

15.2   'A firm should minimise its variances from budget at all costs.' Discuss.

15.3   Job No. 674 on an assembly line has been observed to have a mean time of ten hours, with a standard deviation of one hour. This information was collected by the work-study department during the past year. During a week the following times were observed for three operators:

Job. No. A 674 Times	Mr A hr	Mr B hr	Mr C hr
	10	12	13
	11	10	14
	12	8	10
	13	7	12

(i) Do you consider any of the deviations from the mean time to be significant and worth investigating?

(ii) What time should the firm adopt as its standard?

15.4 'The use of budgets for planning is a form of *ex ante* control.' Explain and analyse this statement.

15.5 'The causes of variances can be explained in terms of controllable and non-controllable at various levels of the organisation.' Discuss.

15.6 To what extent is the analogy of a boiler and thermostat a useful representation of a budgetary control system?

15.7 Variances may be partly due to omissions of important data by the forecaster, partly due to changes in the firm's environment and partly due to factors which can be controlled by the firm. What problems are there in the analysis of variances into these classifications? Are there other classifications which have been omitted from the generalisation? Use the following variances to illustrate your analysis:

(a) wage-rate variance
(b) material-usage variance
(c) fixed-overhead-capacity variance.

15.8 'The numbers in variances are of little use to managers unless they reflect the opportunity cost (or benefit) of actual decisions taken during the budget period which were not budgeted'. Discuss.

16
Interpretation of Financial Statements

16.1 Introduction

In this chapter we examine methods of control which do not necessarily rely on the use of budgets as described in Chapter 15. The criteria against which to judge a firm's performance may include budgets, but may also rely on comparisons with the performance of other firms, or norms for industry as a whole.[1] If managers or shareholders wish to assess whether the performance of a firm is satisfactory they will want to develop a set of criteria against which to gauge the actual results of decisions. To rely on the measurement of performance through periodic profit calculation is, as we have seen earlier, limited by the attachment to accounting concepts. However, it is possible to abstract many of the characterisitics of the firm, e.g. its profitability and liquidity, by examining patterns of relationships shown by the balance sheet and profit statement. These relationships are normally expressed for convenience in the form of ratios, which facilitate comparison between divisions of a firm, or firms within an industry, or with the economy as a whole. As explained in Sect. 14.1 this analysis provides a basis for several aspects of control, for example, the individual investor who uses information for decisions about buying or selling shares, and managers who use information to assess the performance of their firms or to make decisions within them. This chapter will analyse the uses of ratios for these various aspects of control and their limitations in the analysis of financial statements.

Chapter 15 examined budgetary control, which also involved interpreting financial statements by comparing actual results with a criterion, i.e. a budget. Most of the techniques of this chapter can be combined with the techniques of the previous chapter to aid the control process.

The aspects of a firm's performance for which it is necessary to develop a means of measurement will depend on the needs of the users of this information. Various separate groups of users, including owners, creditors and employees will have different informational requirements. This is discussed further in Chapter 17. Thus it is necessary to examine different aspects which may be of use to the various users. Shareholders may be interested in the amount of dividends they might receive in relation to their investment or resources. Managers may wish to appraise budgets before they are implemented. Creditors may be interested in the safety of their loans. These aspects can be expressed in ratios.

16.2 Ratios in financial statements

In Chapter 1 we saw that the interested parties were concerned about the health of the firm. This was mainly represented by the firm's present financial position, how it has performed recently and how it is likely to perform in the future. The purpose of interpretating the balance sheet and profit statement is an attempt to answer these questions.

If we examine a firm's balance sheet and profit statement over a period of years we might expect to find some trends and relationships. These can be expressed in either absolute terms, or as ratios, e.g. a growth in sales revenue could be expressed as £10,000 each year or as a 20% annual increase. Trends which are often disguised in absolute numbers can sometimes be discovered through the use of ratios, e.g. marketing expenditure per £ of sales revenue. From these trends or relationships we can develop a form of control by the analysis of financial statements. Using ratios we can compare the trends with a budget or other criteria.

By calculating a series of ratios for a firm it may be possible to measure the important elements in its performance. For example, the areas of profitability, liquidity, and financial structure can each be broken down into a series of ratios. The ratios for liquidity and financial structure were considered in Chapter 7. Examples relating to profitability are illustrated in the pyramid of ratios in Fig. 16.1. The reason why we analyse these three areas rather than relying on a single-profit number is that, as we have seen throughout, profit alone is not always an adequate proxy for a firm's health or success.

If the management knows that ratios are going to form the basis of analysing their performance it is possible that the ratios could become objectives in themselves. Rather than relying solely on accounting profit as a measure of success the firm may substitute a set of ratios which are intended to correspond to the shareholders' or firm's objectives. In addition, a pattern of ratios may be considered to be desirable in itself because of past experience. Firms which are considered as successful may have been found to demonstrate a particular set of ratios. Conversely, certain ratios may be found or considered to be found, in unsuccessful firms, e.g. poor liquidity ratios and thus may predict performance.[2]

As ratios are abstractions from available data it is necessary that those ratios used to represent the firm's activities are both representative of the firm as a whole and calculated from relevant data. The use of periodic data, e.g. annual accounts,

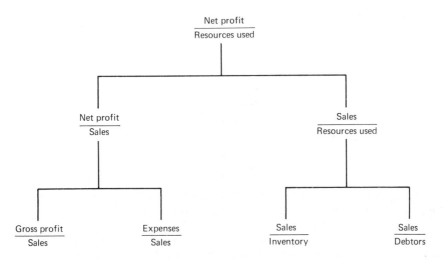

Figure 16.1 A pyramid of profitability ratios

is clearly open to doubts about the representativeness of the data itself and of the period from which it is drawn.

Where the ratios analysis is based on current performance as shown in the balance sheet and profit statement care must be exercised in using this as a predictor of future performance. There is a tendency to quote ratios as if they were expected to remain constant in the future. In this context it should be remembered that conventional accounting data expressly excludes the unrealised effect of current decisions.

16.3   Ratio analysis

Some of the most common profitability ratios which can be calculated from the balance sheet and profit statement can be conveniently brought together in a pyramid of ratios, which is illustrated in Fig. 16.1

The ratios in Fig. 16.1 reflect specific parts of the firm, and together they combine to produce the ratio at the apex of the pyramid which represents the overall profit performance of the firm. The return on investment is the most important ratio in the pyramid and we will now examine it more closely.

Return on Investment
The most common ratio used to measure a firm's overall performance is a ratio comparing the firm's output with its input, where output is net profit and input is resources used. This is related to a general concept of efficiency and can be expressed as:

$$\frac{\text{Net profit}}{\text{Resources used}}$$

This is the general form of return on investment (R.O.I.). The philosophy behind the relationship arises from the needs of providers of finance to receive returns. The measure can be used in many different forms, e.g.:

R.O.I. (Return on long-term finance) =
$$\frac{\text{Net profit}}{\text{Total equity} + \text{long-term debt}}$$

R.O.I. (Return on net assets) =
$$\frac{\text{Net profit}}{\text{Assets} - \text{current liabilities}}$$

R.O.I. (Earnings yield) =
$$\frac{\text{Net profit per share}}{\text{share price}}$$

R.O.I. (Dividend yield) =
$$\frac{\text{Dividend per share}}{\text{share price}}$$

The first two measures (sometimes called return on capital employed or accounting rate of return) relate to the firm, the other two to the investor and provide a comparison of his output, e.g. dividend, with his input, e.g. current share price.

The concept of R.O.I. can be analysed by examining its application to the investment by an individual in a fixed-interest security, e.g. Mr P purchases a debenture for £100, repayable at nominal value after eight years with interest of 10% payable annually. His investment can be shown diagrammatically as:

Years	0	1	2	3	...8
Forecast Cash flow (£s)	−100	+10	+10	+10	... +110

Using the analysis described in Sect. 12.4 the yield of this investment can be shown to be 10%. This means that provided Mr P's cost of finance is no more than 10% the investment is satisfactory. For purposes of appraising the performance of his investment at the end of the first year Mr P has several alternatives. These could include the use of a form of budgetary control, as described in Chapter 15, comparing the actual results with his initial budget or plan. He could also calculate his R.O.I. and compare that with his cost of finance. Assuming his forecast for the first year is attained, his R.O.I. is:

$$\frac{\text{Net profit for Year 1}}{\text{Finance provided}} = £\,\frac{10}{100} = 10\%$$

This shows that the R.O.I. in year 1 is the same as the yield. This is to be expected if the system of appraisal used *ex ante* is consistent with the system used *ex post*.

If, however, the use of R.O.I. is used in situations where the returns arise in different annual amounts through time we may find that the yield of a project calculated *ex ante* differs from R.O.I. calculated *ex post*. For example, let us examine an investment for Mr P where the yield is also 10% but where the pattern of the forecast flows are different:

Years	0	1	2	3	...8
Forecast Cash flow (£s)	−100	+1	+21	−5	... +120
R.O.I.—annual		+1%	+21%	−5%	

If the evaluation of performance is based on R.O.I. we would find the project performing unsatisfactorily in Years 1 and 3 when compared to the cost of finance of 10%, and performing in excess of requirements in Year 2. The reason for this is that R.O.I. is usually based on conventional accounting data and this ignores the unrealised returns in future years. However, as we stated the project has a yield of 10% We thus should not conclude that the performance is unsatisfactory at any stage provided that the annual forecasts are attained. In Sect. 12.5 R.O.I. was rejected as a means of investment appraisal *ex ante,* and its use as a means of measurement *ex post* uses different criteria for decision-making from those used for control.

There are further problems with the application of R.O.I. in practice, i.e. how to measure investment and what to include as returns. We will first examine the measurement of investment. We could measure investment as the amount of long-term finance provided, or as the amount of assets less current liabilities used. These are equivalents, as we have seen from the fundamental accounting equation. The investment used in the calculation must be representative of the whole period, and must be valued on an appropriate basis. One basis could be the total value of the investment given up by the owners and lenders, i.e. total owners' equity and total debt (a finance base). The alternative is to use an asset base. Whatever basis we use, value – as we saw in Chapter 1 – could yield different numbers depending on the concept of value used. Thus, in calculating R.O.I., we could use several bases:

Finance basis
    Balance-sheet value of shares and loans
    Market value of shares and loans

Asset basis
    Balance-sheet value of assets
    Market value of assets (replacement cost or net realisable value)

When using balance-sheet values (see Sect. 9.2) the finance basis is equivalent to the asset basis. However, they will not be equivalent using market values and the investor may be more concerned with the market value of his shares which, as we saw in Chapter 9, may have little relationship to balance-sheet values.

If we use data derived from a conventional balance sheet and profit statement, the calculation will be affected by the way the accounting concepts have been applied in the particular periods under consideration. For example, the use of alternative bases of depreciation described in Sect. 5.4 will affect the calculation of R.O.I. As a result comparisons of R.O.I. can be distorted.

In the use of R.O.I. it is important to ensure that the returns are related to the appropriate investment. If a firm is appraising the effectiveness of its overall use of finance, the calculation of the returns must exclude any charges for the use of finance. Firms should calculate the R.O.I. either based on overall finance used or on equity finance. The difference reflects the results of gearing as illustrated below:

$$\text{Return on total long-term finance employed} = \frac{\text{Net profit before interest payments}}{\text{Owners' equity plus long-term loans}}$$

$$\text{Return on total equity finance employed} = \frac{\text{Net profit after interest payments}}{\text{Owners' equity}}$$

In our analysis of R.O.I. we have so far ignored the effect of taxation. App. B explains the principles of the taxation system in the U.K. In relation to R.O.I. there are some complex problems of taxation,[3] for example, the question of whether the returns used in R.O.I. ratios should be expressed before or after taxation. If returns are expressed before taxation this may make comparison easier between years because the ratio will not be affected by changes in the taxation rates. It is argued that returns should not seem to change because taxation rates change as this is largely out of the control of the firm and does not therefore reflect its con-trollable performance. Against this it is argued that taxation is an expense of the business and returns should be calculated after all expenses.

In our illustration below we will calculate R.O.I. ratios before taxation except where they relate to the returns to owners, e.g. earnings per share, because in these latter ratios we try and reflect the returns they could or will receive.

16.4 Illustration of Ratio Analysis

The balance sheet and profit statement in Ex. 16.1 will serve as the basis of our analysis of ratios.

Example 16.1
The following are balance sheets and profit statements of Pierrepoint Co. Ltd:

Balance Sheets

	At 31 December 19X0	At 31 December 19X1
	£000	£000
Fixed Assets		
Machinery, at cost	30	32
Less: accumulated depreciation	5	6
	25	26
Current Assets		
Inventory	2	6
Debtors	2	3
Cash	2	1
	6	10
Current Liabilities		
Creditors	4	4
Net Current Assets	2	6
	£27	£32
Financed by:		
Owners' Equity		
Share capital (22,000 ordinary shares @ £1)	22	22
Retained profit	5	8
Long-term Liabilities		
Loan at 10%	—	2
	£27	£32

Profit Statements for years ended:

	31 December 19X0	31 December 19X1
	£000	£000
Sales Revenue	20	30
Less: Cost of Goods Sold	10	12
Gross Profit	10	18
Less: Interest	—	0.2
Other Expenses	4	9.8
Net Profit before Tax	6	8
Less: Corporation Tax	3	4
Net Profit after Tax	3	4
Dividends	1	1
Profit Retained	£2	£3

In this section we will analyse some of the important ratios that can be calculated from the above data.

		Ratio Numbers	
Ratio	*Calculation*	*19X0*	*19X1*

PROFITABILITY

1. Return on assets	$\dfrac{\text{Net profit before tax and interest}}{\text{Assets} - \text{current liabilities}}$	$\dfrac{6}{27} = 22\%$	$\dfrac{8.2}{32.0} = 26\%$
2. Return on total finance employed	$\dfrac{\text{Net profit before tax and interest}}{\text{Owners' equity} + \text{loan}}$	$\dfrac{6}{27} = 22\%$	$\dfrac{8.2}{32.0} = 26\%$
3. Earnings per share	$\dfrac{\text{Net profit after tax}}{\text{Number of shares}}$	$\dfrac{3}{22} = £0.14$	$\dfrac{4}{22} = £0.18$
4. (a) Earnings yield	$\dfrac{\text{Net profit after tax per share}}{\text{Share price (Note 1)}}$	$\dfrac{0.14}{2} = 7\%$	$\dfrac{0.18}{2} = 9\%$
(b) Price/earnings ratio	$\dfrac{\text{Share Price (Note 1)}}{\text{Net profit after tax per share}}$	$\dfrac{2}{0.14} = 14$	$\dfrac{2}{0.18} = 11$
5. Ordinary Dividend yield	$\dfrac{\text{Ordinary Dividend per share}}{\text{Share price (Note 1)}}$	$\dfrac{0.05}{2} = 2\%$	$\dfrac{0.05}{2} = 2\%$
6. Ordinary Dividend cover	$\dfrac{\text{Net profit after tax}}{\text{Total Ordinary Dividends}}$	$\dfrac{3}{1} = 3$	$\dfrac{4}{1} = 4$
7. Net profit ratio	$\dfrac{\text{Net profit before tax}}{\text{Sales}}$	$\dfrac{6}{20} = 30\%$	$\dfrac{8}{30} = 27\%$
8. Gross profit ratio	$\dfrac{\text{Gross Profit}}{\text{Sales}}$	$\dfrac{10}{20} = 50\%$	$\dfrac{18}{30} = 60\%$
9. Sales/Assets ratio	$\dfrac{\text{Sales}}{\text{Assets} - \text{current liabilities}}$	$\dfrac{20}{27} = £0.74$	$\dfrac{30}{32} = £0.94$
10. Expense/Sales ratio	$\dfrac{\text{Expenses}}{\text{Sales}}$	$\dfrac{4}{20} = 20\%$	$\dfrac{9.8}{30} = 33\%$
11. Sales/Inventory ratio	$\dfrac{\text{Sales}}{\text{Year-end inventory}}$	$\dfrac{20}{2} = 10$	$\dfrac{30}{6} = 5$

LIQUIDITY

12. Very short-term	$\dfrac{\text{Very liquid assets}}{\text{Current liabilities}}$	$\dfrac{2}{4} = 0.5$	$\dfrac{1}{4} = 0.25$
13. Short-term	$\dfrac{\text{Current assets}}{\text{Current liabilities}}$	$\dfrac{6}{4} = 1.5$	$\dfrac{10}{4} = 2.5$
14. Inventory turnover	$\dfrac{\text{Cost of goods sold}}{\text{Av. inventory}}$	$\dfrac{10}{\text{(Note 2)}} = \text{(Note 2)}$	$\dfrac{12}{4} = 3$
15. Debtors' turnover	$\dfrac{\text{Sales (Note 3)}}{\text{Debtors}}$	$\dfrac{20}{2} = 10$	$\dfrac{30}{3} = 10$
16. Creditors' turnover	$\dfrac{\text{Purchases (Note 3)}}{\text{Creditors}}$	$\dfrac{\text{(note 3)}}{4}$	$\dfrac{16}{4} = 5.0$

FINANCIAL STRUCTURE

17. All debt/equity	$\dfrac{\text{All debt}}{\text{Equity}}$	$\dfrac{4}{27} = 0.15$	$\dfrac{6}{30} = 0.20$
18. Long-term debt/equity	$\dfrac{\text{Long-term debt}}{\text{equity}}$	–	$\dfrac{2}{30} = 0.07$

Notes: (1) The share price was £2.00 per share on 31 December 19X0 and 19X1 (2) This ratio cannot be calculated as we cannot obtain from these figures the average holding of inventory; (3) All sales are assumed to be on credit. Cost of goods sold, plus the increase in inventory, have been used as a proxy for credit purchase.

Fig. 16.2 sets out the main ratios that could be calculated from the data given in Ex. 16.1. The ratios provide an initial analysis of changes in major performance indicators from 19X1 to 19X2. The ratio data could be used in the manner suggested in Sect. 16.2 to identify trends and patterns over time, e.g. increase in expense/sales ratio, or to examine inter-relationships within a period, e.g. return on assets. The ratios provide a neat and concise analytical device which enable us to concentrate our attention on major indicators of performance. In this case we have chosen profitability, liquidity and financial structure. Other indicators could be used to measure other aspects of performance, not computed here, such as the employee turnover ratio.

Ratio analysis of Ex. 16.1 should enable us to learn from data about performance. As a control device, we should attempt to explain the causes of the changes and perhaps develop a scenario which could explain the patterns which have emerged, e.g. lack of administration cost control leading to higher expense/sales ratio. Most important as a control device is the the likely continuation of trends into the future and ratios may highlight the beginning trends, e.g. short-term liquidity is deteriorating.

We would expect the student to examine the data given in Fig. 16.2 in the light of comments in this and previous chapters on accounting concepts, valuation and planning and control considerations, and consider the possible explanations for any patterns which the data reveals.

16.5 Groups of companies

So far in this chapter we have examined individual companies and their financial statements. It is quite common for a number of companies, termed a 'group of companies', to have a common corporate ownership. The owning company is termed a 'holding company'. Indeed any company owning another, partly or wholly, could be termed a holding company, but in this section we are restricting our analysis to the relationships expressed below.

The Companies Act, 1948, Section 154, defines a 'subsidiary' as either:

(1) a company whose voting share capital is more than 50% owned by the holding company, or
(2) a company whose board of directors is controlled by the holding company.

An 'associated company' is defined by the S.S.A.P. no. 1[4] as a company:

(1) in which the holding company's interest is effectively that of a partner in a joint venture, or
(2) in which the holding company owns at least 20% of the voting share capital, and can exercise a significant influence over the associated company. The intention should also be to hold the investment for a long period.

Fig. 16.3 illustrates a possible group of companies. The percentages in this figure relate to the amount of voting shares owned by the immediate holding company. Therefore B, C, D and G are wholly-owned subsidiaries, while F is partially owned (55%) E is only 40% owned by B, therefore it is 40% owned by A and is an associated company.

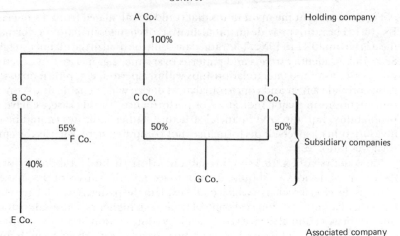

Figure 16.3 An example of a group of companies

Some of the reasons for operating a business as a number of legally separate, though jointly owned companies are:

(1) to take advantage of limited liability available to each separate trading unit (see App. A);
(2) to give the appearance of independence to separate companies, i.e. they have their own name, board of directors, etc.;
(3) for historical reasons, e.g. a business is purchased as a company and is operated in this way for convenience;
(4) to retain an existing company's name for customer goodwill;
(5) to control large amounts of assets without providing a comparable level of finance. It is possible through subsidiaries to invest a relatively small proportion of their total value and yet keep control, e.g. B company owning 55% of the shares of F Co. and thus controlling 100% of its assets.

We will examine first the effect that the existence of subsidiary companies has on interpretation and then consider the effect of associated companies.

Subsidiary companies
The 1948 Companies Act required a holding company to prepare and publish an aggregate balance sheet and profit statement which includes the numbers relating to the holding company and all its subsidiaries. These aggregate statements are called consolidated accounts or group accounts. The reasons for this requirement are:

(a) it will help an owner of the holding company assess the financial health of the group;
(b) the profits of the group could be exaggerated in each individual company's profit statement by sales at a profit within the group which have not been resold outside the group. The realisation concept is applied to the group rather than the individual company;
(c) the assets and liabilities of each individual company within the group could be exaggerated by intra group debts;
(d) the gearing of the whole group will be disclosed;
(e) to prevent the holding company avoiding disclosure of certain details about its subsidiaries for reasons of secrecy, e.g. a loss in one subsidiary, or for reasons of conservation, e.g. a subsidiary that is very valuable;

(f) dividends paid by one company to another within the group could exaggerate the profit of individual companies;

(g) the sales of the group could be exaggerated in each individual company's profit statement by sales within the group.

For these reasons it will be useful to prepare group accounts. Ex. 16.2 is an illustration of some of the techniques involved.

Example 16.2
The Paper Co. owns ordinary shares in the People's Co. which is purchased on 1 January 19X0 for £4000. The summary balance sheets of each company and the group balance sheets at 1 January 19X0 are shown, below in the situation (A) that Paper Co. owns, 100% of the People's Co. shares, and (B) that it owns 60% of the People Co. shares.

	Paper Co.	People's Co.	Group (situation A)	Group (situation B)
	£	£	£	£
Goodwill			1,000	2,200
Fixed Assets	5,000	4,000	9000	9,000
Investment				
Shares in Subsidiary	4,000			
Current Assets	2,000	1,500	3,500	3,500
Current Liabilities	(500)	(800)	(1,300)	(1,300)
	£10,500	£4,700	£12,200	£13,400
Financed by:				
Owners' Equity				
Ord. Share Capital	3,500	1,000	3,500	3,500
Retained Profit	7,000	2,000	7,000	7,000
	10,500	3,000	10,500	10.500
Minority Interest	–	–	–	1,200
				11,700
Loan	–	1,700	1,700	1,700
	£10,500	£4,700	£12,200	£13,400

In Ex. 16.2 the fixed assets, current assets, current liabilities and loans are added together to form aggregate numbers for the group accounts. If there were any intra-group debts or intra-group profits within these numbers they would have to be eliminated. The group balance sheets not only show the total external liabilities of the group but also the total equity held by the external shareholders. Where the Paper Co. owns 100% of the People's Co. the total equity held by these external shareholders is the equity of Paper Co. only. Where the ownership is only 60% the equity held by the external shareholders of the People's Co. is shown under the heading 'minority interests'. This reflects the fact that 40% of the equity of the People's Co. (the total equity is £3000) is owned by shareholders external to the group giving a minority interest of £1200.

The goodwill in the group balance sheets arises because the price paid by the Paper Co. for the shares in the People's Co. exceeded the balance sheet value of the percentage of the assets less liabilities, i.e. owners' equity acquired. The goodwill is calculated thus:

Situation A	Situation B
£4000 − (100% of £3000) = £1000	£4000 − (60% of £3000) = £2200

There are many different ways of treating the aggregation of the numbers in preparing group accounts.[5] See Sect. 9.3 for a further discussion of goodwill.

We have not considered a group profit and loss account[5] (or profit statement) because this is a relatively simple matter of aggregating the total figures. Adjustments may need to be made for intra-group transactions, and the interests of any minority shareholders in the group profits or losses will have to be noted.

Associated companies

Prior to S.S.A.P. no 1 being issued it was usual for a holding company with associated companies to value its investments at cost in its balance sheet and include only the dividends received from the associates in its profit statement. S.S.A.P. no 1 was designed to provide more information for the holding company's shareholders by including additional information in the group accounts about the value and profits of associated companies.

Where a holding company has an associated company the published group balance sheet should show the investment in the associate updated by the holding company's share of any profits or losses of the associate. The published group profit and loss account should also include these profits or losses.

16.6 Summary

In this chapter we have reviewed a further area of control. The control was exercised by interpretation of the financial statements using ratios. These ratios were compared with criteria which could be based on plans, on the past year's performance of the firm, on the performance of other firms, or on norms for industry as a whole. An assessment of the company or part of the company, could be made to help control its performance. The techniques could be used by management or, in the case of published accounts, by external users.

For various reasons many businesses are now run as a group of individual companies under common corporate ownership. This has implications for interpretation and we explored these in the chapter.

This chapter is closely linked to the next chapter because ratios are widely used by external users to interpret published financial information which is the particular concern of Chapter 17.

Notes and References

1. C. A. Westwick, 'The Companies Act 1967 and its Implications for Inter-firm Comparison', *Business Ratios* (Spring 1968).
2. S. Dev, 'Ratio Analysis and the Prediction of Company Failure', in *Debits, Credits Finance and Profits*, Ed. H. Edey and B. Yamey (London Sweet & Maxwell, 1974).
3. Accounting Standards Steering Committee, *SSAP 3. The Treatment of Taxation under the Imputation System in the Accounts of Companies (Including the Effect on Earnings Per Share)* (Institute of Chartered Accountants in England and Wales, 1973).
4. Accounting Standards Steering Committee, *S.S.A.P. 1, Accounting for the Results of Associated Companies* (Institute of Chartered Accountants in England and Wales, 1971).
5. Accounting Standards Steering Committee, *E.D. 3. Accounting for Acquisitions and Mergers* (Institute of Chartered Accountants in England and Wales 1971).

Further Reading

K. W. Bevan, *The Use of Ratios in the Study of Business Fluctuations and Trends* (General Educational Trust of the Institute of Chartered Accountants in England and Wales, 1966).

F. Bailey, *Current Practice in Company Accounts* (London Haymarket, 1973).

D. P. Francis, *The Foundations of Financial Management* (London, Pitman Publishing, 1973).

L. R. Amey, *The Efficiency of Business Enterprises* (London, Allen & Unwin, 1969).

J. Dearden, 'The Case against R.O.I. Control' *The Harvard Business Review,* May–June 1969).

B. Lev, 'Industry Averages as Targets for Financial Ratios', *Journal of Accounting Research,* vol. 7 (Autumn 1969).

D. Solomons, *Divisional Performance: Measurement and Control* (Homewood, Ill,. Urwin, 1965) chap. 5.

E. Solomons and J. Laya, 'Measurement of Company Profitability: Some Systematic Errors in the Accounting Rate of Return', in *Financial Research and Management Decisions,* ed. A. A. Robichek (New York, N.Y., John Wiley & Sons, 1967).

J. Flower, 'Measurement of Divisional Performance', *Accounting and Business Research* (September 1971).

Accounting Standards Steering Committee, *The Corporate Report* (The Institute of Chartered Accountants in England and Wales, 1975).

Questions and Problems

16.1   What do you understand by the following terminology?

A pyramid of ratios	Liquidity ratios
Return on investment	Gearing ratios
Return on assets	Consolidated balance sheet
Accounting rate of return	Consolidated profit statement
Return on capital employed	Group accounts
Return on finance employed	Minority interest
Earnings yield	Associated company
Dividend yield	Goodwill
Dividend cover	
Earnings per share	
Price earnings ratio	

16.2   The following is the balance sheet of Pickle Co. Ltd at 31 December 19X0:

Balance Sheet as at 31 December 19X0

		£
Fixed Assets		
Machine less accumulated depreciation		4000
Current Assets		
Inventory	800	
Debtors	1700	
	2500	
Less: Current liabilities		
Creditors	1100	
Overdraft	300	
	1400	
Net Current Assets		1100
		£5100

Financed by:
Owners' Equity
    Share capital (3000 Ordinary shares of £ 0.50 each)   1500
    Retained profit   2100

                   3600
Loan at 10%   1500
               £5100

Profit Statement for year ending 31 December 19X0

	£
Sales revenue	12000
Less: cost of goods sold	8000
Gross profit	4000
Less: expenses	2000
Net profit	2000
Dividends	500
Retained profit	£1500

Calculate the ratios you would consider important in assessing whether you would buy shares in the company? What criteria would you choose in order to assess the ratios?

16.3   What are the best measures for the following?
    (a)   liquidity
    (b)   effective use of floor space in a retail company
    (c)   the performance of a division of a company
    (d)   profitability, where the owner owns all the shares in the company.

16.4   Calculate measures of return on investment that you consider useful for Mr Illingworth's firm in Ex. 9.3.

16.5   Analyses the performance of Marks & Spencer Ltd, using the data in App. D. What additional information would you like to have?

16.6   The following are balance sheets of Peter Ltd and Paul Ltd. Peter owns 60% of the shares of Paul, the shares being purchased on 31 December 19X0:

Balance sheets at 31 December 19X0

	Peter	Paul
	£	£
Fixed Assets	800	1000
Investment in Paul Ltd	1000	—
Current Assets	3000	2500
Current Liabilities	600	1800
	£4200	£1700
Owners' Equity		
Share capital	1000	500
Retained profit	2200	1000
	3200	1500
Loan at 10%	1000	200
	£4200	£1700

At 31 December 19X0 Paul owes Peter £200. This was included in the current liabilities of Paul and current assets of Peter.

Prepare a consolidated blance sheet at 31 December 19X0. What additional information does it give a shareholder of Peter who had access to the individual balance sheets of Peter and Paul?

17
Disclosure of Accounting Information

17.1 Introduction

A central theme which runs through this book is that accounting information systems should be designed to satisfy the needs of users. In this context we will examine why it is necessary for firms to disclose, in various ways, information about their finances and activities. The development of the analysis will involve an examination of the needs of particular users of information, a study of the background to the current disclosure requirements and an evaluation of the extent to which they are satisfactory.

One of the results of business activity in the U.K. since the Industrial Revolution has been the increasing separation of the providers of finance, i.e. owners and creditors, from those who manage the firm. Where business management and finance is carried out by the owners themselves the requirements of the owners for information about the health of a firm could be easily satisfied by using personal knowledge of the firm and direct reference to the accounts. This latter form of control has become more difficult and complex with the development of modern capitalism and large-scale organisations. The requirement for large amounts of finance and large-scale employment and the enormous significance in national economies led initially to the development of limited liability companies, and more recently to the emergence of the multi-national corporation.

An important concept in political and social theories of control is that without information, control is not possible, and accordingly the requirement for firms to disclose information to various users is an attempt to satisfy the needs of control. The way in which the disclosure of information may facilitate control is that it can be used as a feedback for control, *ex post*, or it may influence behaviour, *ex ante*, because of the knowledge that disclosure of a particular activity may be required. The mechanics of disclosure may operate in many different ways, and the term 'disclosure' does not indicate any particular style of communication. For example, disclosure could mean free access to all information by interested parties, or the filing of summarised information where it would be available for inspection, or publication in the financial press.

The need to preserve the privacy of the individual and the firm has been an important consideration which has been reflected in legislation and case law in the U.K. If firms are to be required to disclose information to various interested parties this may involve lifting the veil of what a firm considers as its private information. To what extent can a firm consider itself a private organisation? The legal distinction between partnerships and companies may assist at this stage of our analysis, as it is in partnerships that we have minimal separation of ownership and management and in the public limited liability company it is at its maximum. We may perhaps expect different disclosure requirements where firms are of different sizes and have different classes of interested parties. The use of the term 'private' enterprise to describe some aspects of modern capitalism may provide a useful indication to the perceived boundaries of disclosure that are applied in current U.K. legislation.

A further factor which influences our analysis is that of accountability. To whom does the firm consider itself responsible and accordingly accountable for its activities? In the nineteenth century there would have been little doubt that owners would have been afforded the prime position in any ranking. However, contemporary opinions suggest that the accountability of the firm is to a far broader community and in consequence this will influence the needs for disclosure.[1,2] In Sect. 17.2 we will examine the needs of the various users of information. Clearly there is room for debate about the extent to which disclosure of all the information is politically and commerically acceptable. We do not make any judgements about the problem of the feasibility of the disclosure suggested, but we examine how the informational objectives of various parties can be satisfied by accounting information.

17.2   Users and their Needs

Before examining the detailed requirements of the various users of accounting information, we will identify certain general principles which should underly any disclosure. It is essential that any bias introduced by the collector and communicator of the information is established and, if possible, eliminated. Historical information can be checked to establish its arithmetical correctness, but clearly problems will arise where information involves forecasts and judgements which necessarily introduce opinions.

Forecasts can be checked *ex post* by comparing them with actual results. A particular problem of forecasts is when they are based on assessments by persons with specialist knowledge, they can only be checked by specialists. The minimum a user of the information might require would be a statement of the underlying assumptions and the knowledge that an independent audit of them had been attempted by such a specialist.

It should be clear from what has been said earlier that many of the measuremert problems in accounting are complex and thus it may not be possible to provide a simple reporting framework for communicating information about such complex business activities. However, minimum standards would aim at eliminating semantic problems caused by imprecise and ambiguous terminology, and varying formats for financial statements.[3] In our examination of the needs of users we will see that the volume of data required may be so substantial that the use of proxies or summaries may be necessary.

In Sect. 14.2 we examined the importance of timeliness of information in any control process. If various users of information rely on feedback information for control purposes, the feedback should be made in time for decisions on appropriate action to be taken. We will now examine the needs of particular users of accounting information.

Owners
The major decision that an owner or potential owner of shares will take relates to increasing or reducing his ownership interest, i.e. purchasing or disposing of his shares. The basis of this decision should be an analysis and comparison of the

value of the share to him with a market valuation. The flow of benefits from his investment will be determined by the size of the potential dividend stream and potential selling price with their associated risks. This information could be communicated to the owner in the form of a dividend forecast, or by profit forecasts and knowledge about the firm's intended profit retention. Evaluation of risks could be in the form of a series of forecasts based on different assumptions or quantification of the dispersion inherent in forecasts (see page 150).

The management of a firm is the trustee of the owners' resources and accordingly the owner must be able to establish whether the best use is being made of the resources. This stewardship relationship can be interpreted on two levels.[2]

Firstly, that the firm is a satisfactory steward and is not abusing the resources through pursuing ultra-vires activities. Furthermore, owners must be assured that managers are not abusing their own inside information for personal gain, to the detriment of the owners. Secondly, that the management is making the 'best use' of resources consistent with the objectives of the owners. The former relationship implies that the firm must merely record how the assets it receives are applied, and that their application, if unsuccessful in generating profits, was not the result of illegal or deceptive intention. The second relationship implies that owners must know about all opportunities that the managers of the firm had available and why they chose a particular set of opportunities and rejected others.

Dissatisfied owners may either sell their shares or retain them and attempt to change the policy of the firm by appointing new directors. The owners may wish to decide whether the assets of the firm should be sold and the proceeds returned to the owners. They may also wish to change the policy of the firm to be consistent with their objectives, e.g. to change the firm's dividend policy or to change the range of activities which affect its risk. Information will be needed about the firm's value and its policy to enable the owners to take such decisions.

Creditors

In Sect. 7.3 we established the major distinctions between debt and equity finance which suggest the basis for different informational requirements. The stewardship function of the firm is to ensure that creditors are repaid their loan and interest when due. To make some assessment of their safety, creditors will need to know if the firm is creditworthy and will be solvent at the time when debts are due for repayment. The limited liability of companies make solvency considerations more important because the creditors can only look to the company and not its members to satisfy their debts. As the financial situation of the firm changes over time, the priority of particular creditors may change. As priority is a major determinant of safety, information about inter-creditor priority will be important. Creditors will also wish to ensure that firms are not paying dividends to owners unless profits have been earned.

Employees

The development of fair collective bargaining depends to a large extent on the information available to the negotiating parties.[4] Employees, perhaps through their trades unions, will wish to make intra- and inter-firm comparisons, which rely on productivity and salary data being available. Employees, as well as owners, will wish to ensure that their share of the benefits is equitable. The capacity of the firm to provide continued employment to the employees is also important.

Consumers

Consumers' interests relate primarily to prices and quality of products. The consumer will wish to ensure prices are fair and that there is no abuse of a firm's monopoly position. This could be achieved, for example, through information about profit margins.[5]

Government

The role of the Government in the control of the company on both a micro- and macro-economic level has become of increasing importance during the last century. The information requirements of Government in its role as owner, creditor, or consumer is not qualitatively different from those previously discussed. However, the Government's interest is much broader than any one particular group, as it must ensure that the allocation of resources such as finance and labour, in the economy is consistent with the objectives of the community it represents. Where a Government relies on the market mechanism, information about prices, profits and opportunities, will be needed to allow resources to be transferred freely through the economy.

Where governments do not rely entirely on market mechanisms to achieve their objectives and intervene in the operation of resource allocation they, too, rely on information. They may wish to encourage (*ex ante* control) firms to attain governmental objectives, e.g. by increasing exports, or they may wish to know about, and influence, the plans of large firms (e.g. the Industry Act, 1975). Information about a firm's exports, or a firm's plans will be required to achieve this.

Public interest

In the application of the 'entity concept' firms tend to ignore externalities – that is, the costs and benefits they impose on their external environment, e.g. the costs to the community of pollution, or the benefits to the community from employee-training. It is, however, becoming more generally accepted that firms have a wider social responsibility than is implied by the entity concept and that accountability to society could be reinforced by disclosure and evaluation of social costs and benefits. There are a growing number of non-governmental agencies interested in reporting on the social consequences of business.[6]

17.3 Development of disclosure

The development of disclosure to meet the information needs of users could be traced in some detail by examining social history since the South Sea Bubble at the beginning of the eighteenth century. The divorce of ownership and management, the joint-stock company, and growth in equity and debt-financing are all important elements which were reflected in legislation about disclosure. App. A.6 sets out the landmarks in Company Law.

The detailed reporting requirement of the 1948 and 1967 Companies Acts are too numerous to include in this book, but some of the major items to be disclosed by most companies are shown below[7] while in App. D we can see a practical illustration.

Balance Sheet
    Share Capital and Reserves – details about type
    Liabilities and Provisions – short and long term
                    – secured liabilities
                    – dividends payable
                    – contingent liabilities
                    – future capital expenditure

Assets – classified under appropriate headings
  – goodwill
  – land
  – fixed assets less accumulated depreciation
  – movements in fixed assets
  – investments; market value of quoted investments
  – subsidiaries
  – current assets

Profit and Loss Account
  Turnover (sales revenue)
  Income from rents of land, investments
  Depreciation expense
  Interest expense
  Dividends paid and proposed
  Directors' emoluments
  Auditors' remuneration
  Taxation
  Net Profit after tax

Directors' Report
  Directors' names, and financial interests
  Principal activities of firm
  Value of land, if directors consider it materially different from balance-sheet
    value.
  Average number of employees and aggregate annual remuneration
  Political and charitable contributions
  Amount of export turnover
  Proposed dividends
  Issue of shares and debentures

Auditor's Report
  To report on whether the balance sheet and profit statement give a true and fair
  view and comply with the Companies Acts 1948 and 1967.

In addition to a series of Companies Acts which govern disclosure, primarily to satisfy investors and creditors, various other legislation has been suggested. *In Place of Strife* and the Industrial Relations Act (1971) referred to the need for disclosure to assist collective bargaining and protect the interests of employees. In neither case were the disclosure requirements spelt out in detail as in the Companies Act. However, the Commission on Industrial Relations recommended[8] that firms should make voluntary agreements with trade unions about disclosure of relevant information for collective bargaining purposes. The Counter Inflation Act (1973) and Fair Trading Act (1973) include provision for disclosure of information to the Price Commission and Director of Fair Trading. The Industry Act (1975) is also a development of the trend towards increased disclosure. Furthermore, the Government has rights through the Monopolies Commission and various agencies to collect information about companies.

E.E.C. law is concerned with the standardisation of many of the aspects of national company law which affect disclosure requirement to enable the E.E.C. to develop an efficient European finance market. The E.E.C.'s draft fourth directive on published company accounts[9] recognised that 'persons who intend to establish relations with companies in other member states have the greatest interest in being able to obtain certain information concerning assets, financial position and results of such companies'.

Various other quasi-legal authorities are in a position to attempt to develop the disclosure of information by companies. The Stock Exchange, which in the U.K. is a non-government agency, regulates the major finance markets. It has established standards of reporting information, primarily for investors, in excess of the minimum Companies Act requirements.[10] The Stock Exchange has developed these rules to improve the quality of information for investors and has remained a private regulatory agency for finance, partly because it has responded to government pressures for greater disclosure, against the threat of a government agency taking regulatory powers. This latter pattern has been adopted in the U.S.A. through the Securities and Exchange Commision, which was established in 1934.

Further pressure for disclosure, particularly in the area of accounting policies and for improvement in accounting reporting has come from the branch of the accounting profession responsible for auditing (see Sect. 2.3). Various recommendations to accountants who are members of the Institute of Chartered Accountants have been issued since 1942, which guided these accountants in particular reporting problems. The Accounting Standards Steering Committee (A.S.S.C.) was set up in 1970 to continue the process of improving reporting procedures and has issued a series of Statements of Standard Accounting Practice (S.S.A.P.) to which all the relevant members of the accounting organisations must adhere, if they are concerned with preparation or audit of published accounting statements. The statements issued to date are:

S.S.A.P.

Explanatory foreword (issued January 1971, revised May 1975)
1. Accounting for Results of Associated Companies (January 1971 revised August 1974)
2. Disclosure of Accounting Policies (January 1971)
3. Earnings per Share (February 1972, revised August 1974)
4. The Accounting Treatment of Government Grants (April 1974)
5. Accounting for V.A.T. (April 1974)
6. Extraordinary Items and Prior-year Adjustments (April 1974)
7. Accounting for changes in the Purchasing Power of Money (May 1974) (Provisional)
8. The Treatment of Taxation under the Imputation System in the Accounts of Companies (August 1974)
9. Stock and Work in Progress (May 1975)
10. Statements of Source and Application of Funds (July 1975)
11. Accounting for Deferred Taxation (August 1975)

Further draft statements have been issued for comment on various subjects. Development of accounting standards on an international scale began in 1973 with the establishment of the International Accounting Standards Committee, which has issued various exposure drafts and statements.

In some cases users of information have the power to obtain information from firms, although it is not required by any legal authority. Potential shareholders or lenders could make disclosure of information a prerequisite to the provision of finance; consumers acting individually or in concert may be able to secure information about costs and insist on price reductions. Furthermore, the development of intermediary financial agencies, such as unit trusts and investment trusts, is a means open to investors to improve their information as these agencies can provide professional analysis, which may not be available to the individual small investor. Financial agencies may also be able to obtain a more direct control of a firm's activities through appointment of directors.

17.4   Disclosure requirements evaluated

The current disclosure requirements can be evaluated against criteria derived from the examination of needs of users of information. The chief criticism of the accounting information that is currently disclosed by companies for owners and creditors is that in many aspects it is based on the original cost concept of value, which is inappropriate for much individual decision-making. The current disclosure requirements are primarily designed to satisfy owners and creditors that their resources are not being misused, i.e. the first of the stewardship concepts explained earlier. The bases of valuation of assets and liabilities, and profit calculation give very little guidance to owners who wish to value their investment, e.g. no dividend forecasts (see Sect. 9.4) and little guidance to creditors as to the safety of their loans, e.g. no valuations based on selling price (see Sect. 9.2) Although much detailed information has to be disclosed to various parties much of the information can be criticised as irrelevant for individual decision-making purposes. There is no requirement for an evaluation of the performance of the firm by its management nor are the auditors required to make an assessment of the management and performance of the firm.

Company financial statements are not required to follow any particular format, terminology or sequence. As an exercise in communication current disclosure requirements must be criticised for their failure to require standardisation of format.[3] In Sect. 9.2 we examined how one set of accounting data could yield various profit computations, according to the particular set of accounting policies selected. Although it can be argued that standardisation of accounting policies is not desirable as it may deny firms the right to reflect their own particular financial positions, it is difficult to adapt this argument to the failure to specify an exact format for financial statements. As can be seen by examining sets of published accounts prepared to satisfy current statutory and other requirements, communication may easily be impeded by the problems of multifarious terminology and presentations.

The current legislation and the requirements of non-statutory bodies which have some control of the development of disclosure have been acting primarily on behalf of investors and creditors except perhaps for some detailed data in the 1967 Companies Act, e.g. average employee pay. However, employees and trade unions are in a relatively unprivileged position, except in firms where trade unions are able to use their powers to extract useful data in collective bargaining. It is a very noticeable absence in current legislation that their information rights are not specified in detail.[12]

Although we have been concerned primarily with companies in our analysis of disclosure requirements we should not ignore other forms of legal entities such as partnerships and sole traders. Until 1967 private companies could avoid most disclosure requirements by virtue of exemption afforded to them because of their restricted ownership. This exemption was removed in 1967 because it was considered that they were of sufficient significance for other users of information that disclosure should be mandatory. Thus it is only firms which have unlimited liability which are exempt from the majority of disclosure requirements. The justification is that these firms do not have limited liability and thus that creditors have direct claims against the owners if necessary and that owners usually have access to management information. However, there are many partnerships or sole traders with a significant number of non-partner employees, e.g. accountants and solicitors, where full disclosure should be necessary to satisfy creditors – and, in particular, employees – that the firms are operating in the best interests of these groups.

The independent role of the auditor is likely to be crucial in any external disclosure. If the importance of the auditor's report increases it is likely that the maintenance of their independence will become more significant. The liability for mis-statements of the auditor, in addition, may be crucial, particularily if the auditors have to report on forecasts.

17.5 Improvements in disclosure

We will examine how improvements in disclosure of accounting information can be afforded through various philosophies of disclosure, how these improvements could be brought about and, finally, some of the problems and criticisms that the proposals have engendered.

At one end of the spectrum firms could be required to make available to interested parties any information which management had available. This would include information about the firm's plans and expectations, past failures and successes. More particularily it would include information such as budgets and dividend forecasts which would satisfy the needs of owners and creditors.[13] To satisfy users this information would have to be audited to meet our general requirements for comprehensibility, timeliness and freedom from bias.

As an alternative to full detailed disclosure the various users could have their interests protected by a representative, such as an auditor, thus extending the responsibility for commenting on broad issues such as profitability, liquidity and financial structure (as examined in Chapter 16) and who should report to interested parties on his findings. This may be a means of full public disclosure of all information which retains a degree of confidentiality while ensuring that all matters *can* if necessary be investigated.

Improvements in disclosure can be effected through legislation or by relying on the efforts of legal or quasi-legal organisations. Current developments seem to be in the hands of several bodies, e.g. the U.K. Government, the E.E.C., the Accounting Standards Committee, and the Stock Exchange. There could be an argument for drawing together these groups into a comprehensive unified structure.[14]

It is clear that the Government will have to decide whether it leaves improvement in disclosure to quasi-legal groups or whether legislation is the solution. The major problem facing the quasi-legal interests is that of the enforceability of their proposals. Although some companies exceed current minimum legal requirements in their reports to shareholders – most particularly in the customary, though not legally required, 'Chairman's report', – it is clear that there is a large gulf between the historically based current disclosure requirements and future-based information so important for individual decision-making.

Companies are required to produce audited profit forecasts in such cases as the public issue of shares and debentures, and there would seem little real justification for the resistance to extending this requirement to annual published accounts.

Any suggestions for a change in emphasis from the past to the future could be subject to criticism. For instance, it can be argued that disclosure which involves forecasts introduces uncertainty and makes auditing impossible. This ignores the information that management uses for decision-making which may be equally useful for investors, etc. It is also argued that disclosure implies an increase in governmental interference in private enterprise, although it could probably also be argued that the price mechanism (which relies on information) is the most efficient resource allocator in the economy. It is also clear that disclosure on a large scale is a costly exercise because of the need to provide a volume of information to many interested parties. However, substantial sums are currently spent on publication of company accounts to high graphical standards. Disclosure may lose a particular firm a competitive advantage if information, particularly about budgets, is made available, although if all firms were required to publish it may break down barriers to competition.

17.6 Summary

In this chapter we have examined the role of disclosure of information about firms, and the pattern of current disclosure in the U.K. The importance of firms in the economies of countries demands that information is available to all who are affected by their decisions and performance.

To enable firms to make this information available it is necessary to establish the needs of users. At the basis of these needs is the necessity to have information that is independant and free form bias.

Current disclosure requirements meet some of the perceived needs of users, but much more information is still needed, particularly about the future prospects of the firm. We reviewed some of the problems raised by an increased emphasis on the future. We concluded that firms could disclose their plans and expectations about the future and thus provide much useful information to various users. This would emphasise the remarks made in Chapter 1 about accounting information providing a basis for future decision-making.

Notes and References

1. D. Solomons, 'Corporate Social Performance: A New Dimension in Accounting Reports?', *Debits, Credits, Finance and Profits*, ed. H. Edey and B. Yamey (London, Sweet & Maxwell, 1974).
2. P. Bird, *Accountability: Standards in Financial Reporting* (London, Haymarket, 1973).
3. P. Bird, 'Standard Accounting Practice', *Debits, Credits, Finance and Profits*, ibid.
4. R. Smith and P. Manley, 'Company Information and the Development of Collective Bargaining', *Three Banks Review* (September 1973).
5. K. Buckley Edwards, 'The Fair Trading Act, 1973', *Accountancy* (November 1973).
6. For example, Social Audit, Counter Information Services, Friends of the Earth.
7. For further details see *Guide to Accounting Requirements of the Companies Acts 1948–1967* (General Educational Trust of Institute of Chartered Accountants; London, Gee & Co., 1967).
8. C.I.R. Report No. 31, *Disclosure of Information* (London, H.M.S.O., 1972).
9. *Proposal for a Fourth Directive on the Annual Accounts of Limited Liability Companies*, supplement 7/71, Annex to Bulletin 12–1971, Commission of the European Communities.
10. *Blank Company Ltd* (Burni Mathieson & Co. Ltd, 1974).
11. *Accounting Policies* (Institute of Chartered Accountants in England and Wales, April 1974).
12. *The Corporate Report* (Accounting Standards Steering Committee, London, 1975).
13. H. C. Edey, 'Accounting Principles and Business Reality', reprinted in *Modern Financial Management*, ed. B. Carsberg and H. C. Edey (Harmondsworth, Penguin Books, 1969).
    G. H. Lawson, 'Cash Flow Accounting' *The Accountant* (28 October, 4 November 1971).
    T. A. Lee, 'The Case for Cash Flow Reporting' *Journal of Business Finance*, No. 2 (1972).
14. For further criticism see C. J. Jones, 'Accounting Standards – a Blind Alley', *Accounting and Business Research* (Autumn 1975).

Further Reading

R. C. Morris, *Corporate Reporting Standards and the 4th Directive* (Research Committee of the Institute of Chartered Accountants, 1973).

P. R. A. Kirkman, 'What Can We Learn from Published Accounts in the U.S.A.', *Accounting and Business Research*, no. 4 (Autumn 1971).

K. W. Wedderburn, *Company Law Reform* (London, Fabian Society, 1965).

H. Rose, *Disclosure in Company Accounts* (London, Institute of Economic Affairs, 1963).

M. Fogarty, *A Companies Act 1970* (P.E.P., 1970).

R. H. Parker, 'The Structure and Content of Annual Accounts in the E.E.C.', *The Accounting Magazine* (March 1972).

D. Flint, 'The Role of the Auditor in Modern Society: An Exploratory Essay', *Accounting and Business Research*, no. 4 (Autumn 1971).

The Corporate Report (Accounting Standards Steering Committee, London, 1975).

Sandilands, *Inflation Accounting – Report of the Inflation Accounting Committee*, Cmnd 6225 (1975).

Questions and Problems

17.1   What to you understand by the following terminology?

Disclosure	Stewardship	Market economy
Accounting information	Audit	Standard of accounting practice
Accountability	Social audit	Profit forecasts
Private information	Auditors' report	
Chairman's report	Directors' report	

17.2   (i) Identify specifically what information you could require from a limited liability company if you were:

   (a) an ordinary shareholder
   (b) a preference shareholder
   (c) a secured creditor (fixed charge)
   (d) a secured creditor (floating charge)
   (e) an unsecured creditor
   (f) an employee
   (g) a major customer
   (h) a potential customer
   (i) government
   (j) an anti-pollution pressure-group

   (ii) would your analysis be different if you were concerned with:

   (a) an unlimited liability company
   (b) a partnership
   (c) a sole trader

17.3   'More disclosure of information about firm's activities will prove a disincentive to new development of private enterprise?' Do you agree?

17.4   'Firms should be obliged to disclose their plans for the next ten years.' Discuss.

17.5   'The development of disclosure should be left to the Stock Exchange and the accounting profession?' Do you agree?

17.6   The scope of the auditor should be extended to commenting on the performance of management.' Do you agree?

17.7 Explain why the Companies Acts require a company to disclose the following information:

    (*a*) political and charitable contributions
    (*b*) directors' emoluments
    (*c*) depreciation
    (*d*) auditors' remuneration
    (*e*) the Chairman's or highest-paid director's salary
    (*f*) export turnover
    (*g*) its principal activities

Appendix A Legal Aspects of Accounting for Companies

A.1 Introduction

This appendix is a guide to the law relating to companies with particular emphasis on the law's affect on accounting information. It is not a detailed examination of the subject; for this reference should be made to specialist texts.[1]

Three legal classifications of the firm were introduced in Chapter 1, i.e. sole traders, partnerships and companies. This appendix is primarily concerned with companies, but we begin with a brief explanation of these common forms of business entity.

(a) Sole trader

The term 'sole trader' is commonly used to describe a business owned by one person. There is no legal distinction between the financial affairs of the business entity and those of the owner. However, it may be found convenient to make such a distinction in the preparation of the accounting statements of the business.

(b) Partnerships

A partnership consists of a number of people who own a business jointly. These owners will have a collective responsibility and authority for the affairs of the business. As with a sole trader there is no legal distinction between the actual partnership and the individual members of the partnership. The partners are free to make whatever arrangements they choose about their business matters, e.g. profit-sharing and voting rights, but where a matter is not covered by such an arrangement it is regulated by the Partnership Act, 1890.

(c) Company

A company is an artificial legal person separate from its owners. It can thus sue and be sued in its own right. There are many ways for a company to be formed but in this appendix we consider only companies formed under one of the various Companies Acts.[2]

A.2 Limited liability[2]

A company can choose to be incorporated as a company with limited or unlimited liability. This refers to the liability of the shareholders. Whatever the choice, all the assets of the company are available to repay its liabilities. If, however, these assets are not sufficient to repay all the liabilities the creditors can look to the shareholders for their debts in the case of a company with unlimited liability. If the company has limited liability the creditors cannot sue the owners to satisfy their unpaid debts. The existence of limited liability is important because it enables shareholders to restrict their commitments and finance to a specified known amount. This possibility is essential if a large number of people are to be attracted to involvement in the ownership of companies.

A.3 The advantages of operating as a company

Some of the advantages of operating as a company are as follows:

(1) A company has a perpetual legal existence not dependent on the life of its owners, managers or employees.
(2) The liability of a company's owners can be limited making it attractive to shareholders and investors.
(3) There is no upper limit (apart from private companies mentioned below) to the numbers that can participate in the ownership of a company. There is a legal limit on the number of partners in a partnership.
(4) Because of the possibility of a number of people participating in the ownership of the company, its potential sources of finance are wider.
(5) There may be tax advantages in trading through a company rather than as a sole trader or partnership.

A.4 The classification of companies

In addition to the classification of companies into those with limited or unlimited liability there are also further common classifications.

Private and public Companies

A private company is one which:

(a) restricts the right of its owners to transfer their shares to other potential owners;
(b) limits the maximum number of its owners to fifty; and,
(c) prohibits any invitation to the public to subscribe for any shares or debentures of the company.

A public company is one that does not have these limitations of ownership. As a consequence it has access to a wider ownership and greater sources of finance. Because of this extra demands are placed on public companies especially in the area of disclosure.[3]

Quoted and unquoted Companies

A quoted company is one whose shares are quoted on a recognised stock exchange. Other companies are not quoted either because the companies choose not to seek a quotation, or because they cannot fulfil the requirements of the stock exchange in question. All quoted companies are public companies but not all public companies are quoted. One of the advantages of a company's shares being quoted is that there is a recognised price for the shares. This makes the shares more easily marketable.

Holding and subsidiary Companies

This classification was explained in Sect. 16.5. These companies can be either public or private, and quoted or unquoted.

A.5 The formation and termination of a company

A company is formed by being registered with the Registrar of Companies. The registration process requires legal documents to be filed with the Registrar, the most important being the constitution of the company.

Memorandum and Articles of Association

This constitution is divided into two parts, a memorandum of association, and the articles of association.[4] The memorandum contains fundamental information such as the name of the company, its objects, and the amount of the share capital. The articles contain the rules governing the internal management of the firm, e.g. the frequency of general meetings, the terms of office of the directors, and the quorums for meetings.

Audit

An auditor has to be appointed to audit a company's financial statements, and to report on them to the shareholders.[5] The Companies Acts give various responsibilities and duties to an auditor.[6] To be appointed, an auditor must meet the qualifications laid down in the Companies Acts. He is answerable to the shareholders, though he may be appointed by the directors between meetings. An auditor may not be removed from his appointment except by the shareholders at the annual general meeting.

Liquidations

The legal existence of a company may be perpetual but it can be terminated in certain situations. The termination of the life of a company is known as its liquidation, or winding up.[7] Sect. 211 of the Companies Act, 1948, outlines three methods of terminating the life of a company:

(1) A voluntary liquidation by either the owners or creditors.
(2) A compulsory liquidation by the court.
(3) A liquidation under the supervision of the court.

If a company is solvent all its liabilities will be paid. If it is insolvent then special rules apply to the order of the repayment of the liabilities. The proceeds of the liquidation will be used in order of preference to pay:

(1) The secured creditors out of the proceeds of their security (i.e. their fixed charge).
(2) The costs of the liquidation.
(3) The preferential debts, e.g. unpaid wages, and taxes.
(4) Holders of floating charges.
(5) Unsecured creditors.

If there are any assets left after these debts have been paid the remainder will be paid to the shareholders.

A.6 Landmarks in company law

The legal concept of a registered company was introduced in 1844 and the law relating to companies has evolved since that date. Initially the legal emphasis was on the protection of the creditor but as investment in companies became extended to cover a wider group of people the emphasis expanded to include the need for more information for the shareholders. In recent years the emphasis has expanded further to consider the responsibility of companies to the general public interest. The landmarks of company law can be summarised as follows:

1844 Joint Stock Companies Act introduced the registration of companies.
1855 Limited Liability Act introduced the limited liability of companies.
1862 Companies Act extended law relating to companies.
1900 Companies Act required auditors to be appointed to report to shareholders.
1908 Companies Act required companies to file a balance sheet with their annual return each year.
1929 Companies Act laid down further rules about the information to be included in the balance sheet.
1932 The Royal Mail Case,[8] which led to increased disclosure of information especially regarding reserves.
1945 Cohen Committee on company law.[9]
1948 Companies Act, which was a major development consolidating company law to that date. It introduced further specific requirements regarding financial statements and audit.
1962 Jenkins Committee on company law.[10]
1967 Companies Act requiring considerable additional information to be published by companies.
1973 European Communities Act, which means the U.K. will be affected by the articles of the Treaty of Rome. The directives and draft directives under this Treaty concern:

(1) the contractual capacity of the company and its directors and the question of publicity of the company;
(2) the formation of the company and maintenance of capital;
(3) mergers;
(4) the annual accounts of limited companies;
(5) the structure of the company.

1975   Industry Act, 1975.

A.7   The law relating to profits and dividends[11]

Profit is not defined by Act of Parliament, but a considerable body of case law has arisen because of the need to define profit. This need arises in various situations, e.g. an employee's salary may be ascertained by reference to profits, dividends may be payable at certain profit levels, taxes are levied on profits. Normally the Courts will accept a profit calculated using generally accepted accounting principles as the starting-point for the assessment in a particular case.[12]

Notes and References

1. For example, K. Smith and D. J. Keenan, *Company Law*, 2nd edn (London, Pitman, 1971), and L. C. B. Gower, *Principles of Modern Company Law* (London, Stevens, 1969).
2. Smith and Keenan, ibid., chap. 1.
3   For example, *The Requirements of the Companies Act 1947 and 1967* (General Educational Trust of the Institute of Chartered Accountants of England and Wales, 1967).
4. Smith and Keenan, op. cit., chap. 3.
5. Ibid., chap. 13.
6. Ibid. chap. 13
7. Ibid., chaps 14, 15 and 16.
8. W. T. Baxter and S. Davidson (eds), *Studies in Accounting Theory*, 2nd edn (London, Sweet & Maxwell, 1962) pp. 452–62.
9. Report of the Committee on Company Law Amendment, Cmd 6659 (London, H.M.S.O., 1945).
10. Report of the Company Law Committee, Cmnd 1749 (London, H.M.S.O., 1962).
11. G. Macdonald, *Profit Measurement: Alternatives to Historical Cost* (London Haymarket, 1974) chap. 1.
12. F. Bailey, *Current Practice in Company Accounts* (London, Haymarket, 1974) chap. 7.

Appendix B Taxation

B.1 Introduction

This appendix is primarily concerned with tax in so far as it relates to companies. It is not a comprehensive analysis but selects specific topics which relate to the content of this book. Most business decisions are affected by tax considerations. Taxes are levied by governments through the Finance Acts; it follows that the decision-maker must have an understanding of the relevant law.

The major U.K. taxes are listed in Fig. B.1. The taxes have been classified in relation to the departments responsible for collecting them. The Inland Revenue are responsible for the administration of direct taxes, the Customs and Excise for indirect taxes. Taxes levied directly on individuals and firms are termed 'direct taxes'. When levied on goods and services and thus indirectly on individuals and firms who purchase the goods and services, they are called 'indirect taxes'.

	Yield 1973/4 £ million	Description
INLAND REVENUE		
Unified income tax	7443	Tax on individual's income
Corporation tax	2262	Tax on company's income
Capital gains tax	324	Tax on capital gains
Death duties*	412	Tax on property passing at death
Stamp duties	190	Tax on certain types of contracts, e.g. house-purchase contracts
CUSTOMS AND EXCISE		
Alcohol duty	953	Included in the price of wines spirits, etc.
Tobacco duty	1085	Included in the price of cigarettes
Value-added tax	1469	Included in the price of goods and services
Betting and gaming duty	185	Tax on gambling transactions
Hydrocarbon oils duty	1585	Tax on petrol, etc.
Import duty	462	Tax on imports of certain goods
Car Tax	117	Tax on purchase of cars
OTHER DEPARTMENTS		
Motor vehicle tax	507	Annual tax on vehicles

* Incorporated in the Capital Transfer Tax since 1975.

Figure B.1   Taxes levied by the UK central government in 1973/4

Fig. B.1 does not include local government taxes, such as general rates on property. The figure shows the relative volume of each tax. The year 1973/4 refers to 6 April 1973 to 5 April 1974. The year to 5 April of each year is the fiscal year on which government income and expenditure is based.

In this appendix we will examine Unified Income Tax and Corporation Tax. In addition we consider the investment incentives that can be claimed by companies from the Government; the effect of profits for tax purposes differing from accounting profit; and the presentation of taxation in the financial statements of companies.

The taxes examined are based on income.[1] In the case of companies it is their profits from business which are taxed. In the case of individuals it includes, for example wages and salaries, and profits from a business. In both cases losses from a business are treated as negative profits for taxation purposes and can normally be set against current or future profits thus reducing the tax payable on those profits.

In the case of firms (whether companies or not) there are a number of differences between accounting profits and profits calculated for tax purposes. The most important difference is due to the method of computing depreciation for tax purposes. For tax purposes the rates of depreciation (called 'capital allowances') may be determined for a variety of reasons, e.g. to encourage investment in a particular area. For accounting profit purposes depreciation rates are determined by the application of accounting principles.

Taxes are assessed by reference to a series of schedules which contain rules for taxing different types of income. The schedules are:

Schedule	Examples of sources covered
A	Rent from the occupation of land
B	Rent from woodlands
C	Interest from government stock
D Case I	Profits of trade
D Case II	Profits of profession
D Case III	Interest from a bank account
D Case IV	Interest on securities (held overseas)
D Case V	Income from foreign possessions
D Case VI	Interest from any other source
E	Salaries and wages of employed person

B.2 Unified Income Tax[2]

This tax, introduced on 6 April 1973, is so named because it replaced income tax and surtax, which was the basis of individual tax up to that date. It is the basis of taxing all individuals on their income as calculated from the rules relating to the above tax schedules.

The taxpayer is given certain allowances which are dependent on his circumstances, to set against his income, e.g. he receives a child allowance for each of his children.[3] These allowances will be deducted from his taxable income to give the income subject to tax. This is subject to graduated taxation, for example in 1974/5 the first £4500 was taxed at 33%, the next £500 at 38% rising by steps to a maximum of 83% for the balance over £20,000. The calculation of an individual's tax liability is illustrated in Ex. B1.

Example B.1

A married man with two children earns £7000 in 19X0/1. The computation of his tax liability would be calculated as:

	£	£
Total income		7000
Less: married man's allowance	865	
Allowance for 2 children	480	1345
Income subject to tax		£5655
Tax liability:		£
first £4500 at 33%		1485
next £ 500 at 38%		190
next £ 655 at 43%		282
		£1957

B.3 Company taxation[4]

The profits made by a company are taxed at a corporation tax rate fixed by the relevant Finance Act. The calculation of profits for this purpose is based on the Schedule D rules[5] for profit assessment, e.g. trading profits under Schedule D, Case I, and interest under Case III.

The taxation of companies has evolved in a different way from that of individuals. As we have seen, companies are legal entities separate from their owners. Tax is therefore levied directly on the company rather than the owners. In this appendix we consider only the current U.K. Legislation.[6]

The accounting profit of a company is the starting-point in calculating profits for corporation tax purposes. After the necessary adjustments have been made the prevailing rate of corporation tax is used to calculate the tax liability of the company. This liability is not normally paid until nine months after the end of the company's financial year.

When a company pays a dividend it is required to pay an amount of corporation tax. This payment is known as advanced corporation tax (A.C.T.), the rate of this tax being set in the Finance Act. It is known as A.C.T. because it is payable in advance of what would otherwise be the payment of corporation tax nine months after the end of the financial year. A.C.T. paid in the financial year is usually deductible from the corporation tax liability for that year, the balance being known as mainstream corporation tax.

As far as the shareholders are concerned the A.C.T. paid by the company which relates to his dividend is a tax credit which will be available to offset his personal tax liability. His personal tax liability will be calculated in the way outlined in Ex. B.1, but his total income will include the dividend he receives plus his tax credit.

The current corporation tax system (known as the imputation system), as it affects the company and the shareholder, is illustrated in Ex. B.2 below. This shows the company paying A.C.T. (£132) at the time they pay the dividend. The corporation tax liability (£500) is reduced by this A.C.T. and the company pays the mainstream tax (£368) at a later date.

Example B.2

A company's taxable profit is £1000. Assume the corporation tax rate is 50%, the A.C.T. rate is 33/67th's of the dividend, and that the personal tax rates and allowances are those that applied in Ex. B.1. The company's calculation:

	£
Net profit before tax	1000
Less: corporation tax	500 (note 1)
	500
Dividend (note 1)	268
Retained Profit	£ 232

Note (1)   The £500 is the calculation of the corporation tax liability. This will be paid as A.C.T. of £132 when the dividend is paid and a later amount of £368, totalling £500.

Assuming that all the dividends go to the individual illustrated in Ex. B.1 the shareholders calculation of his tax would be:

	£
Dividend plus tax credit	400
Other income	7000
	7400
Less: allowances	1345
Income subject to tax	£6055
Tax liability:	
first £4500 at 33%	1485
next £ 500 at 38%	190
next £1000 at 43%	430
next £55 at 48%	26
Total tax liability	2131
Less: tax credit on dividend	132
Additional tax payable	£1999

Note the effect of this is that the shareholder pays tax on the dividend (£400) at his marginal tax rate (i.e. £345 at 43% and £55 at 48% in this case). The A.C.T. deducted does not determine the tax ultimately paid on the dividend but is a form of interim payment made by the company on the shareholder's behalf.

It is interesting to note the different treatment for tax purposes of dividend payments (on equity) and interest payments (on debt). The latter are a deduction before arriving at the profits liable to corporation tax, but the former are a distribution of profit after corporation tax. If a company is considering raising finance an important consideration will be the tax implications when choosing between debt and equity (see Chapter 7 for other considerations).

Ex. B.3 shows the relative cost of raising finance by borrowing (debt), and by issuing more share capital (equity). The company needs to earn more profit to provide the same rate of return to equity rather than debt.

Example B.3

A company wishes to raise £1000. The required rate of return by equity and debt finance is 10% before tax (6.7% after tax assuming the standard rate of 33%). Assume corporation tax is 50% and basic rate income tax is 33%. The profit required to pay the required interest and required dividend leaving in both cases a nil retained profit is:

Company	Debt	Equity
	£	£
Net profits before tax, interest and dividends	100	134
Less: interest	100	
	—	
Corporation tax*	—	67
	—	67
Less: dividend		67
(A.C.T. paid £33*)		
Retained profit	—	—

Investor	Debt	Equity
	£	£
Received gross of tax	100	—
Less: tax paid	33	—
Received net of tax	67	67

From this we can see that the before tax cost of the debt to the company was 10%, i.e. the profits required on the £1000 investment in order to pay the interest was £100. In the case of equity the before tax cost is 13.4%

B.4 Investment grants and capital allowances

Successive Governments have encouraged investment by firms with grants and allowances. Investment in certain regions of the country qualified the firm for a cash grant (termed an 'investment grant') based on the cost of the asset. In itself this grant is an incentive to firms to investment. In addition most firms can deduct 100% of the cost of the asset from profits for tax purposes in the year of their choice, e.g. it can all be taken in the first year. These deductions are in place of the firm's depreciation expense and are called 'capital allowances'.

Ex. B.4 illustrates the application of these grants and allowances.

Example B.4

A company with profits of £10,000 purchases an asset for £5000 at start of 19X5. This asset qualifies for an investment grant of 20% and capital allowances of 100% calculated on the cost of the asset to be taken when the company chooses. The company depreciates the asset for accounting purposes at 10% of cost. The investment grant received would be £1000. The corporation tax is calculated as:

	£
Net profit before tax	10,000
Add: depreciation disallowed	500
	10,500
Less: capital allowances (100% of cost)	5,000
Taxable profit	£5,500
Corporation tax at 50%	£2,750

The profit statement for 19X5 would be presented as follows:

	£
Net profit before tax	10,000
Less: corporation tax (50%)	2,750
Net profit after tax	£7,250

S.S.A.P. no. 4 'The Accounting Treatment of Government Grants'[7] explains the way the investment grant should be presented in the financial statements.

B.5 Deferred taxation

We have noted that adjustments have to be made to accounting profit in order to calculate tax profits. Some differences, known as permanent differences, arise because certain types of income are tax free or certain expenses are disallowed for tax purposes. Others arise from timing differences; that is, some items are included for accounting profit purposes in a period different from that in which they are dealt with for tax purposes. This means that the tax on parts of the accounting profit may be deferred to later periods.

The matching concept implies that costs and revenues are matched in the profit statement of the period to which they relate. This suggests that the taxation expense in the profit statement should be related to the accounting profit rather than be based on the tax profit, i.e. profits for tax purposes. In order to do this the taxation expense in the profit statement will include a part relating to the tax profits of the current period and a part reflecting the tax deferred in the current period but payable in future periods (or vice versa). This latter adjustment is related to a number in the balance sheet of the total taxation deferred to date. By their nature these adjustments relate only to timing differences.

In Ex. B.4 a calculation was shown in which capital allowances were substituted for depreciation expenses. It could be said that the profit statement for 19X5 was misleading because it showed an abnormally low tax expense. This arose because the taxable profits were £5500 and the accounting profits £10,500.

S.S.A.P. no. 11 'Accounting for Deferred Taxation'[8] recommends either of two methods of making adjustments to rectify this misleading impression. There are, however, other possible methods. The recommendations can best be illustrated by an example:

Example B.5

A company's accounting profits before tax was £2000 for each of the four years from 19X1. At the start of 19X1 it had bought a machine for £4000 and depreciated it on a straight-line basis over the four years. The capital allowances were 75% in 19X1 and 25% in 19X2.

The profits and tax paid by the company would be reported as follows:

(a) *No adjustment for timing differences*

	19X1	19X2	19X3	19X4	Total
	£	£	£	£	£
Accounting profit before tax, after depreciation	2000	2000	2000	2000	8000
Corporation tax liability— (50% of taxable profit) (A.C.T. + mainstream)	–	1000	1500	1500	4000
Profits after tax	£2000	£1000	£500	£500	£4000

(b)   Adjusted for timing differences

	19X1	19X2	19X3	19X4	Total
	£	£	£	£	£
Accounting profit before tax	2000	2000	2000	2000	8000
Corporation tax					
—current liability (A.C.T. + mainstream)	—	1000	1500	1500	4000
—deferred tax liability	1000	—	(500)	(500)	—
Profits after tax	£1000	£1000	£1000	£1000	£4000

It can be seen in Ex. B.5 that when the tax liability is adjusted for timing differences the costs and revenues are more appropriately matched in each year. The total tax over the four years is the same in both cases.

B.6   Presentation of taxation in financial statements

S.S.A.P. no. 8 'The Treatment of Taxation under the Imputation System in the Accounts of Companies'[9] provides a standard for the presentation of taxation in the financial statements of companies (see Sect. D.3, notes 1 (C) and 4). The parts of the standard relevant to this Appendix includes the following:

In the profit statement
(a)   amount of the corporation tax expense of the period;
(b)   any transfers to and from the deferred taxation account;
(c)   dividends should not include the related A.C.T.;
(d)   the rate of corporation tax should be disclosed.
In the balance sheet
(e)   dividends proposed (net of tax) should be shown in current liabilities;
(f)   A.C.T. not yet paid to the Inland Revenue should be shown separately as a current liability;
(g)   deferred taxation total should be shown where relevant.

The Companies Acts require the corporation tax liability to be shown in the balance sheet.

Notes and References

1. J. M. Cope, *Business Taxation* (London, Nelson, 1972) chaps 6 and 7.
2. D. J. Ironside, *Personal Taxation – the New Unified System* (General Educational Trust of the Institute of Chartered Accountants in England and Wales, 1972).
3. Apart from child allowances there are several others. The allowances normally change each year in the Finance Act.
4. L. H. Clark, *Coporation Tax – the Imputation System* (Institute of Chartered Accountants, 1972).
5. K. S. Carmichael (ed.), *Spicer & Pegler's Income Tax*, 28th rev. edn (London, H. F. L. (Publishers) Ltd, 1972) chap. 7.
6. There are several alternatives to this current system, e.g. see *Reform of Corporation Tax* (H.M.S.O., 1971).
7. Accounting Standards Steering Committee, *S.S.A.P., 4: The Accounting Treatment of Government Grants* (Institute of Chartered Accountants, 1974).
8. Accounting Standards Steering Committee, *S.S.A.P., 11: Accounting for Deferred Taxation* (Institute of Chartered Accountants, 1975).
9. Accounting Standards Steering Committee, *S.S.A.P., 8: The Treatment of Taxation under the Imputation System in the Accounts Companies* (Institute of Chartered Accountants, 1974).

Appendix C Compound Interest Computations

C.1 Introduction

Many aspects of financial management require computations which make adjustments for timing. This recognises that in most cases numerically equal benefits and costs have different values according to the point in time at which they occur. These different valuations arise because of preferences, sometimes termed 'time preferences', derived from different weightings that are attached to benefits and costs arising at different points in time. As most benefits and costs are expressed in monetary terms, we normally refer to this preference as the time value of money. Preferences can be measured in terms of interest rates, not only because of the mathematical convenience of this procedure, but also because benefits and costs may arise from the opportunity cost of uses of cash in interest yielding capacities.

Time preferences may arise from the additional benefits which can be derived from earlier receipt of resources, and costs can be incurred by deferment of receipts. They may also occur because of uncertainties in the data, e.g. a bird in the hand may be worth two in the bush, or because of changes in the price level, e.g. preference for £1 in 1976 currency to £1 in 1990 currency. When we use the term 'time value of money' we will include a combination of the valuation differences arising from these various considerations.

There are four types of calculations which will concern us:

(1) The future (or terminal) value of a sum of money, e.g. how much would we have in the bank in ten years' time if we invested £1000 now at 10% per annum compound interest?
(2) The present value of a sum of money, e.g. how much would we have to invest in the bank now at 8% per annum compound interest to give us £2000 in four years' time?
(3) The future value of an annuity (an annuity is a series of equal flows at equal intervals in the future, for our purposes annually), e.g. how much would we have in the bank if we invested £10 per annum for three years commencing in one year's time at 10% per annum compound interest?
(4) The present value of an annuity, e.g. how much would we pay now for an annual receipt of £600 per annum for four years commencing in one year's time at 10% per annum compound interest?

Calculations which involve future values are normally termed 'compounding and those which involve present values are termed 'discounting'. We will assume for simplicity that interest is compounded annually.

C.2 Arithmetic of future value of one amount

If we denote the present value as V_0, the interest rate as r, then at the end of the first year we will have V_1 such that:

$$V_1 = V_0 + V_0 (r)$$
$$V_1 = V_0 (1 + r)$$

(subscripts show time in years).

One period later we will have

$$V_2 = V_0 (1 + r) + V_0 (1 + r)(r)$$
$$V_2 = V_0 (1 + r)(1 + r)$$
$$V_2 = V_0 (1 + r)^2$$

This accumulation process can continue for as many periods as required, say n. From the previous equation the general form is:

$$V_n = V_0 (1 + r)^n$$

V_n is the future value of V_0 invested at time 0 (now) at an annual compound interest rate of r for n periods.

Example

What is the future value of £80 invested at 10% p.a. for three years?

$$V_n = \text{unknown}$$
$$V_0 = £80, r = .10, n = 3$$
$$V_3 = 80 (1.10)^3$$
$$V_3 = £80 (1.331) = £106$$

C.3 Arithmetic of present Value of one Amount

Using the general formula previously derived we are interested in the present value, V_0, which will give us a future value, V_n. As the future amount is known and the present value unknown:

then $\qquad V_n = V_0 (1 + r)^n \quad V_n$ known, $\quad V_0$ unknown

rearranging $V_0 = \dfrac{V_n}{(1 + r)^n}$

V_0 is the present value of V_n receivable in n years' time at an annual interest rate of r. The rate r is also termed the 'discount rate'.

Example

What is the present value of £242 receivable in two years' time at an interest rate of 10% p.a.?

$$V_0 = \text{unknown}$$
$$V_2 = £242, r = 0.10, n = 2$$
$$V_0 = \frac{242}{(1.10)^2} = £200$$

Table A at the end of this appendix gives the present value of £1, thus the present value of £242 is: £242 × 0.8264 = £200

C.4 Arithmetic of the future Value of an Annuity

An annuity could be shown diagramatically as

Cash flow	0	F_1	F_2	F_n
Year	0	1	2	n

where F_1 etc. are equal flows and the annuity is of n periods commencing after one year. To calculate the sum of this series we can use the following expression:

$$V_n = F \frac{(1 + r)^n - 1}{r}$$

Example

What is the future value of five receipts of £20 per annum commencing in one year's time at an interest rate of 10% p.a.?

$$V_n = \text{unknown}$$
$$F = £20, r = 0.10, n = 5$$
$$V_5 = 20\left(\frac{(1.10)^5 - 1}{0.10}\right) = £122$$

C.5 Arithmetic of the present Value of an Annuity

The formula for the present value of an annuity is:

$$V_0 = F\left(\frac{1 - (1 + r)^{-n}}{r}\right)$$

Example

What is the present value of an annuity of four receipts of £1000 per annum commencing in one year's time at an interest rate of 10% p.a.?

$$V_0 = \text{unknown}$$

$$F = £1000, r = 0.10, n = 4$$
$$V_0 = 1000\left(\frac{1 - (1.10)^{-4}}{0.10}\right)$$
$$V_0 = £3170$$

Table B shows the present value of an annuity of £1, commencing after 1 year, thus the present value of the annuity is: £1000 × 3.1699 = £3170.

Where we have a series of equal flows which are considered as endless we will have a perpetuity. In the previous formula the effect of n becoming very large is to reduce $(1 + r)^{-n}$ towards zero in the limit and hence as an approximation

$$V_0 = F\frac{(1 - 0)}{r}$$
$$V_0 = \frac{F}{r}$$

Example

What is the present value of a perpetuity of £500 at 10% p.a.?

$$V_0 = \text{unknown}$$
$$F = £500, r = 0.10$$
$$V_0 = \frac{£500}{0.10} = £5000$$

C.6 Present Value Tables

As most valuation problems discussed in this text involve the calculation of present value, rather than future value, we have included only present value tables. Future value (normally termed 'compound interest') tables, are of course available, but are not widely used in an accounting context.

An appreciation of the effect of time and discount rate can be developed by inspection of Table A. The sensitivity of present value to changes in discount rate can be seen on the horizontal axis, and to changes in timing on the vertical axis. Clearly the user of these tables must always be critically aware of the effect on his calculations of the accuracy of his data about discount rates and timing.

Table A

Present value of 1 at compound interest: $\dfrac{1}{(1+r)^n}$

Periods (n) Interest rates (r)

(n)(r%)	1	2	3	4	5	6	7	8	9	10	11	12	13	14	15
1	0.9901	0.9804	0.9709	0.9615	0.9524	0.9434	0.9346	0.9259	0.9174	0.9091	0.9009	0.8929	0.8850	0.8772	0.8696
2	0.9803	0.9612	0.9426	0.9246	0.9070	0.8900	0.8734	0.8573	0.8417	0.8264	0.8116	0.7972	0.7831	0.7695	0.7561
3	0.9706	0.9423	0.9151	0.8890	0.8638	0.8396	0.8163	0.7938	0.7722	0.7513	0.7312	0.7118	0.6931	0.6750	0.6575
4	0.9610	0.9238	0.8885	0.8548	0.8227	0.7921	0.7629	0.7350	0.7084	0.6830	0.6587	0.6355	0.6133	0.5921	0.5718
5	0.9515	0.9057	0.8626	0.8219	0.7835	0.7473	0.7130	0.6806	0.6499	0.6209	0.5935	0.5674	0.5428	0.5194	0.4972
6	0.9420	0.8880	0.8375	0.7903	0.7462	0.7050	0.6663	0.6302	0.5963	0.5646	0.5346	0.5066	0.4803	0.4556	0.4323
7	0.9327	0.8706	0.8131	0.7599	0.7107	0.6651	0.6227	0.5835	0.5470	0.5132	0.4817	0.4523	0.4251	0.3996	0.3759
8	0.9235	0.8535	0.7894	0.7307	0.6768	0.6274	0.5820	0.5403	0.5019	0.4665	0.4339	0.4039	0.3762	0.3506	0.3269
9	0.9143	0.8368	0.7664	0.7026	0.6446	0.5919	0.5439	0.5002	0.4604	0.4241	0.3909	0.3606	0.3329	0.3075	0.2843
10	0.9053	0.8203	0.7441	0.6756	0.6139	0.5584	0.5083	0.4632	0.4224	0.3855	0.3522	0.3220	0.2946	0.2697	0.2472
11	0.8963	0.8043	0.7224	0.6496	0.5847	0.5268	0.4751	0.4289	0.3875	0.3505	0.3173	0.2875	0.2607	0.2366	0.2149
12	0.8874	0.7885	0.7014	0.6246	0.5568	0.4970	0.4440	0.3971	0.3555	0.3186	0.2858	0.2567	0.2307	0.2076	0.1869
13	0.8787	0.7730	0.6810	0.6006	0.5303	0.4688	0.4150	0.3677	0.3262	0.2897	0.2575	0.2292	0.2042	0.1821	0.1625
14	0.8700	0.7579	0.6611	0.5775	0.5051	0.4423	0.3878	0.3405	0.2992	0.2633	0.2320	0.2046	0.1807	0.1597	0.1413
15	0.8613	0.7430	0.6419	0.5553	0.4810	0.4173	0.3624	0.3152	0.2745	0.2394	0.2090	0.1827	0.1599	0.1401	0.1229
16	0.8528	0.7284	0.6232	0.5339	0.4581	0.3936	0.3387	0.2919	0.2519	0.2176	0.1883	0.1631	0.1415	0.1229	0.1069
17	0.8444	0.7142	0.6050	0.5134	0.4363	0.3714	0.3166	0.2703	0.2311	0.1978	0.1696	0.1456	0.1252	0.1078	0.0929
18	0.8360	0.7002	0.5874	0.4936	0.4155	0.3503	0.2959	0.2502	0.2120	0.1799	0.1528	0.1300	0.1108	0.0946	0.0808
19	0.8277	0.6864	0.5703	0.4746	0.3957	0.3305	0.2765	0.2317	0.1945	0.1635	0.1377	0.1161	0.0981	0.0829	0.0703
20	0.8195	0.6730	0.5537	0.4564	0.3769	0.3118	0.2584	0.2145	0.1764	0.1486	0.1240	0.1037	0.0868	0.0728	0.0611
25	0.7798	0.6095	0.4776	0.3751	0.2953	0.2330	0.1842	0.1460	0.1160	0.0923	0.0736	0.0588	0.0471	0.0378	0.0304
30	0.7419	0.5521	0.4120	0.3083	0.2314	0.1741	0.1314	0.0994	0.0754	0.0573	0.0437	0.0334	0.0256	0.0196	0.0151
35	0.7059	0.5000	0.3554	0.2534	0.1813	0.1301	0.0937	0.0676	0.0490	0.0356	0.0259	0.0188	0.0139	0.0102	0.0075
40	0.6717	0.4529	0.3066	0.2083	0.1420	0.0972	0.0668	0.0460	0.0318	0.0221	0.0154	0.0107	0.0075	0.0053	0.0037
45	0.6391	0.4102	0.2644	0.1712	0.1113	0.0727	0.0476	0.0313	0.0207	0.0137	0.0091	0.0061	0.0041	0.0027	0.0019
50	0.6080	0.3715	0.2281	0.1407	0.0872	0.0543	0.0339	0.0213	0.0134	0.0085	0.0054	0.0035	0.0022	0.0014	0.0009

Table B

Present value of an annuity of 1: $\dfrac{1-(1+r)^{-n}}{r}$

Periods (n) Interest rates (r)

(n)(r%)	1	2	3	4	5	6	7	8	9	10	11	12	13	14	15
1	0.9901	0.9804	0.9709	0.9615	0.9524	0.9434	0.9346	0.9259	0.9174	0.9091	0.9009	0.8929	0.8850	0.8772	0.8696
2	1.9704	1.9416	1.9135	1.8861	1.8594	1.8334	1.8080	1.7833	1.7591	1.7355	1.7125	1.6901	1.6681	1.6467	1.6257
3	2.9410	2.8839	2.8286	2.7751	2.7232	2.6730	2.6243	2.5771	2.5313	2.4869	2.4437	2.4018	2.3612	2.3216	2.2832
4	3.9020	3.8077	3.7171	3.6299	3.5460	3.4651	3.3872	3.3121	3.2397	3.1699	3.1024	3.0373	2.9745	2.9137	2.8550
5	4.8534	4.7135	4.5797	4.4518	4.3295	4.2124	4.1002	3.9927	3.8897	3.7908	3.6959	3.6048	3.5172	3.4331	3.3522
6	5.7955	5.6014	5.4172	5.2421	5.0757	4.9173	4.7665	4.6229	4.4859	4.3553	4.2305	4.1114	3.9975	3.8887	3.7845
7	6.7282	6.4720	6.2303	6.0021	5.7864	5.5824	5.3893	5.2064	5.0330	4.8684	4.7122	4.5638	4.4226	4.2883	4.1604
8	7.6517	7.3255	7.0197	6.7327	6.4632	6.2098	5.9713	5.7466	5.5348	5.3349	5.1461	4.9676	4.7988	4.6389	4.4873
9	8.5660	8.1622	7.7861	7.4353	7.1078	6.8017	6.5152	6.2469	5.9952	5.7590	5.5370	5.3282	5.1317	4.9464	4.7716
10	9.4713	8.9826	8.5302	8.1109	7.7217	7.3601	7.0236	6.7101	6.4177	6.1446	5.8892	5.6502	5.4262	5.2161	5.0188
11	10.3676	9.7868	9.2526	8.7605	8.3064	7.8869	7.4987	7.1390	6.8052	6.4951	6.2065	5.9377	5.6869	5.4527	5.2337
12	11.2551	10.5753	9.9540	9.3851	8.8633	8.3838	7.9427	7.5361	7.1607	6.8137	6.4924	6.1944	5.9176	5.6603	5.4206
13	12.1337	11.3484	10.6350	9.9856	9.3936	8.8527	8.3577	7.9038	7.4869	7.1034	6.7498	6.4235	6.1218	5.8424	5.5831
14	13.0037	12.1062	11.2961	10.5631	9.8986	9.2950	8.7455	8.2442	7.7862	7.3667	6.9819	6.6282	6.3025	6.0021	5.7245
15	13.8651	12.8493	11.9379	11.1184	10.3797	9.7122	9.1079	8.5596	8.0607	7.6061	7.1908	6.8109	6.4624	6.1422	5.8474
16	14.7179	13.5777	12.5611	11.6523	10.8378	10.1059	9.4466	8.8514	8.3126	7.8237	7.3792	6.9740	6.6039	6.2651	5.9542
17	15.5623	14.2919	13.1661	12.1657	11.2741	10.4773	9.7632	9.1216	8.5436	8.0216	7.5488	7.1196	6.7291	6.3729	6.0472
18	16.3983	14.9920	13.7535	12.6593	11.6896	10.8276	10.0591	9.3719	8.7556	8.2014	7.7016	7.2497	6.8399	6.4674	6.1280
19	17.2260	15.6785	14.3238	13.1339	12.0853	11.1581	10.3356	9.6036	8.9501	8.3649	7.8393	7.3658	6.9380	6.5504	6.1982
20	18.0456	16.3514	14.8775	13.5903	12.4622	11.4699	10.5940	9.8181	9.1285	8.5136	7.9633	7.4694	7.0248	6.6231	6.2593
25	22.0232	19.5235	17.4131	15.6221	14.0939	12.7834	11.6536	10.6748	9.8226	9.0770	8.4217	7.8431	7.3300	6.8729	6.4641
30	25.8077	22.3965	19.6004	17.2920	15.3725	13.7648	12.4090	11.2578	10.2737	9.4269	8.6938	8.0552	7.4957	7.0027	6.5660
35	29.4086	24.9986	21.4872	18.6646	16.3742	14.4982	12.9477	11.6546	10.5668	9.6442	8.8552	8.1755	7.5856	7.0700	6.6166
40	32.8347	27.3555	23.1148	19.7928	17.1591	15.0463	13.3317	11.9246	10.7574	9.7791	8.9511	8.2438	7.6344	7.1050	6.6418
45	36.0945	29.4902	24.5187	20.7200	17.7741	15.4558	13.6055	12.1084	10.8812	9.8628	9.0079	8.2825	7.6609	7.1232	6.6543
50	39.1961	31.4236	25.7298	21.4822	18.2559	15.7619	13.8007	12.2335	10.9617	9.9148	9.0417	8.3045	7.6752	7.1327	6.6605

16	17	18	19	20	21	22	23	24	25	26	27	28	29	30
0.8621	0.8547	0.8475	0.8403	0.8333	0.8264	0.8197	0.8130	0.8065	0.8000	0.7937	0.7874	0.7812	0.7752	0.7692
0.7432	0.7305	0.7182	0.7062	0.6944	0.6830	0.6719	0.6610	0.6504	0.6400	0.6299	0.6200	0.6140	0.6009	0.5917
0.6407	0.6244	0.6086	0.5934	0.5787	0.5645	0.5507	0.5374	0.5245	0.5120	0.4999	0.4882	0.4768	0.4658	0.4552
0.5523	0.5337	0.5158	0.4987	0.4823	0.4665	0.4514	0.4369	0.4230	0.4096	0.3968	0.3844	0.3725	0.3611	0.3501
0.4761	0.4561	0.4371	0.4190	0.4019	0.3855	0.3700	0.3552	0.3411	0.3277	0.3149	0.3027	0.2910	0.2799	0.2693
0.4104	0.3898	0.3704	0.3521	0.3349	0.3186	0.3033	0.2888	0.2751	0.2621	0.2499	0.2383	0.2274	0.2170	0.2072
0.3538	0.3332	0.3139	0.2959	0.2791	0.2633	0.2486	0.2348	0.2218	0.2097	0.1983	0.1877	0.1776	0.1682	0.1594
0.3050	0.2848	0.2660	0.2487	0.2326	0.2176	0.2038	0.1909	0.1789	0.1678	0.1574	0.1478	0.1388	0.1304	0.1226
0.2630	0.2454	0.2255	0.2090	0.1938	0.1799	0.1670	0.1552	0.1443	0.1342	0.1249	0.1164	0.1084	0.1011	0.0943
0.2267	0.2080	0.1911	0.1756	0.1615	0.1486	0.1369	0.1262	0.1164	0.1074	0.0992	0.0916	0.0847	0.0784	0.0725
0.1954	0.1778	0.1619	0.1476	0.1346	0.1228	0.1122	0.1026	0.0938	0.0859	0.0787	0.0721	0.0662	0.0607	0.0558
0.1685	0.1520	0.1372	0.1240	0.1122	0.1015	0.0920	0.0834	0.0757	0.0687	0.0625	0.0568	0.0517	0.0471	0.0429
0.1452	0.1299	0.1163	0.1042	0.0935	0.0839	0.0754	0.0678	0.0610	0.0550	0.0496	0.0447	0.0404	0.0365	0.0330
0.1252	0.1110	0.0985	0.0876	0.0779	0.0693	0.0618	0.0551	0.0492	0.0440	0.0393	0.0352	0.0316	0.0283	0.0254
0.1079	0.0949	0.0835	0.0736	0.0649	0.0573	0.0507	0.0448	0.0397	0.0352	0.0312	0.0277	0.0247	0.0219	0.0195
0.0930	0.0811	0.0708	0.0618	0.0541	0.0474	0.0415	0.0364	0.0320	0.0281	0.0248	0.0218	0.0193	0.0170	0.0150
0.0802	0.0693	0.0600	0.0520	0.0451	0.0391	0.0340	0.0296	0.0258	0.0225	0.0197	0.0172	0.0150	0.0132	0.0116
0.0681	0.0592	0.0508	0.0437	0.0376	0.0323	0.0279	0.0241	0.0208	0.0180	0.0156	0.0135	0.0118	0.0102	0.0089
0.0596	0.0506	0.0431	0.0367	0.0313	0.0267	0.0229	0.0196	0.0168	0.0144	0.0124	0.0107	0.0092	0.0079	0.0068
0.0514	0.0433	0.0365	0.0308	0.0261	0.0221	0.0187	0.0159	0.0135	0.0115	0.0098	0.0084	0.0072	0.0061	0.0053
0.0245	0.0197	0.0160	0.0129	0.0105	0.0085	0.0069	0.0057	0.0046	0.0038	0.0031	0.0025	0.0021	0.0017	0.0014
0.0116	0.0090	0.0070	0.0054	0.0042	0.0033	0.0026	0.0020	0.0016	0.0012	0.0010	0.0008	0.0006	0.0005	0.0004
0.0055	0.0041	0.0030	0.0023	0.0017	0.0013	0.0008	0.0007	0.0005	0.0004	0.0003	0.0002	0.0002	0.0001	0.0001
0.0026	0.0019	0.0013	0.0010	0.0007	0.0005	0.0004	0.0003	0.0002	0.0001	0.0001	0.0001	0.0001	0.0000	0.0000
0.0013	0.0009	0.0006	0.0004	0.0003	0.0002	0.0001	0.0001	0.0001	0.0000	0.0000	0.0000	0.0000	0.0000	0.0000
0.0006	0.0004	0.0003	0.0002	0.0001	0.0001	0.0000	0.0000	0.0000	0.0000	0.0000	0.0000	0.0000	0.0000	0.0000

16	17	18	19	20	21	22	23	24	25	26	27	28	29	30
0.8621	0.8547	0.8475	0.8403	0.8333	0.8264	0.8197	0.8130	0.8065	0.8000	0.7937	0.7874	0.7812	0.7752	0.7692
1.6052	1.5852	1.5656	1.5465	1.5278	1.5095	1.4915	1.4740	1.4568	1.4400	1.4235	1.4074	1.3916	1.3761	1.3609
2.2459	2.2096	2.1743	2.1399	2.1065	2.0739	2.0422	2.0114	1.9813	1.9520	1.9234	1.8950	1.8684	1.8420	1.8161
2.7982	2.7432	2.6901	2.6386	2.5887	2.5404	2.4936	2.4483	2.4043	2.3616	2.3202	2.2800	2.2410	2.2031	2.1662
3.2743	3.1993	3.1272	3.0576	2.9906	2.9260	2.8636	2.8035	2.7454	2.6893	2.6351	2.5827	2.5320	2.4830	2.4356
3.6847	3.5892	3.4976	3.4098	3.3255	3.2446	3.1669	3.0923	3.0205	2.9514	2.8850	2.8210	2.7594	2.7000	2.6427
4.0386	3.9224	3.8115	3.7057	3.6046	3.5079	3.4155	3.3270	3.2423	3.1611	3.0833	3.0087	2.9370	2.8682	2.8021
4.3436	4.2072	4.0776	3.9544	3.8372	3.7256	3.6193	3.5179	3.4212	3.3289	3.2407	3.1564	3.0758	2.9986	2.9247
4.6065	4.4506	4.3030	4.1633	4.0310	3.9054	3.7863	3.6731	3.5655	3.4631	3.3657	3.2728	3.1842	3.0997	3.0190
4.8332	4.6586	4.4941	4.3389	4.1925	4.0541	3.9232	3.7993	3.6819	3.5705	3.4648	3.3644	3.2689	3.1781	3.0915
5.0286	4.8364	4.6560	4.4865	4.3271	4.1769	4.0354	3.9018	3.7757	3.6564	3.5435	3.4365	3.3351	3.2388	3.1473
5.1971	4.9884	4.7932	4.6105	4.4392	4.2784	4.1274	3.9852	3.8514	3.7251	3.6059	3.4933	3.3868	3.2859	3.1903
5.3423	5.1183	4.9095	4.7147	4.5327	4.3624	4.2023	4.0530	3.9124	3.7801	3.6555	3.5381	3.4272	3.3224	3.2233
5.4675	5.2293	5.0081	4.8023	4.6106	4.4317	4.2648	4.1082	3.9616	3.8241	3.6948	3.5733	3.4587	3.3507	3.2487
5.5755	5.3242	5.0916	4.8759	4.6755	4.4890	4.3152	4.1530	4.0013	3.8593	3.7261	3.6010	3.4834	3.3726	3.2682
5.6685	5.4053	5.1624	4.9377	4.7296	4.5364	4.3567	4.1894	4.0333	3.8874	3.7509	3.6228	3.5026	3.3896	3.2832
5.7487	5.4746	5.2223	4.9897	4.7746	4.5755	4.3908	4.2190	4.0591	3.9099	3.7705	3.6400	3.5177	3.4028	3.2948
5.8178	5.5339	5.2732	5.0333	4.8122	4.6079	4.4187	4.2431	4.0799	3.9279	3.7861	3.6536	3.5294	3.4130	3.3037
5.8775	5.5845	5.3162	5.0700	4.8435	4.6346	4.4415	4.2627	4.0967	3.9424	3.7985	3.6642	3.5386	3.4210	3.3105
5.9288	5.6278	5.3527	5.1009	4.8696	4.6567	4.4603	4.2786	4.1103	3.9539	3.8083	3.6726	3.5458	3.4271	3.3158
6.0971	5.7662	5.4669	5.1951	4.9476	4.7213	4.5139	4.3232	4.1474	3.9849	3.8342	3.6943	3.5640	3.4423	3.3286
6.1772	5.8294	5.5168	5.2347	4.9789	4.7463	4.5338	4.3391	4.1601	3.9950	3.8424	3.7009	3.5693	3.4466	3.3321
6.2153	5.8532	5.5386	5.2512	4.9915	4.7559	4.5411	4.3447	4.1644	3.9984	3.8450	3.7028	3.5708	3.4478	3.3330
6.2335	5.8713	5.5482	5.2582	4.9966	4.7596	4.5439	4.3467	4.1659	3.9995	3.8458	3.7034	3.5712	3.4481	3.3332
6.2421	5.8773	5.5523	5.2611	4.9986	4.7610	4.5449	4.3474	4.1664	3.9998	3.8460	3.7036	3.5714	3.4482	3.3333
6.2463	5.8801	5.5541	5.2623	4.9995	4.7616	4.5452	4.3477	4.1666	3.9999	3.8461	3.7037	3.5714	3.4483	3.3333

Appendix D Published Financial Statements of Marks & Spencer Limited

D.1 Profit and Loss Account for the year ended 31 March 1975

	Notes	1975 £000	1974 £000
TURNOVER	2	721,876	571,650
OPERATING PROFIT	3	81,857	76,825
TAXATION	4	42,500	39,900
PROFIT AFTER TAXATION		39,357	36,925
EXTRAORDINARY ITEM			
Surplus on disposal of fixed assets		49	2,383
		39,406	39,308
DIVIDENDS			
Preference shares		73	73
Ordinary shares			
Interim of 2·25p per share	5	7,271	6,680
Final of 4·2244p per share		13,708	12,255
		21,052	19,008
UNDISTRIBUTED SURPLUS		18,354	20,300
EARNINGS PER SHARE	6	12·2p	11·4p

D.2   Balance Sheet as at 31 March 1975

	Notes	1975 £000	1974 £000
FIXED ASSETS			
PROPERTIES	1 (a) & 8	393,624	221,895
FIXTURES AND EQUIPMENT	1 (a) & 9	20,688	19,825
		414,312	241,720
INVESTMENT IN ASSOCIATED COMPANY	10	3,493	1,170
INVESTMENT IN SUBSIDIARY COMPANIES	11	3,047	1,040
CURRENT ASSETS			
STOCK	1 (b)	37,687	31,472
AMOUNTS OWING BY SUBSIDIARY COMPANIES		859	—
DEBTORS AND PREPAYMENTS		11,433	10,502
CASH AND SHORT TERM DEPOSITS		20,132	18,460
		70,111	60,434
TOTAL ASSETS		490,963	304,364
CURRENT LIABILITIES			
CREDITORS AND ACCRUED CHARGES		33,481	28,055
CORPORATION TAX		30,450	28,237
PROPOSED FINAL DIVIDEND		13,708	12,255
		77,639	68,547
NET ASSETS		413,324	235,817
DEFERRED TAXATION	1 (c) & 12	21,150	18,400
DEBENTURE STOCK	13	45,000	45,000
		66,150	63,400
SHAREHOLDERS' INTERESTS		347,174	172,417
PREFERENCE SHARES	14	1,350	1,350
ORDINARY SHAREHOLDERS' INTERESTS	15	345,824	171,067

MARCUS J. SIEFF ⎫
⎬ *Directors*
M. M. SACHER ⎭

D.3 Notes to the Accounts

1. ACCOUNTING POLICIES

(a) DEPRECIATION

Buildings, short leasehold land (under 50 years) and fixtures and equipment, with the exception of certain minor items which are written off in the year of acquisition, are depreciated evenly over their expected remaining life.
No depreciation is provided on freehold and long leasehold land (over 50 years).

(b) STOCK

Stock is valued at the lower of cost and replacement value.

(c) DEFERRED TAXATION

Deferred taxation is provided at the appropriate rate of corporation tax for each year on the amount by which taxation allowances exceed the charge for depreciation on those assets qualifying for allowances.

(d) REPAIRS AND RENEWALS

Expenditure on repairs and renewals is written off in the year in which it is incurred.

(e) FOREIGN CURRENCIES

Assets, liabilities, sales and results of overseas subsidiary and associated companies are converted into sterling at the rates of exchange ruling at the balance sheet date. Assets and liabilities of the company in foreign currencies are also converted at the same rates of exchange.

(f) GROUP ACCOUNTS

Consolidated accounts are not prepared. A statement of the state of affairs of the subsidiaries at the balance sheet date is included in Note 11 to the accounts.

(g) ASSOCIATED COMPANY

The accounts include the company's share of the profits of an associated company.

2. TURNOVER

	1975 £000	1974 £000
Store sales in the United Kingdom	739,451	591,488
Less: Value Added Tax	39,014	33,421
	700,437	558,067
Direct export sales	21,439	13,583
Net sales	721,876	571,650

Store sales are shown after deduction of refunds to customers.

3. OPERATING PROFIT

In arriving at the profit for the year, charges and income taken into account include the following:

	1975 £000	1974 £000
CHARGES		
Repairs, renewals and maintenance of properties, fixtures and equipment	3,789	3,728
Depreciation of properties, fixtures and equipment	7,470	5,464
Debenture stock interest	3,178	3,178
Contribution to employees' pension scheme	1,982	1,611
Directors' emoluments (Note 7)	574	507
Auditors' remuneration	30	23
INCOME		
Bank and other interest received	1,640	2,128
Share of profit of associated company (Note 10)	147	180

4. TAXATION

	1975 £000	1974 £000
The taxation charges comprises:		
Corporation tax at 52% (*last year* 52%)	39,750	34,500
Deferred taxation (Note 12)	2,750	5,300
	42,500	39,800
Taxation on share of profit of associated company (Note 10)	—	100
	42,500	39,900

5. DIVIDENDS

The amount of £7,271,000 in respect of the interim dividend for the year includes £1,608,000 capitalised or retained in reserves by the issue of 1,348,122 ordinary shares of 25p each fully paid pursuant to elections made by certain holders of ordinary shares to receive shares in lieu of a cash dividend.

6. EARNINGS PER SHARE

The calculation of earnings per share is based on earnings of £39,284,000 (*last year* £36,825,000) and 323,324,377 ordinary shares (*last year* 323,154,477), which is a weighted average of the number of ordinary shares in issue during the year.

7. EMOLUMENTS

The numbers of directors and employees whose annual salaries are within the following range is:

DIRECTORS

Gross Salary £	After Tax £		1975	*1974*
35,001–37,500	12,500	....	1	–
30,001–32,500	11,600	....	3	*2*
27,501–30,000	11,200	....	2	–
25,001–27,500	10,800	....	–	*2*
22,501–25,000	10,300	....	6	*3*
20,001–22,500	9,900	....	4	*2*
17,501–20,000	9,400	....	5	*6*
15,001–17,500	8,700	....	3	*8*
10,001–12,500	7,200	....	–	*1*
Under 2,500		....	2	*1*
			26	*25*

Included in the above are the Chairman's emoluments of £35,995 *(last year £32,250)*

EMPLOYEES

Gross Salary £	After Tax £		1975	*1974*
15,001–17,500	8,700	....	5	–
12,501–15,000	8,000	....	26	*4*
10,001–12,500	7,200	....	64	*40*
			95	*44*

The after tax figures are based on Income tax rates for 1974/75 at the higher end of each band and assume that the recipient is a married man without children and without any other source of income.

8. PROPERTIES

		1975 £000	*1974 £000*
(a)	As valued at 31 March 1964	—	*87,232*
	As valued at 31 March 1974 (see (d) below)	377,079	—
	Subsequent additions at cost	18,925	*143,180*
		396,004	*230,412*
	Less: Accumulated depreciation	2,380	*8,517*
		393,624	*221,895*
(b)	Additions in the year, at cost	19,204	*41,206*
	Disposal of properties in the year	279	*848*
		18,925	*40,358*
(c)	Properties after depreciation:		
	Freeholds	237,455	*141,163*
	Long leaseholds (over 50 years)	152,196	*78,780*
	Short leaseholds (under 50 years)	3,973	*1,952*
		393,624	*221,895*

(d) A professional valuation of the company's properties was made by Gerald Eve & Co., Chartered Surveyors, as at 31 March 1974 which placed a value on the freehold and leasehold properties of £443,623,000. The valuation was made on the basis of a sale in the open market with vacant possession of those properties (or parts of properties) which were in the company's occupation, having regard to the fact that the stores and other operational properties form part of a retail chain.

In view of the decline in property values since the date of the valuation the directors have obtained a further opinion from Gerald Eve & Co. as to the approximate overall reduction in value since 31 March 1974. Gerald Eve & Co. are of the opinion that if their valuation were reduced by 15% overall the result would be to state conservatively the value of the properties as a whole as at 31 March 1975.

The overall value of the company's properties has accordingly been reduced by 15% from £443,623,000 to £377,079,000, which revised value has been incorporated into the books and records of the company.

(e) No provision has been made for the liability to capital gains tax, amounting in total to approximately £46,500,000, which would arise if the properties were to be sold at their revised book of £377,079,000.

9. FIXTURES AND EQUIPMENT

The fixtures and equipment are shown at cost, less accumulated depreciation.

	1975 £000	1974 £000
Additions less sales in the year	5,953	8,385

10. INVESTMENT IN ASSOCIATED COMPANY

The company has a 50% interest in 210,000 common shares without par value which comprise the total issued share capital of St Michael Shops of Canada Limited, incorporated in Canada. There has been included in the profit and loss account, by reference to the audited accounts to 31 July 1974 and unaudited management accounts to 31 March 1975, the share of the profits and of the taxation charges of the associated company attributable to Marks & Spencer Limited. No dividend has been paid by the associated company since it was incorporated in July 1972.

This investment is stated at cost (£1,090,000) plus amounts advanced by the company, together with its share of the retained profits. The directors consider the investment to be worth this value.

11. INVESTMENT IN SUBSIDIARY COMPANIES

With the exception of the following the company's subsidiaries have not operated during the year and are not represented in the company's balance sheet. A schedule of interests in subsidiaries is filed with the Annual Return.

Name of Company	Country of Incorporation	Proportion of shares (all ordinary) held by	
		Company	Subsidiary
Marks & Spencer (Nederland) B.V.	The Netherlands	100%	—
Marks & Spencer (France) S.A.	France	—	100%
S.A.Marks & Spencer (Belgium) N.V.	Belgium	—	100%

The state of affairs of these subidiaries at 31 March 1975 was as follows:

	1975 £000	1974 £000
FIXED ASSETS		
Property	4,502	1,316
Fixtures and Equipment	898	—
	5,400	1,316
CURRENT ASSETS		
Stock	1,070	—
Debtors and Prepayments (see below)	1,282	245
Cash	63	3
	2,415	248
TOTAL ASSETS	7,815	1,564
CURRENT LIABILITIES		
Creditors and Accrued Charges	2,410	71
Amounts owing to Marks & Spencer Limited	859	—
Bank Overdrafts	1,540	453
	4,809	524
	3,006	1,040
Comprising:		
Shares at Cost	150	75
Advances from Marks & Spencer Limited	2,897	965
	3,047	1,040
Less: Losses for the Year	41	—
	3,006	1,040

Marks & Spencer (France) S.A. Commenced trading on 25 February 1975 and S. A. Marks & Spencer (Belgium) N.V. on 24 March 1975. Total turnover to 31 March 1975 amounted to £535,000.

Debtors and Prepayments primarily comprise pre-trading expenses which have been deferred and will be written off over the next three years.

12. DEFERRED TAXATION	1975 £000	1974 £000
At 1 April 1974	18,400	13,100
Provided in the year	2,750	5,300
At 31 March 1975	21,150	18,400

13. FIRST MORTGAGE DEBENTURE STOCK	1975 £000	1974 £000
$5\frac{1}{2}$%—1985/1990	5,000	5,000
$6\frac{1}{2}$%—1989/1994	10,000	10,000
$7\frac{1}{4}$%—1993/1998	15,000	15,000
$7\frac{3}{4}$%—1995/2000	15,000	15,000
	45,000	45,000

14. PREFERENCE SHARES—Authorised, issued and fully paid

	1975 £000	1974 £000
350,000 7% cumulative preference shares of £1	350	350
1,000,000 4.9% cumulative preference shares of £1	1,000	1,000
	1,350	1,350

15. ORDINARY SHAREHOLDERS' INTERESTS

	1975 £000	1974 £000

ORDINARY SHARES
At 1 April 1974 the authorised ordinary share capital amounted to £81,250,000 consisting of 325,000,000 25p ordinary shares of which 323,154,477 were issued and fully paid...

	1975 £000	1974 £000
	80,789	80,789

At an Extraordinary General Meeting held on 13 December 1974, the authorised ordinary share capital was increased from £81,250,000 to £82,500,000, consisting of 330,000,000 ordinary shares of 25p each of which a further 1,348,122 ordinary shares were issued as fully paid during the year to those shareholders electing to take shares in lieu of a cash dividend ....

	337	—

Making, at 31 March 1975, a total of 324,502,599 shares issued and fully paid ....

	81,126	80,789

RESERVES
Surplus arising on valuation of the company's properties, after deduction of valuation fees (Note 8) ....

	154,795	—
Retained profits at 1 April 1974	90,278	69,978
Add: Undistributed surplus for the year	18,354	20,300
Amount retained in respect of shares issued in lieu of cash dividend (Note 5)	1,271	—
Retained profits at 31 March 1975	109,903	90,278

TOTAL ORDINARY SHAREHOLDERS' INTERESTS AT 31 MARCH 1975 .

345,824	171,067

16. PROPERTY AND OTHER COMMITMENTS

At 31 March 1975 there were commitments in respect of properties in the course of development of approximately £37,250,000 (*last year £38,500,000*).

Capital expenditure authorised by the directors, but not yet contracted for, amounted to approximately £30,000,000 (*last year £35,250,000*).

There were also commitments at 31 March 1975 in respect of forward contracts for purchases of raw materials and stocks in the normal course of business.

The company has guaranteed the bank borrowings of the subsidiary companies trading abroad up to £3,000,000.

D.4 Report of the Auditors to the Members of Marks & Spencer Limited

We have examined the annexed accounts and supplementary statements.

In our opinion

(i) the accounts set out on pages 00 to 00 give, so far as concerns the members of Marks & Spencer Limited, a true and fair view of the state of affairs at 31 March 1975 and of the results for the year ended on that date and comply with the Companies Acts 1948 and 1967.

(ii) the statement set out on pages 00 and 00 has been properly prepared to restate, in summary form, the results of the company for the year ended 31 March 1975 and its financial position at that date in terms of the general purchasing power of money at 31 March 1975.

(iii) the statement set out on page 00 gives a true and fair view of the sources and applications of funds for the year ended 31 March 1975.

LONDON,   DELOITTE & CO.,
10 April 1975   *Chartered Accountants*

D.5 Directors' Report (*extract*)

ACTIVITIES OF THE GROUP
The group sells clothing, foods and other merchandise under the 'St Michael' trade mark in its chain of 252 retail stores throughout the United Kingdom and in its stores in Paris and Brussels. Merchandise is also sold for export.

SALES
The net sales of the company for the year were £721,876,000 compared with £571,650,000 last year, made up as follows:

	1975 £000	1974 £000
Store sales in the United Kingdom:		
Clothing and other merchandise	574,271	453,699
Foods	210,612	171,292
	714,883	624,991
Less: Refunds	45,432	33,503
	739,451	591,488
Less: Value Added Tax	39,014	33,421
Total net sales in the United Kingdom	700,437	558,067
Direct export sales	21,439	13,583
	721,876	571,650

Store sales in Paris and Brussels not included above amounted to £535,000 (*last year £ nil*).

PROFIT AND DIVIDENDS	1975	1974
	£000	£000
Excluding the results of the subsidiary companies, the operating profit before taxation for the year amounts to	81,857	76,825
which, after making provision for taxation of	42,500	39,900
leaves a balance of	39,357	36,925
to which is added an extraordinary item arising in the year of	49	2,383
making a balance available for distribution of	39,406	39,308

It is proposed to apply this year's profit as follows:

	£000
Dividends:	
Preference Shares	73
Ordinary Shares	
Interim dividend paid of 2.25p per share *(last year 2.0671p)*	7,271
Final dividend proposed of 4.2244p per share *(last year 3.7922p)*	13,708
Total ordinary dividend for the year of 6.4744p per share	20,979
(last year 5.8593p)	
Total cost of dividends	21,052
Undistributed surplus for the year	18,354
	39,406

The amount of £7,271,000 in respect of the interim dividend for 1975 includes £1,608,000 capitalised or retained by way of issuing 1,348,122 ordinary shares of 25p each fully paid pursuant to elections made by certain shareholders to receive shares in lieu of cash.

The proposed final ordinary dividend will be paid on 18 July 1975 to shareholders whose names are on the register as at the close of business on 16 May 1975.

FIXED ASSETS

A professional valuation of the company's properties was made as at 31 March 1974. After an adjustment to take account of the decline in property values since the date of the valuation, the revised value of £377,079,000 has been incorporated into the books and records of the company.

The directors have no intention at present of making any major sales of the properties, which are held for long-term use in the company's business and, therefore, no provision has been made for any liability to taxation on capital gains which would arise if the properties were sold at their revised book value.

SCRIP ISSUE

It is proposed to capitalise the sum of £81,125,650 being part of the reserves by making a scrip issue to the Ordinary Shareholders of 324,502,599 shares of 25p each fully paid in the proportion of one Ordinary Share for each Ordinary Share held. It is intended that renounceable share certificates will be posted on Friday 25 July 1975 to those members whose names are on the register at the close of business on Friday 16 May 1975. Application will be made to The Stock Exchange for dealing in the New Ordinary Shares to commence on 14 July, 1975 for deferred settlement on 29 July 1975.

ORDINARY SHARE CAPITAL

At 31 March 1975 the company had not been notified that any person held more than 10% of the issued ordinary share capital.

EMPLOYEES

The average weekly number of employees during the year was 39,840 which included 22,784 part-time staff. The aggregate remuneration paid to all employees was £54,169,000.

CHARITABLE AND POLITICAL CONTRIBUTIONS

Donations to charitable organisations amounted to £325,000.

Political contributions totalling £22,750 were made to the following:

British United Industrialists	£20,000
The Liberal Party	£2,500
Lincoln Democratic Labour Association	£250

INCOME AND CORPORATION TAXES ACT 1970

The close company provisions of this Act do not apply to the company.

AUDITORS

The auditors, Deloitte & Co., will continue in office in accordance with Section 159 (2) of the Companies Act 1948.

MARCUS J. SIEFF ⎫
                ⎬ *Directors*
M. M. SACHER ⎭

LONDON,
10 April 1975

D.6 Ten-year Statement

Year Ended 31 March

	1966	1967	1968	1969	1970	1971 (53 weeks)	1972	1973	1974	1975
	£000	£000	£000	£000	£000	£000	£000	£000	£000	£000
TURNOVER*	219,354	235,809	260,296	289,244	325,693	371,928	417,266	495,655	571,650	721,876
OPERATING PROFIT	29,618	30,659	33,871	38,123	43,705	50,115	53,766	70,036	76,825	81,857
PROFIT AFTER TAXATION	18,268	18,959	20,121	21,773	26,005	31,215	34,416	45,136	36,925	39,357
Corporation Tax Rate	40%	40%	42½%	45%	42½%	40%	40%	40%	52%	52%
EARNINGS PER SHARE	5.6p	5.8p	6.2p	6.7p	8.0p	9.6p	10.6p	13.9p	11.4p‡	12.2p‡
DIVIDEND PAYMENTS TO SHAREHOLDERS	9,928	9,950	10,266	10,609	11,928	13,904	15,528	17,826	19,008	21,052‡
RETAINED PROFIT	4,322	2,461	2,536	3,667	5,747	8,220†	9,132	23,924	17,917†	19,962§
DEPRECIATION	1,993	2,177	2,488	2,987	3,534	4,177	4,620	5,055	5,464	7,470
ORDINARY SHARE CAPITAL AND RESERVES	109,790	112,251	114,788	118,455	123,152	127,711	136,843	150,767	171,067	345,824¶
TOTAL SALES AREA (square feet—000)	3,471	3,635	3,929	4,214	4,408	4,708	4,944	5,059	5,489	5,712

* After deduction of refunds and V.A.T./Purchase Tax.
† Excluding surplus on disposal of assets—1971 £2,393,000: 1974 £2,388,000.
‡ Earnings per share in 1974 and 1975 are not comparable with earlier years by reason of the change in basis of taxation.
§ Including amounts capitalised or retained by the issue of ordinary shares in lieu of cash dividends.
¶ Including surplus arising from property valuation—£155,184,000.

D.7 Summary of Results and Financial Position Adjusted for the Effects of Inflation (Note A)

	Historical pounds (pages 00 and 00)		Current pounds as at 31 March 1975	
	1975 £000	1974 £00	1975 £000	1974 £000
RESULTS FOR THE YEAR ENDED 31 MARCH 1875				
Turnover	721,876	571,650	787,204	736,460
Operating Profit (Note B)	81,857	76,825	82,706	92,402
Taxation	42,500	39,900	42,500	48,279
Profit after taxation	39,357	36,925	40,206	44,123
Extraordinary item	49	2,383	52	2,260
Monetary gain attributable to Debenture Stock and Preference Shares	—	—	9,733	7,290
	39,406	39,308	49,991	53,673
Dividends	21,052	19,008	21,202	23,002
Undistributed surplus	18,354	20,300	28,789	30,671
Earnings per share	12.2p	11.4p	12.4p	13.6p
FINANCIAL POSITION AT 31 MARCH 1975				
Fixed assets (Note C)	414,312	241,720	422,777	405,988
Investment in subsidiary and associated companies	6,540	2,210	6,540	2,674
Net current liabilities	(7,528)	(8,113)	(7,528)	(10,287)
	413,324	235,817	421,789	398,375
Less: Deferred taxation	21,150	18,400	25,014	22,264
Debenture stock	45,000	45,000	45,000	54,450
Preference shares	1,350	1,350	1,350	1,633
	67,500	64,750	71,364	78,347
Ordinary shareholders' interests (Note D)	345,824	171,067	350,425	320,028

A. BASIS OF ADJUSTMENT

As a result of inflation the company's accounts on pages 00 to 00 are stated in a mixture of pounds of different purchasing power ('Historical pounds'). The summary on page 00 shows the effect of converting the results and the financial position in Historical pounds into pounds of current purchasing power as at 31 March 1975 ('Current pounds').

The figures in Historical pounds have been converted into Current pounds by using factors derived from the index of retail prices, which in January 1974 was 100 and at 31 March 1975 was estimated to have been 123.9, compared with 102.6 at 31 March 1974.

B. OPERATING PROFIT

The difference between the operating profit in Historical pounds and the operating profit in Current pounds is made up as follows:

	1975 £000	1974 £000
OPERATING PROFIT IN HISTORICAL POUNDS	81,857	76,825
ADJUSTMENTS TO CONVERT TO CURRENT POUNDS:		
Increase in the cost of opening stock	(6,690)	(3,853)
Increase in the charge for depreciation	(2,857)	(1,716)
Sales, purchases and expenses	7,839	7,523
	80,230	78,779
Gain/(Loss) on monetary items (excluding Debenture Stock and Preference Shares)	2,476	(2,414)
	82,706	76,365
Adjustment to update last year's profit to Current pounds	—	16,037
OPERATING PROFIT IN CURRENT POUNDS	82,706	92,402

C. FIXED ASSETS

A valuation of properties was made as at 31 March 1974, which, following professional advice, has been revised to take account of the overall decline in property values in the year to 31 March 1975. This revised value has been included in the statement of the financial position of the company in Current pounds at 31 March 1975, and at 31 March 1974, but has only been incorporated in the accounts in Historical pounds as at 31 March 1975. Subsequent net additions of properties during the year have been converted into Current pounds using the factors described in Note A.

D. ORDINARY SHAREHOLDERS' INTERESTS

	Historical pounds £000	Current pounds £000
At 1 April 1974	171,067	320,028
Amount capitalised or retained in respect of shares issued in lieu of cash dividend	1,608	1,608
Surplus arising on valuation of the company's properties	154,795	—
Undistributed surplus for the year	18,354	28,789
At 31 March 1975	345,824	350,425

D.8   Statement of Sources and Application of Funds

SOURCES AND APPLICATIONS OF FUNDS for the year ended 31 March 1975

	1974/5 £000	1973/4 £000
CASH AND SHORT-TERM DEPOSITS AT 1 APRIL 1974	18,460	48,612
SOURCES OF FUNDS		
Profit before taxation earned in the United Kingdom	81,710	76,645
Depreciation	7,470	5,464
Sales of Fixed Assets	334	3,231
	89,514	85,340
	107,974	133,952
APPLICATIONS OF FUNDS		
Dividends paid in cash	17,991	28,036
Taxation	37,537	29,622
Purchase of Fixed Assets	25,552	49,654
Investment in Subsidiary and Associated Companies overseas .	4,183	2,078
Increase in Stock	6,215	1,834
Increase in Debtors	1,790	2,352
Decrease in Creditors	—	1,916
	93,268	115,492
Less: Increase in Creditors	5,426	—
	87,842	115,492
CASH AND SHORT-TERM DEPOSITS AT 31 MARCH 1975	20,132	18,460

Author Index

Subject Index